The industrialised world has recently witnessed a dramatic increase in the volume of international capital movements in the forms of borrowing and lending, bond transactions and foreign direct investment. At the same time, many non-OECD countries have embarked on extensive programmes of capital market liberalisation.

This volume, drawn from the proceedings of a CEPR conference with the Bank of Israel and the Pinhas Sapir Center for Development, Tel-Aviv University, examines the implications of this increased international capital mobility for both industrialised and developing countries. The contributors look at the effect of recent developments on economic fluctuations, and on fiscal and monetary policies under alternative exchange rate regimes. They also address the erosion of capital taxation as a source of government revenue, the contribution of mobile capital to development with 'endogenous growth', the role of mobile capital in reducing unemployment where there are large-scale population flows, and the convergence of national growth rates.

Capital mobility: the impact on consumption, investment and growth

Pinhas Sapir Center for Development

The Pinhas Sapir Center for Development was established in 1975 as a research centre, to promote independent analysis and public discussion of all aspects of development and growth, with a special emphasis on economics. The Center, bearing the name of Israel's third minister of finance (1963–74) is affiliated with Tel-Aviv University.

The Centre for Economic Policy Research

The Centre for Economic Policy Research is a network of over 200 Research Fellows, based primarily in European universities. The Centre coordinates its Fellows' research activities and communicates their results to the public and private sectors. CEPR is an entrepreneur, developing research initiatives with the producers, consumers and sponsors of research. Established in 1983, CEPR is already a European economics research organisation with uniquely wide-ranging scope and activities.

CEPR is a registered educational charity. Institutional (core) finance for the Centre is provided through major grants from the Economic and Social Research Council, the Esmée Fairbairn Charitable Trust, the Bank of England, Citibank, the Baring Foundation, 33 other companies and 14 other central banks. None of these organisations gives prior review to the Centre's publications, nor do they necessarily endorse the views expressed therein.

The Centre is pluralist and non-partisan, bringing economic research to bear on the analysis of medium- and long-run policy questions. CEPR research may include views on policy, but the Executive Committee of the Centre does not give prior review to its publications, and the Centre takes no institutional policy positions. The opinions expressed in this volume are those of the authors and not those of the Centre for Economic Policy Research.

Centre for Economic Policy Research

[illegible]

Board of Trustees

[illegible]

Officers

[illegible]

Capital mobility: the impact on consumption, investment and growth

Edited by

LEONARDO LEIDERMAN

and

ASSAF RAZIN

Published by the Press Syndicate of the University of Cambridge
The Pitt Building, Trumpington Street, Cambridge CB2 1RP
40 West 20th Street, New York, NY 10011-4211, USA
10 Stamford Road, Oakleigh, Melbourne 3166, Australia

First published 1994

Printed in Great Britain at the University Press, Cambridge

Capital mobility: the impact on consumption, investment, and growth /
edited by Leonardo Leiderman and Assaf Razin.
p. cm.
Proceedings of a CEPR conference with the Bank of Israel and the
Pinhas Sapir Center for Development, Tel Aviv University.
Includes index.
ISBN 0 521 45438 7
1. Capital movements – Congresses. 2. Foreign exchange – Congresses.
3. Capital investments – Congresses. 4. Investments, Foreign – Congresses.
I. Leiderman, Leonardo, 1951– . II. Razin, Assaf.
III. Centre for Economic Policy Research (Great Britain).
IV Bank Yiśra'el. V. Merkaz le-fituaḥ 'al-shem P. Sapir.
HG3891.C37 1994
332'.041 – dc 20 93-50839 CIP

ISBN 0 521 45438 7 hardback

CE

Contents

Figures

Tables

Preface

Financial market integration is at the centre stage of current world economic developments. Economic theory suggests that increased capital mobility could either smooth or increase the volatility of economic activity for the individual countries. A conference on 'International Capital Mobility and Development' was held in Tel-Aviv, Israel, on 20–22 December 1992, to provide a forum for the discussion of recent research in this area. The conference was jointly sponsored by the Bank of Israel, CEPR and the Pinhas Sapir Center for Development at Tel-Aviv University. This volume is based on the papers and discussions presented at the conference.

Throughout the organisation of the Tel-Aviv conference we received invaluable advice and support from CEPR (in particular from Richard Portes, Stephen Yeo, David Guthrie, and Kate Millward) and from the Pinhas Sapir Center (in particular from Nava Ganor and Laura Bundt). We are grateful to all of them for the help they have provided, and to the Bank of Israel for additional financing. We thank our Production Editor, Barbara Docherty, for her very valuable input into the production of this book.

May 1993

Leonardo Leiderman
Tel-Aviv University

Assaf Razin
Tel-Aviv University

Acknowledgements

The editors and publishers wish to thank the following for permission to reproduce copyright material.

Oxford University Press, for data in Table 2D.1, from A. Maddison, *Phases of Capitalist Development* (1982).
Review of Income and Wealth, for data in Table 2D.1, from R. Summers and A. Heston, 'A new set of international comparisons of real product and price levels estimates for 130 countries, 1950–1985' (1988).
IMF, for data in Tables 3.1 and 12.1, from *Annual Report on Exchange Arrangements and Exchange Restrictions* (various years); in Table 12.2, from *Balance of Payments Yearbook*; in Tables 12.1 and 12.2, from *International Financial Statistics*; in Table 12.1, from *World Economic Outlook*; and in Table 9.1, from L. Bovenberg and G. Kopits, 'Harmonization of Taxes on Capital Income and Commodities in the European Community' (October 1989).
IBRD, for data in Table 3.2, from L. Pritchett, 'Measuring outward orientation in developing countries' (1991).
Banco de Mexico, for data in Table 4.1, from *Indicadores Economicos*.
CANSIM, for data in Table 4.1.
Price Waterhouse, for data in Table 9.1, from *Individual Taxes: A World-wide Summary* (1989).

List of conference participants

Avi Ben Bassat, *Bank of Israel*
Benjamin Bental, *Technion*
Giuseppe Bertola, *Princeton University and CEPR*
Daniel Cohen, *Université de Paris I, Ecole Normal Superieure, Paris, and CEPR*
Alex Cukierman, *Tel-Aviv University*
Zvi Eckstein, *Tel-Aviv University*
Jay Epstein, *Tel-Aviv University*
June Flanders, *Tel-Aviv University*
Jacob A. Frenkel, *Bank of Israel, Tel-Aviv University and CEPR*
Vittorio Grilli, *Birkbeck College, London, and CEPR*
Elhanan Helpman, *Tel-Aviv University and CEPR*
John Huizinga, *University of Chicago*
Shmuel Kandel, *Tel-Aviv University*
David Klein, *Bank of Israel*
Leonardo Leiderman, *Tel-Aviv University and CEPR*
Donald J. Mathieson, *IMF*
Rafi Melnick, *Bank of Israel*
Enrique G. Mendoza, *IMF*
Gian Maria Milesi-Ferretti, *LSE*
Maurice Obstfeld, *University of California at Berkeley and CEPR*
Marco Pagano, *Università Bocconi, Milano, and CEPR*
Shula Pessach, *Bank of Israel*
Richard Portes, *CEPR and Birkbeck College, London*
Assaf Razin, *Tel-Aviv University and CEPR*
Andrew K. Rose, *University of California at Berkeley*
Efraim Sadka, *Tel-Aviv University*
Ron Shachar, *Tel-Aviv University*
Nathan Sussman, *Hebrew University of Jerusalem and University of Western Ontario*

Oren Sussman, *Hebrew University of Jerusalem*
Zvi Sussman, *Tel-Aviv University*
Lars E.O. Svensson, *Institute of International Economic Studies, Stockholm, and CEPR*
Manuel Trajtenberg, *Tel-Aviv University*
Daniel Tsiddon, *Hebrew University of Jerusalem*
Philippe Weil, ECARE, *Université Libre de Bruxelles, and CEPR*
Eran Yashiv, *Tel-Aviv University*
Chi-Wa Yuen, *Hong Kong University of Science and Technology*
Joseph Zeira, *Hebrew University of Jerusalem and CEPR*

1 Introduction

LEONARDO LEIDERMAN and
ASSAF RAZIN

The recent turbulence in the European Monetary System has added new impetus to issues of international capital flows, such as macroeconomic volatility, exchange rate fluctuations, capital controls, and international convergence of growth rates. Key questions about international capital mobility which require a fresh look are:

(1) Is there rigorous evidence in support of the notion that international capital markets have become more integrated?;
(2) Does more capital mobility contribute to smoothing or volatilising of the macroeconomy?
(3) Are the comovements between national saving and investment weaker under increased capital mobility?
(4) Does enhanced capital mobility magnify the transmission of financial shocks from country to country and thereby raise the likelihood that governments will renege on their exchange rate commitments, such as target zones?
(5) Is there a link between the drop in investment growth in industrialised countries and the increase in exchange rate flexibility?
(6) What is the role of foreign finance in the growth of indebted countries?
(7) Is there stronger convergence in growth rates across countries when capital markets are more integrated?
(8) What are the political factors and institutions that are most likely to result in liberalisation of existing capital controls?

This list of questions constitutes the agenda for the research on capital mobility presented in this volume. Part One deals with macroeconomic volatility. Exchange rate volatility is discussed in Part Two. Part Three focuses on investment and growth, and Part Four provides policy perspectives.

1 Macroeconomic volatility

There are two basic approaches that have been used to assess the extent to which world financial markets have become more integrated in recent years. A first, direct, approach consists of examining whether asset returns on comparable assets traded at different locations exhibit lower cross-country differentials than before; e.g., the comparison between offshore–onshore interest rate differentials. That is, the removal of barriers to international capital mobility can be expected to result in stronger convergence of asset returns. Similarly, one could examine the extent to which the volume of international trade in assets has risen relative to GNP or other indicators of the real economy. A second, indirect, approach focuses on the implications of enhanced capital mobility for comovements of other economic variables across countries.

Chapter 2 by Maurice Obstfeld adopts this second approach. In particular it looks at changes in the comovement between domestic consumption and rest-of-world consumption for the seven largest industrial countries. If individuals in different countries are allowed to share their idiosyncratic risks by trading in the world capital market, then their consumption will tend to be correlated because trade in assets will tend to cancel out the country-specific shocks. If, on the other hand, individuals are allowed to trade only part of their country-specific risk, e.g. due to capital controls, then the correlation of consumption growth will be weakened.

Based on correlation and regression analysis, Obstfeld reaches the conclusion that for most of the countries in the sample there appears to be a post-war trend of increasing coherence between domestic and world consumption growth. For all countries, except Canada, the correlation of domestic with rest-of-world consumption growth rises in the most recent sample period, most sharply in the cases of Germany and Japan. While in principle the evidence is consistent with increased capital mobility, other interpretations could be provided. Specifically, increased coherence may have resulted from common shocks impinging on the various countries for a given degree of capital mobility. The chapter addresses this issue, at least partially, by explicitly accounting for one possible common factor, namely oil-price shocks. Clearly, these useful findings would have to be supplemented by more detailed evidence on common factors before one could reach decisive conclusions about the extent to which there has been a rise in capital mobility.

Chapter 3 by Assaf Razin and Andrew Rose examines whether the cyclical variability of consumption, investment and output in various countries is related to the degree of openness in financial and goods markets in a manner that is consistent with the predictions of basic intertemporal trade models. In this sense, the chapter belongs to the second, indirect, approach mentioned above. Reductions in barriers to capital mobility are expected to enhance investment opportunities, and therefore to raise the volatility of investment, and at the same time to improve the ability to diversify country-specific shocks, and thereby to facilitate consumption smoothing. A reduction in trade barriers (e.g., import tariffs or nontariff barriers) tends to enhance comparative advantage and thereby to increase output volatility.

Based on data from the IMF and World Bank, the authors used factor analysis to construct measures of capital and goods mobility for the countries in their sample. Moreover, the authors characterised the time-series properties of consumption, investment, and production in terms of transitory vs. permanent and country-specific vs. global (common) components. For the most part, the information in the sample was not powerful enough to deliver clearcut implications. Except for some evidence on the impact of openness on consumption smoothing, there is no strong link between openness and the volatility of investment and output. This could well be an indication that most of the fluctuation in these variables is due to permanent factors, and to common shocks, as some of the earlier evidence in the chapter tends to indicate. Perhaps more conclusive evidence could be derived from a more detailed set of indicators of openness, which would measure not only the existence of restrictions but also their intensity. Similarly, it would be useful to explore further alternative measurements of the transitory, and idiosyncratic, components.

According to the neoclassical model of a small open economy there is no necessary link between savings and investment as is familiar from closed economy analysis. That is, if capital is fully mobile and risk is internationally diversified investment is determined by technology and world cost of capital while domestic saving is determined by the world return on assets and the country's wealth and productivity. Empirical studies such as Feldstein and Horioka (1980), however, have found positive savings–investment correlations to be the rule, and have thus concluded that there is a limited degree of capital mobility. This, somewhat indirect, evidence on capital mobility is at variance with the notion that international financial markets have become more integrated, as directly evidenced by narrowing interest rate differentials. Experience with other indicators such as consumption smoothing and investment variability provided mixed results. Similarly, the evidence on portfolios indicates a bias toward home country investment which is a bit surprising if indeed there is high capital mobility and investors attempt to globalise their portfolios.

Overall, then, there are difficulties in designing appropriate measures for the degree of capital mobility.

Chapter 4 by Enrique G. Mendoza argues that the existence of strong links between saving and investment should not be interpreted as showing a low degree of capital mobility. In fact, the author shows that in a neoclassical framework calibrated to Canada and Mexico certain types of shocks will give rise to a comovement of savings and investment even under perfect capital mobility. Mendoza's simulations are derived under the assumptions of persistent productivity and terms-of-trade shocks. These shocks created business cycles comparable to those realised in Canada and Mexico. Mendoza then examines the accuracy of saving–investment correlations and the degree of consumption smoothing as indicators of capital mobility under several sets of parameters and assumptions about the true degree of capital mobility. This work thus belongs to the second, indirect, approach of measuring capital mobility. Mendoza found the indicators to be more sensitive to the parameters that describe the stochastic process and the preference than to the true degree of capital mobility.

2 Exchange rate volatility

There are various important channels of interaction between capital mobility and the exchange rate regime. On the one hand, in the presence of some degree of commitment to exchange rate management, such as target zones, increased capital mobility can reduce the scope for independent monetary policy. Since the authorities may have several other commitments and exchange rate management is only one of them, there could be sufficiently large shocks that would result in increased exchange rate volatility and the inability of the authorities to fulfil their commitments. In such circumstances, realignments and adjustments to the exchange rate regime would be observed. On the other hand, to restore monetary independence in the presence of strong exchange rate commitments countries may choose to limit the degree of capital mobility via exchange and capital controls.

Chapter 5 by Lars E.O. Svensson deals with the most widely used exchange rate regime in Europe in the present period of capital mobility: target zones. It provides a useful survey of the most recent work in this area which began with Krugman's (1987) study. Although the model provided useful insights into the mechanics of a target zone regime, most of the testable implications derived under the benchmark case of full credibility and marginal interventions have been rejected by the data. For example, the assumptions of perfect credibility and marginal interventions only suggest that exchange rates will spend most of their time near the edges of their bands. This indicates that a 'U-shaped' density function should describe the distribution of actual exchange rates in the band over time. The data, however, generates a 'hump-shaped' distribution whereby exchange rates tend most often to be realised near the central parity. This suggests that intra-marginal intervention is the rule. Another implication of the Krugman model is a strong negative correlation between the exchange rate and uncovered interest differentials. Under perfect credibility, if the actual exchange rate is near the weaker edge of its band it can only appreciate, thus resulting in a lower differential between domestic and foreign interest rates. However, the observed relationship between exchange rates and the uncovered interest differential is diffuse, with no apparent correlation of any sort. Svensson explains this by the imperfect credibility of the band. When the exchange rate is near the edge of the band, realignment expectations are high, thus distorting the effect of mean reversion on the data. Svensson surveys recent literature, which has been able to incorporate imperfect credibility and intra-marginal interventions in order to better describe exchange rate behaviour in a target zone regime.

The September 1992 currency crisis in Europe highlights the type of strains that can arise in a world of high capital mobility in the presence of policy commitments about exchange rates. Some countries, such as Italy and the United Kingdom, abandoned their earlier exchange rate commitments, thus confirming the expectations of those who stressed the lack of credibility of these policies. This classic episode of a speculative attack strengthens the need for incorporating endogenous policy choices about the exchange rate regime under imperfect credibility into the analysis.

Chapter 6 by Alex Cukierman, Miguel Kiguel, and Leonardo Leiderman provides a positive theory of how a policymaker determines the width of an exchange rate band and the timing and size of realignments of the central parity. Exchange rate bands are understood as a limited commitment device in a world where realignment may involve a political cost. The chapter models bandwidth as endogenously determined by a policymaker who weighs the benefits of higher short-run real depreciation of the exchange rate, and hence higher employment, against the costs in terms of higher level and volatility of inflation. The authors show that the choice of bandwidth is mainly affected by the strength of the policymaker's reputation, the cost of reneging on its commitments, and the volatility of the underlying shocks. The credibility of the band is shown to decrease as the exchange rate moves toward its weaker edge. While a wider band allows a greater range of flexibility, the choice of a narrow band increases the credibility of the policymaker. The tension between these goals of flexibility and credibility determines optimal bandwidth for a given set of parameters. Simple tests based on data for Chile, Finland, Israel, Norway, and Sweden (i.e., countries with unilateral exchange rate bands) provided evidence in support of the model's implication that the contribution of expected realignments to expected depreciation increases as the exchange rate increases toward the upper limit of the band.

High capital mobility and some flexibility of exchange rates are likely to be associated with substantial exchange rate uncertainty. Since the volatility of nominal exchange rates is likely to exceed that of prices in the goods and labour markets, nominal exchange rate uncertainty may have consequences for important real economic variables such as investment. In his Chapter 7, John Huizinga examines the effects on investment of the increased nominal exchange rate volatility, and thus uncertainty, which accompanied the transition from Bretton Woods to a flexible exchange rate regime. The research strategy consisted of breaking the sample into two periods, one when the exchange rate variability was high and the other when it was low. Huizinga finds that the move to a flexible exchange rate regime induced increased uncertainty in exchange rates as well as in a variety of price and quantity measures from data on four-digit US manufacturing industries. That an important causal role was played by the increased exchange rate volatility is evident from the nature of cross-industry diversity in changes in uncertainty: the increase in uncertainty was much more pronounced in those industries which were particularly exposed to international trade. Regarding investment, high uncertainty about real output prices is found to be negatively correlated with investment and productivity growth rates and positively correlated with the share of equipment in the capital stock. While the move toward flexible exchange rates could explain some of these findings (as stressed by Huizinga), the increase in investment volatility could be partly due to the impact of increased capital mobility per se.

3 Investment and growth

An important manifestation of capital mobility for many developing countries is the availability of foreign finance for their domestic investments. Daniel Cohen in Chapter 8 investigates the channels through which foreign finance has influenced the growth pattern of debtor countries. In a traditional Solow-type model in which total factor productivity is exogenous, foreign finance can only raise growth through capital accumulation. Cohen argues that in addition a country that gains new access to the world financial markets could use an important part of these resources to increase productivity. His evidence points to the importance of both these channels.

Assaf Razin and Chi-Wa Yuen in Chapter 9 provide a quantitative assessment of the role played by two factors, capital mobility and tax policies, in explaining the observed diversity rates of growth of per capita and total incomes, in the long run. Under free capital mobility, the law of diminishing returns implies that capital will move from the capital rich to the capital poor countries. Over time, therefore, such international capital flows will equalise the marginal productivity of capital prevailing in all countries. In the long run (with balanced growth), the authors argue that total income growth rates must be equalised across countries, regardless of national policy differences. However, this is not necessarily the case for per capita growth rates. Indeed, in the presence of capital mobility the implications that follow are: (i) long-term growth rates of population and per capita incomes should be negatively correlated across countries; and (ii) total income growth rates should exhibit less variation than per capita income growth rates across countries. The chapter provides evidence in support of these implications based on a cross-section of LDCs and DCs.

When capital is mobile the choice of the international tax principle and tax rates applied to capital incomes is shown by the authors to be crucial for the convergence of per capita growth rates. This was done by employing a calibrated model of the world economy. Simulations based on this model involve switching from a state where cross-country capital flows are perfectly mobile to a state where capital movements are nonexistent, and altering the tax rate on capital income with compensating changes in lump-sum taxes to balance the fiscal budgets. Razin and Yuen's numerical results show that although the long-run effects of liberalising capital flows may not be all that sizeable, the growth effects of tax policy changes are magnified in the presence of free capital mobility.

It has been observed that capital flows typically follow a cyclical pattern. That is, some regions are the recipients of capital inflows for a few periods and the pattern is reversed for several periods afterwards. For example, there was a marked capital outflow from Latin America in most of the 1980s, but there were pronounced capital inflows in the late 1970s and early 1990s. While external factors could partially explain these facts, Giuseppe Bertola and Allan Drazen argue in Chapter 10 that regional productivity shocks and the policies that they induce may also give rise to this pattern. In their chapter, they suggest that variability of government policies may be responsible for the observed volatility of capital flows. In a framework where productivity shocks can induce persistent effects on investment and capital flows, the authors show how government policies can magnify the effects of these shocks. That is, they stress the existence and role of procyclical government policies. This procyclical behaviour is attributed to the failure of governments to respond to domestic supply shocks by cutting government expenditures so as to keep the tax rates and the deficit unchanged. Bertola and Drazen discuss a mechanism by which the tax base shrinks during the low productivity state and a higher tax rate is required to maintain government expenditure. Increased tax rates mean a lower after-tax return on investment and thus a decreased capital inflow.

4 The political economy of controls and liberalisation

In their Chapter 11, Alberto Alesina, Vittorio Grilli and Gian Maria Milesi-Ferretti study, using simple regression analysis, the institutional and political determinants of capital controls in a sample of twenty OECD countries for the period 1950 to 1989. The authors focus on two main factors: the political strength of government (indicated by whether it is a majority or a minority government) and the exchange rate regime. In principle, political strength of a government can have two opposite effects on the extent of capital controls. On the one hand, strong governments are able to increase tax revenue via inflation tax and thus tend to rely on controls more heavily. On the other hand, in a political war of attrition situation the inflation tax is a residual tax and thus strong governments are likely to rely on this tax and on controls. The authors bring some evidence, based on their sample, which indicates that capital controls are more likely to be imposed by strong governments.

As far as the exchange rate regime is concerned, it is well known that greater fixity of exchange rates comes together with less autonomy of monetary policy under capital mobility. Capital controls thus help restore monetary policy efficacy under fixed exchange rates. The authors find that capital controls are empirically more likely to be introduced when the exchange rate is pegged or managed, a finding that is in line with the theory.

The use of capital controls has been motivated by various factors: to reduce volatility of capital flows, to ensure that domestic saving leads to domestic investment, to limit foreign ownership of domestic assets and to prevent currency appreciations due to capital inflows during periods of stabilisation and reform. While these controls have never been fully effective, Donald Mathieson and Liliana Rojas-Suarez argue in Chapter 12 that the ability of governments to prevent the flow of capital across borders deteriorated significantly in the 1980s, and that it is now extremely costly to maintain effective barriers. They attribute this change to several factors, including technological advances and learning-by-doing. The authors examine the policy implications of this reduction of the effectiveness of capital controls. They reach the conclusions that the sequencing and speed of liberalisation matters less than 'fundamentals' policy, and that fiscal adjustment is a crucial element in any stabilisation programme. It would be interesting to relate these findings to the political factors discussed above. In particular, strong government are most likely to exert a tight control over fundamentals, which may create a tendency toward liberalisation of the capital account.

REFERENCES

Feldstein, M. and C. Horioka (1980) 'Domestic savings and international capital flows', *Economic Journal*, **90** (June), 314–29.

Krugman, P. (1987) 'Trigger strategies and price dynamics in equity and foreign exchange markets', NBER, *Working Paper*, **2459**.

Part One
Macroeconomic volatility

2 Are industrial-country consumption risks globally diversified?

MAURICE OBSTFELD

1 Introduction

This chapter develops consumption-based tests of alternative hypotheses about countries' participation in world financial markets. The underlying methodology in principle can throw light both on the efficiency of international trade in noncontingent assets, and on the range of contingent assets countries use to diversify idiosyncratic national risks.

My empirical analysis of aggregate consumption behaviour in the seven largest industrial countries is consistent with the hypothesis that most became increasingly integrated into world markets for risk sharing over the 1973–88 portion of the post-World War II era. In this group of economies, Germany stands out as having reduced idiosyncratic consumption risk through trade to an exceptional degree. For France, Italy, Japan, and the United Kingdom, the interpretation of aggregate consumption behaviour after 1973 is more ambiguous, as one might expect given these countries' comparatively late capital account liberalisation drives. Country size makes the United States' record difficult to assess, while Canada throws up a puzzle, an apparent sharp reduction after 1973 in the global diversification of its consumption risks.

Empirical studies of international trade in consumption risk generally reach the conclusion that markets for risk function imperfectly at the international level, and certainly less efficiently than do domestic markets. Atkeson and Bayoumi (1992), for example, argue that the national diversification of regional incomes within the United States is significantly greater than the international diversification of European national incomes.[1] French and Poterba (1991), Golub (1991), and Tesar and Werner (1992) document what appears to be a domestic asset bias in the security portfolios of major industrial countries.

Yet another approach, proposed by Leme (1984) and Scheinkman (1984), starts from the observation that national consumption levels should move in a synchronised fashion when aggregate preferences are stable and mutual insurance against idiosyncratic risks is feasible. Consumption-based analysis of international risk sharing has been refined and extended by Stockman and Tesar (1990), Devereux, Gregory and Smith (1992), Backus, Kehoe and Kydland (1992), Backus and Smith (1992), and Baxter and Crucini (1993), among others. The basic message of this work is that correlations among international consumption movements are too low to be fully explained within a setting of free international asset trade and complete markets.

This chapter draws on the consumption-based approach to develop an empirical framework for evaluating international financial integration. My framework recognises explicitly that the *ex post* covariation in national consumptions depends not only on the freedom residents of different countries have to transact in securities markets, but also on the completeness of those markets – that is, on the range of contingencies on which cross-border contracts can be written. The empirical methodology can accommodate the two extreme cases of noncontingent asset trade and complete markets, as well as the broad middle ground where only a subset of national consumption risks is insurable. Once identifying assumptions are made, the consumption effects of noninsurable risks can be separated empirically from those of restrictions on international asset trade. (The necessary identifying assumptions are unlikely to be innocuous, however.)

Section 2 below sets out a model of international consumption comovements under possibly incomplete asset markets. Section 3 develops an econometric framework for testing the predictions of this model. The framework generalises the one based on free international trade in bonds that has been applied to industrial countries by myself (1989) and by Kollmann (1992).

The data and estimation strategy are discussed in section 4, where a central question is the treatment of country-specific preference shocks. Section 5 tests successively less restrictive versions of the model. One test in section 5 is inspired by Feldstein and Horioka's (1980) analysis of economies' saving and investment rates, but leads to a different perspective on the post-war evolution of world capital markets. Section 6 draws some conclusions.

2 Market completeness and international consumption correlation

This section develops a general method for analysing international consumption comovements when there is cross-border trade in assets. The approach illustrates that empirical predictions about consumption comovements depend not only on the opportunity to trade assets freely, but also on the range of events on which assets' payoffs can be conditioned. In the model I develop it is approximately true (and under one set of assumptions, exactly true) that *ex post* consumption-growth differentials between countries are uncorrelated with any random variable on which contingent contracts can be written. The model thus yields a potentially powerful method for discriminating empirically among different hypotheses about market completeness.

To simplify matters I assume that there is a single tradable consumption good and that each country i, $i = 1, \ldots, N$, is inhabited by a representative infinitely-lived individual.

Modelling the evolution of uncertainty is critical to the developments that follow. For every date t there is a set of possible states of nature $\mathcal{S}_t$, a generic element of which is denoted s_t. Transitions between states obey a Markovian probability law: the probability that state s_t occurs depends on the realised value s_{t-1} and possibly on calendar time. Conditional expectations are thus straightforward to compute.

Let C_{it} be the date-t consumption of the country-i individual. This individual's objective function at $t = 0$ is

$$U_0 = \mathrm{E}\left\{\sum_{t=0}^{\infty} \beta_i^t u(C_{it}, \theta_{it}) \,|\, s_0\right\}, \qquad 0 < \beta_i < 1, \tag{1}$$

where $\mathrm{E}\{\cdot|s_t\}$, given the Markov structure assumed, is an expectation conditional on the information observed up to time t. In (1), θ_{it} is a preference shock, the realised value of which is one element determining the world economy's state.[2]

Let $\mathcal{V}_t$ be a minimal countable partition of $\mathcal{S}_t$ into *verifiable* events.[3] For any $v_t \in \mathcal{V}_t$, contracts can be written on the event $s_t \in v_t$, but not on the event that s_t lies in some element of a partition of $\mathcal{S}_t$ strictly finer than $\mathcal{V}_t$. I make no attempt in this chapter to model the nonverifiability of some events. The notion $q(v_t|s_{t-j})$ will be used to denote the price on date $t-j$ of the asset that pays 1 consumption unit in the event $s_t \in v_t$ and 0 in the event $s_t \notin v_t$.

Predictions about consumption dynamics are derived from the Euler equations associated with transactions in these state-contingent assets. Let $C_{it} = C_i(s_t)$ be country i's per capita consumption level contingent on event s_t. The stochastic Euler equation associated with the asset described in the last paragraph is

$$\begin{aligned} &q(v_{t+1}|s_t)u'[C_i(s_t), \theta_{it}] \\ &\quad = \beta_i \mathrm{E}\{u'[C_i(s_{t+1}), \theta_{it+1}]\,|\, v_{t+1}, s_t\} \cdot \pi(v_{t+1}|s_t), \end{aligned} \tag{2}$$

where $\pi(v_{t+1}|s_t)$ is the date-t conditional probability that event v_{t+1} occurs. The left-hand side of this equation is the current utility cost of buying the state-contingent asset, the right-hand side the discounted expected utility value of its payoff.

If people in different countries i and j face the same asset prices and have rational expectations, then equation (2) implies that for all $s_t \in \mathcal{S}_t$, $v_{t+1} \in \mathcal{V}_{t+1}$,

$$\mathrm{E}\left\{\frac{\beta_i u'[C_i(s_{t+1}),\theta_{it+1}]}{u'[C_i(s_t),\theta_{it}]} - \frac{\beta_j u'[C_j(s_{t+1}),\theta_{jt+1}]}{u'[C_j(s_t),\theta_{jt}]} \middle| v_{t+1}, s_t\right\} = 0. \qquad (3)$$

Equation (3) provides the central link between national intertemporal rates of substitution and insurable risks.

The main prediction of (3) is that *ex post* differences in individuals' rates of intertemporal substitution are statistically uncorrelated with variables on which contractual payoffs can be conditioned, and with variables known as of date t. To set the stage for a proof, let $D_{ij}(s_{t+1}, s_t)$ denote the *ex post* difference in marginal rates of intertemporal substitution between representative agents of countries i and j, so that (3) becomes:

$$\mathrm{E}\{D_{ij}(s_{t+1}, s_t) \mid v_{t+1}, s_t\} = 0 \qquad (\forall s_t \in \mathcal{S}_t, v_{t+1} \in \mathcal{V}_{t+1}). \qquad (4)$$

Since only events in $\mathcal{V}_{t+1}$ or countable unions thereof are verifiable, contingent contracts payable on date $t+1$ can be written only on random vectors $f: \mathcal{S}_{t+1} \rightarrow \mathbb{R}^n$ that are *measurable* with respect to $\mathcal{V}^*_{t+1}$, the smallest set containing the null set $\emptyset$ and all countable unions of members of $\mathcal{V}_{t+1}$. Measurability of f means that the inverse image $f^{-1}(I)$ of any product of half-open intervals $I \subseteq \mathbb{R}^n$ is a member of $\mathcal{V}^*_{t+1}$, i.e. that the event $f(s_{t+1}) \in I$ is verifiable for all I. Measurability implies that $f(s_{t+1})$ is constant on every $v_{t+1} \in \mathcal{V}_{t+1}$, since $f^{-1}(z) \in \mathcal{V}^*_{t+1}$ for every point $z \in \mathbb{R}^n$. Similarly, variables known as of date t are functions on $\mathcal{S}_t$ that are measurable with respect to $\mathcal{S}^*_t$, which is defined analogously to $\mathcal{V}^*_t$.[4]

To prove the main result, notice that for any $\mathcal{V}^*_{t+1}$-measurable function $f: \mathcal{S}_{t+1} \rightarrow \mathbb{R}^n$,

$$\begin{aligned}\mathrm{E}\{D_{ij}(s_{t+1}, s_t) f(s_{t+1})\} &= \mathrm{E}\{\mathrm{E}\{D_{ij}(s_{t+1}, s_t) f(s_{t+1}) \mid v_{t+1}, s_t\}\} \\ &= \mathrm{E}\{f(s_{t+1}) \mathrm{E}\{D_{ij}(s_{t+1}, s_t) \mid v_{t+1}, s_t\}\} = 0.\end{aligned}$$

The first equality follows from the law of iterated conditional expectations, the second from the constancy of $f(s_{t+1})$ on each element $v_{t+1} \in \mathcal{V}_{t+1}$, and the third from (4). A similar argument shows that $D_{ij}(s_{t+1}, s_t)$ is uncorrelated with date-t information.

The discussion can be summarised by the following:

Theorem: The date-$t+1$ *ex post* marginal rate of intertemporal substitution difference between any two countries i and j,

$$D_{ij}(s_{t+1}, s_t) = \frac{\beta_i u'[C_i(s_{t+1}), \theta_{it+1}]}{u'[C_i(s_t), \theta_{it}]} - \frac{\beta_j u'[C_j(s_{t+1}), \theta_{jt+1}]}{u'[C_j(s_t), \theta_{jt}]} \tag{5}$$

is statistically uncorrelated with any random variable on which date-$t+1$ contracts can be written, as well as with any variables realised on date t or before.

Two simple examples will help to clarify this theorem's meaning:

1. As a first example, suppose that $\mathcal{V}_t = \mathcal{S}_t$ on all dates, which is the case of *complete* markets. In this case contracts can be made contingent on *any* state of nature, so the theorem states that the random variable $D_{ij}(s_{t+1}, s_t)$ must be uncorrelated with any random variable realised at time $t+1$. This can be true, however, only if $D_{ij}(s_{t+1}, s_t)$ is a constant and, by (4), that constant must be zero. So by (5), for all states of nature,

$$\frac{\beta_i u'[C_i(s_{t+1}), \theta_{it+1}]}{u'[C_i(s_t), \theta_{it}]} = \frac{\beta_j u'[C_j(s_{t+1}), \theta_{jt+1}]}{u'[C_j(s_t), \theta_{jt}]} \tag{6}$$

in the case of complete markets. Marginal rates of intertemporal substitution must be equalised after the fact.[5]

2. As a second example consider the opposite extreme in which $\mathcal{V}_t = \{\mathcal{S}_t\}$, i.e., in which the minimal verifiable partition of $\mathcal{S}_t$ consists of $\mathcal{S}_t$ alone. Now only noncontingent contracts can be written, so that the only assets traded are indexed bonds. The theorem above implies the weaker result that $D_{ij}(s_{t+1}, s_t)$ is uncorrelated with information available as of time t, or that

$$\mathrm{E}\left\{\frac{\beta_i u'[C_i(s_{t+1}), \theta_{it+1}]}{u'[C_i(s_t), \theta_{it}]} - \frac{\beta_j u'[C_j(s_{t+1}), \theta_{jt+1}]}{u'[C_j(s_t), \theta_{jt}]} \middle| s_t\right\} = 0 \tag{7}$$

(compare with equation (3)). Hence, the *ex post* rate of substitution differential is uncorrelated with information known as of date t. But its correlation with date-$t+1$ variables is unrestricted. Relations similar in spirit to (7) have been tested empirically by me (1989) and by Kollmann (1992).[6]

Intermediate between these two extreme possibilities is a range of cases in which partial insurance renders $D_{ij}(s_{t+1}, s_t)$ uncorrelated with some, but not all, date-$t+1$ variables. The intuition for the theorem is easy. Any idiosyncratic consumption risk systematically related to some verifiable random event is traded, leaving *ex post* differentials in marginal intertemporal substitution rates as functions of nonverifiable events only.

3 Econometric implications of the model

Empirical testing of the models presented in section 2 requires additional identifying assumptions. Here I describe how restrictions on utility functions and on the distributions of preference shocks lead to simple econometric specifications of the models. These specifications, which I will apply to time-series data below, are related to specifications tested against panel microdata by Townsend (1989) and Mace (1991) and against cross-sectional microdata by Cochrane (1991).

3.1 Complete asset markets

Assume tentatively that there is free international trade in a *complete* set of Arrow–Debreu securities.

As a first possibility, assume that the period utility function takes the isoelastic form

$$u(C_i, \theta_i) = \frac{1}{1-\rho}(C_i)^{1-\rho}\exp(\theta_i) \qquad (\rho > 0). \tag{8}$$

Let $t = 0$ be the initial period and let θ_{i0} be normalised, for all countries i, so that $\theta_{i0} = 0$. Under complete markets equation (6) holds true; it implies that $\forall t \geq 0$,

$$\frac{\beta_i^t \exp(\theta_{it}) C_{it}^{-\rho}}{C_{i0}^{-\rho}} = \frac{\beta_j^t \exp(\theta_{jt}) C_{jt}^{-\rho}}{C_{j0}^{-\rho}}. \tag{9}$$

The assumption that countries share a common risk-aversion coefficient ρ is not innocuous, but is a central maintained hypothesis in the analysis and tests that follow. In my 1989 paper I found little evidence against this hypothesis in quarterly 1973–85 data for Germany, Japan, and the United States.[7]

Taking natural logarithms in (9) yields the time-series model

$$\log C_{it} = \log C_{jt} + \log(C_{i0}/C_{j0}) + \log(\beta_i/\beta_j)(t/\rho) + \frac{1}{\rho}(\theta_{it} - \theta_{jt}). \tag{10}$$

In (10), $\log(\beta_i/\beta_j)$ measures the extent to which country i's residents are more patient than those of country j, while $\log(C_{i0}/C_{j0})$ reflects relative impatience as well as the initial wealth of i relative to j.

A main implication of (10) is that when national time-preference rates coincide ($\beta_i = \beta_j$) and there are no differential preference shocks across countries ($\theta_{it} - \theta_{jt} = 0, \forall t$), national per capita consumption levels display equal proportional *ex post* comovements. In the analysis below, however, country-specific taste shocks will play a role. Equation (10) then makes the weaker prediction that *other things the same*, $\log C_{it}$ *and* $\log C_{jt}$ *should move by equal amounts*. Equation (10) also implies that *no date-*t *variable that is uncorrelated with* $\theta_{it} - \theta_{jt}$ *will be correlated with* $\log C_{it} - \log C_{jt}$.

In the many-country framework of this chapter, an alternative estimation strategy has some potential advantages that section 4 will discuss in detail. Let n_{it} be country i's share in world population and let C_{Wt} be world per capita consumption, so that

$$C_{Wt} \equiv \sum_{j=1}^{N} n_{jt} C_{jt}. \tag{11}$$

Let μ_t be the common value of the marginal rates of substitution in equation (9). Using (9) and (11), one finds that

$$\mu_t = \left[\frac{C_{Wt}}{\Sigma_j \beta_j^{t/\rho} \exp(\theta_{jt}/\rho) n_{jt} C_{j0}}\right]^{-\rho},$$

from which it follows that

$$\begin{aligned}\log C_{it} = \log C_{Wt} + \log C_{i0} + (\log \beta_i)(t/\rho) \\ + \{\theta_{it}/\rho - \log[\Sigma_j \beta_j^{t/\rho} \exp(\theta_{jt}/\rho) n_{jt} C_{j0}]\}.\end{aligned} \tag{12}$$

(Notice that the consumption time trend is zero when $\beta_i = \beta_j$, $\forall i, j$, and when countries' population shares contain no time trend.) Equation (12), which provides an alternative and more compact mode of summarising the main message of equation (10), likewise implies proportional movements between each country's consumption and world consumption, all else equal. It also implies that date-t variables independent of preference and population shocks will also be uncorrelated with $\log C_{it} - \log C_{Wt}$.

The isoelastic-utility specification (8) is an appropriate one in a context of ongoing economic growth, and the log-consumption specification in equations (10) and (12) will therefore be the basis for the tests carried out below. An alternative, exponential form of the period utility function helps simplify some of the econometric arguments I make in section 4 in favour of a testing strategy based on (12) rather than (10). It is therefore useful to develop briefly the empirical implications of complete asset markets under exponential utility,

$$u(C_i, \theta_i) = -\exp(-\rho C_i + \theta_i)/\rho \qquad (\rho > 0). \tag{13}$$

If we assume that $\theta_{i0} = 0$, $\forall i$, equation (6) now implies that

$$\frac{\beta_i^t \exp(-\rho C_{it} + \theta_{it})}{\exp(-\rho C_{i0})} = \frac{\beta_j^t \exp(-\rho C_{jt} + \theta_{jt})}{\exp(-\rho C_{j0})}$$

$\forall t \geq 0$. Taking natural logarithms yields

$$C_{it} = C_{jt}(C_{i0} - C_{j0}) + \log(\beta_i/\beta_j)(t/\rho) + \frac{1}{\rho}(\theta_{it} - \theta_{jt}), \tag{14}$$

the 'levels' version of (10). The analogue of (12) is

$$\log C_{it} = C_{Wt} + (C_{i0} - \Sigma_j n_{jt} C_{j0}) + (\log \beta_i - \Sigma_j n_{jt} \log \beta_j)(t/\rho) + (\theta_{it} - \Sigma_j n_{jt} \theta_{jt}). \quad (15)$$

As noted above, the results I report below are for equations involving consumption logs, not consumption levels. Equations estimated in levels, however, led to very similar results.

3.2 Incomplete asset markets

This section has proceeded under the tentative assumption of complete asset markets. If consumption depends on idiosyncratic uninsured risks, however, equation (4) shows that equations like (10), (12), (14), and (15) must be modified by the addition of extra error terms reflecting those risks.

In the extreme case that only noncontingent assets are traded on date $t-1$, the extra error term can reflect any new date-t information relevant to current consumption decisions. Generally, however, at least some state-contingent assets are traded. Their payoffs are functions of events that do not generate *ex post* international differences in the growth of the discounted marginal utility of consumption.

The econometric implications of market incompleteness are discussed further in context below (equations (19) and (20)).

4 Specification and data

There are two preliminary specification issues to be settled before estimation. First, should one investigate pairwise regressions such as (10) and (14), or are there advantages to working with a world consumption measure as in (12) and (15)? Second, should consumption data be differenced prior to regression? This section discusses these two issues and then describes the data.

4.1 Reducing least-squares bias through use of world consumption data

Several studies have attempted to test relations like (10) and (14). Generally these studies assume that $\beta_i = \beta_j$ and that there are no preferences shocks, and then proceed to examine pairwise correlations between C_{it} and C_{jt} (or between various transforms of those variables). These correlations turn out to be low in many cases – generally lower, for industrialised countries, than the correlations between national output levels.[8] The finding of low pairwise consumption correlation is often taken as evidence of imperfect international financial market integration or of missing markets.

Such low international consumption correlations are not surprising, even under complete markets, when there are significant country-specific preference shocks. Yet regression equations such as (10) or (14) can mask the possibility that international consumption changes due to factors other than preference shifts are closely synchronised. One way to think of this problem is as an *endogenous-regressor* problem: country-j consumption in (10) or (14) is likely to be positively correlated with θ_{jt} – a high realisation of θ_{jt} raises the marginal utility of country j's time-t consumption – and so least-squares estimates will tend to produce downward-biased estimates of slope coefficients.

One can reduce this bias by estimating equations of form (12) or (15), in which world consumption is the independent variable explaining country i's consumption. Particularly if country i is small, the degree to which its taste shock θ_i diverges from an average world taste shock should be approximately uncorrelated with world consumption. The composite errors $\theta_{it}/\rho - \log[\Sigma_j \beta_j^{t/\rho} \exp(\theta_{jt}/\rho) n_{jt} C_{j0}]$ in (12) and $\theta_{it} - \Sigma_j n_{it} \theta_{it}$ in (15) are thus more plausibly weakly correlated or uncorrelated with their respective regressors than is the error $(\theta_{it} - \theta_{jt})/\rho$ in (10) and (14).

An example based on exponential utility clarifies this intuition. Imagine a pure exchange economy in which world per capita output on date t, Y_{Wt}, is an exogenous random variable. Under complete markets either of (14) or (15) describes the equilibrium consumption allocation; if we simplify the notation by assuming that $\rho = 1$, that $C_{i0} = C_{j0}$ and $\beta_i = \beta_j \; \forall i, j$, and that $n_{it} = 1/N \; \forall i, t$, then these two equations become, respectively,

$$C_{it} = C_{jt} + \theta_{it} - \theta_{jt}, \tag{16}$$

$$C_{it} = C_{Wt} + \theta_{it} - (1/N)\Sigma_j \theta_{jt}. \tag{17}$$

Since in equilibrium $(1/N)\Sigma_j C_{jt} = C_{Wt} = Y_{Wt}$, country i's equilibrium consumption level is, by (17),

$$C_{it} = Y_{Wt} + \theta_{it} - (1/N)\Sigma_j \theta_{jt}. \tag{18}$$

Let $\hat{a}_{ij}$ be the slope estimate derived from applying ordinary least squares to the pairwise regression equation (16). I make the further simplifying assumptions that the taste shocks θ_{it} are distributed independently of Y_{Wt} and that $\forall i, j$, θ_{it} and θ_{jt} have identical but independent distributions. By (18), it follows that

$$\text{plim } \hat{a}_{ij} = 1 - (\sigma_\theta^2/\sigma_C^2),$$

where σ_θ^2 is the variance of preference shocks and σ_C^2 the variance of national consumption levels. If preference shocks account for part of the overall variance of national consumption, least-squares regressions of country-*i* on country-*j* consumption can produce slope estimates that are asymptotically biased below the true value of 1.

Consider next the least-squares slope estimate $\hat{a}_{iW}$ from (17). Under the distributional assumptions just made, plim $\hat{a}_{iW} = 1$. Least-squares estimation of (17) thus gives an asymptotically accurate picture of how national consumptions and world consumption covary holding preferences constant. Furthermore, date-*t* variables uncorrelated with the error $\theta_{it} - (1/N)\Sigma_j\theta_{jt}$, other than C_{Wt}, should be insignificant in (17) when it is estimated by least squares.

In section 5 I will try to reduce least-squares bias by relying on a specification like (17), in which world per capita consumption is a regressor. In situations other than the simple one-good pure-exchange economy of my example, however, some bias can remain. Preference shocks may alter the division of world output between consumption and saving, so in principle a nonzero correlation between the regressor and error term in (17) is possible in an economy with investment. This possibility is most important when country *i* in (17) is large, a point I will revisit in analysing results for the United States below.

4.2 *Should the data be differenced?*

As mentioned above, the estimates reported below will be derived from the logarithmic specification (12). Tests could in principle be based on equations such as (12) itself or on the implied equations in log-differences. In their microdata studies, Mace (1991) and Cochrane (1991) use differenced specifications to remove fixed household effects corresponding to the terms in period-0 consumption in (12).[9] In the present time-series context another reason for considering a differenced model is the danger of spurious correlations and asymptotically invalid inferences.

Per capita consumption data are well known to be generated by integrated or near-integrated processes, a feature rationalised by forward-looking consumption theories. A regression of country *i* consumption on world consumption, as in equation (12), might give a misleading impression of close correlation if these series are not cointegrated. Such a spurious relationship could also result in erroneous statistical inferences.

For most of the countries examined below, logarithmic regressions of national on world consumption do give rise to R^2 statistics that are above Durbin–Watson statistics – the informal diagnostic indicator of spurious regression suggested by Granger and Newbold (1974). More formally, for a typical country *i*, $\log C_{it}$, $\log C_{Wt}$, and $\log C_{it} - \log C_{Wt}$ all appear to be nonstationary processes; indeed, $\log C_{it}$ and $\log C_{Wt}$ are often not cointegrated.[10] These findings suggest that a specification in log-differences will be more informative than one in log-levels.

Taking a linear approximation to (12) (which assumes complete markets) and differencing yields

$$\Delta \log C_{it} = \delta + \Delta \log C_{Wt} + \epsilon_{it}; \tag{19}$$

the disturbance ϵ_{it}, which is assumed to follow a stationary process, is a function of taste shocks and, possibly, errors in measuring consumption.[11] I will generally assume that ϵ_{it} and $\Delta \log C_{Wt}$ are approximately uncorrelated, but will also remark on cases where some correlation seems likely.[12]

Equation (19) may lead to unbiased least-squares slope estimates even when asset markets are incomplete. To understand this possibility, notice that in the present context and under incomplete markets, equation (19) would become

$$\Delta \log C_{it} = \delta + \Delta \log C_{Wt} + \epsilon_{it} + \eta_{it}, \tag{20}$$

where η_{it} is a function of date-t innovations that are not verifiable and thus cannot be insured. If such innovations are uncorrelated with $\Delta \log C_{Wt}$, least-squares estimation of (20) gives a consistent slope estimate provided $\mathrm{E}(\Delta \log C_{Wt} \epsilon_{it}) = 0$. The converse of this implication should also be noted, however: if markets are incomplete and the uninsurable factors η_{it} *are* correlated with $\Delta \log C_{Wt}$, then the least-squares slope estimator is not consistent for (20). Further, insured factors correlated with η_{it} might display nonzero estimated coefficients if included on the right-hand side of (20).

Equation (20) will be the workhorse for the empirical analysis in section 5. A test of financial integration asks if the coefficient of $\Delta \log C_{Wt}$ in (20) is 1 once the uninsurable risk factors underlying η_{it} are added as regressors (assuming these, like $\Delta \log C_{Wt}$, are uncorrelated with ϵ_{it}). At the same time, random variables uncorrelated with ϵ_{it}, and on which contracts can be written, should not enter significantly into (20). It is thus possible in principle to identify the uninsured factors contributing to idiosyncratic national consumption fluctuations.

4.3 Data description

The annual national income and product account and population data used in this study come from the Penn World Table (Mark 5), as described by Summers and Heston (1991). The national account components studied below – gross domestic product (GDP), consumption (C), private plus public investment (I), and government consumption (G) – are all measured in real per capita terms at 1985 international prices.[13]

Table 2.1. *Correlation coefficients for per capita consumption growth rates, 1951–72 and 1973–88*

	Canada	France	Germany	Italy	Japan	UK	US
Rest-of-world	0.43	0.26	− 0.11	− 0.02	0.06	0.29	0.26
	0.10	0.50	0.72	0.27	0.62	0.59	0.31
Canada		0.07	0.04	0.04	0.03	− 0.22	0.60
		0.00	0.38	− 0.12	0.03	− 0.15	0.17
France			0.21	0.28	0.18	− 0.21	0.05
			0.44	0.42	0.65	0.21	0.30
Germany				− 0.12	0.19	− 0.13	− 0.04
				0.36	0.45	0.39	0.46
Italy					0.54	− 0.15	− 0.03
					0.37	0.19	− 0.02
Japan						− 0.23	0.05
						0.68	0.46
UK							0.39
							0.49

World per capita consumption is as defined in equation (11). For my purposes the 'world' consists of the 47 Penn World Table countries with data extending over the entire 1950–88 sample, and awarded a quality grade of at least $C-$ by Summers and Heston.[14] The major oil exporters are not part of this group.

To allow convenient comparison with the findings in other studies of international consumption comovements, I report in Table 2.1 correlation coefficients for changes in the logarithms of annual national per capita consumption rates. Each box in the table contains two estimated correlation coefficients one (above the diagonal) for the period 1951–72 and a second (below the diagonal) for the period 1973–88. The sample split is motivated by independent evidence that the first subperiod was on the whole an era of considerably lower global asset market integration than the second. The individual-country sample is the Group of Seven (G-7), consisting of the largest industrial nations. Obviously it is feasible and desirable to apply tests such as those done here to additional countries.

The first row of Table 2.1 shows the correlation coefficient between the change in each G-7 country's log consumption per capita and the change in the rest of the world's log consumption per capita.[15]

Table 2.2. *Standard deviation of domestic consumption growth relative to standard deviation of world consumption growth, 1951–72 and 1973–88*

	Canada	France	Germany	Italy	Japan	UK	US
1951–72	2.61	1.66	2.54	1.99	2.65	2.32	2.02
1973–88	3.92	1.84	1.50	1.90	1.99	2.63	1.84

$$\text{Standard deviation of annual world consumption growth} = \begin{cases} \overset{\%}{0.85} & (1951\text{–}72) \\ 1.13 & (1973\text{–}88) \end{cases}$$

Three main facts are apparent from Table 2.1. First, as the recent empirical literature has shown, pairwise correlations between national consumption growth rates, as well as correlations between national growth rates and rest-of-world growth rates, are typically far below the unit correlation that would characterise a world with costless asset and commodity trade, complete markets, no preference shocks, and no errors in measuring real consumption per head. Second, in most cases the country-to-country correlation coefficients for the second sample sub-period are higher than those for the first (most of the exceptions involve Canada). Third, for all countries except Canada, the correlation of domestic with world consumption growth rises in the second sample period – dramatically so in the cases of Germany and Japan.

Taken as a whole, Table 2.1 is consistent with the hypothesis that increased international trade in a broader range of financial assets took place after 1973. Table 2.2 offers some additional evidence pertinent to this question. Financial diversification makes it feasible for every country to reduce the variability of its consumption growth relative to that of world average consumption growth; Table 2.2 shows that only Japan and Germany have done so in a big way. World consumption growth became a third more variable after 1973, but Germany actually reduced the absolute variability of its consumption growth rate while Japan held the variability of its rate about constant. Canada is again an outlier, with a massive increase in relative consumption growth variability.

A potential alternative explanation for the results in Tables 2.1 and 2.2, one that does not rely on international diversification, comes from looking at changes over time in the behaviour of national per capita *outputs* (that is, gross domestic products). The results indicate that Tables 2.1 and 2.2 are easily explained by a model in which consumption growth closely (and naively) tracks domestic output growth.

Table 2.3 shows the output correlations corresponding to the entries in

Table 2.3. *Correlation coefficients for per capita output growth rates, 1951–72 and 1973–88*

	Canada	France	Germany	Italy	Japan	UK	US
Rest-of-world	0.42 0.30	0.41 0.56	0.31 0.87	0.35 0.61	0.43 0.71	0.49 0.66	0.19 0.67
Canada		0.49 −0.11	0.09 0.29	−0.11 −0.03	0.10 0.23	−0.21 0.14	0.63 0.37
France			0.07 0.63	0.10 0.82	0.52 0.52	−0.07 0.50	0.25 0.33
Germany				0.22 0.70	0.09 0.70	0.26 0.66	0.18 0.80
Italy					0.46 0.43	0.22 0.32	0.15 0.43
Japan						0.33 0.73	0.26 0.63
UK							0.29 0.66

Table 2.1. As in Table 2.1, the correlations have a tendency to increase over time. Furthermore, as noted by Backus, Kehoe and Kydland (1992) and Stockman and Tesar (1990), the international output correlations in Table 2.3 tend to be higher than the consumption correlations in Table 2.1.

Table 2.4 does the calculations in Table 2.2 using output rather than consumption growth rates. For all the countries but the UK, there is a decline in domestic relative to world output-growth variability after 1973. For Japan and Germany in particular, the declines in domestic relative to world output-growth variability match the corresponding declines in relative consumption-growth variability shown in Table 2.2.

Tables 2.2 and 2.4 reinforce the finding that even though world consumption growth is smoother than world output growth, the industrial countries' output growth risks appear better 'diversified' than their consumption growth risks. This fact leads to a fundamental ambiguity, since the data do not obviously refute the view that apparent changes over time in international consumption correlations are entirely due to exogenous shifts in output correlations rather than improved risk sharing.

Table 2.5 presents some relevant additional information. The table shows correlation coefficients between domestic per capita consumption

Table 2.4. *Standard deviation of domestic output growth relative to standard deviation of world output growth, 1951–72 and 1973–88*

	Canada	France	Germany	Italy	Japan	UK	US
1951–72	2.20	1.04	2.11	1.75	2.01	1.13	1.84
1973–88	1.94	0.99	1.30	1.71	1.35	1.59	1.69

$$\text{Standard deviation of annual world output growth} = \begin{cases} \%\\ 1.31 & (1951\text{–}72) \\ 1.75 & (1973\text{–}88) \end{cases}$$

Table 2.5. *Correlation coefficients between domestic consumption growth and rest-of-world output growth, 1951–72 and 1973–88*

	Canada	France	Germany	Italy	Japan	UK	US
1951–72	0.13	0.59	0.11	0.17	0.43	− 0.09	0.07
1973–88	− 0.07	0.34	0.58	0.49	0.49	0.51	0.36

growth and the rest of the world's per capita output growth. Comparing this table with Table 2.1, one sees that for all countries save Italy and the United States, the post-1973 correlation of domestic consumption growth with rest-of-world output growth is below the corresponding correlation with rest-of-world consumption growth (though sometimes only barely so). This is weak evidence that for some countries more may be going on in the data than a simple proportionality of output and consumption.

The implications of these data for global financial markets depend critically on the importance of preference shocks and uninsured risks. The empirical model developed above provides a framework within which the various factors generating the changes in Tables 2.1 and 2.2 can potentially be identified. I therefore turn to tests of that model's predictions.

5 Empirical results

The model developed above has a number of empirical implications. This section reports tests of the model based on equation (19), which assumes complete markets, and on the less restrictive equation (20), which allows for some uninsurable risks.

5.1 National consumptions and world consumption

The first application of the model is to estimate directly equations of form suggested by (19),

$$\Delta \log C_{it} = \delta + a_{iW} \Delta \log C_{Wt} + \epsilon_{it},$$

and test the hypothesis that $a_{iW} = 1$. Table 2.6 reports the results of least-squares estimation over the 1951–72 (panel A) and 1973–88 (panel B) subsamples.[16]

For countries other than Canada and the United States, the coefficient on world consumption growth rises, usually sharply, in the second subperiod. (Canada's behaviour is consistent with the results of Table 2.1; however, the unusually big increase in the variability of Canada's consumption growth after 1973 lowers the precision of estimation.) The equation's $\bar{R}^2$ rises for the countries outside North America, also suggesting a greater coherence between domestic and world consumption growth.

For 1951–72, the hypothesis $a_{iW} = 1$ can be rejected at the 5% level only for Italy and the United States, but this is in most cases the result of low-precision estimates $\hat{a}_{iW}$, not of estimates near 1 (panel A). Thus, the hypothesis $a_{iW} = 0$ also is not rejected at the 5% level for three of the seven over 1951–72. Over 1973–88 (panel B), however, $a_{iW} = 1$ is rejected only for the United States, despite more precise estimates of a_{iW} for Germany and Japan. The hypothesis $a_{iW} = 0$ is now rejected in five of seven cases.

The US estimates pose a special problem in light of the country's size. Because US consumption makes up a sizable fraction of world consumption, positive realisations of the US preference shock θ_{US} are likely to have a large positive correlation with the world consumption measure used in Table 2.2; as a result, the least-squares slope estimate in Table 2.2 probably has an upward bias. In fact, the most likely explanation for the fall in that estimate between the first and second subperiods is the shrinking weight of US consumption in world consumption.

To a lesser degree, this problem could plague the non-US equations as well: in a world with investment, we may exaggerate the link between a given country's consumption and world consumption when we do not remove the country from the world consumption index. Let C^i_{Wt} be world per capita consumption outside country *i*. Table 2.7 shows the results of regressing $\Delta \log C_{it}$ against $\Delta \log C^i_{Wt}$ for each of the G-7 countries.[17]

All slope coefficients and all but one of the $\bar{R}^2$s drop, but the substance of the results changes little. Comparing Table 2.7 with Table 2.6, the results seem in general somewhat less compatible with global financial

Table 2.6. *Regressions of national on world consumption growth rates, 1951–72 and 1973–88*

A. 1951–72

	Canada	France	Germany	Italy	Japan	UK	US
$\Delta \log C_W$	**1.29**	**0.55**	0.06	0.13*	0.45	**1.00**	**1.77***
	(0.34)	(0.27)	(0.51)	(0.44)	(0.58)	(0.47)	(0.22)
$\bar{R}^2$	0.20	− 0.05	− 0.05	− 0.05	− 0.02	0.14	0.75
Lags	1	3	1	0	0	0	0

B. 1973–88

	Canada	France	Germany	Italy	Japan	UK	US
$\Delta \log C_W$	0.84	**0.63**	**1.14**	0.68	**1.45**	**1.77**	**1.53***
	(1.02)	(0.26)	(0.37)	(0.47)	(0.36)	(0.49)	(0.20)
$\bar{R}^2$	− 0.02	0.07	0.54	0.07	0.50	0.41	0.67
Lags	0	0	1	0	0	0	1

Note: Standard errors appear below estimates of the coefficient of world consumption growth. **Boldface entries** of this estimate are those differing from 0 at the 5% significance level or below. An asterisk (*) marks coefficients that differ from 1 at the 5% level or below. 'Lags' shows the moving-average order assumed for the equation disturbance in calculating standard errors.

integration in panel A, but not more so in panel B. For the United States a_{iW} is no longer estimated to be significantly above 1 in either subperiod, but neither panel's estimate differs significantly from 0 (at the 5% level) either. Furthermore, regardless of period the rest-of-world consumption growth rate accounts for the same very small fraction of the variation in the US rate. The post-1973 results for Italy are ambiguous, those for Canada even less decisive.

Notice that by changing the regressor in Table 2.7, an opposite bias may be introduced, one especially relevant for large countries like the United States. Positive realisations of the preference shock θ_{US} are likely to lower rest-of-world consumption growth and thus lead to *downward*-biased slope estimates. Without more information, it is impossible to know how large this bias is, or the extent to which it affects the other G-7 countries.

A concern raised by the data description above (section 4.3) is that the results in Table 2.7 reflect nothing more than the typical high correlation

Table 2.7. *Regressions of national on rest-of-world consumption growth rates, 1951–72 and 1973–88*

A. 1951–72

	Canada	France	Germany	Italy	Japan	UK	US
$\Delta \log C^i_W$	**1.13**	0.41	– 0.27*	– 0.04*	0.16	0.67	0.64
	(0.41)	(0.32)	(0.53)	(0.43)	(0.59)	(0.50)	(0.54)
$\bar{R}^2$	0.15	0.02	– 0.04	– 0.05	– 0.05	0.04	0.02
Lags	1	0	0	0	0	0	0

B. 1973–88

	Canada	France	Germany	Italy	Japan	UK	US
$\Delta \log C^i_W$	0.38	**0.57**	**1.08**	0.50	**1.26**	**1.60**	0.63
	(0.71)	(0.26)	(0.35)	(0.48)	(0.43)	(0.62)	(0.40)
$\bar{R}^2$	– 0.06	0.20	0.48	0.01	0.34	0.30	0.02
Lags	1	0	1	0	0	1	2

Note: Standard errors appear below estimates of the coefficient of rest-of-world consumption growth. **Boldface entries** of this estimate are those differing from 0 at the 5% significance level or below. An asterisk (*) marks coefficients that differ from 1 at the 5% level or below. 'Lags' shows the moving-average order assumed for the equation disturbance in calculating standard errors.

between domestic consumption growth and domestic output growth, coupled with the typical high correlation between domestic output growth and world output growth. To address this concern, Table 2.8 reports the results of estimating

$$\Delta \log C_{it} = \delta + a_{iW} \Delta \log C^i_{Wt} + \gamma_i \Delta \log GDP^i_{Wt} + \epsilon_{it},$$

where GDP^i_{Wt} is world per capita output outside country i. The right-hand variables in this equation are quite collinear, so sharp conclusions are not expected. Nonetheless, the estimates suggest that for the G-7 countries other than Italy and the United States, it is world consumption growth rather than world output growth that was more closely related to domestic consumption growth after 1973. For France, Germany, and Japan, the reversal of this relationship between the two sample periods is noteworthy. The results in Table 2.8 are consistent with the simple correlations in Tables 2.1 and 2.5, and provide weak evidence that the patterns

Table 2.8. *Domestic consumption growth, world consumption growth, and world output growth, 1951–72 and 1973–88*

A. 1951–72

	Canada	France	Germany	Italy	Japan	UK	US
$\Delta \log C^i_W$	**1.61**	− 0.32*	− 0.77*	− 0.45*	− 0.90*	**1.64**	1.47
	(0.58)	(0.38)	(0.70)	(0.57)	(0.67)	(0.64)	(0.92)
$\Delta \log GDP^i_W$	− 0.46	**0.75**	0.52	0.41	**1.09**	**− 0.86**	− 0.60
	(0.27)	(0.24)	(0.47)	(0.38)	(0.44)	(0.40)	(0.54)
Lags	1	0	0	0	0	0	0
H_1	0.24	0.01	0.05	0.05	0.03	0.11	0.45

B. 1973–88

	Canada	France	Germany	Italy	Japan	UK	US
$\Delta \log C^i_W$	2.51	0.94	**1.22**	− 1.00*	1.51	1.48	0.00
	(2.05)	(0.52)	(0.40)	(0.81)	(0.85)	(0.96)	(0.95)
$\Delta \log GDP^i_W$	− 1.59	− 0.28	− 0.11	**1.17**	− 0.18	0.09	0.54
	(1.33)	(0.34)	(0.39)	(0.54)	(0.53)	(0.50)	(0.64)
Lags	0	0	1	0	0	1	1
H_1	0.43	0.23	0.85	0.08	0.80	0.60	0.53

Note: Standard errors appear below coefficient estimates. **Boldface entries** of coefficient estimates are those differing from 0 at the 5% significance level or below. An asterisk (*) marks coefficients on $\Delta \log C^i_W$ that differ from 1 at the 5% level or below. 'Lags' shows the moving-average order assumed for the equation disturbance in calculating standard errors. Marginal significance levels are reported for tests of the hypothesis: H_1: $a_{iW} = 1$, $\gamma_i = 0$.

in the data are not driven entirely by changing output correlations as opposed to improved international risk sharing.

5.2 *The role of oil-price shocks*

For four of the G-7 countries, the rest of the world's consumption growth appears to play a statistically significant and economically important role in explaining domestic consumption growth after 1973. Table 2.8 notwithstanding it is still possible that this finding is not due to international asset market integration at all, but is the result of common shocks to the world macroeconomy that hit all industrialised economies simultaneously and with similar effects on consumption growth. Over the 1973–88 sample period, a leading probable source of such common shocks is the real price of petroleum. The simple correlation coefficient over the period between the change in the log real price of oil and the change in the log of world real per capita consumption is -0.6.[18]

To explore this possibility I add the change in the log real oil price between years t and $t-1$, ΔOIL_t, to the basic estimating equation:

$$\Delta \log C_{it} = \delta + a_{iW}\Delta \log C^{i}_{Wt} + \gamma_i \Delta OIL_t + \epsilon_{it}.$$

If the countries making up the world consumption index I use optimally insured each other against the idiosyncratic effects of oil-price shocks, then $\gamma_i = 0$ holds because oil prices affect an individual country's consumption only by affecting group consumption (recall the theorem in section 2 above); otherwise $\gamma_i \neq 0$ in general.[19] If the results in Tables 2.6 and 2.7 are *entirely* due to the common effect of oil prices on group consumption, but idiosyncratic risks have not been shared within the group, then a_{iW} should become insignificant with ΔOIL added to the regression.

Table 2.9 reports the estimation results for 1973–88. The oil variable enters significantly in the regressions for Italy, the United Kingdom, and the United States, suggesting that these countries did not fully trade to the rest of the 47-country world sample the idiosyncratic consumption risk due to oil-price changes. For all of the countries but Canada and the United States, however, a_{iW} is now estimated to be fairly close to 1; it is significantly different from 0 at the 5% level for Germany, Italy, and Japan, and at the 10% level for France. The estimate $\hat{a}_{iW}$ is not significantly different from 1 for any country.

5.3 *Modelling imperfect allocation*

A simple heuristic model of international asset market inefficiency produces a more stringent test of the hypothesis that world financial market integration increased during the period after 1973.

Table 2.9. *Effects of oil-price changes on consumption growth, 1951–72 and 1973–88*

	Canada	France	Germany	Italy	Japan	UK	US
$\Delta \log C^i_W$	− 0.07	0.64	**1.29**	**1.40**	**1.06**	0.88	0.31
	(1.30)	(0.34)	(0.50)	(0.29)	(0.54)	(0.52)	(0.36)
$\Delta\, OIL$	− 0.02	0.00	0.01	**0.04**	− 0.01	**− 0.04**	**− 0.04**
	(0.04)	(0.01)	(0.01)	(0.01)	(0.02)	(0.01)	(0.01)
Lags	0	0	1	1	0	2	3
H_1	0.71	0.29	0.19	0.00	0.68	0.00	0.00

Note: Standard errors appear below estimates of regressor coefficients. **Boldface entries** of these estimates are those differing from 0 at the 5% significance level or below. An asterisk (*) marks coefficients on $\Delta \log C^i_W$ that differ from 1 at the 5% level or below. 'Lags' shows the moving-average order assumed for the equation disturbance in calculating standard errors. The reported marginal significance levels are for the F or χ^2 test of the hypothesis: H_1: $a_{iW} = 1$, $\gamma_i = 0$.

The quantity $TR_i \equiv C_i - (GDP_i - I_i - G_i)$ measures the net resource transfer from the rest of the world to country *i* due to foreign borrowing, interest/dividend earnings and capital gains on assets held abroad, and all other state-contingent payments on foreign wealth. Of course, $TR_i = 0$ when international capital markets are closed. I define the *domestic resource limit*, DRL_i, as

$$DRL_i \equiv GDP_i - I_i - G_i, \tag{21}$$

i.e., as the consumption level at $TR_i = 0$ given GDP_i, I_i, and G_i.

Let C_i^*, I_i^*, and TR_i^* be the hypothetical consumption, investment, and net resource transfer levels under free-asset trade. To simplify I will suppose that in the short run GDP_i and G_i do not depend on the extent of trade, but that actual date-*t* investment is related to potential investment by

$$I_{it} = I_{it}^* - \kappa(TR_{it}^* - TR_{it}) \qquad (0 \le \kappa \le 1). \tag{22}$$

Assume next that actual transfers are given by

$$TR_{it} = \lambda TR_{it}^* + \zeta_{it} \qquad (0 \le \lambda \le 1), \tag{23}$$

where ζ_{it} is an exogenous mean-zero disturbance. Combine the definition of TR_i, the assumption $TR_{it}^* = C_{it}^* - (GDP_i - I_i^* - G_i)$, (21), (22), and (23). Apart from an error term, actual date-*t* consumption is a weighted average of C_{it}^* and $GDP_{it} - I_{it} - G_{it}$;

$$C_{it} = \frac{\lambda}{1 - \kappa(1 - \lambda)} C^*_{it} + \frac{(1 - \lambda)(1 - \kappa)}{1 - \kappa(1 - \lambda)} DRL_{it} + \frac{(1 - \kappa)}{1 - \kappa(1 - \lambda)} \zeta_{it}. \tag{24}$$

If $\lambda = 1$ consumption is at its efficient level (apart from the error term). If $\kappa = 1$ investment bears all the burden of any fall in net resource transfers, so consumption need not differ from C^*_{it}. If $\lambda = 0$ consumption equals DRL_i (apart from the fraction of ζ_i that does not go into home investment). Other cases, however, imply that both C^*_{it} and DRL_{it} will systematically affect consumption, with positive partial derivatives that sum to 1.

Now suppose that equation (20) characterises the free-trade level of consumption and that (24) can be expressed in log-differences. The resulting equation is

$$\Delta \log C_{it} = \delta' + a_{iW} \Delta \log C_{Wt} + \gamma_i \Delta \log DRP_{it} + v_{it}, \tag{25}$$

where v_{it} is a linear combination of the preference shock ϵ_{it} from (19) and the net resource transfer shock ζ_{it} from (23). In estimating (25) we would expect to find that $a_{iW} = 0$ and $\gamma_i = 1$ under a regime of limited global financial integration. Under high financial integration, however, we would expect that $a_{iW} = 1$ and $\gamma_i = 0$.

The regression framework (25) is closely related to one developed by Feldstein and Horioka (1980) for estimation of the cross-sectional correlation between saving and investment. Intuitively, equation (25) gives an indication of whether domestic consumption growth is more closely correlated with global or with domestic factors. If domestic investment is constrained by domestic saving, then domestic consumption is constrained by the domestic resource limit and the hypothesis $a_{iW} = 0, \gamma_i = 1$ should not be rejected. An advantage of the present framework is that it avoids the use of national income and product account data on national saving which (among other problems) fail adequately to measure the international asset–income flows central to the present inquiry.[20]

Table 2.10 presents estimates of equation (25). I used the variable ΔOIL in some of the regressions to control for associated uninsured risks η_{it} from (20).[21]

In panel A the hypothesis that $a_{iW} = 1$ and $\gamma_i = 0$ is rejected at a very low significance level every time. Only for the United States is it possible to reject the hypothesis that $a_{iW} = 0$ and $\gamma_i = 1$, but the reason is a coefficient on $\Delta \log C^i_W$ that is significantly *negative*. Only in that case, and in the case of Canada, is the latter coefficient estimated at far from 0. In contrast, all coefficients on $\Delta \log DRL_i$ (with France a marginal exception) are insigni-

Table 2.10. *Domestic consumption growth, world consumption growth, and the domestic resource limit, 1951–72 and 1973–88*

A. 1951–72	Canada	France	Germany	Italy	Japan	UK	US
$\Delta \log C_W^i$	**0.62**	0.27*	−0.18*	−0.32*	−0.15*	0.20*	**−0.64***
	(0.31)	(0.17)	(0.33)	(0.28)	(0.37)	(0.28)	(0.25)
$\Delta \log DRL_i$	**0.81**	**0.57***	**0.76**	**0.82**	**0.76**	**0.95**	1.08
	(0.12)	(0.20)	(0.13)	(0.16)	(0.13)	(0.14)	(0.10)
Lags	0	3	0	2	0	0	0
H_1	0.00	0.00	0.00	0.00	0.00	0.00	0.00
H_2	0.10	0.06	0.21	0.18	0.18	0.77	0.05

B. 1973–88	Canada	France	Germany	Italy	Japan	UK	US
$\Delta \log C_W^i$	−0.25*	**0.57**	**1.07**	1.00	**1.18**	−0.16	**−1.27***
	(0.47)	(0.26)	(0.32)	(0.53)	(0.42)	(0.51)	(0.52)
$\Delta \log DRL_i$	**0.86**	0.21*	0.02*	0.47*	0.35*	**1.10**	**1.54**
	(0.12)	(0.22)	(0.20)	(0.27)	(0.26)	(0.28)	(0.43)
Lags	0	0	1	0	0	0	0
H_1	0.00	0.20	0.97	0.19	0.37	0.01	0.00
H_2	0.40	0.00	0.00	0.11	0.01	0.92	0.05

Note: Standard errors appear below coefficient estimates. **Boldface entries** of coefficient estimates are those differing from 0 at the 5% significance level or below. An asterisk (*) marks coefficients that differ from 1 at the 5% level or below. 'Lags' shows the moving-average order assumed for the equation disturbance in calculating standard errors. Marginal significance levels are reported for tests of the hypotheses: H_1: $a_{iW} = 1$, $\gamma_i = 0$ and H_2: $a_{iW} = 0$, $\gamma_i = 1$.

ficantly different from 1. The picture that emerges for the years 1951–72 is one of an industrialised world in which financial markets essentially provide no consumption insurance.

While panel B falls short of portraying the opposite extreme of full financial integration, its results are quite different from those of panel A (perhaps surprisingly so, in view of the Feldstein–Horioka findings). For four countries – France, Germany, Italy, and Japan – the hypothesis $a_{iW}=1$ and $\gamma_i=0$ cannot now be rejected; for France, Germany, and Japan, the hypothesis $a_{iW}=0$ and $\gamma_i=1$ is rejected decisively (and it fails at the 11% level for Italy). Germany stands out as showing most strongly the characteristics we would expect of an economy well integrated into world financial markets. Because Japan maintained capital controls until the start of the 1980s while France and Italy did so until past the middle of that decade, this result is plausible.

The United Kingdom's appearance of financial insularity may be due to its own controls on resident capital movements, which were dismantled only in 1979. If equation (25) is estimated for the United Kingdom over 1979–88, the result (with the intercept suppressed) is:

$$\underset{}{\Delta \log C_{\mathrm{UK}}} = \underset{(1.03)}{1.45\, \Delta \log C_W^{\mathrm{UK}}} + \underset{(0.45)}{0.40\, \Delta \log DRL_{\mathrm{UK}}} - \underset{(0.03)}{0.02\, \Delta\, OIL}.$$

Neither hypothesis, $a_{\mathrm{UK},W}=0$ and $\gamma_{\mathrm{UK}}=1$ nor $a_{\mathrm{UK},W}=1$ and $\gamma_{\mathrm{UK}}=0$, can be rejected; but insofar as one can draw conclusions from only 10 observations, the results above seen more compatible with international financial integration of the United Kingdom than do those in Table 2.10, panel B.

The US results in panel B may be due to strong negative correlation between world consumption growth and the residual in the US equation. The results for Canada are a mystery, especially in view of other, independent evidence suggesting a high degree of openness for Canadian financial markets.[22]

5.4 *A closer look at Germany and Japan*

Having come this far, it is tempting to carry out further tests on the diversification of idiosyncratic macroeconomic shocks. For example, does consumption growth respond to idiosyncratic output risk or can such risk in large part be traded away? I will argue in this section, using Germany and Japan as examples, that severe endogeneity problems prevent such tests from giving unambiguous answers. The argument suggests that the econometric results of the last section are potentially consistent with contradictory structural interpretations.

Table 2.11. *Regressions of German consumption growth on rest-of-world consumption growth and various macroeconomic shocks, 1973–88*

	1	2	3	4	5	6	7
$\Delta \log C_W^{GY}$	**0.73**	**0.99**	**0.95**	0.72	**0.93**	**0.77**	**1.04**
	(0.32)	(0.37)	(0.23)	(0.55)	(0.45)	(0.37)	(0.44)
$\Delta \log GDP$	0.20	—	—	0.41	0.01	—	− 0.54
	(0.25)	—	—	(0.46)	(0.23)	—	(0.48)
$\Delta \log I$	—	0.02	—	− 0.06	—	0.03	0.13
	—	(0.05)	—	(0.10)	—	(0.05)	(0.11)
$\Delta \log G$	—	—	**0.49**	—	**0.49**	**0.50**	**0.68**
	—	—	(0.17)	—	(0.18)	(0.17)	(0.23)
$\bar{R}^2$	0.46	0.44	0.66	0.43	0.63	0.65	0.65
Lags	1	1	0	0	0	0	0
H_1	0.66	0.94	0.03	0.81	0.09	0.08	0.10
H_2	0.42	0.75	0.01	0.65	0.05	0.04	0.06

Note: Standard errors appear below coefficient estimates. **Boldface entries** of coefficient estimates are those differing from 0 at the 5% significance level or below. An asterisk (*) marks first-row coefficients differing from 1 at the 5% level or below. 'Lags' shows the moving-average order assumed for the equation disturbance in calculating standard errors. Marginal significance levels are reported for tests of two hypotheses: H_1 is the hypothesis that the coefficient of rest-of-world consumption growth is 1, those of all other variables 0; H_2 is the hypothesis that the coefficients of variables other than rest-of-world consumption growth are all 0.

Table 2.11 presents 1973–88 regressions of German consumption growth on world consumption growth and key domestic macroeconomic variables: changes in output, total investment, and government consumption. Since output is in part a function of possibly unobservable effort, we would expect some income components to be uninsurable, as the micro-level studies of Mace (1991) and Cochrane (1991) confirm. Changes in investment profitability could widen any wedge between domestic and rest-of-world consumption growth if world savings cannot flow costlessly to their most productive uses. Finally, considerations of moral hazard make it implausible that government spending shocks are completely insurable abroad: such insurance would present governments with an irresistible incentive to overspend. If uninsured idiosyncratic consumption risks are uncorrelated with aggregate preference shocks, they should enter significantly into the Table 2.11 regressions.

Table 2.11 strongly supports the basic model of financial integration for

Table 2.12. *Regressions of Japanese consumption growth on rest-of-world consumption growth and various macroeconomic shocks, 1973–88*

	1	2	3	4	5	6	7
$\Delta \log C_W^{JN}$	− 0.01*	0.36	**1.21**	− 0.04*	0.02*	0.13	0.04
	(0.43)	(0.53)	(0.48)	(0.46)	(0.44)	(0.59)	(0.50)
$\Delta \log GDP$	**0.82**	—	—	**0.77**	**0.85**	—	**0.88**
	(0.20)	—	—	(0.29)	(0.21)	—	(0.36)
$\Delta \log I$	—	**0.23**	—	0.03	—	**0.25**	− 0.01
	—	(0.09)	—	(0.11)	—	(0.10)	(0.14)
$\Delta \log G$	—	—	0.10	—	− 0.12	0.23	− 0.14
	—	—	(0.29)	—	(0.20)	(0.25)	(0.26)
$\bar{R}^2$	0.69	0.50	0.29	0.67	0.65	0.50	0.64
Lags	0	0	0	0	0	0	0
H_1	0.00	0.08	0.80	0.01	0.01	0.12	0.03
H_2	0.00	0.03	0.76	0.01	0.01	0.07	0.02

Note: Standard errors appear below coefficient estimates. **Boldface entries** of coefficient estimates are those differing from 0 at the 5% significance level or below. An asterisk (*) marks first-row coefficients that differ from 1 at the 5% level or below. 'Lags' shows the moving-average order assumed for the equation disturbance in calculating standard errors. Marginal significance levels are reported for tests of two hypotheses: H_1 is the hypothesis that the coefficient of rest-of-world consumption is 1, those of all other variables 0; H_2 is the hypothesis that the coefficients of variables other than rest-of-world consumption growth are all 0.

Germany, but suggests that government consumption shocks are not fully insurable abroad. Regression 3, for example, strongly rejects any hypothesis setting the coefficient on government consumption growth to zero. The results show that domestic and rest-of-world consumption move in proportion except for shocks to German government consumption, which actually raise domestic growth relative to world growth, contrary to the prediction of a neoclassical Ricardian model of purely wasteful government spending. Output and investment shocks, however, seem to play no role. It should be noted that the output and investment variables are highly correlated with rest-of-world consumption growth (the simple correlation coefficients are 0.84 and 0.77, respectively).

Is it possible that ouput shocks really do contribute to 'excess' domestic consumption growth in regressions 1, 4, 5, and 7, but that their effect is masked by a correlation with the preference shocks in the equation disturbance? This seems implausible, as the correlation between preference shocks that raise home consumption and output would likely have to be negative to bias downward the coefficient of $\Delta \log GDP$.

The results for Japan in Table 2.12 present a quite different picture. Here domestic GDP growth is significant; moreover, its presence reduces the influence of rest-of-world consumption growth to zero. Over 1973–88, Japanese output growth and rest-of-world consumption growth are highly correlated (the correlation coefficient is 0.72). One interpretation of our earlier results suggesting substantial financial integration for Japan is that world consumption growth was merely proxying the true factor driving Japan's consumption growth, namely, the country's own domestic output growth. On this view, the Japan regressions in Tables 2.6–2.10 are not strong evidence in support of a financial market link between Japanese and foreign consumption growth.[23]

This interpretation of Table 2.12 relies, however, on an assumption that $\Delta \log GDP$ is uncorrelated with the unobservable Japanese preference shocks. A different possible interpretation is suggested, however, by the hypothesis that preferences shocks that raise Japanese consumption growth also raise Japanese GDP growth (through Keynesian or other mechanisms).

To investigate the effects of such a correlation, write regression 1 in Table 2.12 (for example) as

$$\Delta \log C_{\mathrm{JN},t} = a_{\mathrm{JN},W}\, \Delta \log C_{W,t}^{\mathrm{JN}} + \gamma \Delta \log GDP_t + \epsilon_{\mathrm{JN},t},$$

where $\epsilon_{\mathrm{JN},t}$ is a pure relative-preference shock. Suppose that $\Delta \log GDP_t$ and $\epsilon_{\mathrm{JN},t}$ have covariance $\sigma_{2\epsilon}$, that ρ_{12} is the correlation coefficient between $\Delta \log C_{Wt}^{\mathrm{JN}}$ and $\Delta \log GDP_t$, and that these two regressors have standard deviations σ_1 and σ_2, respectively. If $\sigma_{2\epsilon} > 0$, the least-squares estimate $\hat{\gamma}$ of γ is upward biased, and at the same time $\hat{a}_{\mathrm{JN},W}$ is a *downward*-biased estimate of $a_{\mathrm{JN},W}$ if $\rho_{12} > 0$:

$$\operatorname{plim} \hat{\gamma} = \gamma + \frac{\sigma_{2\epsilon}}{\sigma_2^2(1-\rho_{12}^2)}, \tag{26}$$

$$\operatorname{plim} \hat{a}_{\mathrm{JN},W} = a_{\mathrm{JN},W} - \frac{\rho_{12}\sigma_{2\epsilon}}{\sigma_1\sigma_2(1-\rho_{12}^2)}. \tag{27}$$

So when both $\sigma_{2\epsilon}$ and ρ_{12} are positive, it is theoretically possible that $a_{\mathrm{JN},W} = 1$ notwithstanding a large-sample regression like 1 in Table 2.12 with $\hat{a}_{\mathrm{JN},W} = -0.01$.

The discussion illustrates the identification problems bedevilling attempts to measure international financial integration and market completeness using aggregate data. The results of this section seem uniformly consistent with the proposition that the German economy is tightly meshed into international financial markets: its consumption moves in proportion to the rest of the world's, and appears not to rise more quickly when domestic output is high or more slowly when domestic investment is high. German government consumption does, however, have an idiosyncratic positive effect on German private consumption. Japan, which liberalised its financial markets more recently than did Germany, shows ambiguous evidence of financial openness. Only under much stronger identifying assumptions than those invoked in the German case can Table 2.12's results be made consistent with the hypothesis that Japan is as well integrated into world financial markets as Germany. If these assumptions are false, explanations other than increasing financial integration must be found for the fall in relative Japanese consumption-growth variability after 1973 (Table 2.2).

6 Concluding remarks

This chapter has studied the relationship between domestic consumption growth and world consumption growth for the G-7 industrial countries. For most of these countries there appears to be a post-war trend of increasing coherence between domestic and world consumption growth, as predicted by models of international financial integration. But the correlation between those variables remains far from perfect – as one would expect, even in a world of unrestricted international asset trade, when asset markets are incomplete, national preferences are subject to shocks, and consumption is measured with error.

Another set of factors underlying empirical international consumption correlations has not been discussed in this chapter: nontraded goods and services, including leisure. These factors' influences were impounded into the error terms of my econometric equations, but an attempt to measure and model them explicitly is an obvious next step that could alter the conclusions reached above.

It is worth emphasising again that the empirical patterns reported in the chapter could have been generated by developments other than increasing financial interdependence. In comparing 1951–72 with 1973–88 we see, for example, a marked rise in the correlations between British, German, and Japanese output growth and rest-of-world consumption growth. Conceivably these changes give the false appearance of greater financial integration, when all that has really happened is that the potential gains from asset trade have fallen exogenously. My conclusion that for Germany and perhaps other countries there is more to the story than this is based on identifying assumptions that certainly warrant further investigation. More could be learned as well by augmenting the limited data sample used here, and by studying additional types of disturbance, such as terms-of-trade and interest-rate shocks.

NOTES

This chapter was originally prepared for the conference on 'International Capital Mobility and Development', sponsored by the Bank of Israel, the Centre for Economic Policy Research, and the Pinhas Sapir Center for Development, Tel-Aviv University (Tel-Aviv, 20–22 December 1992). I thank Matthew Jones for excellent research assistance. The editors of this volume, Benjamin Bental, Andrew Rose, and participants in seminars at the Federal Reserve Bank of San Francisco, the University of Washington and Princeton provided helpful comments. All errors are my own. National Science Foundation grant SES-9022832 and a Ford Foundation grant to the Center for International and Development Economics Research (CIDER) at UC-Berkeley provided generous financial support.

1 van Wincoop (1992) examines the degree of risk sharing evident in Japanese regional consumption data.
2 Stockman and Tesar (1990) stress the potential importance of country-specific preference shocks in matching a real business cycle model to industrial-country data.
3 See Radner (1972) for a similar approach to modelling possibly incomplete markets.
4 For applications of measure-theory concepts in economics and finance, see Stokey and Lucas (1989) and Duffie (1992).
5 Because the complete-markets case yields Pareto-optimal allocations, this efficiency condition could alternatively be derived by considering the choices a benevolent social planner would make (see, e.g., Cole and Obstfeld, 1991).
6 If indexed bonds were widely traded, which they are not, a rejection of the implications of (7) could be construed as evidence of imperfect capital mobility, i.e., of impediments to free-asset trade. My 1989 paper tested the implications of free trade in nominal bonds between the United States and Japan and Germany. I found evidence of substantial trade impediments before the early 1970s, but not afterward. To conserve space, I do not carry out analogous tests in the present chapter.
7 My preferred point estimate for ρ was 1.52.
8 See the studies listed in section 1 above. Simple correlations of log-consumption differences for this chapter's sample are presented at the end of this section.
9 In their setups, these fixed effects arise from planner utility weights in a social welfare function.
10 Kollmann (1992) reports similar findings for different consumption data sets.
11 Equation (19) could have been derived from (6).
12 An alternative estimation approach would be to use instrumental variables correlated with the growth in world consumption. Lagged variables are plausible candidates for instruments, but the inherent near-unpredictability of consumption changes makes it difficult to find lagged variables that are closely correlated with $\Delta \log C_{Wt}$. Tim Cogley has suggested, in analogy with Hall (1986), that a contemporaneous variable such as world military expenditures

might provide a suitable instrument for $\Delta \log C_{Wt}$. I plan to pursue this suggestion in future work.

13 These are variables 3 through 6 from Appendix A.1 of Summers and Heston (1991). I also used population (variable 1).

14 The countries included are Kenya, Morocco, South Africa, Canada, Costa Rica, the Dominican Republic, El Salvador, Guatemala, Honduras, Mexico, Trinidad and Tobago, the United States, Argentina, Bolivia, Chile, Colombia, Ecuador, Paraguay, Peru, Uruguay, India, Japan, Pakistan, the Philippines, Thailand, Austria, Belgium, Cyprus, Denmark, Finland, France, West Germany, Greece, Iceland, Ireland, Italy, Luxembourg, the Netherlands, Norway, Portugal, Spain, Sweden, Switzerland, Turkey, the United Kingdom, Australia, and New Zealand.

15 Thus, in Table 2.1's first row I report the correlation of $\Delta \log C_{it}$, not with $\Delta \log C_{Wt}$, but with $\Delta \log C^{i}_{Wt}$, where $\Delta \log C^{i}_{Wt} \equiv (1 - n_{it})^{-1}(C_{Wt} - n_{it} C_{it})$.

16 The estimates were done in RATS. When there was strong evidence of serial correlation, standard errors were corrected using the 'lags' option in LINREG, with a damping factor of 0.8. In the tables, 'Lags' indicates the order moving-average process assumed for the equation disturbance. Because the time-series sample under study here is so small, the autocorrelation corrections suffer from a small-sample bias that seems to understate standard errors. I have therefore tried to be conservative in using the correction and in drawing inferences from corrected estimates.

17 The theoretically expected slope coefficient is still 1 because (12) is replaced by:

$$\Delta \log C_{it} = \log C^{i}_{Wt} + \log C_{i0} + (\log \beta_i)(t/\rho) + \left\{\theta_{it}/\rho - \log\left[\frac{1}{1 - n_{it}} \Sigma_{j \neq i} \beta_j^{t/\rho} \exp(\theta_{jt}/\rho) n_{jt} C_{j0}\right]\right\}.$$

18 The price of oil is an index of the US dollar prices of Saudi Arabian crude petroleum exports, as reported in the International Monetary Fund's *International Financial Statistics*. These dollar prices are deflated by the US GNP deflator reported in the *Economic Report of the President*.

19 Even though there are no major oil exporters in my 47-country index, the countries do not all depend on oil imports to the same extent. Countries face differential levels of oil-price risk, and can benefit from reallocating that risk through trade.

20 Let F be net factor payments from abroad, CA the current account balance, and S national saving. One version of the national income identity is $I = CA + (GDP + F - C - G) = CA + S$; Feldstein and Horioka (1980) in effect regress I on S to determine whether CA has an impact on domestic investment independent of S. Another way to write the national income identity – one that highlights the dependence of consumption and investment on *all* net resources from abroad – is as $C = (F - CA) + (Y - I - G) = TR + (Y - I - G)$; when $a_{iW} \approx 0$ because of low capital market integration, F should be negligible too and regression (25) should lead to the same result ($\gamma_i \approx 1$) as a time-series version of the Feldstein–Horioka regression. Notice that data on F, which are notoriously inaccurate, are *not* required for (25), as they are for accurately measuring S. For a discussion of the biases lack of accurate data on F could cause, see my (1986) paper.

21 The log oil-price change was entered into the regressions for Italy and the

United Kingdom in panel B (the only cases in which oil entered significantly). Coefficient estimates for oil are not reported.

22 See Boothe, Clinton, Côté and Longworth (1985).

23 In the Table 2.10 (panel B) regression for Japan involving the domestic resource limit $DRL = GDP - I - G$, it is possible that the strong correlation between output and investment growth (the 1973–88 correlation coefficient is 0.85) reduced the composite variable to insignificance. Notice in Table 2.12 (regressions 2 and 6) that investment is significant when it, instead of output, is entered into the regression.

REFERENCES

Atkeson, A. and T. Bayoumi (1992) 'Do private capital markets insure against regional risk? Evidence from the United States and Europe', University of Chicago and International Monetary Fund, mimeo.

Backus, D. and G. Smith (1992) 'Consumption and real exchange rates in dynamic exchange economies with nontraded goods', New York University and Queen's University, mimeo.

Backus, D.K., P.J. Kehoe and F.E. Kydland (1992) 'International real business cycles', *Journal of Political Economy*, **100** (August), 745–55.

Baxter, M. and M. Crucini (1993) 'Explaining saving/investment correlations', *American Economic Review*, **83** (June), 230–78.

Boothe, P., K. Clinton, A. Côté and D. Longworth (1985) *International Asset Substitutability: Theory and Evidence for Canada*, Ottawa: Bank of Canada.

Cochrane, J. (1991) 'A simple test of consumption insurance', *Journal of Political Economy*, **99** (October), 957–76.

Cole, H. and M. Obstfeld (1991) 'Commodity trade and international risk sharing: How much do financial markets matter?', *Journal of Monetary Economics*, **28** (August), 3–24.

Devereux, M., A. Gregory and G. Smith (1992) 'Realistic cross-country consumption correlations in a two-country, equilibrium, business cycle model', *Journal of International Money and Finance*, **11** (February), 3–16.

Duffie, D. (1992) *Dynamic Asset Pricing Theory*, Princeton, NJ: Princeton University Press.

Feldstein, M. and C. Horioka (1980) 'Domestic saving and international capital flows', *Economic Journal*, **90** (June), 314–29.

French, K. and J. Poterba (1991) 'International diversification and international equity markets', *American Economic Review*, **81** (May), 222–6.

Golub, S. (1991) 'International diversification of social and private risk: The U.S. and Japan', Swarthmore College, mimeo.

Granger, C. and P. Newbold (1974) 'Spurious regressions in econometrics', *Journal of Econometrics*, **2**, 111–20.

Hall, R. (1986) 'The role of consumption in economic fluctuations', in R. Gordon (ed.), *The American Business Cycle: Continuity and Change*, Chicago: University of Chicago Press.

Kollmann, R. (1992) 'Consumptions, real exchange rates and the structure of international asset markets', Université de Montréal, mimeo.

Leme, P. (1984) 'Integration of international capital markets', University of Chicago, mimeo.

Mace, B. (1991) 'Full insurance in the presence of aggregate uncertainty', *Journal of Political Economy*, **99** (October), 928–56.

Obstfeld, M. (1986) 'Capital mobility in the world economy: Theory and measurement', *Carnegie–Rochester Conference Series on Public Policy*, **24** (Spring), 55–104.

(1989) 'How integrated are world capital markets?: Some new tests', in G. Calvo, R. Findlay, P. Kouri and J. Braga de Macedo (eds), *Debt, Stabilization and Development: Essays in Memory of Carlos Diaz-Alejandro*, Oxford: Basil Blackwell, 134–55.

Radner, R. (1972), 'Existence of equilibrium of plans, prices, and price expectations in a sequence of markets', *Econometrica*, **40** (March), 289–303.

Scheinkman, J. (1984) 'General equilibrium models of economic fluctuations: A survey of theory', University of Chicago, mimeo.

Stockman, A. and L. Tesar (1990) 'Tastes and technology in a two-country model of the business cycle: Explaining international comovements', *NBER, Working Paper*, **3544** (December).

Stokey, N. and R. Lucas (1989) *Recursive Methods in Economic Dynamics*, Cambridge, MA: Harvard University Press.

Summers, R. and A. Heston (1991) 'The Penn World Table (Mark 5): An expanded set of international comparisons, 1950–1988', *Quarterly Journal of Economics*, **106** (May), 327–68.

Tesar, L.L. and I.M. Werner (1992) 'Home bias and the globalization of securities markets', *NBER Working Paper*, **4218** (November).

Townsend, R. (1989) 'Risk and insurance in village India', University of Chicago, mimeo.

van Wincoop, E. (1992) 'Regional risksharing', Boston University and IGIER, Milan (November), mimeo.

Discussion

BENJAMIN BENTAL

The point of Chapter 2 is compelling – world financial markets become more integrated over time. Of course, all of us 'know' that this is so, and there is little point in arguing against this thesis. But Obstfeld's goal is to *prove* that this is indeed the case by using economic theory and clever econometrics. My discussion will, therefore, concentrate solely on the proof Obstfeld suggests. I will pretend that I know nothing about the world economy, and ask: are there other possible explanations (according to economic theory) which may account for the reported phenomena in the data, other than increased financial integration?

The model used in this chapter is quite simple and appealing. Consider two individuals who are given random consumption streams. Suppose that each individual is shocked by idiosyncratic random shocks which are uncorrelated with the shocks of any other individual. Then the consumption streams will be uncorrelated. If we allow the individuals to share their idiosyncratic risks by trading in contingent claims, then their consumption will be highly correlated since the trade will, in a sense, cancel out the idiosyncratic shocks. If, on the other hand, the individuals can trade away only part of the idiosyncratic risk, the correlation of the individual consumption levels will be less than perfect. However, the expected value of the intertemporal marginal rates of substitution, conditioned on any set of random variable that can be traded, must be the same for any pair of individuals which is engaged in trade. In particular, it must be uncorrelated with any random variable which can be traded (see the Theorem on p. 16). If we use the representative consumer approach to model country behaviour, the same must hold for aggregate consumption streams of countries.

Obstfeld takes this approach, assumes that preferences in each country are of the CRRA form, but subject to a country-specific preference shock. With such a specification the intertemporal marginal rates of substitution are simply logarithmic differences of consumption levels, so that the similarity of these MRSs could be directly tested. For various technical reasons, Obstfeld differences the logs of the consumption levels, so that all his tests are carried out in the terms of rates of growth of consumption. In addition, instead of testing the similarity pairwise, Obstfeld tests each of the G-7 against the world growth rate of consumption. Essentially, higher correlations between each country's consumption growth rate and the world growth rate are interpreted as supporting the hypothesis that the degree of worldwide financial integration has increased.

Table 2.1, which reports simple pairwise correlations among the G-7 as well as the correlation between each of them and the rest-of-world, basically tells the whole story. In it we see that (except for Canada) these correlations are much higher in the 1973–88 than in the 1951–72 period. These results are then tested in more elaborate regressions, but the same picture emerges.

Obstfeld is quite careful in the interpretation of these results; he remarks that 'Taken as a whole, Table 2.1 is consistent with the hypothesis that increased international trade in a broader range of financial assets took place after 1973'. At this point of the argument the natural question to ask is whether this result is due to a common factor affecting all these countries. The most natural candidate is, of course, the oil shock. Obstfeld is, of course, aware of this question. He adds the yearly changes in the

Table 2D.1. *Per capita GDP growth rates, 1948–72 and 1972–88, 1973–80 and 1980–88*

	CA	*F*	*D*	*I*	*J*	*UK*	*US*	*mean*	*sd*
1948–72	2.9	4.3	5.7	4.9	8.2	2.4	2.2	4.4	1.98
1972–88	2.6	2.1	2.2	2.8	3.3	2.1	1.7	2.4	0.49
1973–80	2.6	2.1	2.2	3.8	2.7	1.1	1.1	2.2	0.88
1980–88	2.1	1.1	1.7	2.0	3.0	2.7	2.3	2.1	0.58

Sources: Maddison (1982); Summers and Heston (1988).

real oil price in the 1973–88 period as regressors and finds that the results are not affected in any essential way. Now, this may be a minor point, but I am not quite convinced by the way Obstfeld tests the impact of the oil shocks. When one looks at the oil prices of the relevant period one observes that this series does not display very much variation. If I am correct, then it is not very surprising that it did not do much in the regressions. Taking this to the extreme – suppose oil prices jumped to a new and much higher level in 1973, staying at that constant (real) level ever after. Then oil prices will not affect Obstfeld's regressions. However, think of the enormous shock waves this increase in oil prices sends through the G-7 economies – with technological adjustments which take 'time to build' and so on. Obviously there is something in the story which is simply not captured!

Let me turn now to an alternative (possible) explanation for the phenomenon reported (i.e., the increased correlations between consumption growth rates). Suppose that growth processes are described by some version of the Solow model, with three key features. First, even though countries in the world are quite isolated from one another, and may be quite different in almost every aspect of their economies, they are all somehow subject to a decreasing returns to scale technology which makes growth rates in all countries *converge*: it is not essential, I think, that they converge to the *same* growth rate. Second, consumption in all countries is closely related to output, so that growth rates in consumption and output are closely related. Finally, the growth processes are affected by some (country-specific) shocks which diminish in some well-specified way in importance as the countries approach the (stochastic) steady states. There are several models which can provide environments of this nature, such as Bental and Peled (1992). In this model the stochastic nature of the growth process arises from an endogenous search for technological improvements, and it posseses all the desired features.

There is plenty of evidence that the predictions of models of the class mentioned above are not contradicted by the data. Table 2D.1 gives some numbers pertaining to the G-7.

It is quite clear from Table 2D.1 that growth rates of these countries have become much more similar in the later subperiods. There is also additional evidence which tells us something about the variation of the growth rates. Bental and Peled (1992) report yearly average growth rates and their standard deviations, conditioned on per capita income. If we look at the relevant range of that figure (not the poorest countries), one may believe that the average growth rates are indeed declining, and (admittedly, with some stretch of the imagination) that the standard deviation of the growth rates is also declining. So countries *do* become more similar, and again – this need *not* be a result of financial integration!

Obstfeld is aware that something like this may be going on. He looks at Germany and Japan, and regresses the rate of growth in each of these countries on the world rate of growth *and* on domestic variables such as the rate of growth of domestic GDP. Now, for Germany the GDP growth rate does not do much to explain German consumption growth, once the world growth is included. But the correlation between German GDP growth and world consumption growth is 0.84! In Japan the picture is reversed – here GDP growth takes over from world consumption in explaining Japanese consumption growth. The correlation between Japanese GDP growth and world consumption growth is 0.72.

So, what do we learn? Let me quote from Obstfeld's conclusions: 'For most of [the G-7] countries there appears to be a post-war trend of increasing coherence between domestic and world consumption growth, as predicted by models of international financial integration'. However, 'the empirical patterns reported in the chapter could have been generated by developments other than increasing financial interdependence'. Obstfeld mentions that it is possible that 'all that has really happened is that the potential gains from asset trade have fallen exogenously'. I am not quite sure what Obstfeld has in mind in this final remark. However, I am sure that his basic assertion that financial integration has significantly increased is indeed correct, although I agree that the evidence presented remains inconclusive.

REFERENCES

Bental, B. and D. Peled (1992) 'Endogenous Technological Progress and Growth: A Search Theoretic Approach', Technion mimeo.

Maddison, A. (1982) *Phases of Capitalist Development*, Oxford: Oxford University Press.

Summers, R. and A. Heston (1988) 'A New Set of International Comparisons of Real Product and Price Levels Estimates for 130 Countries, 1950–1985', *Review of Income and Wealth*, **35** (March), 1–26.

3 Business-cycle volatility and openness: an exploratory cross-sectional analysis

ASSAF RAZIN and ANDREW K. ROSE

1 Motivation and introduction

Countries which reduce international barriers to movements in either goods or capital sacrifice domestic autonomy in the hope of a higher standard of living. The elimination of trade barriers should result in increased opportunities to exploit country-specific comparative advantages, and hence higher income on average. However, in reducing barriers to trade, countries also become more susceptible to shocks from the rest of the world (e.g., terms of trade shocks). In this chapter, we explore the link between openness and domestic economic conditions, focusing on the impact of international openness on business-cycle volatility.

Our work is empirical in nature, and exploits a panel of data which covers some 130 countries over the post-war period. We distinguish between barriers to capital mobility and barriers to goods mobility, since openness in goods flows and capital flows often have different theoretical implications. We first develop theoretical arguments which informally link the effects of increased accessibility to international goods and capital markets to business-cycle volatility. We then examine the empirical validity of these theoretical effects.

There are a number of different motivations for our interest in the links between mobility and business-cycle volatility. Recently, closer ties in both goods and capital markets have been established through a variety of regional arrangements such as the European Community's Single Market and the North American Free Trade Agreement (NAFTA). Regionally-based trade liberalisation may have an important effect on business-cycle volatility of member countries if volatility and openness are interrelated, and shocks are common across countries within a region.

Further, regionally-based trade liberalisation may potentially be explained by the political–economic aversion to the effects of openness-induced macroeconomic shocks. Virtually all of the EC, NAFTA and ASEAN countries are included in our sample.

The collapse of the Eastern Bloc has resulted in substantial openness in foreign trade of the former CMEA countries. Exchange controls have virtually disappeared on current account transactions, barter trade has given way to market-determined trade, and so far only relatively light import tariffs have been put in place. The potentially important effects of these trade policies on volatility has yet to be determined, but could have important effects on the economic and political success of the transition process. Along similar lines, several Latin American countries have recently unilaterally slashed trade barriers as an integral part of their inflation stabilisation programme. The possibility that this regime switch may have changed the business-cycle process in these countries is worthy of investigation. Our cross-sectional analysis includes a wide range of countries which are comparable in wealth and size to the former socialist and Latin American countries.

Surveying trade reforms in developing countries the 1991 *World Development Report* (p. 103) concluded that 'Despite the difficulties in implementing reform and sustaining it once introduced, liberalizing countries outperformed the others. Growth rates of the reforming countries exceeded the rest when other factors have been taken into account, including external financing, changes in the terms of trade, real exchange rate movements and faster growth in OECD countries'. However, the issue of business-cycle volatility has not yet been addressed and may bring related economic costs to liberalising countries even to the point of threatening the political sustainability of the programmes.

Our theoretical arguments are presented in section 2 of the chapter. This is followed by a description of the data in section 3, and presentation of our empirical methodology and some preliminary diagnostics in section 4. Our results on cross-country volatility are then presented in section 5. Some conclusions are offered in section 6.

2 Theoretical considerations

2.1 Introduction

This chapter is a preliminary exploration into some of the linkages which might exist between business-cycle volatility and barriers to international flows of goods and capital. It would be premature for us to develop and estimate a completely specified general equilibrium model. Our goal is much more modest, and should be viewed as an attempt to determine whether a more involved inquiry is warranted. Rather than specify and estimate a stochastic general equilibrium model, we investigate the sort of linkages between volatility and openness that economic theory suggests; we then perform nonstructural empirical analysis in an attempt to discover stylised facts and see whether the links are even close to what is suggested. Promising positive results would certainly not result in strong conclusions without further investigation; the weak links between openness and business-cycle volatility which we find may warrant additional, more refined analysis. This is especially true given the results of Mendoza (1992) who emphasises the sensitive nature of our cross-country statistical analysis to structural differences in the underlying economies.

We use theory informally to pin down the links between three different aspects of business-cycle volatility (output, consumption, and investment volatility) and two distinct concepts of openness, since reduced barriers to international trade in goods across countries often have different implications from international trade in goods across time. For simplicity, we refer to the former as barriers to current account or goods mobility, while the latter are referred to as barriers to the capital account, or simply capital mobility.

We take care below to treat four different sorts of shocks distinctly. Our shocks can be transitory or persistent in duration; in addition, they may also be either common across countries, or idiosyncratic (country-specific).

Our heuristic reasoning about the effects of trade and capital flow barriers on volatility is as follows. Reductions in barriers to capital mobility provide for enhanced investment opportunities and allow countries to diversify country-specific productivity shocks. Increased capital mobility can thus be expected to enhance the volatility of investment. At the same time, the ability to use the current account for international borrowing and lending facilitates consumption smoothing. Hence, *enhanced capital mobility should be associated, ceteris paribus, with smoother consumption and more volatile investment*. This intuition is well known in the literature (e.g., Backus *et al.*, 1992); we then seek to quantify the relationship between the degree of capital mobility and the volatility in both consumption and investment.[1]

Turning to goods markets, international economic integration of goods markets intuitively allows national economics to specialise in (final) goods in which they have some comparative advantage. A reduction in trade barriers (e.g., import tariffs or non-tariff barriers (NTBs)) through either the use of comparative advantage or the exploitation of external economies, will lead to geographical concentration of industries and to export specialisation. Random non-diversifiable industry-specific shocks that lead to erratic shifts in exports will thus make output volatility more pronounced as international trade transactions are liberalised; Krugman (1992) discusses the same phenomenon at the regional level. Succinctly, *increased goods mobility should be associated, ceteris paribus, with increased output volatility*. Of course, if most of these shocks are persistent in nature, then consumption volatility should also be expected to rise with reductions in barriers to trade.

In the subsections which follow, we sketch out these ideas in more detail. Our objective is to outline the effects that differing shocks will have on each of our three measures of business-cycle volatility, under varying levels of both goods and capital mobility.

2.2 *Investment*

Restrictions on international capital flows directly affect the intertemporal trade opportunities of a country, and consequently the volatility of its investment and consumption. Investment theory predicts that reduction in barriers to the free flow of capital would enhance investment volatility as the substitution between investment at home and investment abroad becomes larger.

The point can be made simply with a diagram like Figure 3.1. We imagine a small open economy which experiences productivity shocks and analyse the implications of restrictions on international capital flows for the volatility of the country's investment and consumption. In the upper panel we show the familiar Solow model. The concave schedule represents the constant saving rate, s, times output, $hF(k)$, where h is a Hicks-neutral technological coefficient, $F(\cdot)$ denotes the production function, and k denotes the stock of capital. The ray from the origin represents the depreciation rate, g, times the capital stock, k. In the steady state, the level of capital is k^*. Without international capital mobility the steady-state condition is:

$$shf(k^*) = gk.$$

The downward-sloping schedule in the bottom panel portrays the marginal productivity of capital. To facilitate comparison with the perfect capital mobility case, we assume that at the steady-state stock of capital k^*, the schedule intersects a line representing the exogenous world rate of interest, r^*. The home country's marginal productivity of capital is thus

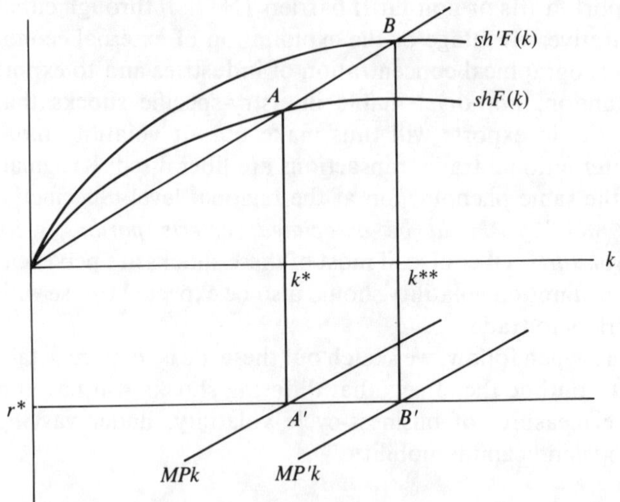

Figure 3.1 Capital mobility and investment

equal to the world rate of interest in every period. Therefore, in the perfect capital mobility case, the equality:

$$hf_k(k^*) = r^*$$

holds at all times, while in the zero-capital mobility case, it holds only at the steady state.

Now, suppose that a productivity-enhancing shock takes place.[2] The shock shifts both the saving schedule in the upper panel and the marginal productivity schedule in the bottom panel outward. If the production function is Cobb–Douglas, the change in the steady-state capital stock is given by (both in the case of free capital mobility and in the case of no capital mobility):

$$dk^*/dh = k^*/h(1-a)$$

where a is the income share of capital. That is, a permanent country-specific shock generates the same *long-run* investment response, whether or not there is capital mobility.

However, the short-run response may be quite different, depending on the degree of capital mobility. Under free capital mobility the capital stock is quickly adjusted from point A' to point B' in the bottom panel. In contrast, if no international capital flows are allowed, the capital stock is slow to adjust since the country's investment is rigidly tied to its savings, and the latter typically adjusts slowly along the transition path so as to smooth out consumption over time.

A comparable *global* shock need not change world saving patterns. However, since the demand for investment rises after an unanticipated productivity increase, an upward pressure on the rate of interest is exerted. Thus, if the productivity shock is common to the home country and the rest of the world, both the world interest rate and the marginal productivity schedule must rise. As the costs and payoffs of the investment project both go up, the effect on domestic investment is ambiguous. If the proportional increases in productivity and the rate of interest are the same, investment spending will remain unchanged. Hence, reductions in barriers to capital flows will enhance investment volatility to the extent that shocks are both persistent and country-specific.

Transitory shocks will have little effect on investment behaviour, whether or not they are common across countries, since investment responds to a change in the expected discounted sum of future profits, which cannot be altered significantly by a nonpersistent shock. To the extent that investment is irreversible, a nonpersistent shock may have no effect at all.

2.3 Consumption

To highlight the effect of capital mobility on consumption behaviour we show in Figure 3.2 the standard Fisherian two-period diagram. We assume that the subjective rate of time preference is equal to the rate of interest and let point *A* in Figure 3.2 describe the initial autarky equilibrium, in which the consumption point coincides with the GDP point. Restrictions on capital flows are therefore, initially, irrelevant.

Suppose that a *country-specific permanent* shock to productivity takes place, shifting the GDP point from *A* to *B*. At the same time assume that the world rate of interest remains unchanged. With homothetic preferences, the new consumption point moves to point *B*, so that capital-mobility restrictions are of no consequence. If, however, the shock is transitory, as indicated by the move from *A* to *B′* in Figure 3.2 without capital mobility the intertemporal consumption pattern must be tilted in favour of the period in which the supply shock is experienced. Capital mobility, however, facilitates consumption smoothing. Thus, in the presence of nonpersistent country-specific shocks, reductions in barriers to capital flows should lower the volatility of consumption.

Consider now what happens if the productivity shock is common across countries. A persistent, common, positive shock raises the world rate of interest, as the saving patterns in the world economy remain unchanged

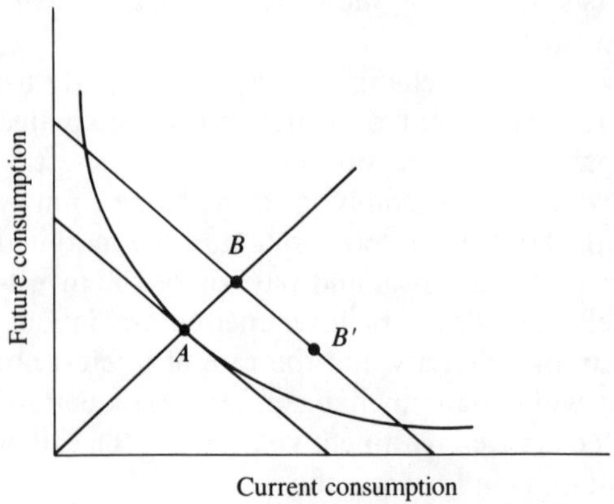

Figure 3.2 Capital mobility and consumption

but the world demand for investment demand rises. This is also true in a closed economy facing a persistent shock. Consequently, the degree of capital mobility does not affect consumption volatility, in the case of persistent global shocks.

A common *transitory* increase in productivity tends to create excess world saving that consequently lowers the world rate of interest. If capital is not allowed to move across countries, consumption rises to follow the temporary blip in output. Under free capital mobility, however, there are two conflicting forces at work: consumption smoothing and the tilting of the consumption path from future to current periods, resulting from the fall in the world rate of interest. Whether or not capital mobility reduces the volatility of consumption in this case depends on the relative magnitude of these conflicting effects.

To sum up, when shocks are common across countries, the role that capital mobility plays in reducing consumption volatility is likely to be relatively weak.

2.4 *Output*

Trade theory predicts that barriers to trade (whether 'artificial' tariffs or NTBs, or 'natural' transport costs) lead to a greater diversification in production (by establishing a range of commodities that are not traded); specialisation is encouraged by market broadening. To highlight this effect, we consider the familiar one-period many-commodity Ricardian trade model of Dornbusch, Fischer and Samuelson (1977).

We assume a continuum of goods and arrange the unit labour require-

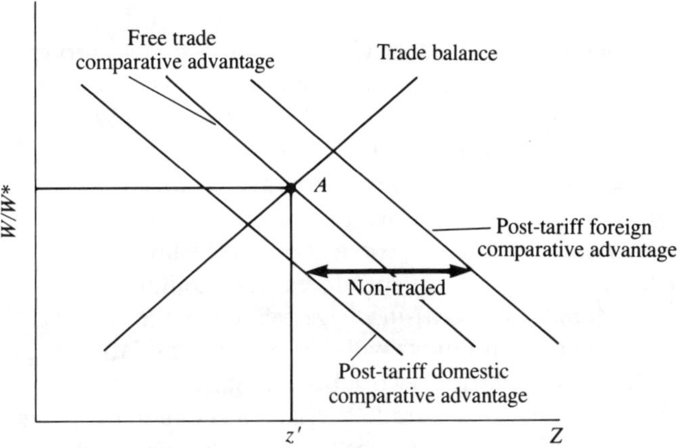

Figure 3.3 Goods mobility and output

ment ratio $a(z)/a^*(z)$ in order of diminishing home-country comparative advantage (where $a(z)$ is the domestic unit labour requirement associated with commodity z, and a^* is the corresponding foreign requirement). In trade equilibrium, goods will be produced where it is cheapest to make them; given a ratio of domestic to foreign wages w/w^*, commodity z will be produced at home so long as:

$$a(z)/a^*(z) > w/w^*.$$

The range of commodities produced by the home country will be between the commodity with the lowest relative unit labour requirement and the borderline commodity, z', for which the wage ratio is just equal to the relative unit labour requirement. This is portrayed by the free trade comparative advantage schedule in Figure 3.3.

In the one-period model, trade must be balanced. Assuming constant expenditure shares, the trade balance equilibrium condition is:

$$[1 - l(z')]wL = l(z')w^* L^*$$

where z' is the border line commodity and $l(z')$ is the fraction of income spent on home produced goods. The fraction of income spent on domestic goods will be larger, the larger is z' simply because a larger fraction of the total range of commodities is produced domestically. Consequently, one can draw an upward-sloping schedule in Figure 3.3 to portray the relationship between the borderline commodity and the relative wage which maintains trade balance equilibrium. Point A in Figure 3.3 indicates the unique relative wage at which simultaneously the world is efficiently specialised and trade is balanced.

A country-specific increase in productivity shifts the relative productivity schedule up. The range of goods that the home country produces rises, and its relative wage rises as well. A global productivity shock, however, will have no effect on relative productivity, and therefore will not change the range of goods that the home country produces.

The introduction of trade barriers gives rise to a range of nontraded commodities. As a result of a tariff (or a NTB, measured in tariff-equivalent terms), the home country produces commodities that are cheap relative to the (domestic) tariff-inclusive relative wage. Similarly, the foreign country's range of products will depend on the relative wage ratio inclusive of the foreign tariff. Two labour requirement schedules thus exist after the introduction of a trade barrier; the commodity range that separates them corresponds to the sector of nontraded goods (see Figure 3.3). The trade balance condition on the demand side is also modified to account for the effect of changes in wages on the range of commodities that are domestically produced.

The post-tariff trade equilibrium has a larger range of commodities that are produced domestically, compared with the free-trade equilibrium; trade barriers enhance product diversification. This implies that the imposition of trade barriers will reduce output volatility in the presence of idiosyncratic supply shocks. A similar prediction applies to the standard (Dixit–Stiglitz) model of intra-industry trade, where increased openness leads to greater output specialisation in certain varieties.

The analysis has thus far assumed that the goods produced and consumed are final goods. To the extent that trade takes place in intermediate inputs, openness may contribute to greater stability of aggregate output, insofar as access to a more diversified set of inputs alleviates supply disruptions. As we will not be able to distinguish between barriers to international trade in final and intermediate goods, we expect our results to be muddied to an uncertain extent.

3 Data

Our empirical work uses data drawn from three different sources. Our regressands are national accounts data taken from the Penn World Table; our measures of goods and capital mobility are taken from two different sources.

3.1 National accounts

The national accounts data is taken from the Penn World Table (Mark 5), hereafter referred to as PWT5. This data base is documented in Summers and Heston (1991). The PWT5 data span 1950 through 1988, though some of the 138 countries do not have data for the complete sample.[3] We use GDP per capita for our measure of output, this series is estimated using a chain index and computed in real terms at 1985 international prices. Our (real per capita) investment series includes both private and public investment. Our data have been transformed by natural logarithms throughout.

The theoretical arguments presented in section 2 deal with investment shocks, and consumption and output business-cycle fluctuations. As we are interested in linking estimates of consumption and output business-cycle volatility to measures of openness, we are forced to detrend these series, while also removing transitory investment influences. We take a relatively agnostic view about appropriate statistical representations of long-run growth, and use two different but standard approaches to decompose series into transitory (business-cycle) and permanent components. First, we examine a standard linear time trend, hereafter the 'TS' model. We also examine first-differences, implicitly adopting a random walk model of trends, hereafter the 'DS' model.

The raw volatility data is exhibited in Figure 3.4. We use standard deviations (of (de)trended variables) as measures of volatility. The graphs on the top (bottom) plot consumption (investment) volatility against output volatility; the graphs on the left (right) use the TS (DS) (de)trending method. In each graph, the datum for each country is marked by the first three letters of the country's name.

A number of points can be gleaned from Figure 3.4. Unsurprisingly, the method of (de)trending is important in that different techniques yield different results, especially with respect to the volatility of investment and output. Permanent investment shocks seem, unsurprisingly, much more volatile than transitory output shocks, but the volatility of (business-cycle fluctuations in) consumption is comparable to that of output. This may reflect: durability of consumption goods; the fact that much of the sample is composed of developing countries with imperfect capital markets; or the nature and persistence of output shocks.

3.2 *IMF data on trade and capital restrictions*

We use two sources for most of our data on capital and trade flow restrictions. The first data set is extracted from the summary tables at the back of the IMF's *Annual Report on Exchange Arrangements and Exchange Restrictions*. This data is available from 1967 through 1990. The data takes the form of country-specific annual dummy variables for seven different variables. The variables are: (1) 'Restrictions [in the form of quantitative limits, undue delay, or other official action which directly affects the availability or cost of exchange which] exist on payments [to

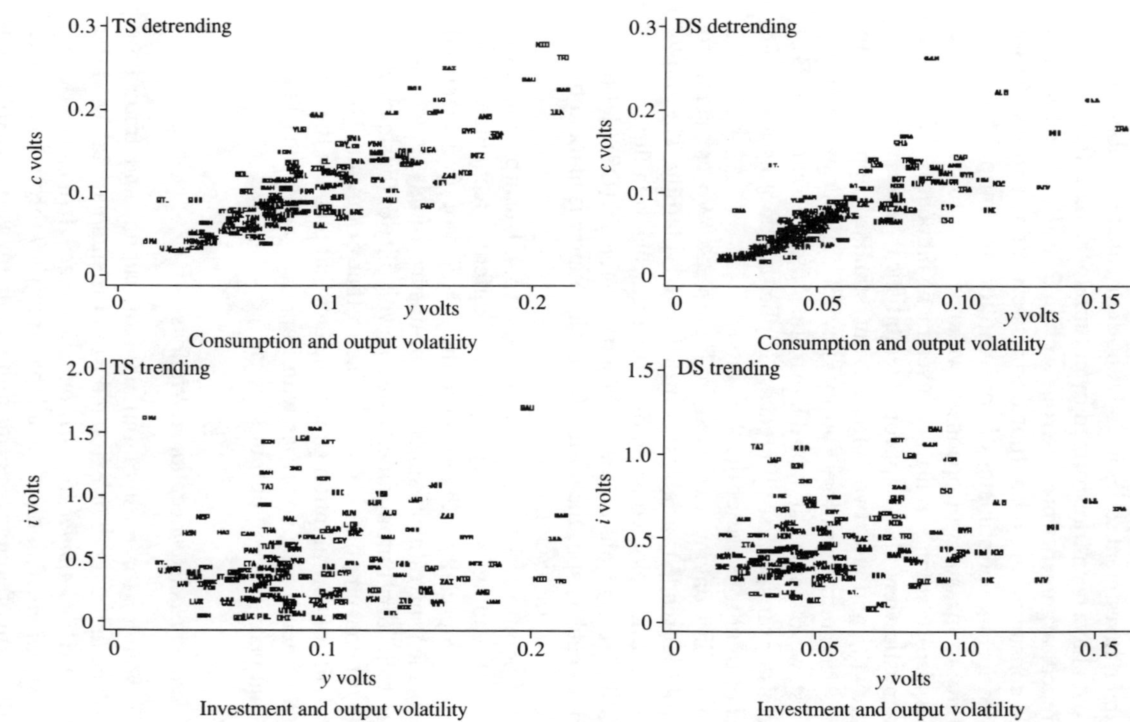

Figure 3.4 Raw volatility data for investment and consumption

Table 3.1. *Descriptive statistics on data from Annual Report on Exchange Arrangements and Exchange Restrictions*, 1967, 1975 and 1990

	1967		1975		1990	
	N	Mean	N	Mean	N	Mean
Current account	104	0.65	118	0.53	136	0.56
Capital account	104	0.77	118	0.79	136	0.79
Bilateral, members	104	0.41	118	0.33	136	0.27
Bilateral, nonmembers	104	0.43	118	0.32	136	0.18
Import surcharges	104	0.21	118	0.30	136	0.35
Import deposit	104	0.24	118	0.22	136	0.13
Export surrender	104	0.77	118	0.74	136	0.82
Prescribed currency	104	0.83	118	0.70	0	n/a
Payments arrears	0	n/a	0	n/a	0	0.36

IMF member countries] in respect of *current* (account) transactions [other than restrictions imposed for security reasons]'; (2) 'Restrictions [in the form of quantitative limits, undue delay, or other official action which directly affects the availability or cost of exchange] exist on payments [of resident-owned funds to IMF member countries] in respect of *capital* (account) transactions' [other than restrictions imposed for security reasons]; (3) '*Bilateral* payments arranged with [IMF] *members*'; (4) '*Bilateral* payments arrangements with *nonmembers*'; (5) 'Import surcharges'; (6) 'Advance import deposits'; (7) 'Surrender of export proceeds required'. In addition, there are two other variables which we cannot use because of limited data availability: (8) 'Prescription of currency' (a series which was discontinued after 1986); and (9) 'Payments Arrears' (a series which is available only after 1986).

The data taken from the *Annual Report* are summarised in Table 3.1, which tabulates cross-country sample sizes and means for 1967, 1975 and 1990. It is worthy to note that the measures indicate that the majority of countries have both current account and (to an even larger degree) capital account restrictions throughout the sample. Other controls are less prevalent, with the exception of the fact that most countries require surrender of export proceeds.

This data set has a number of problems. First, the variables are binary indicators, and do not take into account the severity of the controls. Second, many countries entered the sample relatively late, in a nonrandom fashion, leading to problems with missing data.[4] Latecomers were

Table 3.2. *Descriptive statistics on data from Pritchett (1991)*

Description	N	Mean	Std Dev.
Total overall charges	73	30.5	21.7
Total overall NTB charges	73	47.0	35.7
General FX licence dummy	73	0.178	0.385
General import licence dummy	73	0.178	0.385
Overall openness measure	45	0.038	0.152
Overall intervention rates	45	0.296	0.144
Overall distortion index	94	124.0	42.1
1982 Overall import penetration	97	28.5	23.4
1985 Overall import penetration	97	27.2	20.8
1982 Adjusted overall import penetration	96	56.2	81.7
1985 Adjusted overall import penetration	97	49.7	36.3

especially likely to be developing countries; clearly, simply truncating our cross-country sample by excluding countries with missing data might lead to nontrivial selection problems. Third, capital controls and/or trade barriers may be put in place as a result of business-cycle shocks of unusual magnitude, so that controls clearly cannot be taken as exogenous with this respect to business-cycle volatility. This potentially serious endogeneity issue will be addressed below.

3.3 Pritchett openness data

Our second source of data on trade and capital restrictions is the recent study by Pritchett (1991). Pritchett presents and discusses a number of different new and existing measures of outward orientation for a variety of both developing and industrial countries. As Pritchett convincingly demonstrates, these measures are very imperfectly correlated; there is no single good measure of trade openness. Among Pritchett's measures are: (1) average total overall charges on imports; (2) NTB frequency; (3) a dummy variable for general foreign exchange licensing; (4) a general import licence dummy; (5) openness, traditionally measured as the ratio of trade flows to GDP; (6) a measure of the overall rate of government intervention in international trade; (7) a measure of price distortion; and lastly (8) two measures (each for both 1982 and 1985) of import penetration, adjusted in different ways for country characteristics (e.g., endowments, geographic and economic size, etc.). Pritchett provides a complete discussion of the data; some descriptive statistics are provided in Table 3.2. It should be noted that the country coverage varies dramatically from country to country.

The empirical strategy that we follow below is to combine the IMF and Pritchett data in a number of different ways to produce plausible overall measures of the degree of goods and capital mobility, explicitly recognising that these measures will be imperfect.

4 Preliminary diagnostics

4.1 Persistence

As demonstrated in section 2, the time-series nature of the shocks is of great importance to our analysis. For instance, capital mobility in the face of persistent shocks is of much less consequence for consumption volatility than it would be if most shocks were transitory, since persistent shocks result in much less consumption smoothing. Hence, we investigate the time-series nature of our variables as a preliminary diagnostic exercise.

We computed simple Dickey–Fuller tests for (the logs of) each of our variables.[5] Unsurprisingly, the data typically do not reject the hypothesis that a single unit-root exists in the univariate representation of output, consumption and investment at conventional levels of statistical significance. We computed three tests (one for each of consumption, output and investment) for each of our 133 countries; of these, 18 (4.5%) tests reject the null hypothesis of a unit root at the 5% significance level, while 5 of these (1.3%) reject the null at the 1% significance level. These results are quite close to what would be expected under the null hypothesis, implying that the data are consistent with the hypothesis of unit-roots in the autoregressive representations of our variables.

It is well known that such tests have low power against stationary alternatives, and that there are serious problems in interpreting our tests results as demonstrating a high degree of persistence (e.g., Quah, 1992). We thus view our findings as consistent with a high degree of persistence in shocks, but by no means definitive. It does not seem worthwhile to use more econometric firepower on our variables, in light of the maximal sample size of less than 40 annual observations.

4.2 Factor analysis of shocks

The theoretical arguments above indicate that many of our results should depend critically on whether shocks are common across countries, or country-specific. To get a handle on this issue, we used standard factor-analytic techniques to test for the nature of the shocks striking our economies. Our factor analysis is performed cross-country on our

Table 3.3. *Cross-country factor analysis of shocks*
Proportions of total variance explained

Countries with at least 20 annual observations

	Output		Consumption		Investment
	TS	DS	TS	DS	DS
1 factor	43	20	37	16	46
4 factors	85	49	80	45	81

Countries with at least 35 annual observations

	Output		Consumption		Investment
	TS	DS	TS	DS	DS
1 factor	41	18	38	15	64
4 factors	79	41	74	37	86

(de)trended measures of output, consumption and investment. Our results are displayed in Table 3.3. Since the national accounts data in PWT5 are sometimes unavailable for the entire 1950–88 period, Table 3.3 tabulates results for two sets of countries: those with at least 20 annual observations, and those with at least 35 observations; results for different sets of countries (with different minimum sample lengths) are quite comparable.[6]

Our results depend critically on the technique used for (de)trending. When the variables are (de)trended using the TS method, four factors (the factors corresponding to the largest four eigenvalues) typically account for around three-quarters of the variation in all three series; the first factor alone accounts for over a third of the total variation. This seems to indicate that there may be a small number of important global shocks that are common across countries. However, these fractions fall by approximately one-half when the DS method of (de)trending is employed. Further, for both methods of (de)trending, the factor loadings (on the important factors) are by no means uniformly positive; the mixed signs indicate that the factors are not consistent with a global business-cycle shock which affects all economies in a similar fashion.

We interpret these results as implying that a significant fraction of the shocks in question are common, although the exact proportion is very far from clear. However, a large fraction of our shocks is also clearly idiosyncratic, especially when the DS method of (de)trending is used. While a reliable delineation of shocks into common and idiosyncratic shocks would be expected to improve our statistical results, we are wary of pursuing such a classification at this stage, for two reasons. First, such a decomposition is not clearly required, since it only improves statistical power. Second, decomposing shocks into idiosyncratic and common elements is extremely problematic, as indicated by the sensitivity of our factor analysis results to (de)trending technique. For instance, factor analysis is unlikely to deliver reliable results, given the well-known sensitivity of factor-analytic work of this style. On the other hand, simply constructing a global shock by adding up country-specific shocks seems even more problematic; weighting country-specific shocks by, e.g., real per capita GDP would not reflect the openness of the economy, which is central to our investigation. For these reasons, we resist classifying our shocks into global or idiosyncratic. However we keep the uncertain but substantial importance of common shocks in mind when we proceed on to our primary object of interest, namely the cross-country volatility work.

4.3 Other issues

One of the most striking features of our data is that much of it is missing, in clearly nonrandom ways. In particular, many developing countries have data gaps for the measures of capital and goods mobility. (Our problem is missing regressors rather than a censored regressand, so that sample selection of the traditional (Heckit) type is not the issue.) We attempt to test for the sensitivity of this issue by comparing our results with results which use imputed regressors, thereby allowing for a larger, more complete sample.

The omnipresent issue of simultaneity exists. We are interested in questions such as 'Does freer access to international capital allow domestic agents to smooth their consumption more effectively?' However, it is plausible, especially in the case of developing countries, that unusually large shocks lead to the imposition of capital controls. We attempt to handle this potentially serious issue by using instrumental variable techniques. (As mentioned above, instrumental variables are also essential insofar as nontrivial measurement error issues are associated with our measures of openness, a point stressed by Pritchett, 1991.) However, it is, as usual, difficult to choose plausible instrumental variables. We use a variety of sets of instrumental variables, discussing each explicitly, in order to check explicitly for the sensitivity of our results.

As should be clear from the discussion of the raw data in section 3, no single measure of openness in either trade or capital flows seems to dominate the available alternatives. We choose not to use a single flawed measure of, e.g., barriers to trade (such as the ratio of exports and imports to GDP, however adjusted). Instead, we use factor analysis to extract factors for goods and capital mobility which are correlated with our various indicators of openness, and treat these as statistical measures of openness with measurement error.[7]

We use 11 variables in constructing our current account openness factor: (1) the sample average value of the IMF dummy for current account restrictions; (2) the sample average value of the IMF dummy for import surcharges; (3) Pritchett's measure of total tariff charges; (4) Pritchett's NTB frequency variable; (5) Pritchett's measure of price distortions; (6) Pritchett's measure of import distortion; (7) Pritchett's traditional measure of openness; and (8)–(11) the 1982 and 1985 measures of openness adjusted in two different ways for country-specific characteristics.

Seven variables were used to construct our factor measuring capital account openness: (1) Pritchett's dummy variable for general foreign exchange licensing; (2) the sample average of the IMF dummy for capital account restrictions; (3) the sample average of the IMF dummy for bilateral balance of payments arrangements with members; (4) the sample average of the IMF dummy for bilateral balance of payments arrangements with nonmembers; (5) the sample average of the IMF dummy for deposit restrictions; (6) the sample average of the IMF dummy for export surrender; and (7) the sample average absolute value of the current account imbalance as a percentage of GDP.

The factor analysis used to generate the measures of goods and capital mobility seems to work well in two senses. First, a high fraction of the variance is absorbed in the single estimated factor (65% in the case of barriers to goods mobility, 75% in the case of capital mobility). Second, the factor loadings seem sensible. For instance, the first six (and the last five) variables which are used to construct the goods mobility factor have the same signs. The only mysterious result is the fact that the general foreign exchange licence dummy variable takes on a sign different from the next five measures of capital barriers.

Our extracted factors for current and capital account openness are presented in Figure 3.5 (there are two versions; one uses the data set which is complete, while the other uses imputed data). Higher value of either factor indicates more barriers to trade. As is clear (especially from Figure 3.5b with imputed data) the extracted factors seem sensible. For

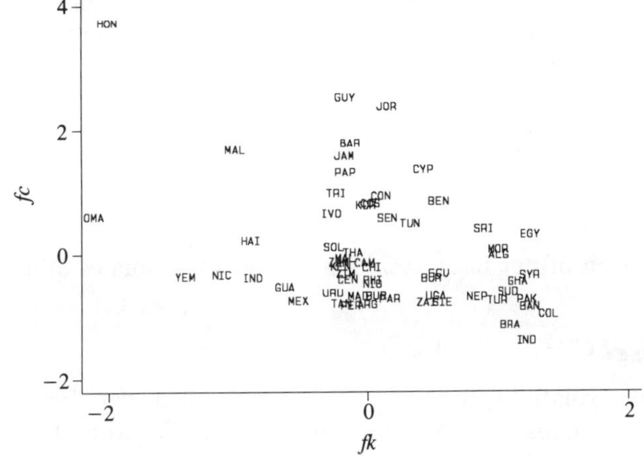

(a)

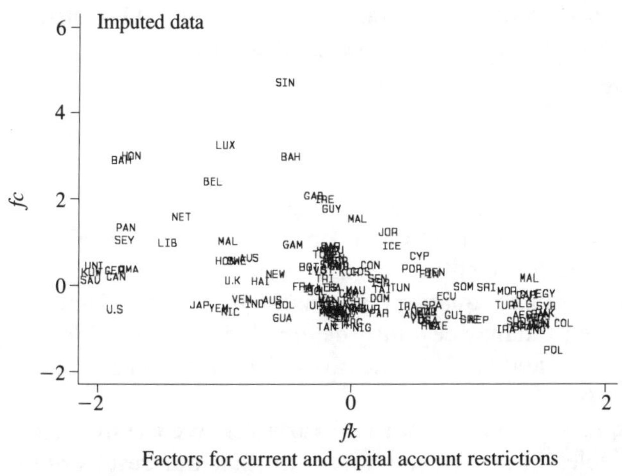

(b)

Figure 3.5 Factors for current and capital account openness

(*a*) Factors, from raw data
(*b*) Factors, from imputed data

instance, Canada, Germany, the United States and the United Kingdom have low barriers to both goods and capital mobility; developing countries tend to have high barriers to openness, especially on the capital side. The two measures of openness are negatively and significantly correlated (the simple correlation coefficient is −0.41 for the sample of 60 countries with complete data; the correlation is −0.48 for the complete sample of 133 countries with imputed data).

5 Empirical results on cross-country volatility

5.1 Basic results

We begin the discussion of our basic results by reporting estimates of a linear regression:

$$\sigma_{j,i} = a + \beta_{j,C} FC_i + \beta_{j,K} FK_i + \epsilon_{j,i}$$

where: σ represents volatility for our three (de)trended variables, $j = Y, C, I$ (for output, consumption, and investment); i denotes the country in question; FC and FK denote our factors for current and capital account mobility respectively; and ϵ represents a host of factors which determine country-specific volatility, and are hopefully orthogonal to our (included) measures of current and capital account mobility. Our theoretical arguments above lead us to the following hypotheses:

Ho: $\beta_{Y,C} < 0$
Ho: $\beta_{C,K} > 0$
Ho: $\beta_{I,K} < 0$

We are primarily interested in the effect of FK on investment and consumption volatility, and the effect of FC on output. However, given the preliminary, reduced-form nature of this work, we include both factors as regressors in all three equations, especially since the two factors are imperfectly measured and may be jointly determined. The inclusion of FK in the output equation and of FC in the investment equation can also be interpreted as specification tests.

We estimate this equation with instrumental variables. We use five sets of instrumental variables in an attempt to ensure that our results are insensitive to the exact choice of instrumental variables. The first set of instrumental variables is most extensive and includes: (1) the logarithm of the level of real GDP in 1985; (2) dummy variables for African, Asian, Latin American and OPEC countries; (3) the CIF/FOB ratio; (4) the ratios of total, private and official external debt to GDP; (5) the ratios of credit, private credit, M1 and M2–M1 to GDP; and (6) the 1985 values of the IMF dummies for current and capital account restrictions, bilateral payments arrangements with both members and nonmembers, required deposit restrictions, required export surrender, and import surcharges. The second set of instrumental variables excludes: (1) the real GDP level;

Table 3.4. *Basic results*
Basic cross-country volatility results (all estimates weighted)

	Output		Consumption		Investment	
	$\beta_{Y,C}$	$\beta_{Y,K}$	$\beta_{C,C}$	$\beta_{C,K}$	$\beta_{I,C}$	$\beta_{I,K}$
TS (de)trending						
IV Set 1	0.007	0.001	0.011	0.013	0.048	− 0.081
(se)	(0.010)	(0.010)	(0.011)	(0.011)	(0.080)	(0.077)
IV Set 2	0.005	− 0.009	0.015	0.024	0.161	0.134
(se)	(0.014)	(0.019)	(0.016)	(0.021)	(0.120)	(0.160)
IV Set 3	0.002	− 0.004	0.009	0.038	0.106	0.120
(se)	(0.014)	(0.019)	(0.017)	(0.023)	(0.115)	(0.158)
IV Set 4	0.002	− 0.004	0.010	0.039	0.112	0.129
(se)	(0.015)	(0.020)	(0.018)	(0.024)	(0.123)	(0.169)
IV Set 5	0.031	− 0.009	0.001	0.056	0.628	0.133
(se)	(0.031)	(0.037)	(0.056)	(0.053)	(0.424)	(0.517)
OLS	0.007	− 0.005	0.006	0.008	0.029	0.126
(se)	(0.006)	(0.008)	(0.008)	(0.010)	(0.049)	(0.061)
DS (de)trending						
IV Set 1	0.006	0.008	0.007	0.013	0.055	− 0.034
(se)	(0.005)	(0.005)	(0.008)	(0.008)	(0.048)	(0.046)
IV Set 2	0.006	0.006	0.015	0.025	0.122	0.092
(se)	(0.007)	(0.009)	(0.012)	(0.015)	(0.072)	(0.096)
IV Set 3	0.001	0.004	0.009	0.027	0.066	0.046
(se)	(0.007)	(0.010)	(0.011)	(0.016)	(0.066)	(0.091)
IV Set 4	0.002	0.007	0.011	0.031	0.091	0.081
(se)	(0.007)	(0.010)	(0.012)	(0.017)	(0.073)	(0.100)
IV Set 5	0.009	0.039	− 0.001	0.057	0.253	0.201
(se)	(0.022)	(0.026)	(0.035)	(0.042)	(0.190)	(0.232)
OLS	0.004	0.007	0.007	0.009	0.033	0.006
(se)	(0.003)	(0.004)	(0.005)	(0.006)	(0.028)	(0.035)

(2) the CIF/FOB ratio; and (3) the 1985 values of the IMF dummy variables. The third set includes: (1) the real GDP level; (2) the debt variables; and (3) the financial variables. The fourth set is the third set without the GDP variable, while the fifth set is merely the set of geographic (and OPEC) dummy variables.

Given the data series of different lengths which are used to construct our volatility (and other) measures, we use weighted procedures throughout, using weights which correspond to the quality of the data (as suggested by Summers and Heston, 1991).

Table 3.4 contains estimates of our basic equation. Results are tabulated for all five sets of instruments; OLS estimates are also presented for

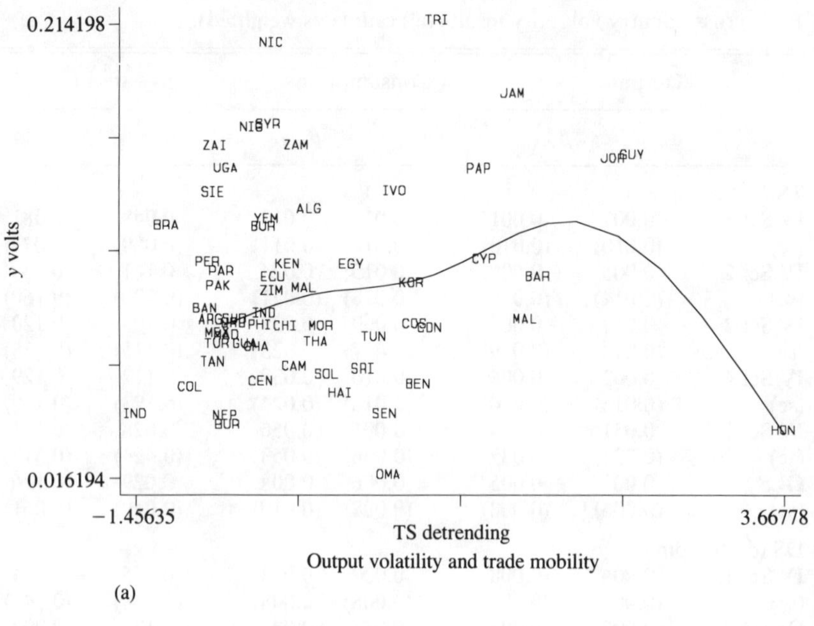

Output volatility and trade mobility

(a)

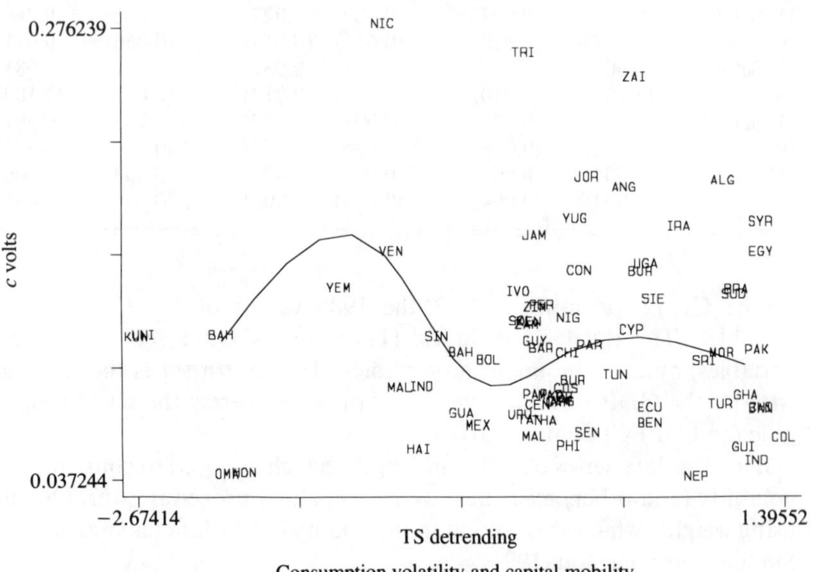

Consumption volatility and capital mobility

(b)

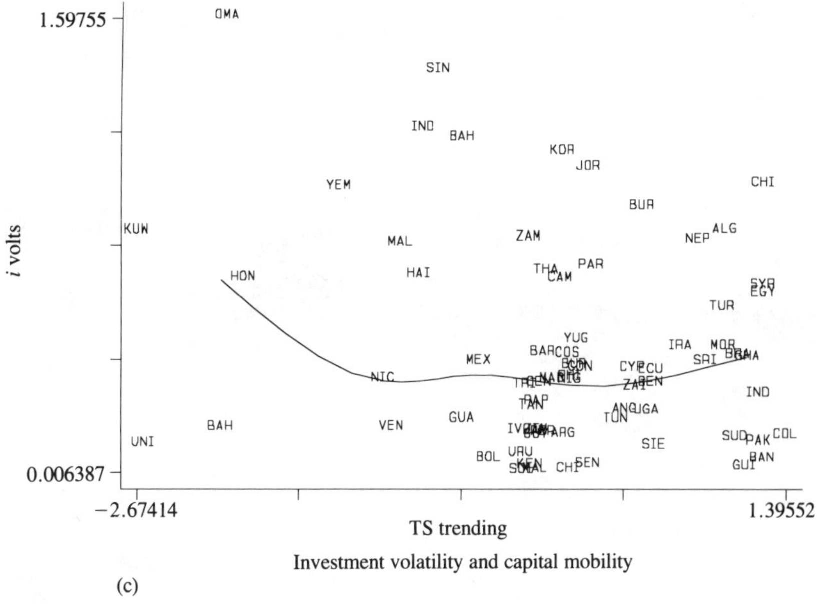

Figure 3.6 Volatility and mobility: TS detrending

(a) a_Y and FC, TS
(b) a_C and FK, TS
(c) a_I and FJ, TS

comparison. These estimates are typically produced using 50–60 observations (the exact number depends on the list of instrumental variables). The clearest finding is the absence of any significant relationship between either of the factors and either of the volatility series for each of our three variables; the coefficients are not significantly different from zero at the 5% significance level in any case, either jointly or individually.[8] The most positive results are the effects of barriers to capital mobility on consumption volatility; each of the coefficient estimates is positive, and they verge on statistical significance at conventional levels for some instrument sets. However, the results for output and investment volatility are not supportive of the null hypothesis. The effects of goods mobility on output volatility are typically positive, although the estimates are not statistically significant. Most of the coefficients linking capital mobility to investment volatility are negative but insignificantly so. Our results appear to be essentially independent of the (de)trending technique.

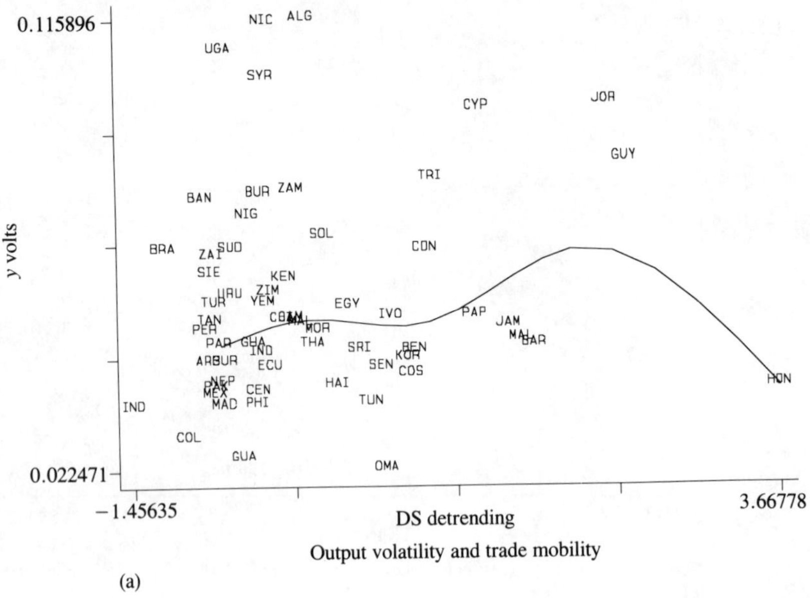

Output volatility and trade mobility

(a)

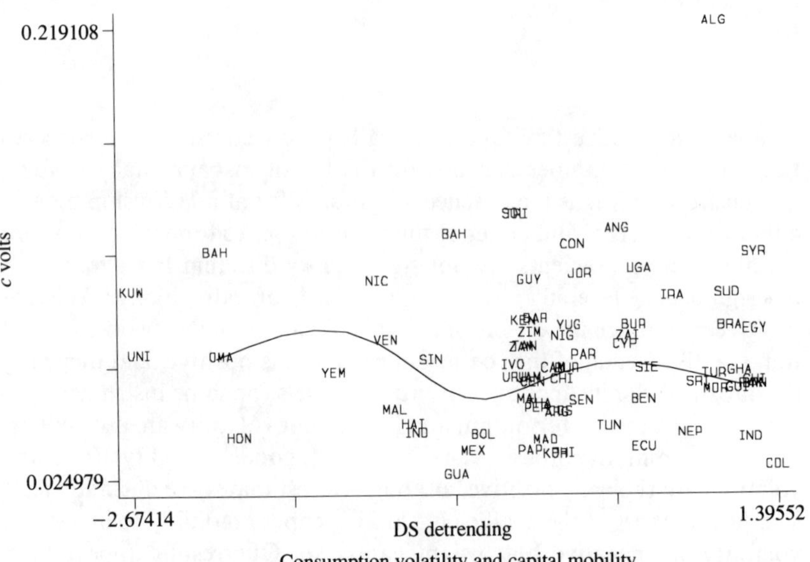

Consumption volatility and capital mobility

(b)

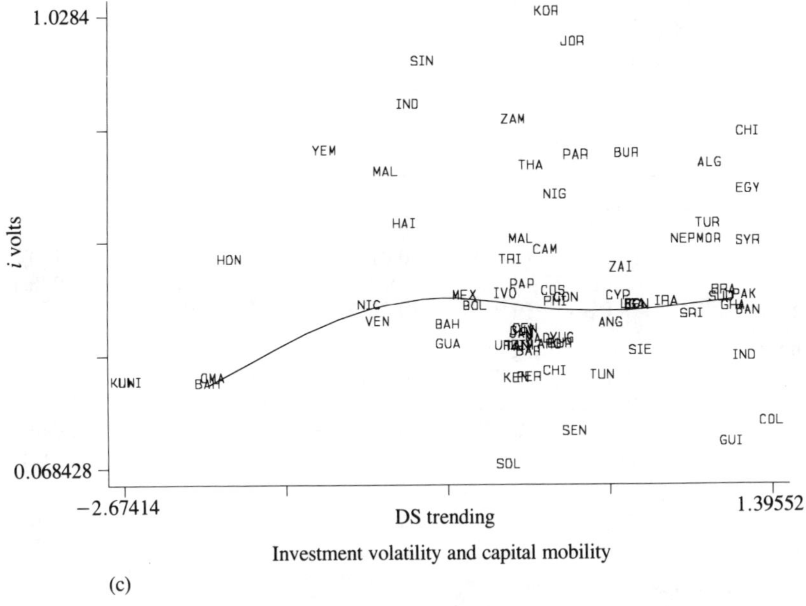

Investment volatility and capital mobility

(c)

Figure 3.7 Volatility and mobility: DS detrending

(*a*) σ_Y and *FC*, DS

(*b*) σ_C and *FK*, DS

(*c*) σ_I and *FK*, SS

We are primarily interested in the bivariate relationships between *FK* on investment and consumption volatility, and *FC* on output. Figure 3.6a shows the output volatility data against the goods mobility factor; Figures 3.6b and 3.6c are comparable graphs of consumption and investment volatility against the capital mobility factor. Figures 3.7a–3.7c are the analogues to 3.6a–3.6c, but using data (de)trended with the DS technique (Figures 3.6a–3.6c use the TS technique). Nonparametric data-smoothers are also provided to assist in gauging the relationships between the variables. These graphs are quite consistent with the results in Table 3.4; there certainly does not appear to be a clear linkage between our measures of goods and capital mobility and business-cycle volatility. These results are consistent with the results of Mendoza (1992), who shows that it is difficult to find correlations of the type we are interested in, even in artificial economies.

We now check the sensitivity of these mostly negative results to a variety of perturbations in our basic methodology, in order to ensure that our findings are robust.

Table 3.5. *Sensitivity analysis*
Sensitivity analysis of cross-country volatility results (all estimates weighted)

	Output		Consumption		Investment	
	$\beta_{Y,C}$	$\beta_{Y,K}$	$\beta_{C,C}$	$\beta_{C,K}$	$\beta_{I,C}$	$\beta_{I,K}$
Imputed data, TS (de)trending						
IV Set 3	0.009	0.021	0.022	0.039	0.248	0.113
(se)	(0.012)	(0.017)	(0.015)	(0.022)	(0.102)	(0.150)
IV Set 5	− 0.083	− 0.046	− 0.121	− 0.051	0.106	− 0.076
(se)	(0.044)	(0.038)	(0.063)	(0.054)	(0.198)	(0.172)
Imputed data, DS (de)trending						
IV Set 3	0.016	0.020	0.031	0.044	0.055	0.077
(se)	(0.008)	(0.012)	(0.014)	(0.020)	(0.060)	(0.088)
IV Set 5	− 0.059	− 0.029	− 0.118	− 0.037	− 0.015	0.040
(se)	(0.031)	(0.027)	(0.063)	(0.055)	(0.128)	(0.111)
Fixed effects, TS (de)trending						
IV Set 1	0.002	0.011	0.024	0.033	0.041	− 0.059
(se)	(0.019)	(0.015)	(0.023)	(0.018)	(0.120)	(0.096)
Fixed effects, DS (de)trending						
IV Set 1	0.009	0.009	0.025	0.023	− 0.030	0.075
(se)	(0.016)	(0.013)	(0.024)	(0.020)	(0.090)	(0.072)
IV Set 1	C/acc	K/acc	C/acc	K/acc	C/acc	K/acc
IMF RHS TS	0.017	− 0.029	0.019	− 0.022	− 0.006	− 0.296
(se)	(0.019)	(0.029)	(0.022)	(0.034)	(0.152)	(0.235)
IMF RHS DS	0.006	0.004	0.013	0.006	− 0.006	− 0.121
(se)	(0.010)	(0.015)	(0.015)	(0.024)	(0.094)	(0.145)

5.2 *Robustness*

We have checked the sensitivity of our basic results by perturbing the methodology implicit in Table 3.4 in a number of different ways. However, our results do not appear to be sensitive. For instance, our results hold if we estimate our basic equation without weighing observations, or if we weight by the number of annual observations used to compute the regressands. Adding squared terms for both factors (which might be relevant if there were some nonlinear relationships between the factors and volatility) does not deliver significant results. Conditioning the consumption and investment volatility equations on either output volatility or the average level of output (the latter proxying for country size) also does not lead to different conclusions.

Table 3.5 presents a variety of other estimates which check the robustness of the results in Table 3.4. First, the cross-sectional sample is extended by imputing missing values; IV results (using the third set of instrument variables) are tabulated.[9] While some of the results are consistent with the hypotheses implied by our theoretical work, these estimates are sensitive in that they depend both on the exact choice of instruments and on the use of imputed data; we view this as weak evidence consistent with our theoretical priors. Next, 'fixed-effect' results are displayed; for these results, the estimating equation is first-differenced, so that the difference between, e.g., 1970–88 and 1950–69 consumption volatility is regressed on the difference between the 1970–88 and 1950–69 factors (i.e., the factors derived from the time-varying data). The first set of instrumental variables are used; results are uniformly insignificantly different from zero. Finally, results are displayed when the sample averages of the IMF dummy variables for current account and capital account restrictions are used as regressors instead of the estimated factors.[10] There are no strong indications of statistically significant correlations between these measures of goods and capital mobility and the indicators of business-cycle volatility. (Consistent with Pritchett, 1991, the use of different 'raw' measures of mobility leads to wildly varying results depending on the mobility measures chosen.)

6 Conclusion

In this chapter we have made a preliminary cross-country analysis of the effects of restriction of goods and capital mobility on business-cycle volatility. Given that we find that many shocks may be common across countries, it is perhaps unsurprising that we have been unable at this stage to find significant correlations between openness and volatility.

A definitive test of the theory relies on a persuasive four-way delineation of shocks by their nature, which is either global or idiosyncratic, and temporary or persistent. The preliminary diagnostics we conducted indicate pervasive signs of commonality and persistence. Nevertheless, our techniques seem to us to be too crude to deliver a trustworthy algorithm with which to categorise shocks. Our data is also suspect, insofar as we have very imperfect measures of barriers to both capital and goods flows (especially as our data does not distinguish between barriers to trade in final and intermediate goods). We hope that future research may correct these inadequacies.

NOTES

We thank: Lant Pritchett for access to his data; Daniel Cohen, Vittorio Grilli, Elhanan Helpman, David Levine, Richard Meese, and Enrique Mendoza for comments; and especially Leo Leiderman for extensive discussions during the initial stages of the project. This research was completed in part during trips to the Research Department of the IMF and the International Finance Division of the Board of Governors of the Federal Reserve System.

1 Recent empirical literature on the intertemporal approach to the current account (Glick and Rogoff, 1992; Leiderman and Razin, 1991) has also emphasised the distinctions between temporary or persistent and common or idiosyncratic shocks, usually in the context of explaining time-series behaviour of consumption, investment and the current account. Glick and Rogoff analysed data for a variety of industrialised countries; Leiderman and Razin considered Israel. Both papers were somewhat successful in finding different effects from different kinds of shocks.

Some of our objects of interest are similar to those of Backus *et al.* (1992), but our methodology is different; our chapter can be thought of as measuring the importance of some of the 'trade frictions' considered by Backus *et al.*

2 The response of investment to a one-time unanticipated shock in a deterministic world is also relevant for behaviour in a stochastic world. A linear-quadratic approximation of a dynamic stochastic model in which disturbances take place repeatedly can be viewed as a linear combination of responses to one-time shocks, with the nature of the behaviour similar in stochastic and deterministic models.

3 We are forced to drop Comoros, Dominica, Grenada, Tonga, and Vanuata altogether because of inadequate data.

4 The following is a list of the countries which entered the sample after 1967, along with the data at which they entered: Angola (1990); Bahamas (1974); Bahrain (1973); Barbados (1971); Benin (1976); Botswana (1969); Cape Verde Islands (1979); China (1981); Comoros (1978); Dominica (1979); Fiji (1972); Grenada (1976); Guinea-Bissau (1978); Hungary (1982); Lesotho (1969); Malta (1969); Mauritius (1969); Mozambique (1985); Oman (1972); Papua New Guinea (1976); Poland (1987); St. Lucia (1980); St Vincent (1980); Seychelles (1978); Solomon Islands (1979); Swaziland (1970); Tonga (1986); United Arab Emirates (1973); Vanuatu (1982); Western Samoa (1972); Yemen (1971); Zaire (1972); Zimbabwe (1981). In addition, data for Taiwan is not available after 1979.

5 We include a constant intercept so as to allow for a unit-root process with drift as the alternative. Further, we augment our regressions with a lag of the difference term.

6 Results are only tabulated for the DS model of investment, given the perfect cross-country collinearity of permanent TS components.

7 Principal components deliver virtually identical factors.

8 The Mundell–Fleming model (e.g., Frenkel and Razin, 1987) predicts that the effect of capital controls on output volatility depends on whether shocks affect goods or money markets, and whether exchange rates are floating or fixed. Our empirical work encompasses a mixture of exchange rate regimes and demand-side shocks. Thus it may not be surprising that the Mundell–Fleming model does not lead to an unambiguous prediction of the effects of capital controls on output volatility, nor that we do not observe very strong effects.

9 It should be noted that the instrumental variables (and the primitive variables required for the factor analysis) as well as the regressands were imputed.

10 The instrumental variables include: the sample averages of the IMF dummy values for import surcharges, required import deposits, surrender of export revenues, and bilateral arrangements both with members and nonmembers; the measure of price distortion; the general import licence deposit; the conventional measure of openness, and the 1985 adjusted import penetration level; the log of real 1985 GDP; dummy variables for Africa, Asia, Latin America, and OPEC status; and ratios of total debt and private credit to GDP.

REFERENCES

Backus, D.K., P.J. Kehoe and F.E. Kydland (1992) 'International Real Business Cycles', *Journal of Political Economy*, **100** (August), 745–75.

Dornbusch, R., S. Fischer and P.A. Samuelson (1977) 'Comparative Advantage, Trade and Payments in a Ricardian Model with a Continuum of Goods', *American Economic Review*, **67**(5), 823–39.

Frenkel, Jacob A. and Assaf Razin (1987) 'The Mundell–Fleming Model: A Quarter Century Later', *IMF Staff Papers*, **34**(4), 567–620.

Glick, Reuven and Kennet Rogoff (1992) 'Global versus Country-Specific Productivity Shocks and the Current Account', *NBER*, *Working Paper*, **4140**.

International Monetary Fund (various issues) *Annual Report on Exchange Arrangements and Exchange Restrictions.*

Krugman, Paul R. (1992) 'Lessons of Massachusetts for EMU', MIT, mimeo.

Leiderman, Leonardo and Assaf Razin (1991) 'Determinants of External Imbalances: The Role of Taxes, Government Spending, and Productivity', *Journal of the Japanese and International Economies*, **5**, 421–50.

Mendoza, Enrique G. (1992) 'Robustness of Macroeconomic Indicators of Capital Mobility', IMF, *Working Paper*, **WP/92/111**.

Pritchett, Lant (1991) 'Measuring Outward Orientation in Developing Countries' IBRD, *Working Paper*, *WPS*, **566**.

Quah, Danny (1992) 'The Relative Importance of Permanent and Transitory Components', *Econometrica*, **60**(1), 107–18.

Summers, R. and A. Heston (1991) 'The Penn World Table (Mark 5): An Expanded Set of International Comparisons, 1950–1988', *Quarterly Journal of Economics*, **106** (May), 327–68.

World Bank (1987) *World Development Report*, Oxford: Oxford University Press.
(1991) *World Development Report*, Oxford: Oxford University Press.

Discussion

ENRIQUE G. MENDOZA

In their Chapter 3, Assaf Razin and Andrew Rose tackle in an original and interesting manner an issue that has been a key component of the ongoing debate on the theory and measurement of international capital mobility; namely, the quantification of the degree of openness of an economy and the assessment of its macroeconomic effects, particularly at business-cycle frequencies. Defining a specific metric to measure the degree of openness, as is required in a serious cross-sectional study of capital mobility such as this one, is a very difficult issue, and Razin and Rose have handled it with great expertise and care. The manner in which they combine information from the IMF's *Annual Report on Exchange Arrangements and Exchange Restrictions* with the descriptive indicators of openness documented in Pritchett (1991) to create a measure of openness using factor analysis is innovative and unique in this area of research.

There are other aspects of this study that should be commended, but these are not detailed in this Discussion so as to highlight instead the issues that can be a matter of controversy. The main objective of the chapter is to examine whether the cyclical variability of consumption, investment, and output is related to the degree of openness in a manner that is consistent with the predictions of the neoclassical framework of savings and investment. Two sets of questions emerge from this analysis; one is related to methodological issues involving the data and the procedures used to create indicators of cyclical variability, and the second, which is perhaps more important, is concerned with the design of the tests that the authors propose, and with the interpretation given to the results.

With regard to the data, one issue of concern is the fact that all available multinational data bases for national income accounts are created with country data of uneven quality. It is a fact that many developing countries find it difficult to spare the resources that are needed to design and maintain a reliable system of national accounts. This is particularly true in the least developed countries, although even middle-income developing countries have systems of national accounts that are reliable only to a certain extent. This is an important issue because the tests of capital mobility proposed in this study examine the cross-sectional relationship between business-cycle variability indicators and the measure of the degree of openness, and the percentage of the former that could be attributed to measurement error in national accounts is not uniform across countries. It is true, however, that there is not much that a researcher can do regarding the quality of the data available. Nevertheless, it would be interesting to provide results for the Razin–Rose tests for a subset of the 130 countries in the sample that are judged to be the ones where measurement errors are minimal.

The second issue involving the data is the procedure used to separate trend and cyclical components. This is an area where real business-cycle theory has made interesting contributions and has raised important questions. Kydland and Prescott (1990) argue that a complete definition of business-cycle variability must give a precise meaning to the concept of *trend.* They define 'trend' as the low-frequency movements in macro variables that are driven by exogenous labour-augmenting technological change. With this definition, a linear time trend – such as the one used to define some of the variability indicators in the chapter – makes sense only if the rate of technological change is constant over time. However, because the underlying rate of technological change seems to vary over time, detrending with a linear function of time seems inadequate, while a first-difference filter may overestimate the speed at which technological change occurs. The ideal filter is one that lets the mean rate of technological change vary, but not too rapidly; and hence Kydland and Prescott propose to use the well-known Hodrick–Prescott filter. From a more practical standpoint, what seems important is not so much to explain where the trend comes from, but to realise that the data of most countries seem to suggest the presence of low-frequency changes in trends that a linear filter ignores and a random walk filter exaggerates. In addition, it is important to make sure that the cyclical components produced by the filter are truly stationary, which is another feature of the Hodrick–Prescott filter. It would then seem reasonable to suggest that the Razin–Rose tests be applied to data using this filter so as to minimise the risk that the results be affected by the filtering method.

The results of these additional tests should also be viewed with caution, however, in light of the findings of the growing literature devoted to the issue of whether the choice of filter matters. For instance, Canova (1991) takes the data of the US national accounts and decomposes them into trend and cyclical components using a number of different filters – including a linear trend, first differences, Hodrick–Prescott filters, random trend decompositions, and others. He finds that the choice of filter may matter significantly for business-cycle variability measures. Cogley and Nason (1992) encountered the fact that while the Hodrick–Prescott filter has the appealing properties discussed above, it may also induce spurious cross-correlations in cyclical components of different variables. At the same time, however, researchers studying open-economy business-cycle models have compared quadratic time trends, first-difference filters, and Hodrick–Prescott filters and have found that while the choice of filters matters for the level of standard deviations – with the quadratic trend producing the largest variability measures and the Hodrick–Prescott filter the smallest, the ratios of standard deviations relative to the standard deviation of output, or the terms of trade, as well as autocorrelation and correlation coefficients, are fairly stable (see Backus, Kehoe, and Kydland, 1992); Stockman and Tesar, 1990; Mendoza, 1992a). For the work of Razin and Rose, this debate on the use of filters suggests that the best strategy is to continue using more than one filter, with the emphasis on examining whether their results are robust to the application of a filter that allows for low-frequency trend shifts.

The second set of questions raised by the authors' analysis is related to the design of the tests of openness they propose, and the interpretation of their results. One question is whether the tests can be regarded as sufficient, in a theoretical sense, to support the conclusion that the data seem to reject some basic hypotheses of neoclassical theory. Following the arguments in Mendoza (1992b), one could argue that regressing business-cycle variability indicators on measures of the degree of openness may yield the negative results obtained by the authors and still be fully consistent with the predictions of a neoclassical business-cycle model – even if the model is driven by pure country-specific shocks. To illustrate the point, one can take the data of the 15 model economies simulated in Mendoza (1992b) and design a crude analogue of the Razin–Rose test by regressing the standard deviation of consumption on a qualitative variable that is zero under perfect mobility, 1 under limited mobility, and 2 under autarky. The resulting slope coefficient has the wrong sign and is not statistically different from zero – even though in this case there is no measurement error in the qualitative variable that measures the degree of openness. However, if we add other dummy variables to control for the structural parameters that change in some of the 15 simulations (the variability and persistence on non-insurable country-specific shocks, the degree of risk aversion, and the price-elasticity of labour supply) the slope coefficient is estimated at 0.13 with a *t*-statistic of about 6.5. In part, this result is in line with the main conclusion of the authors (i.e., that it is necessary to incorporate additional information regarding temporary vs. persistent and idiosyncratic vs. global shocks to strengthen the tests), but it illustrates that the problem may extend to other components that differentiate the structure of economies in the world – particularly in a study that combines industrial and developing countries.

Another important question is whether the tests can separate the degree of *openness* from the degree of *completeness* of world financial markets.

For instance, a developing country subject to large terms-of-trade shocks could experience significant flunctuations in consumption not because the degree of openness of the economy is too low, but simply because international markets of contingent claims are not as complete as necessary to neutralise the effect of that country-specific shock. There is theoretical and empirical evidence suggesting that distinguishing the competitive allocations that result from different regimes of market completeness may be difficult (Helpman and Razin, 1978; Cole and Obstfeld, 1991; Mendoza, 1991; Baxter and Crucini, 1992), and hence this may be an issue that tests like those proposed by Razin and Rose may find hard to deal with.

Finally, the authors' conclusion that there may be an important world-shock component in business cycles is very appealing – and there is some recent empirical work by Head, Gregory and Raynauld (1992) that seems to support this argument. However, detailed analysis is needed to document the extent to which this common shock can overcome the effects of country-specific disturbances, particularly terms-of-trade shocks. Given the large cross-country differences in export bases, common world commodity price changes result in different country-specific shocks to the terms of trade. These shocks are quite large in the data and they seem to have played a significant role in recent episodes of business cycles, particularly for developing economies (see Frenkel and Razin, 1992; Mendoza, 1992a).

REFERENCES

Backus, D.K., P.J. Kehoe F.E. Kydland (1992) 'Relative Price Movements in Dynamic General Equilibrium Models of International Trade', Working Paper, **EC-92-25**, Department of Economics, New York University.

Baxter, Marianne and Mario J. Crucini (1992) 'Business Cycles and the Asset Structure of Foreign Trade', Rochester Center for Economic Research, University of Rochester, unpublished manuscript.

Canova, Fabio (1991) 'Detrending and Business Cycle Facts', Department of Economics, Brown University, Providence RI, unpublished manuscript.

Cogley, Timothy and James M. Nason (1992) 'Effects of the Hodrick–Prescott Filter on Integrated Time Series', Department of Economics of British Columbia, unpublished manuscript.

Cole, Harold L. and Maurice Obstfeld (1991) 'Commodity Trade and International Risk Sharing: How Much Do Financial Markets Matter', *Journal of Monetary Economics*, **28** (August), 3–24.

Frenkel, Jacob A. and Assaf Razin (1992) *Fiscal Policies and the World Economy*, Cambridge, MA: MIT Press, 2nd edn.

Head, Allen, Allan Gregory and Jacques Raynauld (1992) 'Measuring World Business Cycles', Department of Economics, Queen's University, unpublished manuscript.

Helpman, Elhanan and Assaf Razin (1978) *A Theory of International Trade under Uncertainty*, New York: Academic Press.

Kydland, Finn E. and Edward C. Prescott (1990) 'Business Cycles: Real Facts and a Monetary Myth', Federal Reserve Bank of Minneapolis Quarterly Review, **Spring**, 3–18.

Mendoza, Enrique G. (1991) 'Capital Controls and the Gains from Trade in a Business Cycle Model of a Small Open Economy', *IMF Staff Papers*, **38**, 480–505.

(1992a) 'The Terms of Trade and Economic Fluctuations', IMF, *Working Paper*, **WP/92/98** (December).

(1992b) 'Robustness of Macroeconomic Indicators of Capital Mobility', IMF, *Working Paper*, **WP/92/111**, see also Chapter 4 in this volume.

Pritchett, Lant (1991) 'Measuring Outward Orientation in Developing Countries', IBRD, *Working Paper*, **WPS 566**.

Stockman, Alan C. and Tesar, Linda L. (1990) 'Tastes and Technology in a Two-Country Model of the Business Cycle: Explaining International Comovements', NBER, *Working Paper*, **3544** (December).

VITTORIO GRILLI

Chapter 3 is part of a relatively recent, but very important, line of research dedicated to the empirical study of business-cycle models using cross-country data. The business-cycle theories analysed in this chapter are nowadays so familiar to us that we often take their implications and predictions for granted. The authors, however, show that several of the central implication of real business-cycle theories do not find support in the data. The results will be disturbing to many since they challenge a deeply-rooted way of thinking about economic fluctuations. The next challenge is to try to understand the reasons for this rejection. Is the problem in the theory, in the data, or in the power of the empirical test? The sensible answer is, probably, 'all of the above'. If this is the case, the results must be interpreted, as the authors correctly point out, with caution.

The authors recognise the problems of implementing a robust and convincing test of business-cycle theory based on the cross-sectional variation of current and capital account controls. They appropriately alert the reader where they think the problems are especially serious. In the following Discussion I will do the same: isolate the aspects of the empirical analysis which are more problematic. Not surprisingly, there is much agreement with the authors in this respect.

The logic of the chapter is simple. The cyclical behaviour of an open economy should differ from that of a closed economy. The reason is that access to international goods markets gives an open economy the opportunity to specialise its production, while access to foreign capital markets allows a country's investment and consumption decisions to be independent (in the short run) from its savings decisions. Several variations of real business-cycle models suggest that a country moving from autarky to free trade in goods and capital should experience a reduction in consumption volatility and an increase in the volatility of investment and output. The important qualifications are, however, necessary. First, the extent of this change in volatility depends on the degree of persistency of economic shocks and on whether they are country-specific or worldwide. In fact, if shocks were mostly permanent and common to most countries, there would be little change in the volatility of consumption and investment after capital liberalisation. It is therefore very important to distinguish, in the empirical analysis, between temporary and permanent, and between idiosyncratic and common shocks. The second critical qualification is that in order to reinterpret these results in a cross-country instead of a time-series dimension, we have to apply carefully the '*ceteris paribus*' condition. In other words, there are several factors that might explain cross-country differences in volatility beside the degree of goods and capital mobility. In the empirical analysis, therefore, it is important to control for these additional country differences, especially those that could be correlated with the degree of openness of the economy.

The problem of separating permanent from transitory movements is, on paper at least, relatively straightforward. Several forms of data filtering are common practice in the profession. The authors employ two alternative techniques: linear detrending and first differences. The fact that some of the results are sensitive to the particular choice of filtering is a clear warning for future research in this area. For example, there is no real reason (except for ease of computation) for using the same type of statistical decomposition for all countries. If we believe, as the logic of the chapter suggests, that the stochastic behaviour of economic aggregates is driven by country-specific shocks, it may be useful to use a decomposition method which is flexible enough to allow for different, country-specific, degrees of importance of permanent vs. cyclical shocks' variability. The Hodrick–Prescott technique seems an obvious, but not unique, alternative to the ones used in the chapter.

More difficult, essentially because less common in the literature, is the problem of isolating idiosyncratic from common shocks. The standard statistical technique to achieve such decomposition is factor analysis. The authors use this technique in a preliminary stage of their work and they uncover substantial evidence of common, world-wide, components of shocks. However, partly because of the technical difficulty of properly quantifying these components, they do not pursue the issue further. Eventually, they perform the cross-country analysis using the total variability of the detrended variables, i.e. including both idiosyncratic and common shocks. The inability of performing the analysis on the country-specific component of volatility undermines the importance of the results. Further research, and not only in this area, should address the problem of separating common from idiosyncratic shocks, and provide some sensible methodology for performing such decomposition.

Razin and Rose do not address the issue of '*ceteris paribus*' explicitly; no specific effort is made to control for other factors potentially responsible for aggregate volatility. The authors acknowledge the problem, and state that, if other factors are important, they 'are hopefully orthogonal to our (included) measures of current and capital account mobility'. This is a strong, and probably incorrect, presumption. The difficulty in controlling for other possible causes of volatility is, in part, due to the absence of an explicit structural model which could provide some guidance in identifying which other variables should be included in the analysis. A fully specified structural model would be well beyond the scope of the chapter. The authors' goal is a different and equally important one: uncovering some basic stylised facts in an area where little is known. Nonetheless, some guidance could be found elsewhere, in other related papers. Alesina, Grilli and Milesi-Ferretti (Chapter 11 in this volume) show that capital control decisions are affected by both economic and political variables which are, in turn, also likely to affect aggregate volatility. For example, they find that the exchange rate regime plays a crucial role in the decision to introduce capital controls. While the evidence on the relationship between exchange rate regime and economic aggregates is not conclusive, such a relationship cannot be dismissed *a priori*. On a different level, the characteristics of governments, like their durability and their parliamentary support, also affect the decision of introducing capital controls. There is evidence that these government characteristics have an impact on output growth and its volatility.

In conclusion, the chapter is successful in establishing badly needed stylised facts in this area; it has also uncovered several problems obtaining reliable results that future research should address.

4 The robustness of macroeconomic indicators of capital mobility

ENRIQUE G. MENDOZA

1 Introduction

Financial capital has become highly mobile across countries as a result of the gradual globalisation of financial markets that followed from widespread deregulation and innovations in communication and transaction technologies in recent years. This development has renewed interest in the debate on the implications and measurement of international capital mobility. The controversial work of Feldstein and Horioka (1980) initiated the new stage of this debate by arguing that, because savings and investment are positively correlated, additions to savings are primarily allocated to the domestic economy, and hence there is little evidence of the arbitrage in world financial markets that the neoclassical paradigm predicts. These results raised doubts as to whether the efficiency and welfare gains, on the basis of which international financial deregulation was introduced, would materialise.

Further empirical work established the robustness of positive savings–investment correlations in time-series and cross-sectional studies for industrial and developing countries (see, for example, Dooley, Frankel and Mathieson, 1987; Tesar, 1991; Bayoumi and Sterne, 1992; Montiel, 1992; and Chapter IV of the May 1991 issue of *World Economic Outlook* (International Monetary Fund, 1991a). At the same time, however, the theoretical literature casts doubts on whether this stylised fact could be regarded as an indicator of the degree to which capital moves across countries (see Obstfeld, 1986; Zeira, 1987; Summers, 1988; Finn, 1990; Sinn, 1991). Simulations of dynamic stochastic equilibrium models demonstrated that, given productivity or terms of trade shocks of the magnitude observed in the data, these models mimic the same positive relationship between savings and investment that characterises actual economies (Mendoza, 1991a, 1992; Baxter and Crucini, 1993). The controversy surrounding savings–investment correlations motivated other

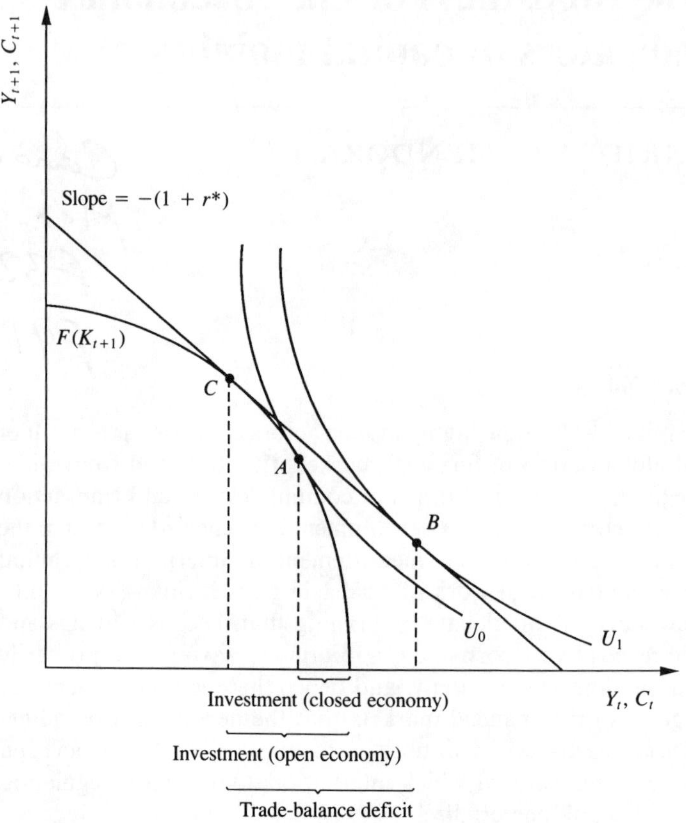

Figure 4.1 The neoclassical model of investment

researchers to focus on alternative indicators of capital mobility, such as the degree of consumption smoothing, the differential in asset returns, and the variability of investment, but the interpretation of these indicators has also been a controversial subject (see Obstfeld, 1986, 1989; Sachs, 1982; Frankel, 1992; Razin and Rose, 1992). Moreover, direct measures of financial capital flows and international portfolio diversification have also added to the debate by showing that, despite heavy trading in international financial markets, there is a significant home bias in portfolio allocation (see Tesar and Werner, 1992).

Perhaps the key element in the debate on the theory and measurement of capital mobility is the connection between the analytical framework from which indicators of capital mobility are obtained and the design of the econometric tests used to study them. Consider the case of the savings–investment correlations. The empirical work advocating the use of this statistic as an indicator of capital mobility is based on the well-known neoclassical model of savings, originally developed in the pioneering work of Irving Fisher (1930) and illustrated in Figure 4.1. In a closed economy, savings and investment are identical and they are determined at the point where the indifference curve between consumption in two periods is tangent to the production possibilities frontier of output in two periods (point *A*). In contrast, when capital is mobile across countries, and households and firms are free to borrow and lend in world markets at the real interest rate r^*, savings and investment decisions are separated (points *B* and *C*). Investment and savings thus move together when capital is not mobile across countries, and hence the rationale for arguing that positive savings–investment correlations are evidence against capital mobility. Nevertheless, this statement is strictly correct only in a deterministic, or perfect-foresight, framework, and is only a rough first approximation in a stochastic economy. Under uncertainty, the marginal product of capital and the world's real interest rate are not equalised exactly each period; there is, instead, an equality that holds in terms of an expected value in which the return of foreign and domestic capital is weighted by the marginal utility of consumption in each state of nature. Shifts in either the indifference curve or the production possibilities frontier in Figure 4.1, given the agents' desire to smooth consumption, could result in movements of investment that coincide with movements in savings. Moreover, even in a deterministic setup, positive comovement between savings and investment could emerge as a result of population growth or technological change (Obstfeld, 1986).

The best approach to determine whether positive savings–investment correlations, as well as other macroeconomic indicators, are robust indicators of capital mobility under uncertainty is to impose a rigorous link between theoretical and empirical work. At the same time, however, deriving the quantitative implications of the intertemporal equilibrium, stochastic framework that has dominated the analytical work in this area in recent years is not straightforward. It is only under particular conditions that this framework produces closed-form solutions from which the properties of macroeconomic indicators can be derived and tested using available economic methods. An alternative, proposed by Obstfeld (1989), is to look for evidence that the optimality conditions, or Euler equations, that characterise consumption behaviour in an intertemporal model of integrated economies hold, instead of trying to extract information from macroeconomic indicators. Another alternative is to examine a dynamic stochastic model by using numerical methods to determine how capital mobility affects the behaviour of macroeconomic variables in general equilibrium. This is the approach proposed here.

This chapter examines various indicators of capital mobility in a stochastic intertemporal equilibrium model of a small open economy. The chapter derives the quantitative implications of the model – i.e., the properties of the equilibrium stochastic processes that characterise the model – and examines which of the model's empirical regularities are better indicators of capital mobility. In contrast with previous work, the exercise does not aim to show whether the data fit a specific prediction of the model, but rather to create macroeconomic time series for a model economy that mimic some properties of actual business cycles, and then to explore the implications of varying the degree of capital mobility on the stylised facts commonly used as measures of capital mobility.

The analysis shows that, for several simulations conducted using a set of reasonable preference and technology parameters, the macroeconomic indicators of capital mobility are not informative. In particular, savings–investment correlations do not provide information about the degree of capital mobility if the magnitude or the persistence of income disturbances changes; consumption variability is not very sensitive to the degree of integration of financial markets; and the stylised facts of investment are robust indicators of capital mobility only in cases in which capital controls are very tight. Most of the indicators are as equally sensitive to differences in structural parameters as to differences in the degree of mobility. Moreover, there is no evidence that preventing agents from accessing world capital markets limits their ability to smooth consumption significantly, suggesting that capital mobility may be difficult to determine using Euler equation tests. These results are consistent with the analytical work of Cole and Obstfeld (1991), the findings of the cross-country analysis undertaken by Razin and Rose (1992), and the simulation analysis of Mendoza (1991b) and Baxter and Crucini (1992).

The chapter is organised as follows. Section 2 describes the model, the parameter specification, and the numerical solution method. Section 3 compares the model's equilibrium comovements with the stylised facts of post-war business cycles in Canada and Mexico. Section 4 examines the performance of the different measures of capital mobility. Section 5 draws some conclusions.

2 The model

The model described here is the standard prototype of the intertemporal equilibrium framework for the small open economy developed by Obstfeld (1981), Helpman and Razin (1982), Svensson and Razin (1983),

Greenwood (1983) and other (see Frenkel and Razin, 1987 for a comprehensive literature review), with the modification that it incorporates stochastic disturbances affecting productivity or the terms of trade – as in the small open economy real business-cycle models of Mendoza (1991a) and Correia, Neves and Rebelo (1991).

2.1 Production technology and financial structure

Firms in the economy produce tradable goods using the following technology:

$$G(K_t, L_t, K_{t+1}) = \exp(e_t)\, K_t^a L_t^{1-a} - \left(\frac{\phi}{2}\right)(K_{t+1} - K_t)^2,$$
$$0 < a < 1, \quad \phi > 0, \tag{1}$$

where L_t is labour services, K_t is the capital stock, e_t is a random shock affecting productivity or the terms of trade,[1] and $(\phi/2)(K_{t+1} - K_t)^2$ is the cost of adjusting the capital stock.[2] The law of motion for capital is

$$K_{t+1} = (1 - \delta)K_t + I_t, \qquad 0 \leq \delta \leq 1, \tag{2}$$

where I_t is gross investment and δ the rate of depreciation.

There are three representations of financial markets in the model that correspond to regimes with different degrees of capital mobility. In a regime of perfect mobility, households and firms exchange one-period noncontingent bonds, A_t, that pay the real interest rate r^*, with the rest of the world in a competitive international capital market.[3] Net holdings of foreign assets evolve according to

$$A_{t+1} = TB_t + A_t(1 + r^*), \tag{3}$$

where TB_t is the balance of trade.[4] In a regime of limited capital mobility, the accumulation of foreign assets faces *binding* constraints for some states of nature. Thus, in every period:

$$\hat{A}_l \leq A_{t+1} \leq \hat{A}_h \tag{4}$$

where $\hat{A}_h$ ($\hat{A}_l$) is a constant lower (higher) than the stock of foreign assets agents would optimally choose to hold under perfect capital mobility in some states of nature. When the constraints are not binding, net foreign assets evolve as in the case of perfect mobility and (4) can be replaced by (3). Finally, in a regime that forcefully obstructs capital mobility by imposing strict capital controls, the range just described collapses into a constraint on foreign asset accumulation that is always binding:

$$A_{t+1} = \hat{A}. \tag{5}$$

In this case, $A_{t+1} = \hat{A}$ for all t and the balance of trade is $TB_t = -r^*\hat{A}$.

The resource constraint states that the sum of consumption, C_t, investment, and the balance of trade cannot exceed output net of adjustment costs:

$$C_t + I_t + TB_t \leq \exp(e_t) K_t^{\alpha} L_t^{1-\alpha} - \left(\frac{\phi}{2}\right)(K_{t+1} - K_t)^2. \tag{6}$$

2.2 *Preferences*

Households are all identical and infinitely-lived. They allocate C_t and L_t intertemporally so as to maximise stationary cardinal utility

(SCU):[5]

$$U = \mathrm{E}\left[\sum_{t=0}^{\infty}\left\{u(C_t - G(L_t))\exp\left(-\sum_{\tau=0}^{t-1} v(C_\tau - G(L_\tau))\right)\right\}\right]. \tag{7}$$

The instantaneous utility and time-preference functions are:

$$u(C_t - G(L_t)) = \frac{\left[C_t - \dfrac{L_t^{\omega}}{\omega}\right]^{(1-\gamma)} - 1}{1-\gamma}, \qquad \omega > 1, \quad \gamma > 1, \tag{8}$$

$$v(C_t - G(L_t)) = \beta \ln\left(1 + C_t - \frac{L_t^{\omega}}{\omega}\right), \qquad \beta > 0. \tag{9}$$

As in Greenwood, Hercowitz and Huffman (1988), (8) and (9) are defined in terms of a composite good described by consumption minus the disutility of labour. The marginal rate of substitution between C and L is a function of the latter only, and hence labour is independent of the dynamics of consumption. This facilitates the quantitative analysis at the cost of neutralising the wealth effect on labour. Labour supply is determined by a condition that equates the marginal product of labour with the marginal disutility of providing labour services, independently of the marginal utility of consumption. This implies that the labour supply choice can be separated from optimal consumption plans in the dynamic programming problem described below.

2.3 *The dynamic programming problem and the solution technique*

Optimal intertemporal plans involve selecting, at each date t, K_{t+1}, A_{t+1}, C_t and L_t, given the state of the economy determined by K_t, A_t and e_t. The usual nonnegativity restrictions on C, K and L, apply and optimal plans must also be consistent with intertemporal solvency. As in Mendoza

(1991a) and Imrohoroglu (1989), Ponzi-type schemes in regimes of perfect or limited capital mobility are ruled out by imposing an upper bound on debt, $A_t \geq \Delta$ for all t, where Δ is a negative constant. If Δ is small enough, the limiting probability of approaching the debt ceiling becomes infinitesimally small. The time-recursive nature of SCU, together with the simplified uncertainty environment described later, implies that the equilibrium of the economy with perfect capital mobility can be characterised by the following stochastic dynamic programming problem:

$$V(K_t, A_t, e_t^s) = \max \left\{ \frac{\left(C_t - \frac{\hat{L}_t^{\omega}}{\omega}\right)^{(1-\gamma)} - 1}{1-\gamma} + \exp\left[-\beta \ln\left(1 + C_t - \frac{\hat{L}_t^{\omega}}{\omega}\right)\right]\left[\sum_{r=1}^{2} \pi_{s,r} V(K_{t+1}, A_{t+1}, e_{t+1}^r)\right]\right\}, \quad (10)$$

subject to

$$C_t = \exp(e_t) Q K_t^{\alpha} \hat{L}_t^{(1-\alpha)} - \left(\frac{\phi}{2}\right)(K_{t+1} - K_t)^2 - K_{t+1} + K_t(1-\delta) + (1+r^*)A_t - A_{t+1},$$

$$\hat{L}_t = \operatorname{argmax}_{(L_t)} \left\{ \exp(e_t) K_t^{\alpha} L_t^{(1-\alpha)} - \frac{L_t^{\omega}}{\omega} \right\},$$

$$A_t \geq \Delta,\ K_t \geq 0,\ L_t \geq 0, \text{ and } C_t \geq 0.$$

Once parameter values for preferences, technology, and the shocks are determined, this problem is solved numerically by making use of an algorithm that iterates on the value function and the state-transition probability matrix using discrete grids to represent the state space.[6] This exact-solution algorithm requires that the dimension of the model's state space be minimised, and hence it often allows only for simple characterisations of the stochastic shocks. In this case, income disturbances are assumed to follow a two-point, symmetric Markov chain. Thus, in every period the shocks take one of two values:

$$e_t \in \mathrm{E} = \{e^1, e^2\}. \quad (11)$$

One-step conditional transition probabilities, denoted as π_{sr}, satisfy the conditions that $0 \leq \pi_{sr} \leq 1$ and $\pi_{s1} + \pi_{s2} = 1$ for $s, r = 1, 2$. The symmetry conditions are $\pi_{11} = \pi_{22} = \pi$ and $e^1 = -e^2 = e$. These conditions simplify the analysis by making the asymptotic standard deviation, σ_e, and the first-order autocorrelation coefficient, ρ_e, of the shocks equal to e and $2\pi - 1$ respectively.

The first-order conditions describing optimal intertemporal plans under perfect capital mobility have the usual interpretation, although with the caveat that changes in current consumption affect the rate of time preference at which future consumption is discounted. From the perspective of any period t, optimal savings are set so as to equate the stochastic marginal rate of substitution between C_t and C_{t+1} with the gross real rate of return on foreign assets $1 + r^*$. Optimal investment is set so as to equalise the expected values of the returns on capital and foreign assets, taking risk factors into account by weighting each possible occurrence of the marginal product of capital by the marginal utility of consumption in each state of nature. Fisherian separation thus holds as a rough approximation; investment is governed by an optimal portfolio allocation decision that equates the returns on alternative assets, and savings are determined by the desire to smooth consumption given its fixed intertemporal relative price. Any need for savings not covered by investment in domestic capital is covered by borrowing or lending in world capital markets.

2.4 Parameter values and calibration

Two sets of parameter values are defined so as to duplicate some of the empirical regularities that characterise business cycles in Canada and Mexico. Canada is viewed as a typical small open economy because of the relatively small set of capital controls in place and the high degree of integration of Canada's financial markets with those of the United States. Data for Mexico are examined to provide some evidence on the stylised facts of business cycles in middle-income developing countries which act as price takers in world markets.

The values of the parameters γ (coefficient of relative risk aversion), ω (1 plus the inverse of the intertemporal elasticity of substitution in labour supply), a (capital's share in output), δ (depreciation rate), β (the consumption elasticity of the rate of time preference), Q (efficiency constant), and r^* (the world's real interest rate), are selected using long-run averages of actual data, the restrictions imposed by the deterministic steady-state equilibrium of the model, and also by approximating some of the estimates obtained in the relevant empirical literature. The values of the parameters are as follows:

$$\begin{aligned}\text{Canada: } & a = 0.32,\ Q = 1.0,\ \delta = 0.1,\ r^* = 0.04,\\ & \omega = 1.455,\ \gamma = 1.6,\ \beta = 0.11,\ \phi = 0.023,\\ & \rho_e = 0.41, \text{ and } \sigma_e = 1.285\%.\end{aligned} \tag{12}$$

$$\begin{aligned}\text{Mexico: } & a = 0.64,\ Q = 0.507,\ \delta = 0.1,\ r^* = 0.04,\\ & \omega = 1.113,\ \gamma = 2.3,\ \beta = 0.56,\ \phi = 0.029,\\ & \rho_e = 0.17, \text{ and } \sigma_e = 2.00\%.\end{aligned} \tag{13}$$

The value of a is set as 1 minus the ratio of labour income to national income at factor prices. The efficiency parameter Q is a scale variable that does not affect equilibrium covariances in the model, but it is used for consistency to correct for relative economy size given the Cobb–Douglas technology and the fact that income per capita in Mexico, adjusted for purchasing power, is one-quarter of that in Canada. δ is the usual 10% depreciation rate of real business-cycle models. r^* at 4% is the real interest rate for the US economy in Prescott (1986). ω for both countries is in the range of estimates discussed in Greenwood, Hercowitz and Huffman (1988) and Mendoza (1991a). γ is set following Prescott's (1986) observation that γ is not much higher than 1, which is in line with some of the existing econometric evidence (see Hansen and Singleton, 1983), and taking into account that agents in developing countries seem to be more risk averse (see Ostry and Reinhart, 1992). β is determined by the steady-state equilibrium condition, considering that the post-war average of the ratio of net foreign interest payments to output, r^*A/Y, is 1.9% for Canada and 2.5% for Mexico. ϕ, ρ_e, and σ_e are calibration parameters set to mimic σ_I, ρ_y, and σ_y respectively as observed in Canada and Mexico for the post-war period (see Table 4.1 on p. 92).

3 The model and the stylised facts

This section establishes how useful the model proposed in the previous section is as a framework to model the implications of capital mobility, by comparing the properties of business cycles in the model with those obtained from Canadian and Mexican data. The data correspond to annual observations for the periods 1946 to 1985 for Canada and 1945 to 1984 for Mexico, expressed in per capita terms of the population older than 15 years, transformed into logarithms and detrended with a quadratic time trend. The statistical moments for the relevant macroeconomic times series are reported in Table 4.1.

Table 4.1 shows that business-cycle facts in Canada and Mexico are consistent with those observed in other industrial and developing countries (see Backus and Kehoe, 1992; Mendoza, 1992) and do not contradict the basic implications of a consumption-smoothing, intertemporal framework. In terms of standard deviations relative to the standard deviation of GDP, consumption is the least variable of all macroaggregates, while savings, investment, and the balance of trade are more variable than output. Regarding the coefficients of correlation with GDP, consumption, savings and investment are procyclical, while the trade balance and real net foreign interest payments are countercyclical or almost uncorrelated with GDP. In both countries savings and investment exhibit a

Table 4.1. *Canada and Mexico, properties of business cycles in the post-war period*[1]

	A			B		
	Canada			Mexico		
Variables	σ^2	ρ^3	ρy^4	σ^2	ρ^3	ρy^4
(1) *GDP*	1.00	0.615	1.000	1.00	0.543	1.000
(2) *C*	0.88	0.701	0.586	0.58	0.384*	0.836
(3) *S*	2.60	0.542	0.662	2.22	0.361	0.399
(4) *I*	3.49	0.314	0.639	3.93	0.524	0.853
(5) *TB*	3.01	0.666	− 0.172*	6.37	0.525	− 0.789
(6) $-r^*A$	5.43	0.727	− 0.175*	4.33	0.369*	− 0.382*
(7) *L*	0.72	0.541	0.799	n.a.	n.a.	n.a.
memo items:						
	SD(GDP) = 2.81			*SD(GDP)* = 3.50		
	CORR(S,I) = 0.445			*CORR(S,I)* = 0.426		

[1] Data measured in per capita terms of the 15 + population (Canada) and total population (Mexico), logged and detrended with a quadratic time trend. (1)–(6) are aggregates from national income accounts, except (6) for Mexico that is from current account data. (2) excludes durables and semidurables for Canada, and includes only food and services for Mexico. Savings are investment plus the balance of trade. Data for Canada are for the period 1946–85 in 1981 dollars (source: CANSIM data retrieval). Data for Mexico are for the period 1945–84, except (2) for 1960–84 and (6) for 1950–84, in 1970 pesos (source: *Indicadores Economicos*, Banco de Mexico).
[2] Standard deviation relative to the percentage standard deviation of output *SD(GDP)*.
[3] First-order autocorrelation coefficient (an asterisk indicates that the coefficient is not statistically significant at the 1% level).
[4] Coefficient of correlation with GDP (an asterisk indicates that the coefficient is not statistically significant at the 1% level).

similar degree of positive correlation, despite differences in the regime governing capital mobility to be detailed later. All macroeconomic aggregates in the two countries also exhibit some degree of positive persistence.

Despite the difference in the size of economic fluctuations between Canada and Mexico – GDP is almost 3/4 of a percentage point more variable in Mexico than in Canada – the *qualitative* properties of business cycles in the two countries are similar. Canada and Mexico exhibit a similar ranking of the coefficients of relative variability, comovement with GDP, and first-order autocorrelation of all macroeconomic aggregates. Moreover, even some *quantitative* regularities appear to be common to the business cycles in the two countries, particularly with regard to the variability of savings, investment and consumption relative to the variability of GDP.

Despite these similarities, the specific characteristics of Mexico, a country with an export base and a production structure less diversified than Canada's and where access to world capital markets has been restricted with varying intensity during the post-war period, should be reflected in the country's stylised facts. The large fluctuations of the balance of trade, the strong negative comovement between the trade balance and GDP, and the lower variability of net foreign interest payments in Mexico compared with Canada may reflect in part some of these characteristics. For instance, the consumption-smoothing principle predicts that, assuming investment remains constant, net foreign assets should fluctuate more in an economy where GDP is more variable because holdings of foreign assets are adjusted more to prevent consumption from being affected by output changes. Nevertheless, real net foreign interest payments, which are used here to approximate the behaviour of net holdings of foreign assets, are more variable in Canada than in Mexico. One possible interpretation of this fact would be that capital controls or capital market imperfections have prevented the optimal adjustment of foreign assets in the Mexican economy.

The regime governing capital mobility currently prevailing in Canada and Mexico is described in detail in the *Annual Report on Exchange Arrangements and Exchange Restrictions* (International Monetary Fund, 1991b). This document suggests that distortions in the exchange arrangement and payments restrictions as of end-December 1990 were more pervasive in Mexico than in Canada. However, the report also notes that Mexico has in recent years introduced a number of reforms to reduce or eliminate many payments restrictions and most of the distortions affecting the foreign exchange market. As of 30 December 1990, there were no exchange controls, nor any prescriptions of currency requirements in Canada. There were no requirements to surrender export proceeds, and no controls over outward direct investment or over inward or outward portfolio investment. There were some import permits and a few quotas on commodities and manufactured goods, a few restrictions on inward foreign direct investment, and ceilings on the ratios of domestic assets to authorised capital of foreign-owned banks operating in Canada. By contrast, in Mexico there was a dual exchange rate system – although with a minimal difference between the controlled and the free-market rates – and there were also a few currency prescriptions, some restrictions on payments for capital transactions, and surrender requirements for export proceeds. Tariffs, licences, and quotas were still present, although at

Table 4.2. *Canada and Mexico, properties of business cycles in artificial economies*[1]

	A			*B*		
	Canada			Mexico		
Variables	σ^1	ρ^2	ρy^3	σ^1	ρ^2	ρy^3
(1) *GDP*	1.00	0.614	1.000	1.00	0.520	1.000
(2) *C*	0.76	0.688	0.943	0.93	0.689	0.931
(3) *S*	2.01	0.602	0.923	1.20	0.437	0.952
(4) *I*	3.57	− 0.045	0.554	3.41	− 0.166	0.433
(5) *TB*	0.98	0.039	0.009	1.38	− 0.220	− 0.092
(6) $-r^*A$	5.58	0.971	− 0.046	4.04	0.859	− 0.063
(7) *L*	0.69	0.614	1.000	0.89	0.520	1.000
memo items:						
	SD(GDP) = 2.81			*SD(GDP)* = 3.59		
	CORR(S,I) = 0.585			*CORR(S,I)* = 0.508		

[1] Standard deviation relative to the percentage standard deviation of output *SD(GDP)*.
[2] First-order autocorrelation coefficient.
[3] Coefficient of correlation with GDP.

much lower levels than in the past. Important restrictions also remained on foreign direct investment, including portfolio investment, but a major reform in this area was introduced in May 1989.

We turn now to examine the ability of the model to explain the stylised facts of business cycles in Canada and Mexico. The first step is to determine which of the three assumptions about capital mobility is most adequate. Given the historical record on capital controls and accessibility to external financing of each country, a reasonable first approximation is to assume that Canada conforms to the view of an economy that has enjoyed free trade in financial assets for most of the post-war period, while Mexico is best characterised as an economy where some capital controls have been in place and access to foreign loans has not always been on competitive terms. These assumptions imply that, for Canada, equation (3) describes the evolution of foreign assets, with Δ set at -1.14 as the upper bound on foreign debt. This limit on external borrowing ensures intertemporal solvency, but is not binding inside the ergodic set of foreign assets in the stochastic steady state. For Mexico, equation (4) is the law of motion of foreign assets, with *binding* upper and lower bounds set at -0.30 and -0.16 respectively. These bounds were determined by starting from non-binding limits under perfect capital mobility, defined as

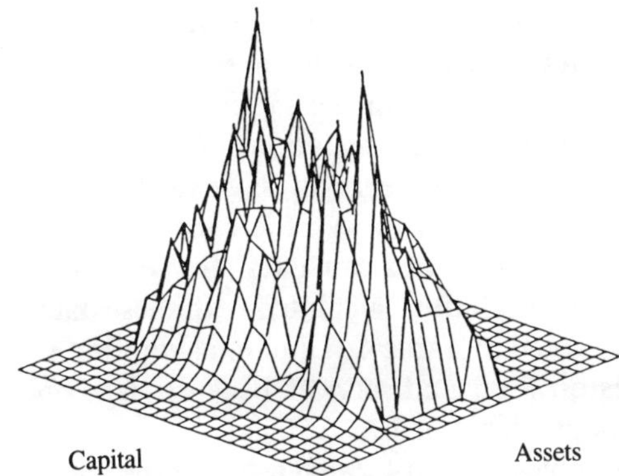

Figure 4.2 Limiting distribution of capital and foreign assets

in the case of Canada to capture the ergodic set of foreign assets, and then adjusting them gradually until the ratio of the standard deviation of net factor payments to the standard deviation of GDP in the model matches that observed in Mexican data (4.3%).

The properties of business cycles in the simulation models representing Canada and Mexico are listed in Table 4.2, and the joint marginal limiting probability distribution of capital and foreign assets in the Canadian benchmark model is depicted in Figure 4.2. Figure 4.2 illustrates clearly how the borrowing constraint is not binding in the stochastic steady state, so that intertemporal solvency is an equilibrium outcome. The statistical moments reported in Table 4.2 can be compared with the corresponding moments obtained from actual data reported in Table 4.1. In general, the model with perfect capital mobility mimics many of the Canadian business-cycle facts – including the positive correlation between savings and investment – except the GDP correlations of consumption and savings, and the first-order autocorrelations of investment and the balance of trade. As shown in Mendoza (1992), the assumption that the intertemporal relative price of aggregate consumption remains fixed at $1 + r^*$ is too strong, and a more realistic structure that decomposes consumption in tradable and nontradable goods would resolve these anomalies.

The model calibrated to the Mexican economy is less successful, but is still capable of mimicking some important stylised facts. Qualitatively, the model is consistent with the data in indicating that savings, investment, and net foreign interest payments are more variable than output, while consumption is less variable. Moreover, consumption, savings, and investment are procyclical, and the trade balance and foreign interest payments are countercyclical, in the model as in the data. By contrast, some large quantitative discrepancies between moments in the model and in the data are observed. The only moments in the model that mimic closely moments in actual data are the standard deviations of investment and net foreign interest payments, the persistence of savings, and the correlation between savings and investment. However, there may be some problems of measurement error with the Mexican data. Some of the coefficients of persistence and GDP correlation calculated with these data are not statistically significant, as noted in Table 4.1, and consumption is defined as personal expenditures on food and services because data on nondurables consumption are not available before 1980.

To conclude, the comparison of Tables 4.1 and 4.2 suggests that the intertemporal equilibrium model proposed in section 2 rationalises several of the stylised facts of business cycles in Canada and Mexico. The model cannot mimic all the stylised facts, particularly for the case of Mexico, but it yields savings plans that embody a pattern of consumption smoothing and allocations of domestic capital and foreign assets similar to that present in the data. The model may thus be viewed as a useful benchmark for evaluating the performance of indicators of capital mobility.

4 Macroeconomic indicators of capital mobility

The extensive literature devoted to measuring capital mobility using data on macroeconomic flows is based on two generalisations of the principle of Fisherian separation of savings and investment already discussed. First, because in an open economy with perfect mobility investment is set to equalise the return on domestic and foreign capital independently of consumption-smoothing considerations, savings and investment should be uncorrelated. Second, because agents make use of the available vehicles of savings to smooth consumption, the variability of consumption relative to output should decline as the degree of capital mobility increases, reflecting the enhanced consumption-smoothing opportunities provided by world capital markets. These two arguments also imply that investment should be more variable and less correlated with output when capital is more mobile, because the resources needed to expand the capital stock according to optimal investment plans can be obtained from world markets and because the influence of consumption-smoothing on those investment plans is reduced.[7] Moreover, the variability of net foreign interest payments relative to output should decrease with the imposition of barriers to capital mobility reflecting suboptimal adjustments in the current account.

Following these arguments, the empirical literature on capital mobility has identified the following stylised facts as indicators of reduced capital mobility in time-series or cross-sectional studies (see Montiel, 1992; Razin and Rose, 1992): (1) an increase in the savings–investment correlation, (2) an increase in the variability of output, (3) an increase in the variability of consumption relative to output, (4) a decrease in the variability of investment relative to output, (5) a decrease in the variability of net foreign interest payments relative to output, and (6) an increase in the correlation between investment and output. The problem with these macroeconomic indicators, as the analysis that follows shows, is that the Fisherian separation argument on which they are based applies strictly only in a deterministic framework, or in tightly-controlled experiments based on stochastic models. Once stochastic elements are taken into account, Fisherian separation holds only as a first approximation and the variability and persistence of exogenous shocks affects the performance of the indicators even if the regime of capital mobility is unchanged. In cross-sectional studies, this problem is compounded by differences in preference and technology parameters across countries which also affect the behaviour of the indicators.

The performance of the above-mentioned indicators of the international mobility of capital is examined next by undertaking a series of experiments in which the model is simulated under alternative regimes of capital mobility and alternative parameter specifications. The benchmark for the analysis is the model parameterised and calibrated to Canadian data. Table 4.3 reports simulated savings–investment correlations that correspond to each of the three regimes of capital mobility discussed in section 2 under five different parameter scenarios; the benchmark model for Canada, an economy with higher risk aversion ($\gamma = 3$), an economy where labour supply is relatively inelastic ($\omega = 3$), an economy where income disturbances are larger ($\sigma_e = 2\%$), and an economy where income disturbances are more persistent ($\rho = 0.6$). Limited capital mobility is defined as a regime under which capital controls force the variability of net foreign interest payments relative to output to decline from 5.6%, as observed under perfect mobility, to 3.6%. Under immobile capital the relative variability of net foreign interest payments to output is set to zero. Tables 4.4–4.8 list the estimates that the same set of simulations produce for other indicators of capital mobility (output variability, consumption variability, investment variability, interest payments variability, and investment–output correlations). Tables 4.3–4.8 are designed so that rows represent alternative specifications of preference parameters and exogenous income disturbances, while columns represent alternative regimes of capital mobility. For a particular indicator of capital mobility to be robust, two

Table 4.3. *Savings–investment correlations in model economies*

	Regime of capital mobility		
Model economy	Perfect mobility	Limited mobility[1]	Immobile capital[2]
Canada benchmark	0.586	0.634	1.0
High risk aversion[3]	0.478	0.518	1.0
Inelastic labour[4]	0.505	0.582	1.0
Large shocks[5]	0.605	0.662	1.0
Persistent shocks[6]	0.457	0.506	1.0

[1] Borrowing and lending ceilings set to reduce the standard deviation of net foreign interest payments from 5.6% under perfect capital mobility for the Canada benchmark to 3.6% under limited capital mobility.
[2] Borrowing and lending ceilings set to reduce the standard deviation of net foreign interest payments to zero.
[3] $\gamma = 3.0\%$.
[4] $\omega = 3.0\%$.
[5] $\sigma^e = 2.0\%$.
[6] $\rho^e = 0.6\%$.

conditions must be satisfied. First, as one moves from left to right in any given row, the indicator should move as predicted by theory. Second, as one moves from top to bottom in any given column, the indicators should remain relatively stable. As Tables 4.3–4.8 show, the first condition is satisfied – except in the case of output variability for simulations with large and persistent shocks – but the second one is not.

According to Tables 4.3–4.8, when the simulation experiments are controlled so as to keep all elements of the model unchanged except the degree of capital mobility, five of the six indicators respond to the imposition of barriers to mobility as theory would predict. As one moves from the regime of perfect mobility to the regime of immobile capital, the savings–investment correlation rises (Table 4.3), consumption variability rises (Table 4.5), investment variability falls (Table 4.6), the variability of net foreign interest payments falls (Table 4.7), and the investment–output correlation rises (Table 4.8). In contrast, output variability in Table 4.4 increases as capital mobility is restricted for the Canada benchmark, the high risk aversion, and the inelastic labour economies, but declines for the economies with large and persistent shocks. This result reflects the fact that, as the shocks become larger or more persistent, the decline in the covariance between the capital stock and the shocks – induced by the inability to borrow from abroad to finance investment – dominates the

Table 4.4. *Output variability in model economies*[1]

	Regime of capital mobility		
Model economy	Perfect mobility	Limited mobility[2]	Immobile capital[3]
Canada benchmark	2.81	2.82	2.83
High risk aversion[4]	2.80	2.82	2.94
Inelastic labour[5]	1.79	1.81	1.88
Large shocks[6]	4.32	4.30	4.29
Persistent shocks[7]	3.33	3.26	3.08

[1] Percentage standard deviations of GDP.
[2] Borrowing and lending ceilings set to reduce the standard deviation of net foreign interest payments from 5.6% under perfect capital mobility for the Canada benchmark to 3.6% under limited capital mobility.
[3] Borrowing and lending ceilings set to reduce the standard deviation of net foreign interest payments to zero.
[4] $\gamma = 3.0\%$.
[5] $\omega = 3.0\%$.
[6] $\sigma^e = 2.0\%$.
[7] $\rho^e = 0.6\%$.

Table 4.5. *Consumption variability in model economies*[1]

	Regime of capital mobility		
Model economy	Perfect mobility	Limited mobility[2]	Immobile capital[3]
Canada benchmark	0.76	0.79	0.85
High risk aversion[4]	0.76	0.79	0.84
Inelastic labour[5]	0.61	0.62	0.70
Large shocks[6]	0.77	0.81	0.87
Persistent shocks[7]	0.80	0.83	0.89

[1] Percentage standard deviation of consumption relative to the percentage standard deviation of GDP.
[2] Borrowing and lending ceilings set to reduce the standard deviation of net foreign interest payments from 5.6% under perfect capital mobility for the Canada benchmark to 3.6% under limited capital mobility.
[3] Borrowing and lending ceilings set to reduce the standard deviation of net foreign interest payments to zero.
[4] $\gamma = 3.0\%$.
[5] $\omega = 3.0\%$.
[6] $\sigma^e = 2.0\%$.
[7] $\rho^e = 0.6\%$.

Table 4.6. *Investment variability in model economies*[1]

Model economy	Regime of capital mobility		
	Perfect mobility	Limited mobility[2]	Immobile capital[3]
Canada benchmark	3.57	3.37	1.76
High risk aversion[4]	3.81	3.51	1.77
Inelastic labour[5]	3.57	3.39	2.48
Large shocks[6]	3.33	3.07	1.70
Persistent shocks[7]	4.00	3.64	1.60

[1] Percentage standard deviation of investment relative to the percentage standard deviation of GDP.

[2] Borrowing and lending ceilings set to reduce the standard deviation of net foreign interest payments from 5.6% under perfect capital mobility for the Canada benchmark to 3.6% under limited capital mobility.

[3] Borrowing and lending ceilings set to reduce the standard deviation of net foreign interest payments to zero.

[4] $\gamma = 3.0\%$.

[5] $\omega = 3.0\%$.

[6] $\sigma^e = 2.0\%$.

[7] $\rho^e = 0.6\%$.

Table 4.7. *Variability of interest payments in model economies*[1]

Model economy	Regime of capital mobility		
	Perfect mobility	Limited mobility[2]	Immobile capital[3]
Canada benchmark	5.59	3.61	—
High risk aversion[4]	9.04	4.21	—
Inelastic labour[5]	9.91	6.22	—
Large shocks[6]	5.61	2.72	—
Persistent shocks[7]	5.70	3.43	—

[1] Percentage standard deviation of net foreign interest payments relative to the percentage standard deviation of GDP.

[2]Borrowing and lending ceilings set to reduce the standard deviation of net foreign interest payments from 5.6% under perfect capital mobility for the Canada benchmark to 3.6% under limited capital mobility.

[3] Borrowing and lending ceilings set to reduce the standard deviation of net foreign interest payments to zero.

[4] $\gamma = 3.0\%$.

[5] $\omega = 3.0\%$.

[6] $\sigma^e = 2.0\%$.

[7] $\rho^e = 0.6\%$.

Table 4.8. *Investment–output correlations in model economies*

Model economy	Regime of capital mobility		
	Perfect mobility	Limited mobility[1]	Immobile capital[2]
Canada benchmark	0.555	0.588	0.938
High risk aversion[3]	0.480	0.502	0.948
Inelastic labour[4]	0.488	0.548	0.919
Large shocks[5]	0.584	0.609	0.933
Persistent shocks[6]	0.441	0.471	0.930

[1] Borrowing and lending ceilings set to reduce the standard deviation of net foreign interest payments from 5.6% under perfect capital mobility for the Canada benchmark to 3.6% under limited capital mobility.
[2] Borrowing and lending ceilings set to reduce the standard deviation of net foreign interest payments zero.
[3] $\gamma = 3.0\%$.
[4] $\omega = 3.0\%$.
[5] $\sigma^e = 2.0\%$.
[6] $\rho^e = 0.6\%$.

increase in the variance of capital that results from the need to use it as the main vehicle of savings.[8]

The usefulness of the macroeconomic indicators of capital mobility is much less clear when slight variations in preference parameters and in the magnitude and duration of income disturbances are taken into account, as one moves from one row to the next in each table. Consider the case of the savings–investment correlations. Table 4.3 shows that an economy where shocks are more persistent would appear to restrict capital mobility less than the Canada benchmark, because savings and investment are less correlated. However, the correlation between savings and investment is smaller, not because of barriers to capital mobility but because, as explained below, the more persistent shocks lengthen the period during which savings decline and investment rises in response to real shocks. Similarly, Table 4.3 shows that economies with higher risk aversion or relatively inelastic labour supply also produce less correlation between savings and investment than the Canada benchmark, while an economy with larger shocks produces the opposite.

The other macroeconomic indicators of capital mobility are also affected by changes in the specification of parameters. Tables 4.4–4.8 show that the variability of output, the output–correlation of investment, and the variability ratios of consumption, investment, and net foreign interest

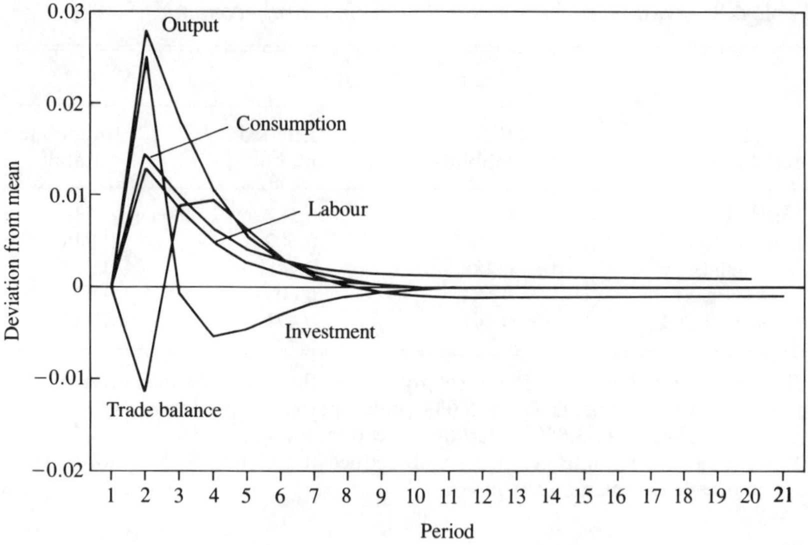

Figure 4.3 Impulse responses under perfect capital mobility

payments relative to output tend to be just as sensitive to changes in parameters as to the imposition of limits on capital mobility. Hence, all countries in the sample of a cross-section study could have identical regimes of capital mobility, and yet be judged as allowing financial capital to flow more or less freely on the basis of differences in macroeconomic indicators that could merely reflect differences in the structure of the economies. Tables 4.3 and 4.8 show that it is only in the extreme case in which capital mobility is totally obstructed that indicators based on savings–investment correlations or investment–output correlations are robust to parameter specifications. However, in a world where neither perfect mobility or absolute immobility are found very frequently, this robustness property may not be useful.

The performance of the indicators of capital mobility in the various experiments summarised in Tables 4.3–4.8 can be examined further by studying the differences in the pattern of adjustment of the economy in response to exogenous shocks due to the imposition of barriers to capital mobility. This is illustrated in Figures 4.3 and 4.4, which depict impulse responses of macroeconomic aggregates to a 1% productivity shock in the regimes of perfect capital mobility and immobile capital respectively.

Under perfect capital mobility (Figure 4.3), the impact effect of the productivity shock on output, consumption, labour supply, and investment is positive, while that on the trade balance is negative. The increase

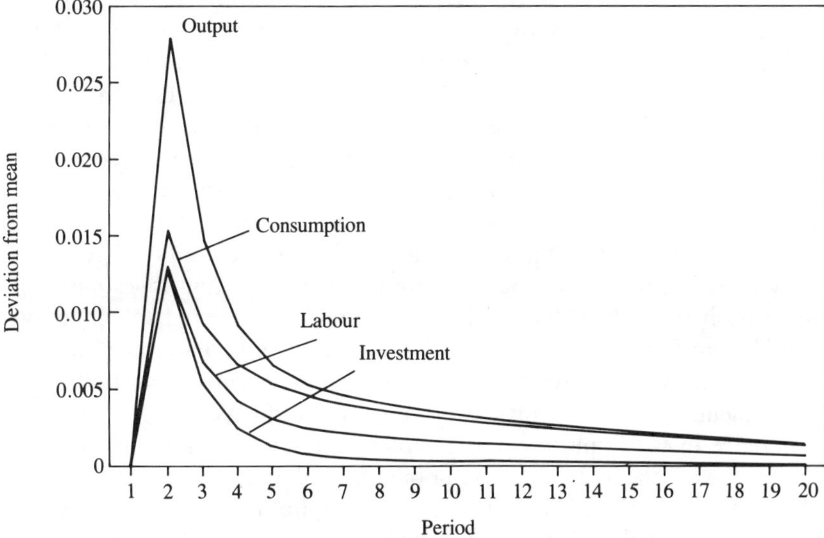

Figure 4.4 Impulse responses under the regime of immobile capital

in labour and consumption is smaller than the surge in output, reflecting the agents' desire to smooth consumption of the composite good *C-G*(*L*). The trade balance worsens to finance additional investment needed to equalise the expected returns on foreign assets and domestic capital. As the effect of the shock fades, output, consumption, and labour revert to their long-run mean values following a downward, monotonic pattern. In contrast, investment declines sharply and becomes negative after the second period, and then it returns to its long-term mean from below zero following upward, monotonic trend. This reflects the extent to which Fisherian separation is still a useful approximation under uncertainty, the volatile behaviour of investment resulting from the agent's ability to borrow and lend as necessary to equalise the expected returns of available assets. The sharp improvement of the trade balance after the negative impact effect is approximately a mirror image of the changes in investment, with the exception that trade surpluses also reflect the accumulation of foreign assets to sustain savings.[9] Savings correspond to the difference between output and consumption; thus, the impulse response of savings would also display a positive impact effect and a downward, monotonic adjustment to the initial equilibrium. Savings and investment are positively correlated, despite perfect capital mobility, because the impact effect on both variables is positive. The correlation is not perfect, however, because after the impact effect savings decline while investment increases. The duration of the disturbances is crucial for this result. If the productivity shock had zero autocorrelation, investment would have little incentive to move – since the expected profitability of future capital is unchanged – and the correlation between savings and investment would be negligible. Hence, a necessary condition for high savings–investment correlations to be interpreted as evidence of imperfect capital mobility is that income disturbances be purely transitory. However, as the analysis that follows shows, this condition is necessary but not sufficient.

The impulse responses under the regime of immobile capital (Figure 4.4) show that in this case output, consumption, labour, and investment all react positively when the shock occurs, and then revert to their initial equilibrium following a downward, monotonic path. The trade balance does not move because the regime of immobile capital prevents any adjustments in the holdings of foreign financial assets. The striking difference in the impulse responses of investment under perfect capital mobility and the regime of immobile capital is again a reflection of Fisherian separation. When international capital mobility is prohibited, agents are forced to formulate savings plans as in a closed economy. Investment must be allocated so as to smooth consumption and not to balance the returns paid by foreign and domestic assets. It is interesting to note, however, that the patterns and magnitudes of the mean deviations of output, consumption, and labour induced by the 1% shock are similar under the two regimes. Moreover, increases in the variability of output and consumption that result from restricting capital mobility in Tables 4.4 and 4.5 are marginal. Thus, as noted by Mendoza (1991b), the agents' ability to smooth consumption is not significantly affected by the imposition of barriers to capital mobility – given the relatively small magnitude of observed business cycles and the assumed low degree of risk aversion. This result suggests that measures of capital mobility based on the variability of output and consumption may be less useful than those based on the cyclical behaviour of investment. The simulation exercises show, however, that the latter are not very informative either.

These results suggest that cross-country studies of capital mobility based on business-cycle volatility indicators may be affected by the noise introduced by differences in risk aversion, labour–leisure preferences, and duration and persistence of random income shocks. To illustrate this point further, the standard deviations of consumption in the 15 simulations reported in Tables 4.3–4.8 are used to construct a simplified version of the test conducted by Razin and Rose (1992). Razin and Rose used direct evidence on the regimes of capital mobility in place in 133 countries, combined with factor analysis, to construct factor variables that measured the openness of the various economies, and then estimated regressions of business-cycle volatility measures on those factors. They concluded that the regressions did not provide strong support for the hypothesis that consumption is less variable and investment more variable as the degree of openness increases. In the experiment conducted here, the standard deviation of consumption is regressed first on a qualitative variable that measures the degree of mobility – this variable is assigned a value of 0 for artificial economies with perfect mobility, 1 for economies with limited mobility, and 2 for economies with immobile capital. Despite the fact that the regimes of capital mobility are identified without error, this regression fails to produce a statistically significant coefficient. However, if additional binary variables are introduced to control for risk aversion, labour elasticity of substitution, and variability and persistence of output shocks, the coefficient on the capital mobility variable is estimated at 0.13 with a t-statistic of 6.5.

In summary, the numerical analysis suggests that cross-country and time-series studies of capital mobility based on macroeconomic indicators are not likely to be illustrative unless differences in preferences, technology, and the nature of shocks across countries and through time periods are taken into account. Otherwise, savings–investment and output–investment correlations, as well as business-cycle variability measures, cannot be interpreted as providing information useful for determining the degree of capital mobility. Given the complexity involved in identifying and incorporating into empirical tests the many differences in economic structure across countries, it is perhaps best to opt for direct measures of mobility such as the transactions and capital account data examined by Tesar and Werner (1992) and Calvo, Leiderman, and Reinhart (1992), or for econometric tests that evaluate directly the implications of the neoclassical framework as the Euler equation tests of Obstfeld (1989).

The results of the numerical simulations also suggest, however, that the results of Euler equation tests of capital mobility should be interpreted with caution. These tests, as proposed in Obstfeld's (1989) work, attempt to establish whether there are systematic differences in the intertemporal marginal rates of substitution in consumption across countries – assuming that agents in different countries have identical preferences, represented by isoelastic-utility functions, and that countries issue one-period, risk-free financial assets. If there is perfect capital mobility, arbitrage in these assets would equalise marginal rate of substitution across countries and, hence, as of date t, variables dated t or earlier should be orthogonal to the difference of the marginal rates of substitution between any two countries. In the context of the model presented in section 2, the Euler equation test can be interpreted as follows. Economies with perfect capital mobility participate in the world's capital market, and hence in equlibrium the intertemporal marginal rates of substitution for economies *A* and *B* equal the world real rate of return:

$$\left[\frac{U'(t)}{\exp(-v(t))\mathrm{E}_t[U'(t+1)]}\right]_a = (1+r^*)$$

$$= \left[\frac{U'(t)}{\exp(-v(t))\mathrm{E}_t[U'(t+1)]}\right]_b . \quad (14)$$

Economies under a regime of immobile capital cannot access world financial markets, and hence the domestic capital stock is the only vehicle of savings. The Euler equations for these economies imply that *each* has a domestic one-period, risk-free real interest rate given by:

$$\frac{U'(t)}{\exp(-v(t))\mathrm{E}_t[U'(t+1)]} = \mathrm{E}_t[(F_k(t+1)+1-\delta)] + \frac{\mathrm{cov}[U'(t+1), F_k(t+1)+1-\delta]}{\mathrm{E}_t[U'(t+1)]}. \quad (15)$$

A researcher can test whether there is perfect capital mobility between two countries by testing the null hypothesis that there are no systematic differences in their marginal rates of substitution, as implied by (14). However, this hypothesis presumes that there are statistically significant differences between the one-period, risk-free interest rates under perfect capital mobility and the regime of immobile capital – i.e. $(1 + r^*)$ and the right-hand side of (15). This implies that the mean return on capital in an economy where capital is immobile must differ from that paid in world markets, and that the economy's risk premium, as measured by the covariance between the marginal utility of consumption and the net marginal product of capital, must be different from zero. If this is the case, one should expect that the equilibrium stochastic process of consumption, in the presence of the same income disturbances, should reflect the limited insurance possibilities of the regime with immobile capital.

Unfortunately, given the parameterisation of preferences, technology, and exogenous shocks, the simulations of the model with immobile capital produce negligible differences in the intertemporal equilibrium allocations for consumption. In the case of the Canada benchmark model, the mean of consumption is neutral to the regime of capital mobility, the standard deviation increases from 0.024 under perfect mobility of 0.027 under immobile capital, and the consumption–output correlation increases by 0.033 from one regime to the other.[10] It thus appears that the ability of agents to smooth consumption is not limited significantly by changes in the regime of capital mobility, and hence it is possible that capital may not move across countries for which the differential in marginal rates of substitution is not statistically different from zero. This result is consistent with previous findings by Cole and Obstfeld (1991), Mendoza (1991b), and Backus, Kehoe and Kydland (1992), suggesting that under particular specifications of preferences and technology, the completeness of financial markets does not significantly affect competitive allocations.

5 Concluding remarks

This chapter examined the performance of several well-known macroeconomic indicators of capital mobility in the context of an intertemporal equilibrium framework of a small open economy. Recursive numerical solution methods were used to compute the equilibrium comovements of a model economy subject to stochastic disturbances affecting productivity or the terms of trade. These equilibrium comovements were compared with the stylised facts of business cycles in Canada and Mexico so as to establish the model's ability to serve as a useful tool for assessing the implications of different regimes of capital mobility. Once it was established that the model rationalises some key characteristics of actual business cycles, several simulation exercises were conducted to examine the performance of the mobility indicators under different regimes of capital mobility and different specifications of the parameters that measure the degree of relative risk aversion, the price elasticity of labour supply, and the variability and persistence of the stochastic shocks.

The results showed that the principle of strong Fisherian separation of savings and investment that holds in a deterministic environment, on which the use of macroeconomic comovements as indicators of capital mobility is based, is only a rough first approximation in a setting with uncertainty. The quantitative implications of this fact affect significantly the robustness of macroeconomic indicators of capital mobility. These indicators generally behave as predicted by theory when the simulation experiments are controlled to modify exclusively the regime of capital mobility, but they prove to be unstable in the presence of small changes in structural parameters. In particular, high savings–investment correlations are found to be a necessary but not sufficient condition for establishing the immobility of capital. Moreover, savings–investment correlations, as well as other indicators based on the cyclical behaviour of output, consumption, and investment, are equally sensitive to slight variations in the parameters that describe preferences and the stochastic process of the disturbances as to changes in the degree of capital mobility.

The findings of this analysis suggest that the evidence presented to date on capital mobility based on macroeconomic indicators cannot be interpreted as showing that the welfare and efficiency gains resulting from the integration of world capital markets have not materialised. Furthermore, empirical tests aimed at establishing the mobility of capital across countries using macroeconomic indicators may be affected by the noise attributed to differences in the structure of the economies under study. Unless this information can be properly incorporated into the tests, an approach based on direct measurement of international flows of financial capital, or the Euler equation tests that evaluate directly the implications of the optimality principles that characterise the neoclassical model, may be the best alternative. The results of the latter should be interpreted with caution, however, because numerical simulations suggest that they can produce favourable results even for economies where capital is in fact immobile.

NOTES

Helpful comments and suggestions by Eduardo Borensztein, Mohsin Khan, Assaf Razin, Andrew Rose, Lars Svensson, Linda Tesar and Peter Wickham, as well as those provided by the discussants of the chapter, John Huizinga and Joseph Zeira, are gratefully acknowledged. The views expressed here are the author's only and do not represent those of the International Monetary Fund.

1 The shock e_t incorporates the effects of fluctuations in the terms of trade because output is a tradable commodity (see Greenwood, 1983). However, the model ignores the existence of nontraded goods and does not model separately importable and exportable commodities. Mendoza (1992) examines a model that relaxes these assumptions.

2 With these adjustment costs, the cost of changing the capital stock by a fixed amount increases with the speed of the desired adjustment, giving agents an incentive to undertake investment changes gradually. This prevents the model from exaggerating the variability of investment relative to what is observed in the data (see Mendoza, 1991a for details).

3 The world's real interest rate is assumed to be fixed for simplicity. This reduces the model to the minimum framework in which to assess the performance of capital mobility indicators under uncertainty. Mendoza (1991a) finds that interest rate shocks do not have significant implications for the model examined here under conditions of perfect capital mobility.

4 Implicit in this financial structure is the assumption that contracts with payment contingent on the realisations of the disturbances cannot be written. Impeding trade in these contingent claims limits the ability of agents to insure

themselves completely against country-specific risks. However, Cole and Obstfeld (1991), Mendoza (1991b) and Baxter and Crucini (1992) found that market incompleteness may not have drastic effects on competitive allocations. This financial structure also assumes that foreigners do not own domestic capital, although it is possible for domestic agents to borrow from world markets to finance investment projects.

5 In this utility function, the rate of time preference, $\exp[\nu(\cdot)]$, increases with the level of past consumption in order to obtain a well-defined unique invariant limiting distribution of the state variables – as demonstrated by Epstein (1983). Obstfeld (1981) used the deterministic analogue of this utility function, following Uzawa (1968), to obtain a well-defined steady state for foreign asset holdings in a small open economy. Epstein also showed that SCU is suitable for dynamic programming, that with it consumption in every period is a normal good, and that the conditions it requires restrain the variability of the rate of time preference so that major deviations from the standard time-separable setup are avoided.

6 This method is due to Bertsekas (1976) and was introduced to macroeconomic models by Sargent (1980). Greenwood, Hercowitz and Huffman (1988) used it to simulate a closed-economy real business-cycle model and Mendoza (1991a) used it to solve a small open-economy model. The technique calculates exactly the unique invariant joint limiting distribution of the state variables, using an algorithm that solves the functional equation problem for a discrete version of the state space.

7 Razin and Rose (1992) also argue that output variability increases with trade liberalisation because of the specialisation trends that follow from perfect mobility of goods.

8 Note that, because of the Cobb–Douglas technology and the separation of consumption and labour in the utility function, the variance of output can be expressed as a linear function of the variance of the shocks, the variance of the capital stock, and the covariance between the capital stock and the shocks.

9 The present value of the trade balance must be zero to satisfy the resource constraint. Hence the initial worsening of the trade balance is offset with several periods of improvement.

10 Even if the exercise is altered to allow for the use of capital controls to target the trade balance, and hence alter the mean of the capital stock, the effects on consumption and welfare are negligible (see Mendoza, 1991b for details).

REFERENCES

Backus, D.K. and P.J. Kehoe (1992) 'International Evidence on the Historical Properties of Business Cycles', *American Economic Review*, **82**, 864–88.

Backus, David K., P.J. Kehoe and Finn E. Kydland (1992), 'International Real Business Cycles', *Journal of Political Economy*, **100** (August), 745–75.

Baxter, M. and M.J. Crucini (1992) 'Business cycles and the asset structure of foreign trade', Rochester Centre for Economic Research, University of Rochester, unpublished paper.

(1993) 'Explaining savings/investment correlations', *American Economic Review*, **83**.

Bayoumi, Tamim and Gabriel Sterne (1992) 'Regional Trade Blocs, Mobile Capital and Exchange Rate Coordination', Research Department, International Monetary fund, unpublished manuscript.

Bertsekas, Dimitri P. (1976) *Dynamic Programming and Stochastic Control*, New York: Academic Press.

Calvo, Guillermo A., Leonardo Leiderman and Carmen M. Reinhart (1992) 'Capital Inflows and Real Exchange Rate Appreciation in Latin America: The Role of External Factors', *IMF Staff Papers*, **40** (March).

Cole, Harold and Maurice Obstfeld (1991) 'Commodity Trade and International Risk Sharing: How Much Do Financial Markets Matter', *Journal of Monetary Economics*, **28** (August) 3–24.

Correia, Isabel H., João C. Neves and Sergio Rebelo (1991) 'Business Cycles in Portugal: Theory and Evidence', *Working Paper*, Research Department, Bank of Portugal.

Dooley, Michael, Jeffrey A. Frankel and Donald J. Mathieson (1987) 'International Capital Mobility: What do Savings–Investment Correlations Tell Us?', *IMF Staff Papers*, **34**, 503–29.

Epstein, Larry G. (1983) 'Stationary Cardinal Utility and Optimal Growth under Uncertainty', *Journal of Economic Theory*, **31**, 133–52.

Feldstein, Martin and Charles Horioka (1980) 'Domestic Savings and International Capital Flows', *Economic Journal*, **90** (June), 314–29.

Finn, Mary G. (1990) 'On Savings and Investment Dynamics in a Small Open Economy', *Journal of International Economics*, **29**, 1–22.

Fisher, Irving (1930) *Theory of Interest*, New York: Macmillan.

Frankel, Jeffrey A. (1992) 'Measuring International Capital Mobility: A Review', *American Economic Review, Papers and Proceedings*, **82**, 197–202.

Frenkel, Jacob A. and Assaf Razin (1987) *Fiscal Policies and the World Economy*, Cambridge, MA: MIT Press.

Greenwood, Jeremy (1983) 'Expectations, The Exchange Rate and The Current Account', *Journal of Monetary Economics*, **12**, 543–69.

Greenwood, Jeremy, Zvi Hercowitz and Gregory Huffman (1988) 'Investment, Capacity Utilization and the Real Business Cycle', *American Economic Review*, **78**, 402–17.

Hansen, Lars P. and Kenneth J. Singleton (1983) 'Stochastic Consumption, Risk Aversion, and the Temporal Behavior of Asset Returns', *Journal of Political Economy*, **91**, 249–65.

Helpman, Elhanan and Assaf Razin (1982) 'Dynamics of a Floating Exchange Rate Regime', *Journal of Political Economy*, **90**, 728–54.

Imrohoroglu, Ayse (1989) 'Cost of Business Cycles with Indivisibilities and Liquidity Constraints', *Journal of Political Economy*, **97**, 1364–83.

International Monetary Fund (1991a) *World Economic Outlook, May 1991*, Washington, DC: IMF.

(1991b) *Annual Report on Exchange Arrangements and Exchange Restrictions*, Washington, DC: IMF.

Mendoza, Enrique G. (1991a) 'Real Business Cycles in a Small Open Economy', *American Economic Review*, **81**, 797–818.

(1991b) 'Capital Controls and the Gains from Trade in a Business Cycle Model of a Small Open Economy', *IMF Staff Papers*, **38**, 480–505.

(1992) 'The Terms of Trade and Economic Fluctuations', IMF, *Working Paper* **WP/92/98** (December).

Montiel, Peter J. (1992) 'Capital Mobility in Developing Countries: Some Measurement Issues and Empirical Estimates', unpublished manuscript, Department of Economics, Oberlin College.

Obstfeld, Maurice (1981) 'Macroeconomic Policy, Exchange Rate Dynamics and Optimal Asset Accumulation', *Journal of Political Economy*, **89** (December), 1142–61.

(1986) 'Capital Mobility in the World Economy: Theory and Measurement', *Carnegie–Rochester Conference Series on Public Policy*, **24** (Spring), 55–104.

(1989) 'How Integrated are World Capital Markets?: Some New Tests', in G. Calvo, R. Findlay, P. Koari and J. Braga de Macedo (eds), *Debt, Stabilization and Development: Essays in Memory of Carlos Diaz-Alejandro*, Oxford: Basil Blackwell.

Ostry, Jonathan D. and Carmen M. Reinhart (1992) 'Private Saving and Terms of Trade Shocks', *IMF Staff Papers*, **39**, 495–517.

Prescott, Edward C. (1986) 'Theory Ahead of Business Cycle Measurement', *Carnegie–Rochester Conference Series on Public Policy*, **25**, 11–44.

Razin, Assaf and Andrew K. Rose (1992) 'Business Cycle Volatility and Openness: An Exploratory Cross-Sectional Analysis, Economics Department, Tel-Aviv University and School of Business Administration, University of California, Berkeley, unpublished manuscript.

Sachs, Jeffrey (1982) 'The Current Account and Macroeconomic Adjustment in the 1970s', *Brookings Papers on Economic Activity*, **12**, 201–68.

Sargent, Thomas J. (1980) 'Tobin's *q* and the Rate of Investment in General Equilibrium', *Carnegie–Rochester Conference Series on Public Policy*, **12**, 107–54.

Sinn, Stefan A. (1991) 'Measuring International Capital Mobility: A Critical Note on the Use of Saving and Investment Correlations', unpublished manuscript, Institut für Weltwirtschaft, Kiel.

Summers, Lawrence (1988) 'Tax Policy and International Competitiveness', in J. Frenkel (ed.), *International Aspects of Fiscal Policies*, Chicago: University of Chicago Press.

Svensson, Lars E.O. and Assaf Razin (1983) 'The Terms of Trade and the Current Account: The Harberger–Laursen–Metzler Effect', *Journal of Political Economy*, **91**, 97–125.

Tesar, Linda L. (1991) 'Savings, Investment and International Capital Flows', *Journal of International Economics*, **31** (August), 55–78.

Tesar, Linda L. and Ingrid M. Werner (1992) 'Home Bias and the Globalization of Securities Markets', NBER, *Working Paper*, **4218** (November).

Uzawa, Hirofumi (1968) 'Time Preference, the Consumption Function and Optimum Asset Holdings', in J.N. Wolfe (ed.), *Value, Capital and Growth: Papers in Honor of Sir John Hicks*, Edinburgh: Edinburgh University Press.

Zeira, Joseph (1987) 'Risk and Capital Accumulation in a Small Open Economy', *Quarterly Journal of Economics*, **102** (May), 265–79.

Discussion

JOHN HUIZINGA

It is well known that the effects of both monetary and fiscal policy depend critically on a country's openness to trade in financial assets, i.e. on its degree of international capital mobility. For this reason, and many others, attempts to measure a country's degree of capital mobility have been numerous and influential. Chapter 4 is an informative and well-written investigation of the important question: how good is our ability to measure the degree of capital mobility in the world economy when macroeconomic indicators are used to conduct the measurement? The fairly convincing answer which is provided to this question is: 'not very'.

I will divide my comments into four sections. Section 1 briefly describes what is done in the chapter. Since the chapter is easy to read and quite clear on this topic, I will be brief. Section 2 describes what can be learned from the chapter. I view it as a sign of a good chapter when (as I believe is the case here) the author and a discussant agree on what can be learned. Section 3 provides my discussion of areas where I disagree with the author. In my opinion these disagreements are primarily in matters of interpretation, not conclusions. Section 4 contains some suggestions on how future work might profitably expand on this study.

1 What is done?

Chapter 4 simulates an open-economy, real business-cycle, model that has been calibrated with Canadian data, to obtain certain variances and covariances which have been examined or proposed in the economics literature as indicators of capital mobility. The potential indicators are the correlation between savings and investment, the correlation between output and investment, the variance of output, and the variance of output relative to the variance of consumption, investment, and international interest payments. The only shock to hit the economy in this model is a two-state productivity shock, which allows numerical solutions to be obtained from the model. Key parameters of the model include the degree of risk aversion, the elasticity of labour supply with respect to the real wage, and the size and persistence of the productivity shock. The degree of capital mobility in the model is captured by establishing bounds on the size of a country's net asset position. Countries with no capital mobility have a fixed net asset position, while countries with perfect capital mobility are restricted only in the sense of not violating a Ponzi scheme constraint. The results of simulating the model appear in Tables 4.3–4.8.

2 What is learned?

The most important thing to be learned from this chapter is that, if the model employed here is an accurate description of the real world then studies of capital mobility based on macroeconomic indicators are not likely to be illustrative unless differences in preferences and technology are taken into account. In short, differences in the key parameters identified above can be just as important as differences in the degree of capital mobility for determining the macroeconomic indicators being studied here. As an example, the correlation between savings and investment in a country with limited capital mobility and highly persistent productivity shocks can be indistinguishable from that same correlation in a country with perfect capital mobility and highly inelastic labour supply.

A secondary finding of the chapter is that if key parameters concerning tastes and technology are quite similar across data sets, macroeconomic indicators such as the variance of output or the relative variances of consumption and output may be less likely to reveal differences in capital mobility than indicators such as the correlation between savings and investment or the relative variance of investment and output.

3 Areas of disagreement

Perhaps the biggest disagreement I see between the author's interpretation and my own concerns what role uncertainty plays in understanding how the key parameters identified here affect the macroeconomic indicators. My opinion is that uncertainty is not crucial, though I get the impression from the chapter that the author feels uncertainty plays a critical role.

Let me illustrate my view with a discussion of what one could learn about the correlation between savings and investment following a temporary productivity shock from a deterministic model which is similar to the stochastic model used in the chapter. With a deterministic model one could, in my opinion, provide diagrams similar to the impulse response functions shown in Figure 4.3 (see, for example, Obstfeld, 1986). Following a temporary productivity shock, output and consumption will rise, with consumption rising less than output due to a desire to smooth consumption in the face of a temporary shock to income. Thus, saving will initially rise, but will then return to its old level after the effects of the shock wear off. Investment will initially rise because the marginal product of capital rises and increases the desired capital shock. Investment turns negative before returning to its original level as the capital built up during the high productivity is consumed after productivity returns to its original level.

What does all this imply about the correlation between savings and investment? During the time immediately after the shock, both investment and savings are high (relative to their long-run value), leading to a positive correlation. Later, investment will be low and savings will still be high, leading to a negative correlation. Overall, the correlation is likely to be positive because observations during the period immediately after the shock get higher weight in computing the correlation. This results from the fact that during this time both savings and investment are further from their long-run value than they are later on.

The temporary nature of the productivity shock is easily seen to be crucial here. With a permanent shock the preference for consumption smoothing will not contribute to increased savings. With no movement in savings there will be no correlation between savings and investment.

What does the introduction of uncertainty add to this analysis? Potentially, if there were time-varying risk and substantial risk aversion, uncertainty could play an important role. In practice, however, adding uncertainty merely allows one to calibrate and obtain numerical results for an economic phenomenon that can be well understood from a deterministic model. The main contribution of this chapter is in presenting carefully constructed numbers which illustrate the importance of concepts which have previously been captured in deterministic models.

Another area of potential disagreement between the author and myself involves the ability of the model used here to explain important macroeconomic data. I have serious doubts about the ability of the model to describe short-run fluctuations accurately. This is important because if the model does a poor job of fitting macroeconomic data, it may give misleading impressions about how key parameters can affect the macroeconomic indicators which are the focus of this chapter. In this regard the term 'model' needs to be broadly interpreted to include both the set of behavioural equations and the variety of shocks which are considered. For example, if fiscal and monetary policy shocks are the dominant forces driving the economy and productivity shocks are relatively unimportant, results such as those presented in this chapter can be very misleading, even if all the behavioural equations are accurate.

4 Suggestions

Future work in this area could provide insights above and beyond those presented in this chapter. As described in section 3, one way in which this could occur is to expand the variety of shocks which drive the economy. Convincing calibration of parameters such as the relative variances of potential shocks, much like convincing calibration of parameters such as the intertemporal rate of substitution, would surely increase interest in the type of results presented in this chapter.

In addition, explorations of alternative methods for modelling limited capital mobility would be interesting. In this chapter, limited capital mobility means both borrowing and lending constraints. It would be informative to consider asymmetric frameworks of borrowing constraints without lending constraints, and vice versa. It would also be informative to consider a characterisation of imperfect capital mobility which involved foreign lending being perceived as more risky than domestic lending (perhaps due to asymmetric information or differences in the possibility of enforcing repayment through the legal system). The risk premium which would arise in such a model could create an interesting form of time-varying impediment to international capital flows.

REFERENCE

Obstfeld, M. (1986) 'Capital mobility in the world economy: Theory and measurement', *Carnegie–Rochester Conferences Series on Public Policy*, **24** (Spring), 55–104.

JOSEPH ZEIRA

Chapter 4 examines a number of macroeconomic indicators which are often used to measure the degree of capital mobility in open economies. The main indicators analysed in the chapter are the savings and investment correlation, and consumption smoothing along time. These indicators have been extensively used to measure capital mobility.

The reasons why these indicators are often used are the following. It capital is fully mobile, and risk is internationally fully diversified, investment is determined solely by technology and by the world's cost of capital. Hence, investment should be completely independent of domestic savings. Empirical studies have, however, shown that correlations between savings and investment are significantly positive.[1] Similarly, if capital is fully mobile, consumption should be fully smoothed along time. This is done by savings decisions which transfer income from period to period, not only individually but on a national level as well, due to capital mobility.

Mendoza claims that these measures do not provide good indicators for capital mobility. He constructs a simulation model of the open economy and examines how these indicators are affected by the imposition of capital restrictions. He shows that under some theoretical assumptions savings and investment are correlated and consumption is not fully smoothed even when capital is fully mobile. Furthermore, it is shown that these indicators are affected by other parameters as well, such as the degree of risk aversion, the elasticity of labour supply, the size of technological shocks and their persistence. Hence, these macroeconomic measures react slightly to restrictions on capital mobility on one hand and react to many other variables as well on the other, and therefore cannot serve as good indicators for capital mobility.

What is the basic intuition behind this conclusion? There are two basic assumptions of the model which account for these results:

(1) Mendoza assumes that the technological shocks are multiplicative and persistent, and thus affect both income and future marginal productivity of capital. As a result, these shocks affect simultaneously both saving and investment decisions. In other words, the correlation of saving and investment is explained by a third factor – productivity – which affects both. This idea has appeared originally in Obstfeld (1986).

(2) The chapter assumes that there is no international trade in shares, namely direct ownership of capital, and no foreign direct investment. Capital mobility is limited to riskless lending and borrowing only. As a result, domestic aggregate risk is not internationally diversified and there is risk premium on holding capital. When savings rise, the risk premium declines and that induces investors to increase investment. This is an additional explanation for greater correlation between savings and investment. This explanation appears in Zeira (1987)

By use of similar arguments we can show that the two above assumptions also tend to reduce consumption smoothing along time. In face of multiplicative shocks, changes in income are accompanied by changes in future income, due to changes in investment. Hence consumption fluctuates by more. If capital ownership is not internationally diversified, the interest rate individuals face reflects a risk premium, which is sensitive to changes in income. This further magnifies fluctuations in consumption.

I have one major criticism on the model which is used in this chapter to evaluate macroeconomic indicators. The definition of imperfect capital mobility as fixed quantity constraints on borrowing and lending is problematic, and is subject to the Lucas critique. If these quantity constraints are endogenous, due to asymmetric information, debt renegotiation schemes, etc. then these constraints should be sensitive to shocks. If income rises, it is reasonable to assume that we could increase collateral and borrow more. This should affect the results significantly. A similar problem arises if the constraint on capital mobility is due not to markets, but rather to government restriction. If the government controls capital mobility, while it has access to the world's capital markets itself, it can manipulate this control in order to become a financial intermediator between the economy and the world, and thus tax capital mobility.[2] It is therefore obvious that in this case as well the government might adjust the constraints to income shocks, for a variety of reasons. Hence, the modelling of imperfect capital mobility by fixed quantity constraints should be replaced by more flexible constraints.

The next move in analysing capital mobility and how to measure it, should thus be to improve the modelling of capital controls. But this chapter is a first step in a more quantitative assessment of the robustness of macroeconomic indicators of capital mobility, and it thus fills a missing gap in our understanding of how good, or rather bad, these indicators are.

NOTES

1 This was first shown by Feldstein and Horioka (1980), and later further established by others, as Mendoza describes.

2 This argument appears in Sussman (1991). A measurement of this implicit tax on capital mobility in many developing countries appears in Giovannini and de Melo (1991).

REFERENCES

Feldstein, Martin and Charles Horioka (1980) 'Domestic Savings and International Capital Flows', *Economic Journal*, **90** *(1980)* (June), 314–29.

Giovannini, Alberto and Martha de Melo (1991) 'Government Revenue from Financial Repression', NBER, *Working Paper*, **3604** (January).

Obstfeld, Maurice (1986) 'Capital Mobility in the World Economy: Theory and Measurement', *Carnegie–Rochester Conference Series on Public Policy*, **24** (Spring), 55–104.

Sussman, Oren (1991) 'Macroeconomic Effects on a Tax on Bond Interest Rates', *Journal of Money, Credit and Banking*, **23** (August), 352–366.

Zeira, Joseph (1987) 'Risk and Capital Accumulation in a Small Open Economy', *Quarterly Journal of Economics*, **102** (May), 265–79.

Part Two
Exchange rate volatility

5 An interpretation of recent research on exchange rate target zones

LARS E. O. SVENSSON

The relative merits of fixed and flexible exchange rate regimes is a classic issue in international economics. The traditional discussion considered a choice between floating exchange rates and fixed exchange rates with occasional discrete jumps. However, fixed exchange rate regimes in the real world typically have explicit finite *bands* within which exchange rates are allowed to fluctuate. For instance, the bands within the exchange rate mechanism of the European Monetary System (EMS) are ± 2.25% around a central parity (except ± 6 for Spain and Portugal), whereas the bands within the Bretton Woods System were ± 1% around dollar parities.

For concreteness, Figure 5.1a shows a typical exchange rate band. The curve shows the logarithm of the French franc/Deutsche mark exchange rate from the start of the EMS in March 1973 through March 1992. The ± 2.25% band around the central parity is shown as the thin horizontal lines. The central parity (not shown) is, of course, in the centre of the band. The vertical axis measures percentage deviation from the initial March 1973 central parity. Realignments, shifts in the central parity, took place in September 1979, October 1981, June 1982, March 1983, April 1986 and January 1987. On all these occasions the franc was devalued against the mark, that is, the FF/DM exchange rate (the number of francs per mark) increased. Figure 5.1b, which I shall refer to below, shows a 3-month FF/DM Euro interest rate differential, that is, the difference between a franc interest rate and a mark interest rate on the Euromarket for deposits with 3 months' maturity.

The existence of such exchange rate bands raises two main questions, one positive and one normative. The first, positive, question is: how do exchange rate bands work compared to completely fixed rates; or, more precisely, what are the dynamics of exchange rates, interest rates and central bank interventions within exchange rate bands? The second, normative, question is: does the difference between bands and completely fixed exchange rates matter and, if so, which of the two arrangements is

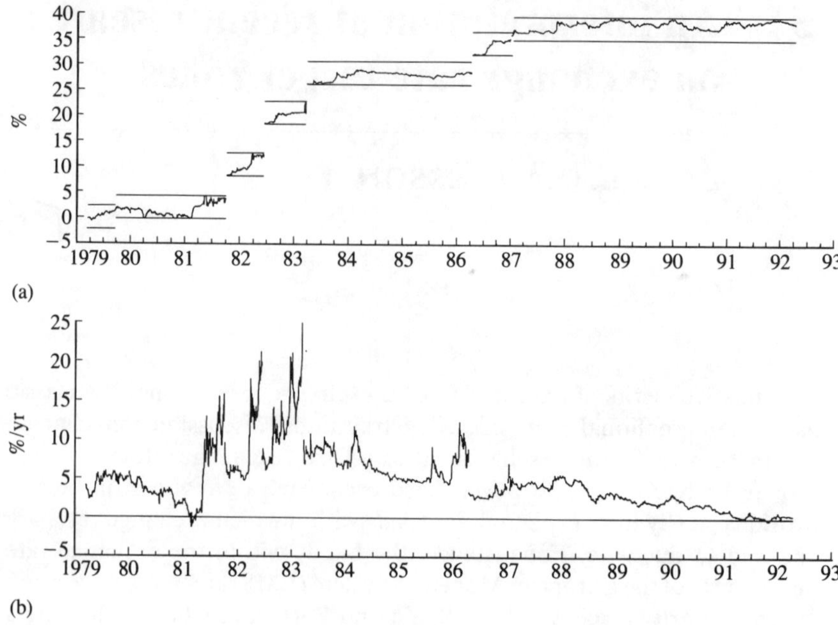

Figure 5.1 A typical exchange rate band
(*a*) Log FF/DM exchange rate
(*b*) FF/DM 3-month interest rate differential

best; or, more precisely, what are the tradeoffs that determine the optimal bandwidth?

Exchange rate target zones – which has become the name given to fixed exchange rates regimes with bands – have been the subject of intensive research in recent years. This research has by now dealt fairly thoroughly with the first, positive, question, whereas the second, normative, question has hardly yet been touched upon. This chapter will present an interpretation of some selected recent theoretical and empirical research on exchange rate target zones, with emphasis on main ideas and results and without technical detail. The chapter is selective and not a survey of the literature. Bertola (1993) gives a comprehensive and detailed survey with an extensive bibliography.[1]

1 The Krugman target zone model

After some earlier work on exchange rate target zones (for instance, Williamson, 1985; Williamson and Miller, 1987; Dumas, 1992)[2] the recent work took off with Paul Krugman's elegant target zone model (Krugman, 1991). This paper, first circulated in 1988, presented what has become the standard target zone model and the starting point for almost all the research that followed.[3]

Krugman started from the presumption that the exchange rate, like any other asset price, depends on both some current fundamentals and expectations of future values of the exchange rate. For instance, for a given level of the current fundamentals, a higher expected future exchange rate (a lower expected future value of the currency) implies a high exchange rate (a lower value of the currency) today.[4] In order to simplify, the exchange rate is actually assumed to depend *linearly* on an aggregate 'fundamental' incorporating the different fundamental determinants of the exchange rate (like domestic output and money supply; foreign interest rate, money supply, price level, etc.) and the expected change in the exchange rate.[5]

The fundamental is assumed to consist of two components: one component, 'velocity', is exogenous to the central bank and stochastic; the other component, 'money supply', is controlled by the central bank and changed by 'interventions'.[6] By controlling the money supply, the central bank can control the aggregate fundamental, and thus the exchange rate: when the currency is weak (the exchange rate is high), the central bank can reduce the money supply ('intervening' either by selling bonds in an open market operation or by selling foreign currency reserves in a foreign exchange intervention) in order to strengthen the currency (reduce the exchange rate), and vice versa when the currency is strong (the exchange rate is low). In an exchange rate target zone, the central bank controls the money supply to keep the exchange rate within a specified band around a specified central parity, for example $\pm 2.25\%$ for most of the EMS bands.[7]

The Krugman model has two crucial assumptions. First, the exchange rate target zone is perfectly credible, in the sense that market agents believe that the lower and upper edges of the band will remain fixed forever, and that the exchange rate will forever stay within the band.[8] Second, the target zone is defended with 'marginal' interventions only. That is, the money supply is held constant and no interventions at all occur as long as the exchange rate is in the interior of the exchange rate band. When the exchange rate reaches the weak edge of the band, the money supply is reduced to prevent the currency from weakening further; vice versa when the exchange rate reaches the strong edge of the band. Both these crucial assumptions are counter to empirical facts, something that we shall return to below.

For an explicit solution to the model, the stochastic process for the exogenous component of the fundamental, velocity, must also be specified. Krugman made the very convenient assumption that velocity is a Brownian motion without drift: the continuous-time analogue of a random walk. The intricacy of Brownian motions is a frequent stumbling block for new students of the target zone literature. However, for the purpose of the present discussion, the reader needs to know only two things about a variable that follows a Brownian motion without drift: its realised sample paths are continuous over time and do not include discrete jumps; and changes in the variable over any fixed time interval are distributed as a normal random variable with a zero mean and a variance that is proportional to the time interval's length.

The assumption of a Brownian motion for velocity is attractive, because it implies that the free-float exchange rate will also be a Brownian motion, which matches the empirical observations that free-float exchange rates seem to behave like random walks (Meese and Rogoff, 1983). In the model the (log) exchange rate actually becomes equal to the aggregate fundamental under a free float: recall that under a free float money supply is assumed to be constant. Therefore, the aggregate fundamental moves only with velocity and is hence also a Brownian motion. Recall also that the exchange rate by assumption depends linearly on the aggregate fundamental and the expected future exchange rate. Equivalently, the exchange rate depends linearly on the aggregate fundamental and the expected future *change* in the exchange rate. If the exchange rate is a Brownian motion without drift, the expected change in the exchange rate is zero, and it follows that the exchange rate just depends linearly on the fundamental. Since the fundamental is a Brownian motion without drift, this is indeed consistent with the exchange rate being a Brownian motion without drift. With a suitable normalisation, the exchange rate is not only a linear function of the fundamental but equal to the fundamental.[9]

The two crucial assumptions mentioned above for the target zone, together with the Brownian motion assumption about velocity, allow the target zone exchange rate to be expressed as a function of the aggregate fundamental, the 'target zone exchange rate function'. Figure 5.2 shows the relation between the exchange rate and the fundamental, both for the free float and the target zone. The fundamental is measured along the horizontal axis, the exchange rate along the vertical axis. The free-float relation is simply the 45-degree dashed line *FF*; the exchange rate is simply equal to the fundamental. The target zone exchange rate function is the S-shaped solid curve *TT*. The horizontal dashed lines show the edges of the exchange rate band.

There are two main results in the Krugman model. These results follow from the shape of the exchange rate function *TT*.

The first main result is that the slope of the S-shaped curve is less than 1

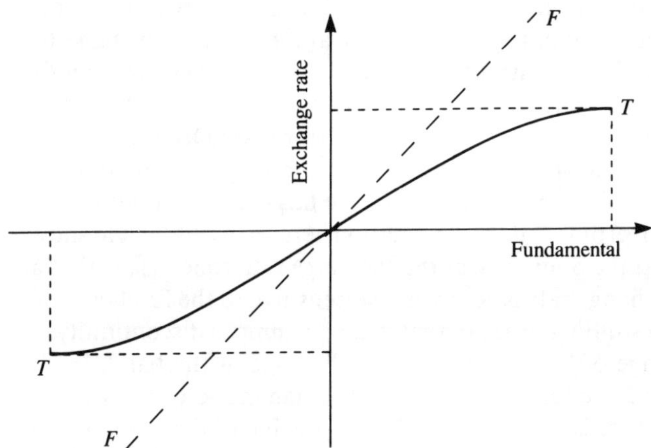

Figure 5.2 The Krugman model

at all times. This result is sometimes called the 'honeymoon' effect, from a reference in Krugman (1987) to a 'target zone honeymoon'. The intuition behind the honeymoon effect is straightforward enough. When the exchange rate is higher (the currency is weaker) and closer to the upper (weak) edge of the exchange rate band, the probability that it will, within a given finite time, reach the upper edge is higher. As a result, the probability of a future intervention to reduce the money supply and strengthen the currency is higher. This means that a future currency appreciation is expected, which the market turns into an immediate appreciation and a lower exchange rate. In this case, the exchange rate is less than the rate predicted by the current fundamental alone, because an expected currency appreciation is being taken into account. In other words, the target zone exchange rate is less than the free-float exchange rate, for a given level of the fundamental. Symmetrically, when the exchange rate is stronger and closer to the lower (strong) edge of the band, a future currency depreciation is expected, implying that the exchange rate is higher (the currency is stronger) than the free-float exchange rate, for a given level of the fundamental.

The honeymoon effect leads to the important insight that a perfectly credible target zone is inherently stabilising: the expectations of future interventions to stabilise the exchange rate makes the exchange rate more stable than the underlying fundamental. Put differently, a target zone means stabilising the fundamentals (between the vertical dashed lines in Figure 5.2), but the exchange rate stabilises even more (between the horizontal dashed lines in Figure 5.2).

The other main result is that the slope of the S-shaped curve flattens to a slope of zero at the edges of the band; that is, at the edges of the band the exchange rate function is tangential to the horizontal lines marking the edges of the exchange rate band. This result is generally called 'smooth pasting', a concept known in option-pricing theory (see Dixit, 1992). The intuition for the smooth-pasting result is far from easy, and another frequent stumbling block for new students of the target zone literature. The reader should not feel put off if the explanation here seems difficult to show.

A slope of zero at the boundary of the exchange rate zone means that at that point, the exchange rate is completely insensitive to the fundamental. Why might this be so? First, we note that there is a jump, a discontinuity, in the expected change of the fundamental at the edge of the band. In the interior of the band, the fundamental is a Brownian motion without drift, so its expected change is zero. At the edges of the band, the fundamental can either remain at the edge or drift back into the band, so its expected rate of change is suddenly *not* zero; at the upper edge it is negative, at the lower edge it is positive. Second, there can be no jump or discontinuity in the expected change of the exchange rate at the edge. To see this, recall that the exchange rate is a linear function of the fundamental and the expected change in the exchange rate. Now there can be no jump in the exchange rate at the edge of the band, otherwise there would be a safe arbitrate (a one-sided bet) since it could only jump one way, into the exchange rate band. Furthermore, the fundamental is continuous and does not jump.[10] Therefore, the expected change in the exchange rate must also be continuous and not take a jump. Third, if the expected change in the fundamental takes a jump, but the expected change in the exchange rate does not, the exchange rate must be completely insensitive to the fundamental at that point.[11]

The smooth-pasting property of the exchange rate function has received considerable theoretical interest. Besides being a neat result, it also has more practical implications. It means that the exchange rate should rather be a nonlinear function of the underlying fundamentals. This could perhaps partially explain why existing linear exchange rate models behaved so badly empirically (Meese and Rogoff, 1983). The theory of exchange rate target zones actually to a large extent became identified with smooth pasting and marginal interventions. Soon after, several researchers clarified and extended the Krugman results, and also confronted the model's implications with data. That confrontation was close to calamitous.

2 Empirical tests of the Krugman model

The Krugman model has clear empirical implications for exchange rates and interest rate differentials. It also has empirical implications for the aggregate fundamental, which is not directly observable but can be estimated from the observed variables. These empirical implications have been tested extensively on data from the EMS, the Nordic countries (especially Sweden), the Bretton Woods system and the gold standard. These tests have consistently rejected the model.

2.1 Exchange rates

The Krugman model implies numerous predictions about the behaviour of exchange rates. One implication is that the distribution of the exchange rate within the band must be U-shaped – that is, the exchange rate must spend most of the time near the edges of the band. To understand this implication, recall the S-shape of the exchange rate function and the 'smoothing pasting' at the edges of the band, which implies that the exchange rate is very insensitive to the fundamental near the edges of the band. Hence the exchange rate will move slowly near the edges of the band; where the exchange rate moves slowly, it will appear often. The fundamental, in contrast, moves with a constant speed between its bounds, hence its distribution is uniform.

The U-shape of the exchange rate's density is clearly rejected by the data. The data shows that the distribution is hump-shaped, with most of the probability mass in the interior of the band and very little near the edges of the band (Bertola and Caballero, 1992; Flood, Rose and Mathieson, 1991; Lindberg and Söderlind, 1991). This is, for instance, the case for the FF/DM exchange rate in Figure 5.1a, which spends most of the time well into the interior of the exchange rate band.

2.2 Interest rate differentials

The Krugman model has specific predictions also for interest rate differentials between domestic and foreign currency interest rates. These predictions are particularly specific under the assumption of 'uncovered interest parity'. Uncovered interest parity is an equilibrium condition on world currency markets. In order to invest in both domestic and foreign currency, investors are assumed to demand that the expected rate of return on an investment in domestic currency equals the expected domestic currency rate of return on an investment in foreign currency. The former is simply the domestic (currency) interest rate. The latter is the sum of the foreign (currency) interest rate and the expected rate of depreciation of the domestic currency. Hence, uncovered interest parity can be expressed as stating that the interest rate differential (between domestic and foreign interest rates) equals the expected rate of (domestic) currency depreciation.[12]

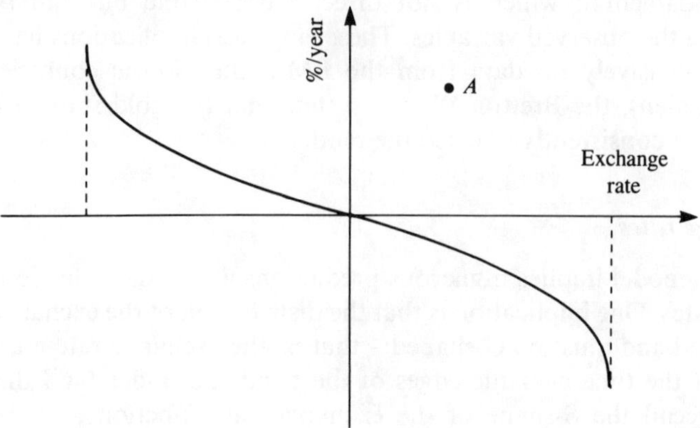

Figure 5.3 The expected rate of currency depreciation within the band

Under the assumption of perfect credibility no realignments (changes in the central parity) are expected to occur, and the expected rate of currency depreciation is the same thing as the expected rate of currency depreciation relative to central parity, which we shall call the expected rate of currency depreciation within the band.

The expected rate of currency depreciation within the band is in the Krugman model negatively related to the exchange rate as shown by the negatively-sloped curve in Figure 5.3. The intuition behind the negative slope is easy (in order to save space, I will skip explaining the particular nonlinear shape). When the exchange rate is high and at the upper edge of the exchange rate band, the currency is weak and cannot depreciate further. The exchange rate can either remain at the weak edge or drift back towards the interior of the band, in which case the currency appreciates. There is an expected currency appreciation: the expected rate of currency depreciation is negative. Analogously, when the exchange rate is at the lower edge of the band, the expected rate of currency depreciation is positive.

The negative relation between the expected rate of currency depreciation within the band and the exchange rate within the band implies that the exchange rate within the band displays *mean reversion*, that is, the expected future exchange rate within the band is closer to the long-run mean of the exchange rate within the band the further away in time it is. This mean reversion is an important general property of target zone exchange rates that is independent of the validity of the specific Krugman model, and it will be important in the discussion of extensions of the model below.

Now, under the two assumptions of uncovered interest parity and perfect credibility, the interest rate differential should equal the expected rate of currency depreciation within the band. Then the Krugman model predicts a negative deterministic relation between the interest rate differential and the exchange rate, and the correlation between the two should be strongly negative (the correlation need not be perfectly negative since the relationship is a bit nonlinear).

However, this deterministic relationship is rejected by the data. Plots of interest rate differentials against exchange rates result in wide scatters of observations. The correlations between exchange rates and interest rate differentials are often positive or zero, and only occasionally negative, depending upon the sample and the sample period (Svensson, 1991c; Flood, Rose and Mathieson, 1991; Lindberg and Söderlind, 1991). It is not difficult to see that a plot of interest rate differentials in Figure 5.1b against the deviations between the exchange rates and the central parity (the centre of the band) in Figure 5.1a results in anything but a negative deterministic relation!

2.3 Fundamentals and exchange rates

Since the Krugman model predicts a characteristic S-shaped relation between the (log) exchange rate and the aggregate fundamental, with smooth pasting at the edges, it is attractive to test this relationship directly by plotting the exchange rate against the fundamental. The problem is that the fundamental is an aggregate of many different determinants of the exchange rate, and not directly observable. The fundamental can, however, be estimated.[13] Plots of the estimated fundamental and the exchange rate show anything but an S-shaped relation but result in a wide scatter of observations[14] (Flood, Rose and Mathieson, 1991).

The nonlinearity of the exchange rate function in the Krugman model has led researchers to try empirical tests for nonlinearities in a variety of ways but no clear pattern of nonlinearities have been found (Meese and Rose, 1990; Flood, Rose and Mathieson, 1991; Lindberg and Söderlind, 1991).[15]

2.4 Testing the crucial assumptions directly

The crucial assumptions of the Krugman model, perfect credibility and only marginal interventions, can be tested separately. Perfect credibility seems unrealistic given the frequency of realignments that have actually occurred, for instance for the FF/DM exchange rate in Figure 5.1a. Furthermore, there is clear direct evidence, for instance in Figure 5.1b, of many of these realignments having been anticipated. The large interest rate differentials observed immediately before some of the realignments must be interpreted as investors demanding very high franc interests as compensation for an anticipated devaluation of the franc. The easiest way of testing the credibility assumption more formally is the 'simplest test' described in Svensson (1991a); it consists of examining whether forward exchange rates for different maturities fall outside the exchange rate band. If forward exchange rates fall outside the exchange rate band for some maturity, under the maintained assumption of international capital mobility the exchange rate target zone cannot be perfectly credible; if it were perfectly credible, unexploited profit opportunities would exist on the forward foreign exchange market. The assumption of perfect credibility is clearly rejected for most exchange rate target zones and most sample periods (Svensson, 1991a; Flood, Rose and Mathieson, 1991).

Tests of the other crucial assumptions, that the central bank undertakes only marginal interventions, require data on (or indications of) central banks' actions. Where those are available, the assumption is clearly rejected. In fact, interventions that occur in the interior of the exchange rate band, 'intra-marginal' interventions, are the rule rather than the exception (Giavazzi and Giovannini, 1989; Mundaca, 1990; Dominguez and Kenen, 1991; Edison and Kaminsky, 1991; Lindberg and Söderlind, 1992).

In summary, the Krugman model with its assumptions of perfect credibility and only marginal intervention has been overwhelmingly rejected by the data. The experience may seem an excellent example of 'the great tragedy of Science – the slaying of a beautiful hypothesis by an ugly fact' (T.H. Huxley). I think it is fair to state that some of the many researchers who had enthusiastically embraced the theory felt some embarrassment and even pessimism because of the glaring mismatch with the data. Nevertheless, the empirical rejection stimulated researchers to get back to the drawing board. It soon appeared that two extensions of the Krugman model seemed to resolve the empirical difficulties. These extensions, examined in sections 3 and 4, involve removing the two crucial assumptions by incorporating imperfect credibility and intra-marginal interventions.

3 Extension 1: imperfect credibility

Clearly, as Figure 5.1a demonstrates, exchange rate bands are sometimes shifted, realigned. Then the central parity – the centre of the band – takes a jump to a new level. If the change in the central parity is so large that the new exchange rate band does not overlap with the old, as in October 1981, the exchange rate must jump as well. If the new band does overlap with the old band, as in September 1979, the exchange rate may or may not jump. Furthermore, the realignments seem, at least to some extent, to be anticipated, as indicated in Figure 5.1b by the large interest rate differentials observed shortly before some of the realignments. One obvious extension of the Krugman model is, therefore, to incorporate time-varying realignment risk. I shall begin by discussing how the theory can be modified, then consider the empirical implications of doing so.[16]

3.1 Time-varying realignment risk

Let us now consider the situation where the exchange rate band can move. The central parity jumps at realignments and remains constant between realignments. Investors are uncertain as to when realignments will occur and how large they will be, and they form expectations of realignments given the available information. This means that we can express the expected rate of (total) currency depreciation as the sum of two components. One component is the expected rate of change of the central parity, which I shall call the expected rate of realignment. The other component is the expected rate of change of the exchange rate relative to central parity, which I have already called the expected rate of currency depreciation within the band. The first component, the expected rate of realignment, should be interpreted as the product of two factors, the first being the probability per unit of time of a realignment, the other being the expected size of a realignment if it occurs.

Recall again that the exchange rate is a linear function of the aggregate fundamental and the expected change of the exchange rate. The exchange rate can then be written as the sum of an aggregate fundamental and the product of a constant a and the expected rate of currency depreciation. If the expected rate of currency depreciation is decomposed into its two components, the terms can be reshuffled so that the exchange rate's deviation from central parity, which I have called the exchange rate within the band, equals the sum of a new composite fundamental and the product of a and the expected rate of currency depreciation within the band. The new composite fundamental is the sum of the old aggregate fundamental and the product of a and the expected rate of realignment.

The new linear relation between the exchange rate within the band, the new composite fundamental and the expected rate of currency depreciation within the band is formally identical to the old linear relation between the exchange rate, the old aggregate fundamental and the expected rate of (total) currency depreciation. This implies that there may exist a relation, an exchange rate function, between the exchange rate within the band and the new composite fundamental that is similar to the relation between the exchange rate and the old fundamental in the Krugman model, the relation displayed in Figure 5.2. (In fact, in the special case in which the expected rate of realignment is perceived to be an exogenous Brownian motion, the new exchange rate function is of exactly the same form as the solution to the Krugman model.)[17]

Despite the similarity with the Krugman model, behind the new composite fundamental there are now *two* fundamentals, the old aggregate fundamental and the expected rate of realignment (which in turn may depend on additional variables). It no longer makes sense to plot the exchange rate against only one of the state variables – the old aggregate fundamental – since it omits the expected rate of realignment, which is another state variable. This provides a possible explanation of why the plots (referred to in the previous section) of exchange rates against estimates of the old aggregate fundamental in Flood, Rose and Mathieson (1991) do not result in a well-behaved exchange rate function.

Rose and Svensson (1991) instead offer plots of exchange rates against estimates of the new composite fundamental that includes the expected rate of realignment.[18] Those plots result in an exchange rate function with a slope less than 1 (that is, they confirm the honeymoon effect), but do not seem to offer the correct flat slope near the edges of the zone (the 'smooth pasting' property). This result will be further discussed in section 4.

The introduction of time-varying realignment risk has important consequences for how interest rate differentials are determined, and how plots of interest rate differentials against exchange rate should be interpreted. Under the assumption of uncovered interest parity, the interest rate differential equals the expected (total) rate of currency depreciation, but this is now equal to the sum of the expected rate of currency depreciation within the band and the new term, the expected rate of realignment.[19] Hence, for an observation of the interest rate differential and exchange rate within the band, such as point A in Figure 5.3, the vertical difference between point A and the downward-sloping curve (the expected rate of currency depreciation within the band) is explained by the expected rate of realignment. Including time-varying realignment expectations hence offers a reason why there need not be a deterministic relation between interest rate differentials and exchange rates. Even though the expected rate of currency depreciation within the band is negatively correlated with the exchange rate within the band, depending upon how the expected rate of realignment fluctuates over time and is correlated with the exchange rate, any correlation pattern between the interest rate differential and exchange rate is possible.

3.2 *The 'drift-adjustment' method to estimate realignment expectations*

The credibility, or rather the lack thereof, of exchange rate target zones is always an issue of great interest, not only for the central bankers and finance ministers directly involved, but also for investors and economics journalists. The approach to determine interest rate differentials presented above has led to a new method to measure realignment expectations and evaluate the credibility of exchange rate target zones. This method has much better precision than the 'simplest test' of target zone credibility referred to above.

Recall that under uncovered interest parity the interest rate differential equals the sum of the expected rate of currency depreciation within the band and the expected rate of realignment. Hence, the expected rate of realignment can be written as the difference between the interest rate differential and the expected rate of currency depreciation within the band. From this two things follow: first, unless the expected rate of currency depreciation within the band is negligible, the interest rate differential is a misleading indicator of realignment expectations. Second, a direct estimate of the expected rate of realignment results in an estimate of the expected rate of currency depreciation within the band is constructed and this estimate is subtracted from the interest rate differential. This method can be called the 'drift-adjustment' method to estimate realignment expectations, since the interest rate differential is adjusted by the 'drift' of the exchange rate within the band.[20]

The difficulty with the method lies in estimating the expected rate of future currency depreciation within the band, that is, to predict the expected future exchange rate within the band. For floating exchange rates, predicting future exchange rate is usually considered a futile exercise, and a simple random walk usually outperforms other forecasting models (Meese and Rogoff, 1983). However, what is at stake here is predicting the expected future exchange rate *within the band*; that is, the future exchange rate's expected deviation from the future central parity. Predicting this has turned out to be much more fruitful than predicting (total) future exchange rates, since – unlike floating exchange rates – exchange rates within the band, both theoretically (see above) and empirically, display strong mean-reversion. In practice, a simple linear regression of future exchange rates within the band on the current exchange rate within the band and current domestic and foreign interest rates seems to predict quite well. This way of estimating the expected rate of realignment has the great advantage that it does not depend on any specific theory of exchange rates; nor does it matter whether expected rates of realignments are exogenous or endogenous (for instance, whether or not they are influenced by the exchange rate's position within the band).

Estimates of expected rates of currency depreciation within the band made for ERM exchange rates and Nordic exchange rates indicate that for time horizons up to 1 year, the estimates are often of the same order of magnitude as the interest rate differentials (up to 2–3% per year). Therefore, the use of interest rate differentials as indicators of target zone credibility, without adjusting for expected rates of depreciation within the band, is potentially misleading for horizons up to 1 year.

Estimating the confidence intervals for expected rates of depreciation within the band results in confidence intervals for expected rates of realignments. These can be used for statistical inference and hypothesis tests. For short horizons, the drift-adjustment method seems to have much better precision and power than the 'simplest test'. In many cases with the drift-adjustment method, the hypothesis that expected rates of realignment are zero can be rejected also for short horizons down to 1 month, whereas the 'simplest test' is usually inconclusive for short horizons (Lindberg, Svensson and Söderlind, 1991). Typically, estimated expected rates of realignment vary quite a bit over time, and they vary more than the interest rate differentials. EMS expected rates of realignment are smaller in later years than in the earliest ones, showing an increase over time in the system's credibility. Even so, the hypothesis of a zero realignment risk vis-à-vis the Deutsche mark can still be rejected for a majority of the EMS currencies (Svensson, 1993).[21]

4 Extension 2: intra-marginal interventions

The earlier discussion pointed out that empirical distributions of exchange rates within the band are hump-shaped, with most of the observations in the middle of the exchange rate band, in contrast to the U-shape predicted by the Krugman model, where most of the observations would occur near the edges of the band. The most obvious explanation for this hump-shape is that the exchange rate is kept in the middle of the band by intra-marginal interventions, that is, central bank interventions that occur in the interior of the exchange rate band.[22]

In the real world, central banks' intervention behaviour is by all accounts both complicated and shifting over time. A first approximation to this complicated behaviour is to propose that in addition to marginal interventions at the edges of the band there are intra-marginal 'leaning-against-the-wind' interventions, that is, interventions that aim at returning the exchange rate to a specified target level within the band. A simple way to model such interventions, in terms of the target zone model

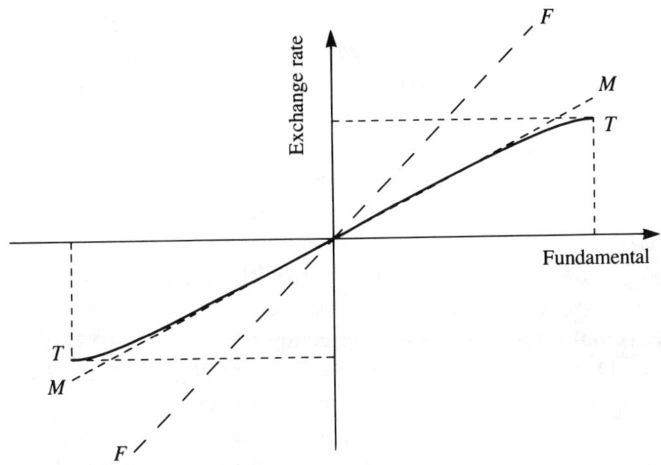

Figure 5.4 Intra-marginal interventions

with imperfect credibility described in the previous section, is to specify that the intra-marginal interventions result in the expected rate of change (the drift) of the composite fundamental towards central parity is proportional to the distance to central parity.[23]

The result of this modification is illustrated in Figure 5.4. The dashed 45-degree line marked *FF* again corresponds to the free-float exchange rate regime, when no interventions are undertaken. Let us then first consider a 'managed-float' exchange rate regime, when interventions are mean-reverting towards a central parity, but there is no specified band and no marginal interventions. The result will be the dashed line *MM* in Figure 5.4, which is less sloped than the free-float line.[24]

In other words, a honeymoon effect operates in the managed-float regime even without an exchange rate band. This effect results in the exchange rate fluctuating less than in the free-float regime, for given fluctuations in the composite fundamental. This is because the mean-reverting interventions imply that when the exchange rate is above the central parity (the currency is weak) the currency is expected to appreciate, which by itself reduces the exchange rate.

Now add an explicit target zone regime to the intra-marginal interventions, which means specifying a band and marginal interventions in case the exchange rate reaches the edge of this band. The resulting exchange rate function is plotted as the solid curve *TT* in Figure 5.4. The curve is close to the *MM* line corresponding to the managed float, except that it has a slight S-shape and smooth pasting at the edges of the band. As drawn here, there is an additional honeymoon effect relative to the managed float, but it is much smaller than the honeymoon effect in the managed float relative to the free float. For the same parameters and a significant degree of mean-reversion, the S-shape is much less pronounced than in the Krugman model of Figure 5.2.

Why is it plausible that the S-shape is less pronounced than in the Krugman model? And why is the exchange rate function so close to that in a managed float?

When the exchange rate is above the central parity (the currency is weak) the currency is expected to appreciate for two reasons. One reason is expected intra-marginal interventions to appreciate the currency towards the central parity. This reason is present also in a managed float. The other is expected future marginal interventions to prevent the exchange rate moving outside the band, in the event that the future exchange rate reaches the upper edge of the band. That reason is present only in the target zone regime. However, the probability of the future exchange rate ever reaching the edges of the band is smaller with mean-reverting interventions than in the Krugman model. The expected currency appreciation caused by the second reason is therefore smaller than that caused by the first.

In a target zone with mean-reverting interventions, the unconditional distribution of the composite fundamental is hump-shaped (Lindberg and Söderlind, 1992 show that it is actually a truncated normal distribution). With sufficiently strong mean-reverting interventions added, the exchange rate function is almost linear and very close to the exchange rate function for a managed float. As a consequence, the unconditional distribution of the exchange rate will be hump-shaped (with possibly some small extra probability mass at the edges of the band).

These predictions square well with the empirical hump-shaped exchange rate distributions. That the exchange rate function may be almost linear is consistent with the difficulty of finding empirical evidence of nonlinearities. In a structural estimation of a target zone model with mean-reverting interventions for the Swedish krona, Lindberg and Söderlind (1992) find reasonable parameter values, fairly strong mean-reversion, and that the overall fit of the model is quite good, much better than the Krugman model.

This analysis leads to the conjecture that the initial emphasis in target zone models on nonlinearities, smooth pasting and infrequent marginal interventions was misplaced. Target zones are better described as similar to managed floats with intra-marginal mean-reverting interventions, with additional marginal interventions defending the target zone in the rare cases when the exchange rate reaches the edge of the band. The honeymoon effect is probably important, whereas smooth pasting and nonlinearities seem empirically insignificant. An official exchange rate band should consequently not be seen as a commitment to mostly marginal interventions, but as a practical way of expressing a verifiable general commitment to limit exchange rate variability with intra-marginal interventions. After all, it would be impractical and unverifiable to announce a commitment to stabilise exchange rates in terms of a degree of mean-reversion or of a standard deviation.[25]

5 Why exchange rate bands?

The issues I have discussed so far all concern the first, positive, question that was posed above: what are the dynamics of exchange rates, interest rates and central bank interventions within exchange rate target zones? Let me now turn to the second, normative, question: are exchange rate bands optimal?

Let me first narrow down the normative question. It can be separated into three consecutive questions: first, when is a fixed exchange rate regime better than floating, where a fixed exchange rate regime in practice means a more or less narrow band around a central parity with possible occasional realignments of the central parity? Second, how often (if ever) and by how much should the central parity be realigned? Third, how narrow should the band be? The first and second questions have been extensively discussed in the traditional literature on exchange rate regimes (see Genberg, 1989 for a survey) and in a recent literature on macroeconomic policy and credibility (see Persson and Tabellini, 1990 for a survey). Space constraints prevent me from summarising that discussion here. Let me hence concentrate on the third question, which has received very little attention in the literature.[26]

Why have a nonzero band instead of just a zero band, since the latter seems simpler?[27] One reason for a nonzero band that was emphasised by Keynes (1930, 319–31) is that it allows some degree of national monetary independence, so that monetary policy can to some extent be used for domestic stabilisation. That monetary independence can arise in a fixed exchange rate regime with free capital mobility may be a surprise to many readers, given the standard textbook result that a fixed exchange rate and free capital mobility implies a complete loss of monetary independence, in the sense that the central bank cannot then set the domestic interest rate at a level different from the foreign interest rate. Let me first explain the textbook result, then show how it is modified with nonzero exchange rate bands.

Recall the assumption that investors, in order to invest in both domestic and foreign currency, demand that the interest rate differential between the domestic and foreign interest rate equals the sum of the expected rate of realignment and the expected rate of currency depreciation within the band. With a zero band, the last term is equal to zero and the interest rate differential is simply equal to the expected rate of realignment. The domestic central bank has then no choice but to let the domestic interest rate fulfil this condition. If it tries to set a lower domestic interest rate there will be a capital outflow because investors shift their investment to the foreign currency, and a loss of foreign exchange reserves will force the central bank to raise the interest rate. If it tries to set a higher domestic interest rate, there will be a capital inflow because international investors shift their investment to the domestic currency, and an increase in foreign exchange reserves will increase liquidity in the economy and force the domestic interest rate down. This is the textbook case of a complete loss in monetary autonomy.[28]

With a nonzero band, the expected rate of currency depreciation within the band is no longer always zero. Now the central bank can control the domestic interest rate via control over the expected rate of currency depreciation within the band. The way to control the expected rate of currency depreciation within the band is to exploit the mean reversion of the exchange rate within the band. If the central bank increases the exchange rate above its mean within the band, the exchange rate is expected to fall in the future towards the mean. That is, an expected currency appreciation within the band is created, which will reduce the domestic interest rate. Similarly, reducing the exchange rate below its mean generates an expected currency depreciation within the band, which increases the domestic interest rate.

This monetary independence allows the central bank some freedom to adjust the domestic interest rates to local conditions, for instance lowering the interest rate in a recession and increasing it during a boom. I believe this degree of monetary independence is the best explanation of why fixed exchange rate regimes have nonzero bands. Put differently, governments and central banks prefer to have some monetary independence, they therefore prefer nonzero bands in fixed exchange rate regimes.[29]

Even if bands result in some monetary independence, it does not follow that this monetary independence in a fixed exchange rate regime is socially optimal. First of all, it does not follow that the degree of monetary independence is sufficiently large to matter, say, in the sense of having significant effects on output or inflation.[30] Second, even if it does matter, there may be some gain from *not* exploiting it. It may be, for instance, that not exploiting the monetary independence for some reason contributes to reducing realignment expectations and hence to increasing the credibility of the exchange rate regime. This is indicated by the experience of the Dutch guilder and the Belgian franc inside, and of the Austrian schilling outside the EMS.[31]

The optimality of exchange rate bands in fixed exchange rate regimes remains an under-researched area. With the improved understanding of the positive questions of how the exchange rate target zones actually work, it should now be possible to deal with the normative issue of their optimality.[32]

6 Conclusion

In summary, the recent work on exchange rate target zones took off in 1988 with Krugman (1991). The Krugman model employs two crucial assumptions: perfect credibility of the target zone and exclusively marginal central bank interventions to defend it. Two main results follow: the 'honeymoon effect' that target zones are inherently stabilising, and 'smooth pasting' – the exchange rate is a nonlinear function of its fundamental determinants and insensitive to these fundamentals at the edge of the exchange rate band. The Krugman model has very specific empirical implications. These have been consistently rejected by the data, as have the two crucial assumptions. New work by several researchers has extended the Krugman model by removing the two crucial assumptions, which has made the theory fit the data very well. Allowing for realignment expectations can explain observed correlations between exchange rates and interest rate differentials, and has led to a new method to empirically estimate realignment expectations, the 'drift-adjustment' method. Allowing for intra-marginal interventions can explain the fact that exchange rate observations tend to cluster in the centre of the bands. Such interventions also imply a strong honeymoon effect but insignificant non-linearities and smooth pasting. A target zone then appears very similar to a 'managed float' with a target central parity but without an explicit band.

From this it appears that the initial emphasis in the target zone literature on exclusively marginal interventions, nonlinearities and smooth pasting was largely misplaced. Real world exchange rate target zones are in practice better understood as managed floats with a target exchange rate level which is mainly defended by frequent mean-reverting intra-marginal interventions, and in addition infrequently supported by marginal interventions at the edges of the band in the very rare cases where the exchange rate actually reaches the edges of the band. The official bands are then best seen as a practical and verifiable way of expressing a general commitment to stabilise exchange rates relative to a central parity (and definitely not as a commitment to marginal interventions only). With this much improved understanding of the actual working of exchange rate target zones, it should be possible to direct future research more towards the under-researched normative issue of the optimality of exchange rate bands.

Much work remains to be done. The models are still extremely simplified, and would surely be more realistic with more state variables, sticky prices, and real effects (perhaps along the lines of Miller and Weller, 1991a, 1991b; Klein 1990; Beetsma and van der Ploeg, 1992). There is certainly room for more realistic intervention policies – for instance, explicit smoothing of exchange rates and interest rates – and for attempts to estimate changes in the intervention policy. The theory for multilateral target zones, as opposed to unilateral and bilateral target zones, is not yet worked out. I suspect there is more to be said on the role of exchange rate uncertainty inside the band, the foreign exchange risk premium, and the degree of substitutability between domestic and foreign currency-denominated assets. The amount of monetary independence that arises in an exchange rate band, and whether it has significant real effects, certainly needs to be clarified further.

Fall 1992 was a dramatic period for fixed exchange rate regimes, with intensive speculative attacks against both ERM and Nordic currencies. At the time of writing (February 1993), Italy and the United Kingdom have left the ERM and allowed their currencies to float, whereas Portugal and Ireland have devalued their currencies. Finland, Sweden and Norway have one after the other abandoned their unilateral fixed exchange rate for flexible rate regimes.

An obvious observation is that these events give clear evidence of imperfect credibility of some fixed exchange rate regimes. I believe that the events also show that it is more difficult than anticipated to defend fixed exchange rate regimes against speculative attacks. From a technical point of view it seems that central banks can always raise short interest rates to a level necessary to contain a speculative attack in the short run. The necessary level may be high, though, as Sweden's experience with a 500% per year overnight interest rate shows. Even if interest rates fall back after a few days to less extreme levels when the speculative attack has blown over, the resulting average interest rates may be considered unacceptable. With limited credibility to start with, the regime suffers resulting high nominal interest rates, which by themselves may reduce the regime's survival time and hence warrant the limited credibility; a vicious circle indeed.

A view that is expressed with increasing frequency is that with free international capital mobility only the extreme regimes of either a common currency or floating separate currencies are viable, whereas the intermediate one of fixed exchange rates between separate currencies are not. This view is contradicted by the experience so far of Europe's hard currency bloc: Germany, Holland, Austria and Belgium, where the latter countries clearly seem able to maintain their fixed rates against the Deutsche mark. The specific reasons why some countries can maintain credible fixed exchange rates should be a fruitful area for further research.

Recent events should lead to renewed interest in the literature on speculative attacks and regime collapses. My chapter does not cover this literature, except by giving a few references to recent research (n. 1, below). This research can be seen as extensions of the Salant and Henderson (1978) and Krugman (1979) view of speculative attacks as eventually resulting after a period of continuous reserve losses caused by a continuous expansion of domestic credit. I believe that the recent collapses of fixed exchange rate regimes are better explained by divergencies other than in domestic credit growth, for instance in fiscal policies, public debt growth, wage formation, and labour market policies. Hence I believe that further theoretical and empirical research is warranted on the precise anatomy of speculative attacks and exchange rate regime collapses.

NOTES

A previous version of this paper was published in *Journal of Economic Perspectives*, **6** (4) (Fall 1992, 119–44). I am very grateful to the *JEP* associate editor Gene Grossman and the *JEP* editors, Carl Shapiro, Joseph Stiglitz and Timothy Taylor, for their excellent suggestions to improve the exposition. I also thank Giuseppe Bertola, Avinash Dixit, Bernard Dumas, Harry Flam, Robert Flood, Paul Krugman, Hans Lindberg, Marcus Miller, Maurice Obstfeld, Torsten Persson, Andrew Rose and Paul Söderlind for comments on earlier drafts; Molly Åkerlund for secretarial and editorial assistance; and the Bank of Sweden Tercentenary Foundation and the Social Science Research Council for financial support. In the present chapter I have benefited from helpful comments by the discussants Shmuel Kandel and Andrew Rose, and by conference participants.

1 Suggestions for further reading would include the following. Bertola (1993) provides a comprehensive and more technical survey of the recent target zone research, including an extensive bibliography. The introduction in Krugman and Miller (1991) also surveys some of the research.

Froot and Obstfeld (1991) give a rigorous presentation of the Krugman model, with several extensions and a treatment of regime shifts. The Krugman model is critically evaluated in Krugman and Miller (1992). Miller and Weller (1991a, 1991b) present an important variant of the Krugman model with sticky prices and real effects. Further extensions along this line are provided by Klein (1990) and Beetsma and van der Ploeg (1992). Flood and Garber (1991) extend the Krugman model to include finite interventions, Perraudin (1990) extends it to include discrete jumps in the fundamental. Svensson (1991b) derives empirical implications of the Krugman model for exchange rates and interest rate differentials; Svensson (1991c) derives and test implications for the term structure of interest rate differentials. Extensive empirical tests of the Krugman model are presented in Flood, Rose and Mathieson (1991), Smith and Spencer (1991), and Lindberg and Söderlind (1991). Pessach and Razin (1991) estimate a Krugman model on Israeli data.

The extension to time-varying realignment risk is made in Bertola and Svensson (1993). The drift-adjustment method is empirically implemented in Rose and Svensson (1991), Svensson (1992a), Frankel and Phillips (1991) and Lindberg, Svensson and Söderlind (1991). An alternative model with realignment risk at the edge of the band that can explain the hump-shaped unconditional exchange rate distribution is presented in Bertola and Caballero (1992) and further extended by Bertola and Caballero (1991) and Bartolini and Bodnar (1992). Weber (1992) uses a Kalman-filter technique to estimate time-varying realignment risk.

The extension to intra-marginal mean-reverting interventions is presented in Froot and Obstfeld (1991), Delgado and Dumas (1992) and Pesenti (1990). Lewis (1990) develops a model with occasional intra-marginal intervention. Intra-marginal interventions are documented in Mundaca (1990), Dominguez and Kenen (1991), Edison and Kaminsky (1991) and Lindberg and Söderlind (1992); the latter contains a structural estimation on Swedish data of an extended target zone model that incorporates both intra-marginal interventions and time-varying realignment risk.

A sizable part of the literature has dealt with regime shifts and regime collapses, the role of reserves, and the problem of bubbles. This includes Froot and Obstfeld (1991), Bertola and Caballero (1992), Krugman and Rotemberg (1991), Delgado and Dumas (1991, 1993), Miller and Sutherland (1991), Buiter and Grilli (1991), Buiter and Pesenti (1990) and Dumas and Svensson (1991). Klein and Lewis (1991) estimate learning about, and shifts in, an implicit dollar/Deutsche mark and dollar/yen exchange rate target zone between the Plaza Agreement (1985) and the stock market crash (1987).

The excessive-volatility argument for a target zone is developed by Williamson (1985, 1989), Corbae, Ingram and Mondino (1990) and Krugman and Miller (1992). The amount of monetary independence in an exchange rate band, which was discussed by Keynes (1930, pp. 319–31), is examined again in Svensson (1992b).

The techniques used, notably stochastic calculus, are discussed, in order of increasing difficulty, in Dixit (1992), Dixit (1991), Bertola (1993), Harrison (1985) and Karatzas and Shreve (1988).

2 Williamson (1985) and Williamson and Miller (1987) advocated a rather wide target zone for *real* exchange rates as a method for international economic policy coordination, without an explicit target zone model. Williamson-type target zones are quite different from the narrow *nominal* exchange rate bands that are the focus of this chapter and it is perhaps confusing that the same name is used for both. Dumas (1992), in a remarkable paper first presented and circulated under a different title in the summer of 1987, developed a general equilibrium model of an endogenous target zone for the real exchange rate, which contained most of the ingredients in the later work on nominal exchange rate target zones. A parallel literature on real investment under certainty, especially contributions by Avinash Dixit, was the source of many of the techniques used in the target zone literature (see Dixit, 1992 for a survey).

3 A forerunner, Krugman (1987), was circulated in the late Fall of 1987. It used a discrete-time model and did not resolve all technical difficulties.

4 The exchange rate, as conventionally defined, is the domestic price of foreign exchange, that is, the number of domestic currency units per foreign currency unit. The exchange rate and the value of domestic currency are therefore inversely related, which sometimes causes confusion.

5 A simple representation of this is 'the exchange rate equation' $s_t = f_t + a\mathrm{E}_t[ds_t]/dt$, for s_t, the log of the exchange rate at time t, f_t, the aggregate fundamental at time t, and $\mathrm{E}_t[ds_t]/dt$, the instantaneous expected rate of currency depreciation. This is a continuous-time analogue of a model where the exchange rate depends on current fundamentals and the expected future exchange rate. Here the positive constant a is the semielasticity of the exchange rate with respect to the instantaneous expected rate of currency depreciation. The instantaneous expected rate of currency depreciation is the limit of $\mathrm{E}_t[s_{t+\Delta t} - s_t]/\Delta t = \mathrm{E}_t[\ln(S_{t+\Delta t}/S_t)]/\Delta_t$ when Δt approaches 0, where E_t denotes expectations conditional upon information available at time t, and S_t is the exchange rate expressed in units of domestic currency per unit foreign currency at time t.

6 In simple notation, this can be written $f_t = v_t + m_t$, where f_t represents the market fundamentals, v_t represents the exogenous velocity, and m_t is the money supply.

7 It does not matter precisely how the central bank implements its monetary policy, for instance whether it is using the interest rate or the money supply as an instrument. Here for correctness we consider money supply to be the instrument.

8 The crucial restriction is actually that the target zone is perfectly credible when the exchange rate is in the *interior* of the band. Krugman discussed the possibility of a collapse to a free float the first time the exchange rate reaches the *edge* of the band.

9 Suppose the exchange rate equals the fundamental, $s_t = f_t$. Then, since the expected change in f_t is zero, so is the expected change in s_t, $\mathrm{E}_t[ds_t] = 0$. Using this in the exchange rate equation in n. 5 above indeed leads to $s_t = f_t$.

10 The velocity component is continuous since it is a Brownian motion. The money supply component is constant except at the edge where it moves just enough to prevent the fundamental from going further in the 'wrong' direction.

11 Formally, by Ito's Lemma we have $\mathrm{E}_t ds_t = S_f \mathrm{E}_t df_t + (1/2) S_{ff} \mathrm{E} df_t^2$, where S_f and S_{ff} denote the first and second derivative of the exchange rate function $s = S(f)$ with respect to the fundamental. By the property of Brownian motions, $\mathrm{E}_t df_t^2 = \sigma^2 dt$, where σ^2 is the instantaneous rate of variance (the variance per unit of time) of the velocity. Now, if $\mathrm{E}_t df_t$ is discontinuous at the edges, but $\mathrm{E}_t ds_t$ is not, the first derivative must be zero at the edges, $S_f = 0$.

12 Uncovered interest parity can be written $i_t - i_t^* = \mathrm{E}_t[ds_t]/dt$, where i_t and i_t^* are the domestic and foreign currency interest rates. Uncovered interest parity is equivalent to a zero (nominal) foreign exchange risk premium, the difference between the expected domestic currency rate of return on a foreign currency investment and the expected rate of return on a domestic currency investment. For floating exchange rates, uncovered interest parity is usually strongly rejected by the data, see Froot and Thaler (1990). For exchange rate target zones, Svensson (1992a) argues that the foreign exchange risk premium is

likely to be small, even if there is some realignment risk, and that hence uncovered interest parity should be a good approximation.

13 Recall that the (log) exchange rate in the Krugman model is taken to be a linear function of an aggregate fundamental and the expected future value of the exchange rate. More precisely it can be written as the sum of the fundamental and the product of a positive constant a, the semielasticity of the exchange rate with respect to the expected rate of currency depreciation, and the expected rate of currency depreciation. Under the maintained assumption of uncovered interest parity, the expected rate of currency depreciation is given by the interest rate differential. Then, given an estimate (or a guess) of a, the fundamental can be estimated by subtracting the product of the estimated a and the interest rate differential from the exchange rate. More formally, the estimate of the aggregate fundamental is $\hat{f}_t = s_t - \hat{a}(i_t - i_t^*)$, where $\hat{a}$ is the estimate of a.

14 Except for very small values of a, when the plot is trivially close to a 45-degree line.

15 The Krugman model has also been tested via sophisticated structural estimation of the parameters of the model, with the method of simulated moments, which involves choosing parameters of the model so that the simulated moments of the model (means, variances, covariances, etc.) match the empirical moments. Tests of the overall fit of the model have led to very strong rejection of the model (Smith and Spencer, 1991; Lindberg and Söderlind, 1991).

16 Bertola and Svensson (1993) presented the first target zone model with time-varying realignment risk. Several papers in the literature (including Krugman, 1991) had previously considered imperfect credibility in the form of possible realignments at the edges of the band but not inside the band. Empirically, perfect credibility has been rejected in periods when the exchange rates have been far from the edges of the band. Actual realignments have occurred both when exchange rates have been near as well as further away from the edges (cf. June 1982 and April 1986 in Figure 5.1a). This supports the presumption that realignment risk is relevant also when exchange rates are away from the edges of the band.

17 A slightly more formal explanation may be helpful to some readers. Since the (log) exchange rate is the sum of the (log) exchange rate within the band and the (log) central parity, $s_t \equiv x_t + c_t$, it follows that the (total) expected rate of currency depreciation can be written as the sum of the expected rate of currency depreciation within the band, $\mathrm{E}_t[dx_t]/dt$, and the expected rate of realignment, $\mathrm{E}_t[dc_t]/dt$, $\mathrm{E}_t[ds_t]/dt \equiv \mathrm{E}_t[dx_t]/dt + \mathrm{E}_t[dc_t]/dt$. Substitution of this equation into the exchange rate equation of n. 5 above, and subtraction of c_t from both sides, leads to the new exchange rate equation for the exchange rate within the band, $x_t = h_t + a\mathrm{E}_t[dx_t]/dt$, where the new composite fundamental h_t is given by $h_t \equiv f_t - c_t + a\mathrm{E}_t[dc_t]/dt$, the sum of the f-fundamental's deviation from central parity and the product of a and the expected rate of realignment, $a\mathrm{E}_t[dc_t]/dt$. The new exchange rate function is formally equivalent to the old exchange rate function in n. 5, except that the exchange rate within the band x_t and the new composite fundamental h_t have replaced the (total) exchange rate s_t and the fundamental f_t.

18 Rose and Svensson estimate the new composite fundamental $h_t = f_t + a\mathrm{E}_t[dc_t]/dt$ by using the Flood, Rose and Mathieson (1991) estimate

of f_t as in n. 3 above and a 'drift-adjustment' estimate of the expected rate of realignment $E_t[dc_t]/dt$ (to be explained below).

19 More formally, $i_t - i_t^* = E_t[ds_t]/dt = E_t[dx_t]/dt + E_t[dc_t]/dt$.

20 The drift-adjustment method was suggested by Bertola and Svensson (1993) and is empirically implemented in Rose and Svensson (1991) and Lindberg, Svensson and Söderlind (1991).

21 When estimation is made for a particular finite maturity or time horizon $\Delta t > 0$, interest rate differentials of that maturity are adjusted by estimates of the expected rate of depreciation within the band over the same horizon, $E_t[x_{t+\Delta t} - x_t]/\Delta t$. The estimated expected rate of realignment $E_t[c_{t+\Delta t} - c_t]/\Delta t$ can then be interpreted in the following way. Suppose the time horizon is 3 months, and that an estimated expected rate of realignment is 12% per year. Conditional upon a given expected size of the realignment if it occurs, the expected conditional realignment size, a probability of a realignment within the time horizon can be constructed. Suppose the expected conditional realignment size is 5%. Then the expected 'frequency', probability per unit of time, of realignment is the expected rate of realignment divided by the expected conditional realignment size, that is, in our case 2.4 per year. Per 3 months, this is one-fourth of 2.4, that is, 0.6. Hence, the market expects a realignment to occur within 3 months with probability 60%, conditional upon the realignment size 5%.

22 Mean-reversion of the fundamental in the Krugman model was first discussed by Froot and Obstfeld (1991) and Delgado and Dumas (1991). Its practical and empirical importance was established by Lindberg and Söderlind (1992). See also Lewis (1990). The drift of the composite fundamental h_t is assumed to fulfil $E_t[dh_t]/dt = -\rho h_t$, where ρ, the rate of mean reversion, is a positive constant.

23 Realignments, which were discussed in the previous section, can be seen as another kind of intervention.

24 The equation for the *MM* line is $x_t = h_t(1 + a\rho)$.

25 That the Krugman model has turned out to be misleading as a model of real world exchange rate bands should not detract from Krugman's important *technical* contribution, namely how to analyse how expectations of *future* infrequent intervention (rather than current continuous intervention) matter for current asset prices.

26 Cukierman, Kiguel and Leiderman (1993) develop a positive theory of when a central bank chooses an exchange rate band, how wide the band is, and when it will be realigned. This is done in a setup where the central bank can make a commitment to a band and faces a given cost if it reneges on the commitment. Their chapter is hence related to the literature on escape clauses and monetary policy – for instance, Flood and Isard (1989) and Lohmann (1992).

27 For simplicity I disregard that for technical reasons the minimum bandwidth is not exactly equal to zero but a small positive number, since the bandwidth must exceed the normal interbank bid–asked spread for exchange rates if the central bank does not want to take over all currency trade. The normal spread is very small, though, say around 0.04%.

28 Strictly speaking, the domestic interest rate equals the foreign interest rate only if the expected rate of realignment is 0, that is, if the exchange rate regime is completely credible. Also, technically the central bank can still control the domestic interest rate if it can somehow manipulate the expected rate of

realignment, but that is not usually considered an example of monetary independence.

29 Another reason for nonzero bands, discussed in De Grauwe (1992, 103–7), is that sufficiently wide bands (and sufficiently small realignments) allow the new and old bands to overlap at realignments. This way realignments are possible without discrete jumps in exchange rates, that is, realignments need not imply one-sided bets on which way the exchange rate will move. This should reduce the amount of speculation and interest rate movements before each realignment. In Figure 5.1a and b, at the two realignments with overlapping bands (September 1979 and January 1987) it appears that the interest rate differential was indeed less volatile than at the other realignments.

30 Note that this monetary independence is limited to interest rates of short maturities, say less than 1 year. The reason is that the expected rate of currency depreciation within the band over a longer maturity is by necessity small: the amount of currency depreciation is bounded by the bandwidth, and it is divided by a long maturity in order to be expressed as a rate. Furthermore, the control is only temporary, in the sense that the average expected rate of currency depreciation within the band must be zero since on average the exchange rate within the band cannot deviate from its mean. The average interest rate differential over a longer period must thus still equal the average expected rate of realignment. Temporarily, expected rates of depreciation within the band can clearly be sizable, though: if the exchange rate is 1% above the central parity, still far from the upper edge of an EMS ± 2.25% band, and is expected to reach the centre of the band in 6 months, the expected rate of appreciation within the band is 2% per year, which is a sizable reduction of the 6-month domestic interest rate. The control over the domestic interest rate is limited even in the short run if the expected rate of realignment is sensitive to exchange rate movements within the band: suppose an increase in the exchange rate above central parity (weakening of currency) leads to an increase in the expected rate of realignment. This by itself increases the domestic interest rates and counters the decrease because of an expected currency appreciation within the band.

The monetary independence can be exploited in order to smooth domestic interest rates, a behaviour often attributed to central banks (Goodfriend, 1991). When there is an increase in the domestic interest rate, say because the foreign interest rate or the expected rate of realignment increases, the central bank can dampen the effect on the domestic interest rate by increasing the exchange rate and create an expected currency appreciation within the band. A tradeoff between domestic interest rate variability and the exchange rate band results. Svensson (1992b) uses Swedish krona to quantify this tradeoff, as a measure of the amount of monetary independence in an exchange rate band. The amount of monetary dependence then appears to be sizable in some instances: an increase in the exchange rate band from 0 to ± 2% allows the standard deviation of the 1-month domestic interest rate to be reduced by a half. This result assumes that the expected rate of realignment is insensitive to the exchange rate's position within the band. If that is not the case, there is much less monetary independence, and the interest rate's variability may even be increasing in the bandwidth.

31 The Dutch guilder has been kept close to its central parity relative to the Deutsche mark since 1983, and to the Belgian franc since 1990. The Bank of

Austria has pegged the Austrian schilling very closely to the Deutsche mark since 1982, without even declaring an explicit band. Some time after these policies were introduced, the interest rate differentals relative to the Deutsche mark all but disappeared. With the simplest test and the drift-adjustment method described above the hypothesis of zero realignment expectations cannot be rejected. Hence, the central banks for these currencies have conspicuously abstained from exploiting their monetary policy and later gained what appears to be complete credibility of their exchange rates.

32 Williamson (1985, 1989) advocates a target zone for the real value of the dollar. He argues that floating exchange rates are subject to irrational destabilising speculation which lead to excessive volatility and 'misaligned' real exchange rates. A target zone would remedy this, but it should be fairly wide (say ± 10%) to allow sufficient latitude for monetary policy, for changes in the central rate without discontinuous changes in exchange rates, and for uncertainty about the correct level of target rate. Recently Corbae, Ingram and Mondino (1990) and Krugman and Miller (1992) have expressed this excess-volatility case for target zones in formal models. Although the excess-volatility argument is sometimes used in general support of fixed rather than floating exchange rates, it does not seem to be very relevant for the choice of bandwidth for EMS-type narrow nominal exchange rate bands. As discussed by Krugman and Miller (1992), the excess-volatility argument may however be important in understanding the G-3 (Germany, Japan and the United States) Louvre agreement in 1987 to stabilise the dollar.

REFERENCES

Bartolini, Leonardo and Gordon Bodnar (1992) 'Target Zones and Forward Rates in a Model with Repeated Realignments', IMF, *Working Paper* **WP/92/22**.

Beetsma, Roel M.W.J. and Frederick van der Ploeg (1992) 'Exchange Rate Bands and Optimal Monetary Accommodation Under a Dirty Float', *Working Paper*, Tilburg University.

Bertola, Giuseppe (1993) 'Continuous-Time Models of Exchange Rates and Intervention', in Frederick van der Ploeg (ed.), *Handbook of International Economics*, London: Basil Blackwell, forthcoming.

Bertola, Giuseppe and Ricardo J. Caballero (1991) 'Sustainable Intervention Policies and Exchange Rate Dynamics', in P. Krugman and M. Miller (eds), *Exchange Rate Targets and Currency Bands*, Cambridge: Cambridge University Press, 186–206.

(1992) 'Target Zones and Realignments', *American Economic Review*, **82** (June), 520–36.

Bertola, Giuseppe and Lars E.O. Svensson (1993) 'Stochastic Devaluation Risk and the Empirical Fit of Target Zone Models', *Review of Economic Studies*, forthcoming.

Buiter, Willem H. and Vittorio U. Grilli (1991) 'Anomalous Speculative Attacks on Fixed Exchange Rate Regimes: Possible Resolutions of the "Gold Standard Paradox"'; in P. Krugman and M. Miller (eds), *Exchange Rate Targets and Currency Bands*, Cambridge: Cambridge University Press, 140–76.

Buiter, Willem H. and Paolo A. Pesenti (1990) 'Rational Speculative Bubbles in an Exchange Rate Target Zone', Centre for Economic Policy Research, *Discussion Paper*, **479**.

Corbae, Dean, Beth Ingram and Guillermo Mondino (1990) 'On the Optimality of Exchange Rate Band Policies', *Working Paper*, University of Iowa.

Cukierman, Alex, Miguel A. Kiguel and Leonardo Leiderman (1994) 'Some evidence on a strategic model of the exchange rate bands', Chapter 6 in this volume.

De Grauwe, Paul (1992) *The Economics of Monetary Integration*, Oxford: Oxford University Press.

Delgado, Francisco and Bernard Dumas (1991) 'Target Zones, Broad and Narrow', in Paul Krugman and Marcus Miller (eds), *Exchange Rate Targets and Currency Bands*, Cambridge: Cambridge University Press, 35–56.

(1993) 'Monetary Contracting Between Central Banks and the Design of Sustainable Exchange Rate Zones', *Journal of International Economics*, **34**.

Dixit, Avinash K. (1991) 'A Simplified Treatment of the Theory of Optimal Control of Brownian Motion', *Journal of Economic Dynamics and Control*, **15** (October), 657–73.

(1992) 'Investment and Hysteresis', *Journal of Economic Perspectives* (Winter), 107–32.

Dominguez, Kathryn M. and Peter Kenen (1991) 'On the Need to Allow for the Possibility that Governments Mean What They Say – Interpreting the Target-Zone Model of Exchange-Rate Behaviour in the Light of EMS Experience', NBER, *Working Paper*, **3670**.

Dumas, Bernard (1992) 'Dynamic Equilibrium and the Real Exchange Rate in a Spatially Separated World', *Review of Financial Studies*, **5**(2), 153–80.

Dumas, Bernard and Lars E.O. Svensson (1991) 'How Long Do Unilateral Target Zones Last?', NBER, *Working Paper*, **3931**.

Edison, Hali and Graciela Kaminsky (1991) 'Target Zones, Intervention, and Exchange Rate Volatility: France 1979–1990', *Working Paper*, Washington, DC: Federal Board of Governors.

Flood, Robert P. and Peter Garber (1991) 'The Linkage Between Speculative Attack and Target Zone Models of Exchange Rates', *Quarterly Journal of Economics*, **106** (November), 1367–72.

Flood, Robert P. and Peter Isard (1989) 'Monetary Policy Strategies', *IMF Staff Papers*, **36** (September), 612–32.

Flood, Robert P., Andrew K. Rose and Donald J. Mathieson (1991) 'An Empirical Exploration of Exchange-Rate Target-Zones', *Carnegie–Rochester Series on Public Policy*, **35**, 7–65.

Frankel, Jeffrey A. and Steven Phillips (1991) 'The European Monetary System: Credible at Last?', NBER, *Working Paper*, **3819**.

Froot, Kenneth A. and Maurice Obstfeld (1991) 'Exchange-Rate Dynamics Under Stochastic Regime Shifts: A Unified Approach', *Journal of International Economics*, **31** (November), 203–29.

Froot, Kenneth A. and Richard H. Thaler (1990) 'Anomalies: Foreign Exchange', *Journal of Economic Perspectives*, **4**(3) (Summer), 179–92.

Genberg, Hans (1989) 'Exchange Rate Management and Macroeconomic Policy: A National Perspective', *Scandinavian Journal of Economics*, **91**, 439–69.

Giavazzi, Francesco and Alberto Giovannini (1989) *Limiting Exchange Rate Flexibility: The European Monetary System*, Cambridge, MA: MIT Press.

Goodfriend, Marvin (1991) 'Interest Rates and the Conduct of Monetary Policy', *Carnegie–Rochester Series on Public Policy*, **34**, 7–30.

Harrison, Michael (1985) *Brownian Motion and Stochastic Flow Systems*, New York: John Wiley.

Karatzas, Ioannis and Steven E. Shreve (1988) *Brownian Motion and Stochastic Calculus*, New York: Springer-Verlag.

Keynes, John Maynard (1930) *A Treatise on Money, Vol. II: The Applied Theory of Money*, London, Macmillan.

Klein, Michael W. (1990) 'Playing with the Band: Dynamic Effects of Target Zones in an Open Economy', *International Economic Review*, **31** (November), 757–72.

Klein, Michael W. and Karen K. Lewis (1991) 'Learning about Intervention Target Zones', NBER, *Working Paper*, **3674**.

Krugman, Paul (1979) 'A Model of Balance of Payments Crises', *Jounal of Money Credit and Banking*, **11** (August), 311–25.

(1987) 'Trigger Strategies and Price Dynamics in Equity and Foreign Exchange Markets', NBER, *Working Paper*, **2459**.

(1991) 'Target Zones and Exchange Rate Dynamics', *Quarterly Journal of Economics*, **106** (August), 669–82.

Krugman, Paul and Marcus Miller (1992) 'Why Have a Target Zone?', *Carnegie–Rochester Series on Public Policy*, **38**, 279–314.

Krugman, Paul and Marcus Miller (eds) (1991) *Exchange Rate Targets and Currency Bands*, Cambridge: Cambridge University Press.

Krugman, P. and Julio Rotemberg (1991) 'Speculative Attacks on Target Zones', in Paul Krugman and Marcus Miller (eds), *Exchange Rate Targets and Currency Bands*, Cambridge: Cambridge University Press, 117–32.

Lewis, Karen K. (1990) 'Occasional Interventions to Target Rates With a Foreign Exchange Application', NBER, *Working Paper*, **3398**.

Lindberg, Hans and Paul Söderlind (1991) 'Testing the Basic Target Zone Model on Swedish Data', Stockholm: Institute for International Economic Studies, *Seminar Paper*, **488**.

(1992) 'Target Zone Models and the Intervention Policy: The Swedish Case', Stockholm: Institute for International Economic Studies, *Seminar Paper*, **496**.

Lindberg, Hans, Lars E.O. Svensson and Paul Söderlind (1991) 'Devaluation Expectations: The Swedish Krona 1982–1991', Stockholm: Institute for International Economic Studies, *Seminar Paper*, **495**.

Lohmann, Susanne (1992) 'Optimal Commitment in Monetary Policy: Credibility Versus Flexibility', *American Economic Review*, **82** (March), 273–86.

Meese, Richard A. and Kenneth Rogoff (1983) 'Empirical Exchange Rate Models of the Seventies: Do they Fit out of Sample?', *Journal of International Economics*, **14** (February), 3–24.

Meese, Richard A. and Andrew K. Rose (1990) 'Nonlinear, Nonparameter Nonessential Exchange Rate Estimation', *American Economic Review*, **80** (May), 192–6.

Miller, Marcus and Alan Sutherland (1991) 'Britain's Return to Gold and Entry into the EMS: Joining Conditions and Credibility', in Paul Krugman and Marcus Miller (eds), *Exchange Rate Targets and Currency Bands*, Cambridge: Cambridge University Press, 82–106.

Miller, Marcus and Paul Weller (1991a) 'Currency Bands, Target Zones, and Price Flexibility', *IMF Staff Papers*, **38** (March), 184–215.

(1991b) 'Exchange Rate Bands with Price Inertia', *Economic Journal*, **101** (November), 1380–99.

Mundaca, Gabriela B. (1990) 'Intervention Decisions and Exchange Rate Volatility in a Target Zone', *Working Paper*, Oslo: Norges Bank.

Perraudin, William R.F. (1990) 'Exchange Rate Bands with Point Process Fundamentals', IMF, *Working Paper*.

Persson, Torsten and Guido Tabellini (1990) *Macroeconomic Policy, Credibility and Politics*, London: Harwood.

Pesenti, Paolo A. (1990) 'Perforate and Imperforate Currency Bands: Exchange Rate Management and the Term Structure of Interest Rate Differentials', *Working Paper*, Yale University.

Pessach, Shula and Assaf Razin (1991) 'Targeting the Exchange Rate: An Empirical Investigation', NBER, *Working Paper*, **3662**.

Rose, Andrew K. and Lars E.O. Svensson (1991) 'Expected and Predicted Realignments: The FF/DM Exchange Rate during the EMS', Stockholm: Institute for International Economic Studies, *Seminar Paper*, **485**.

Salant, Stephen W. and Dale W. Henderson (1978) 'Market Anticipation of Government Gold Policies and the Price of Gold', *Journal of Political Economy*, **86** (August), 627–48.

Smith, Gregor W. and Michael G. Spencer (1991) 'Estimation and Testing in Models of Exchange Rate Target Zones and Process Switching', in Paul Krugman and Marcus Miller (eds), *Exchange Rate Targets and Currency Bands*, Cambridge: Cambridge University Press, 211–39.

Svensson, Lars E.O. (1991a) 'The Simplest Test of Target Zone Credibility', *IMF Staff Papers*, **38** (September), 655–65.

(1991b) 'Target Zones and Interest Rate Variability', *Journal of International Economics*, **31** (August), 27–54.

(1991c) 'The Term Structure of Interest Rates in a Target Zone: Theory and Swedish Data', *Journal of Monetary Economics*, **28** (August), 87–116.

(1992a) 'The Foreign Exchange Risk Premium in a Target Zone with Devaluation Risk', *Journal of International Economics*, **33** (August), 21–40.

(1992b) 'Why Exchange Rate Bands? Monetary Independence in Spite of Fixed Exchange Rates', Stockholm: Institute for International Economic Studies, *Seminar Paper*, **532**, forthcoming.

(1993) 'Assessing Target Zone Credibility: Mean Reversion and Devaluation Expectations in the EMS 1973–1992', *European Economic Review*, **37**.

Weber, Axel A. (1992) 'Time-Varying Devaluation Risk, Interest Rate Differentials and Exchange Rates in Target Zones: Empirical Evidence from the EMS', Centre for Economic Policy Research, *Discussion Paper*, **611**.

Williamson, John (1985) *The Exchange Rate System*, Washington, DC: Institute for International Economics.

(1989) 'The Case of Roughly Stabilizing the Real Value of the Dollar', *American Economic Review*, **79** (May), 41–5.

Williamson, John and Marcus H. Miller (1987) *Targets and Indicators: A Blueprint for the International Coordination of Economic Policy*, Washington, DC: Institute for International Economics.

Discussion

SHMUEL KANDEL

My discussion will focus on the links between Chapter 5 and models in financial economics. At the beginning of the twentieth century a French mathematician called Bachelier wrote a dissertation on the theory of speculation (Bachelier, 1900). Assuming that stock prices follow a Brownian motion with no drift, he tried to derive the price of an option. To the best of my knowledge, this was the first work where continuous-time mathematics of stochastic processes was applied in a study of economic phenomena. The next significant step in this direction took place more than 60 years later, with some important developments in financial economics, such as the developments of optimal rules for consumption allocation and portfolio selection and the theory of option pricing. The financial models have usually excluded the effects of the public sector on the economic system. For example, the processes of short-term interest rate and the exchange rate are usually considered to be exogenous to the models.

In his excellent Chapter 5, Lars Svensson reviews, criticises, and interprets the results of a new line of research, where continuous-time mathematics of stochastic processes is applied to models of currency bands. The paper on which the chapter was based was originally prepared for the *Journal of Economic Perspectives*, and it fits the interest of an 'accidental tourist', like me, to the area of international monetary economics very well. I was amazed to learn how much work has been done in this area in the last 3–4 years. The phenomenon is very similar to what happened in studies of finance after the introduction of the Black–Scholes (1973) formula and the models of Merton (1973) and Cox, Ingersoll and Ross (1985).

The main message from Svensson's chapter is that the general policy of currency bands may reflect more than a single form of intervention by the central bank. Svensson shows that there is a way to derive the exchange rate dynamics in models with target-zones where at least one of the two main assumptions of Krugman's (1991) model are relaxed. These derivations allow for intra-marginal interventions and changing the policy (or its central parity value) after some time ('less than perfect credibility'). In the spirit of Svensson's interpretation, I interpret all these exchange rate dynamics as feasible solutions to an as yet unspecified optimisation problem of the policymakers. In finance we are familiar with band policies (*s–S* policies) that are optimal policies for managing inventory, cash, or portfolio in models with adjustment costs. The problem typically involves an exogenous variable which follows a stochastic process, a policy variable, and two types of costs: a cost of being away from an unconstrained optimum and the costs of transactions, adjustments or rebalancing. The requirement is that the resulting process will be consistent with equilibrium conditions, and in particular with the 'No Arbitrage Condition'.

In many discrete-time models it is impossible to obtain a closed-form solution for the optimal policy. Introducing continuous-time trading usually makes the problem more tractable, resulting in a closed-form solution. It also allows us to check whether a suggested policy results in a feasible solution or not. Obstfeld (1992), for example, shows that a regime with a fixed exchange rate, where the government allows the currency to float if and only if the foreign reserves are zero ('the gold standard'), is not consistent with equilibrium, as it allows arbitrage. The ability to derive the dynamics of the exchange rate explicitly under different sets of assumptions and the associated growth of the set of 'feasible solutions', introduce a challenge to the theoreticians to develop a model where the policy of exchange rate bands serves society best.

Svensson criticises the emphasis given to the 'smooth pasting' conditions. I agree that, *a priori*, without specifying the policymakers' optimisation problem, these conditions are by no means necessary. Nevertheless, I would like to mention here that, in several models, these conditions are linked to the optimality of the solution. These conditions were first encountered by Samuelson (1965) in studying the optimal early-exercise for American-type warrants ('high contact' at the boundary). Early exercise of a call option (or warrant) may be optimal when the stock, for example, pays dividends. The value of the option depends on the optimal exercise, and Merton (1990) shows that the 'high-contact' condition is implied by the maximising behaviour of the warrant holder. Similar optimality considerations are presented in two recent papers by Dumas (1992) and Dumas and Luciano (1991) where the optimal policy is a band-type policy: a model of real exchange rate with costs of transfer of capital from one country to the other and a model of portfolio rebalancing with transactions costs. In both papers the intervention of the central planner is 'marginal' and the 'smooth pasting' conditions require that the derivatives of the value or utility function must be the same at the trigger and the target points.

My last comment is about risk premia. Being a financial economist, I am used to associating a nonzero risk premium with any uncertain payoff whose risk is not diversifiable. However, some of the inferences documented by Svensson are based on the assumption of a zero premium for foreign exchange risk. In particular, the data reject the hypothesis of a negative deterministic relation between the interest rate differential and the exchange rate. This hypothesis is based not only on Krugman's assumptions of perfect credibility and marginal interventions, but also on the assumption of 'uncovered interest parity'. As Svensson explains in n. 12, this last assumption is equivalent to a zero premium for foreign exchange risk. In their derivation of the model from underlying behavioural relationships, Froot and Obstfeld (1992) allow for a nonzero risk premium and show that the aggregate macroeconomic fundamental variable may include the risk premium as one of its terms. It seems to me that a time-varying and mean-reverting risk premium may explain some of the empirical findings Svensson documents here. Based on his empirical study (Svensson, 1992), Svensson argues that, for exchange rate target zones, the premium is likely to be small. Nevertheless, I believe that, as uncertainty and risk are crucial building blocks of the models of this new line of research, more effort should be directed to the incorporation of risk premia in both the theoretical analyses and their empirical testing.

REFERENCES

Bachelier, L.F. (1900) 'Theorie de la speculation', English translation in P.H. Cootner (ed.) (1964), *The Random Character of Stock Market Prices*, Cambridge, MA: MIT Press.

Black, Fischer and Myron Scholes (1973) 'The pricing of options and corporate liabilities', *Journal of Political Economy*, **81**, 637–54.

Cox, John F., Jonathan E. Ingersoll and Stephen A. Ross (1985) 'An intertemporal general equilibrium model of asset prices', *Econometrica*, **53**, 363–84.

Dumas, Bernard (1992) 'Dynamic equilibrium and the real exchange rate in a spatially separated world', *Review of Financial Studies*, **5**(2), 153–80.

Dumas, Bernard and Elisa Luciano (1991) 'An exact solution to a dynamic portfolio choice under transactions costs', *Journal of Finance*, **46**, 577–95.

Froot, Kenneth A. and Maurice Obstfeld (1992) 'Stochastic process switching: some simple solutions', in P.R. Krugman and M. Miller (eds), *Exchange Rate Targets and Currency Bands*, Cambridge: Cambridge University Press.

Krugman, Paul R. (1991) 'Target zones and exchange rate dynamics', *Quarterly Journal of Economics*, **106** (August), 669–82.

Merton, Robert C. (1973) 'An intertemporal capital asset pricing model', *Econometrica*, **41**, 867–87.

(1990) *Continuous-Time Finance*, Cambridge, MA: Basil Blackwell.

Obstfeld, Maurice (1992) 'Discussion of anomalous speculative attacks on fixed exchange rate regimes: possible resolutions of the "gold standard paradox" by W.H. Buiter and V. Grilli', in P.R. Krugman and M. Miller (eds), *Exchange Rate Targets and Currency Bands*, Cambridge: Cambridge University Press.

Samuelson, Paul A. (1965) 'Rational theory of warrant pricing', *Industrial Management Review*, **6**, 13–31.

Svensson, Lars O.E. (1992) 'The foreign exchange risk premium in a target zone with devaluation risk', *Journal of International Economics*, **33** (August), 21–40.

ANDREW K. ROSE

Svensson has provided us in Chapter 5 with a clear and extremely readable study on one of the hottest areas of recent research in international finance, namely the literature on exchange rate target zones. The profession owes him a debt for providing not just a survey, but also an interpretation of this work. He concludes that imperfect credibility and mean-reverting central bank intervention are critical in understanding the actual behaviour of managed exchange rates, while nonlinearities and smooth pasting are not. I find this conclusion to be eminently reasonable. While I have a few quibbles with the chapter (especially the continued use of the inappropriate 'honeymoon effect' expression), I find it to be a well-balanced critique of the current state of the art in the area, and have no substantive points of disagreements with Svensson.

Nevertheless, I do not share the optimism about the state of current and future exchange rate research that is implicit in the study. I see little evidence that the profession really understands either fixed or floating exchange rates very well from an economic point of view. More importantly, the profession does not have a very good idea of the different behaviour of the economy in fixed as opposed to floating exchange rate regimes. While I will comment on a few of these issues, none of this should take away from Svensson's study, which is more narrowly focused.

Most of my remarks concern the underlying 'fundamentals' which are used throughout the target zone literature. These are usually thought of as being derived from a monetary model with flexible prices, although I know of little compelling evidence that shows that this model works well in reality. The target zone literature works off the premise that the (conditional) volatility of the exchange rate is reduced by changing the relationship linking the exchange rate to fundamentals; the models maintain that the volatility of the fundamentals is little changed when a floating rate is fixed. Yet when fundamentals are estimated, the conditional volatility of fundamentals varies dramatically across exchange rate regimes. The conditional volatility of estimated fundamentals also seems to be surprisingly high at even very fine frequencies, compared to what we might expect from monetary model fundamentals. This may reflect measurement error or irrational expectations; it may also reflect the fact that monetary models (and indeed all exchange rate models based on macroeconomic phenomena) just cannot deliver enough conditional volatility to explain high-frequency exchange rate volatility.

On a related note, the volatility of macroeconomic fundamentals (such as money, income, and prices) does not vary much for a given country over time. Yet the volatility of exchange rates does vary substantially, falling when exchange rates are fixed and being higher during floats. But if exchange rates are linear functions of fundamentals (as Svensson encourages us to think of them), how can we explain regime-varying exchange rate volatility with macroeconomic volatility which is unchanging? Similarly, the United States, France and Germany have (to a first approximation) comparable macroeconomic volatility. But why then is the DM/FF exchange rate so much less volatile than the DM/$ exchange rate? The fact that economists have been unable to provide useful insights on such issues leads me to be much more sceptical than Svensson on the current state of knowledge vis-à-vis exchange rates.

My view is that the profession had a good *statistical* understanding of exchange rate processes in floating exchange rate regimes by the mid-1980s; it has since added a variety of stylised facts concerning the statistical behaviour of managed exchange rates. While this is a worthwhile contribution, it should not stop us from reflecting on the paucity of empirical work which validates plausible structural *economic* models.

6 Some evidence on a strategic model of exchange rate bands

ALEX CUKIERMAN, MIGUEL A. KIGUEL and LEONARDO LEIDERMAN

1 Introduction

This chapter develops and tests some of the implications of a framework designed to analyse policymakers' choices regarding unilateral exchange rate bands. The basic model draws on Cukierman, Kiguel and Leiderman (1993), who view exchange rate bands as the outcome of an optimisation problem of a policymaker whose objective function weighs the level of the real exchange rate against the level and variability of the nominal exchange rate. This specification is aimed at capturing an important aspect of exchange rate policy determination in countries such as Chile or Israel where the authorities have shown their concern to preserve and improve the competitiveness of exports and the current account position, while at the same time avoiding the possible inflationary consequences of nominal exchange rate depreciation.[1] Exchange rate bands are seen in this context as a simple and verifiable system for the policymaker to make a credible anti-inflation commitment, while allowing for some degree of exchange rate flexibility needed to shield exports and the current account from the impact of adverse shocks.[2]

It turns out that most of the existing work on currency bands offers little guidance on the policy tradeoffs involved in the choice of such bands. While some of the earlier work on exchange rate target zones partially dealt with these important policy choices,[3] the recent voluminous literature on target zones has taken the existence of bands and their width to be exogeneous. That is, the recent work,[4] although elegant and useful, has not addressed the consideration involved in policy decisions whether or not to adopt an exchange rate band and what could be the characteristics of such a band. The relatively poor empirical performance of standard target zone models (see Chapter 5 in this volume) and the existence of frequent exchange rate realignments provide motivation for shifting to models which endogenise policy decisions about the specifics of the exchange rate regime.

Our model differs from most previous models of exchange rate bands in three main aspects. First, the width of the band is determined endogeneously as the result of maximisation of policymakers' objectives. Since the model allows for bands of any width, it includes as special cases, fixed and floating exchange rates (i.e., bands of zero and infinite size respectively). Second, for a given realisation of exogeneous shocks, the effective 'fundamentals' are interpreted as equal to the difference between the real exchange rate desired by policymakers and the actual real exchange that obtains at the historically given nominal exchange rate. The desired rate depends, in turn, on various shocks to the economy (such as shocks to capital flows or the terms of trade) that policymakers take as exogeneous. Third, we endogenise policymakers' decisions about realignments. That is, we consider conditions under which the realisation of shocks is such that reneging on the existing commitment and setting a new set of parameters for the band is optimal from policymakers' perspective. Since at each point in time there is a nonzero probability of realignment, there is imperfect credibility about the existing exchange rate band.

The determination of optimal bandwidth in our model involves a choice between credibility and flexibility. This policy tradeoff has recently been investigated by Flood and Isard (1989) and Lohmann (1992) for closed economies and by Cukierman, Kiguel and Liviatan (1992) for open economies. The models in the latter paper and in this chapter complement each other. In Cukierman *et al.* the exchange rate is pegged by assumption, but policymakers can set the degree of commitment to the peg by choosing the cost of reneging on it. Here the cost of reneging on the band is taken as given, but policymakers can influence the *ex ante* tradeoff between credibility and flexibility by choosing the width of the band. The existence of a fixed cost of reneging operates as a partial commitment device.[5]

The chapter is organised as follows. Section 2 discusses the basic policy tradeoffs and develops the notion that an exchange rate band can be seen as a partially credible commitment device. Section 3 discusses equilibrium strategies and the range of effective commitment that arises from the band policy. Section 4 derives the relation between the contribution of expected realignments to expected depreciation, interest rate differentials, and the position of the exchange rate within the band. This hypothesised relation is tested in section 5. Section 6 draws some conclusions.

2 A strategic model of exchange rate bands

2.1 *Policy tradeoffs*

In the basic model, exchange rate policy faces a fundamental tradeoff between moving the real exchange in a desired direction on the one hand and exchange rate stability and price stability on the other. This tradeoff arises under shocks affecting the current account and the level of domestic economic activity well as the capital account of the balance of payments.

Because of the stochastic nature of current account, employment and capital account shocks, there is uncertainty about the direction and magnitude of the desired changes in real exchange rates. This uncertainty, as well as the fundamental policy tradeoff, is captured by postulating that policymakers have the following objective function:

$$V(\pi) \equiv x[\pi - \pi^e] - \frac{\pi^2}{2}. \tag{1}$$

Here π and π^e are the actual and the (previously) expected rates of nominal exchange rate depreciation and x is a stochastic variable. Expected depreciation is an important determinant of the rate of increase in domestic wages and prices. To capture the stickiness of domestic prices we assume that current prices are preset on the basis of exchange rate expectations which are formed prior to the choice of exchange rate by policymakers. Those prices are reset immediately after the formation of expectations in the following period.

Given π^e, and the assumed timing for determination of wages and prices, the policymaker can produce a real depreciation by making π larger than π^e and a real appreciation by making it smaller than π^e. If real trade shocks, employment shocks and capital flows are such that the real exchange rate desired by policymakers differs from its level at the historically given nominal exchange rate they can improve the value of their objectives by appropriately adjusting the nominal exchange rate. A positive value of x means that the desired real exchange rate is larger than the existing one. Hence, policymakers derive positive utility from a positive value of unanticipated depreciation. The converse is true when x is negative. In this case the desired real exchange rate is lower than the existing one. Hence, policymakers derive positive utility from overanticipation of depreciation since this reduces the real exchange rate. When $x = 0$ the actual and the desired real exchange rates are equal.

The second term in equation (1) reflects the political costs of inflation and of exchange rate variability when π is positive[6] and only the latter when π is negative. The same functional form for both positive and negative values of π is used for simplicity. In countries with persistent balance of payments deficits the realisations of x are usually positive. We limit our analysis to this case by restricting x to be positive.[7] The mean value of x is a measure of the average degree of dissatisfaction of policymakers with the existing real exchange rate, relative to inflation and exchange rate variability. Thus x can be considered as a measure of misalignment, as perceived by policymakers. We shall therefore refer to it as the *degree of exchange rate misalignment.*

2.2 *Exchange rate bands as a partially credible commitment device*

We consider exchange rate bands as a partial commitment device. It is partial because it commits policymakers to maintain the (nominal) rate of exchange within the band only for some realisations of the degree of misalignment, and not for others. Why would policymakers willingly choose to accept restrictions on their freedom of action? The answer suggested here is that by doing so they increase their credibility. They consequently lower exchange rate depreciation expectations, and thus increase the value of their objective function for positive realisations of x. The cost associated with this gain in credibility is a loss in flexibility which partially prevents policymakers from adjusting the exchange rate in line with the degree of misalignment. The optimal width of the band is determined by balancing the benefits of credibility against the cost of reduced flexibility.

To illustrate the basic considerations involved in the choice of a band, consider the following four-stage sequence of events. In the first stage, policymakers announce a central parity rate and a (symmetric) band around it. In the second stage, the value of x realises. In the third stage, expectations about exchange rate changes are formed (and wages and prices are set in accordance with those expectations). In the last and fourth stage, the actual rate of nominal exchange rate depreciation is chosen by policymakers.

Since typically there is considerable uncertainty about the commitment ability of policymakers, we assume that there are two possible types of policymakers. One, to which we refer as dependable (D), incurs a fixed cost – c – whenever s/he allows the exchange rate to be set outside the band after having preannounced the existence of such a band. The other type, referred to as weak (W) incurs no such cost.[8] We assume that when a given band is announced the public holds a probability a that the policymaker in office is of type D and a probability $1 - a$ that s/he is of type W.

The equilibrium strategies of policymakers and the equilibrium value of expectations can be obtained by using the principle of dynamic programming. Given the choice of band, the realisation of x, and the level of expectations, the policymaker picks π in stage 4 so as to maximise the value of the objective function in equation (1). If the policymaker is of type D s/he also takes into consideration the cost of violating the band. In stage 3 expectations are formed on the basis of the public's knowledge of the objective function in equation (1), the previously realised value of x and the probability, a, that the band has been preannounced by a dependable policymaker. In stage 1 the width of the band is chosen so as to maximise the expected value of the objective function in equation (1), taking into consideration the way expectations are formed and the fact that the policymaker knows, already in stage 1, his decision rule for stage 4 as a function of x. If type D is in office s/he also takes into consideration the cost of reneging on the band which will be incurred for some realisations of x. Policymakers of type W are not subject to this cost. Hence they do not take it into consideration when announcing the band. However, they always prefer to mimic the announcement of D since, if they do not, expectations of depreciation will be larger, and the value of their objectives lower. Hence the band chosen by *both* policymaker types is determined by the solution to the decision problem of the dependable policymaker in stage 1. But, when the time comes to decide whether to maintain the band or to renege on it, the weak policymaker reneges on it whenever the realisation of x makes such a course of action desirable. In other words, the band does not bind him in any way.

3 Equilibrium strategies and the choice of exchange rate band

Suppose type W is in office. Since this policymaker faces no cost for abandoning the band, the value of π is chosen so as to maximise the value of the objective function in (1) for all values of x. This maximisation problem has the solution:

$$\pi = x \qquad \text{for all } x. \tag{2}$$

This is analogous to the well-known Barro–Gordon (1983) discretionary solution for inflation.

When D is in office, s/he also behaves according to the decision rule in equation (2), but only as long as the rate of exchange falls within the band. When the decision rule in equation (2) calls for abandoning the band, D may or may not abandon the band depending on whether the value of his/her objectives, net of the cost of reneging on the band, is larger or smaller than that value when the band is maintained. Which of these two magnitudes is larger depends on the realisation of x, on the width of the band, and on the initial position of the exchange rate within the band. It can be shown that D devalues and adjusts the band upward if and only if[9]

$$x > \pi_m + \sqrt{2c} \equiv \pi_m + d \tag{3}$$

where π_m is the maximisation rate of depreciation that, given the historical level (e_{-1}) of the exchange rate, does not lead to a violation of the band. In the particular case in which the initial exchange rate is at the central parity rate ($e_{-1} = e_c$) this condition reduces to

$$x > B + \sqrt{2c} \tag{3a}$$

where B is the (single-sided) width of the band. When $x \leq B$, D picks the discretionary policy in equation (2). When

$$B < x \leq B + d \tag{4}$$

the dependable policymaker depreciates the currency up to the upper limit of the band but does not renege on the band. Hence the range of values defined by equation (4) is the only range in which the commitment to the band is binding. We therefore refer to it as the *range of effective commitment*. Note that this range is immediately above the upper limit, $\bar{e}$, of the band.[10] The existence of a band produces a range of commitment for realisations of x just outside the upper limit of the band. However, there obviously is no commitment for realisations of x within the band.

Expectations are formed rationally after the realisation of x, taking this realisation, the width of the band, and the fact that the policymaker may be either dependable or not, into consideration. Hence the dependable policymaker can reduce expectations of depreciation by appropriate choice of bandwidth. But by doing so he gives up the flexibility to adjust π to its discretionary value, x, in the effective commitment range and subjects himself to a cost if circumstances make it expedient to renege on the band. The choice of band therefore involves a tradeoff between credibility and flexibility.[11] The optimal bandwidth and its dependence on reputation, on the cost of reneging on the band and on the variability of x are characterised in Cukierman, Kiguel and Leiderman (1993). Here we focus on the implications of this approach for interest rates and the size of expected realignments.

4 The interest rate differential and the contribution of expected realignments to expected depreciation

This section develops the implications of our framework for the contribution of expected realignments to expected depreciation. The model's main empirical implication for this concept is derived here, and it is tested empirically in section 5.

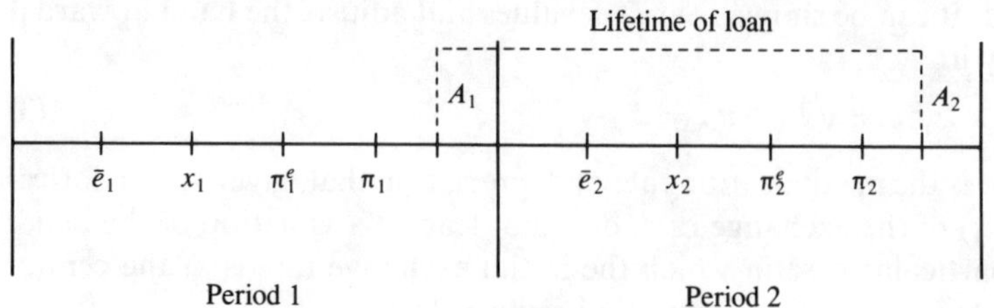

Figure 6.1 A capital market in a two-period framework

A basic premise is that the behaviour of the interest rate differential reflects the expected rate of depreciation of the currency. This expectation is affected in turn by the characteristics of the distribution of the shock x and the reputation of policymakers. To capture the effect of uncertainty about both the realisation of x and the type of policymakers in office on interest rate differentials we consider a framework in which the basic sequence of events repeats twice.[12] We think of each such sequence as occurring within a period. Figure 6.1 illustrates the extended two-period framework. The sequence of shock realisations and of decisions in period 1 is as described in section 2. Changes in political circumstances and in the evaluation, by policymakers, of their chances to stay in office, affect their dependability even without a formal change of government. This prevents the public from discovering the identity of the policymaker after the realisation of π_1. Formally, we assume that the policymaker type in office is drawn anew at the beginning of each period from an i.i.d. of policymakers with stable probability a of being type D.

If the realisations of x_1 and t_1 (the policymaker type in period 1) are such that the band is maintained, $e_1 \leq \bar{e}_1$, $\bar{e}_2 = \bar{e}_1$, and $e_{c1} = e_{c2}$. In such a case the actual exchange rate at the beginning of period 2 usually differs from the centre rate so that $\pi_m \neq B$. Except for this difference in the position of the opening exchange rate, events and decisions in period 2 occur in a manner that is similar to that in period 1.

If x_1 and t_1 are such that the band is violated, $e_1 > \bar{e}_1$ and a new band is instituted at the beginning of period 2, with the new centre rate set at e_1. Since basic parameters such as a and c are unchanged, the width of the band remains as in period 1. But now $\bar{e}_2 = e_1(1 + B)$ since the centre rate has been shifted upward. Except for the fact that they occur within the framework of a different band, events and decisions in period 2 then proceed according to the single-period principles discussed in previous sections.

Suppose now that *after* the choice of π_1 but prior to the realisations of either x_2 or π_2 a one-period loan market opens up. For convenience one can think of the loan as being contracted at point A_1 and being due at point A_2 (see Figure 6.1). Assuming uncovered interest arbitrage holds, the interest rate differential between domestic and foreign rates reflects the expected rate of depreciation. This expectation reflects, in turn, the public's expectation, as of point A_1 about the realisations of x_2 and of the policymaker type in period 2. We focus, without loss of generality, on the case in which the band is not adjusted at the end of the first period.

Following Svensson (1991, 1992a), and as indicated earlier, we refer to situations in which the actual exchange rate is allowed to get out of the prespecified band as a realignment (see also Chapter 5 in this volume). Depreciations that occur without a realignment are referred to as depreciations within the band. Expected depreciation takes into consideration that both realignments and depreciations within the band are possible. More formally,

$$\mathrm{E}\pi = \mathrm{E}\pi_R + \mathrm{E}\pi_{NR} \tag{5}$$

where R stands for 'realignment' and NR stands for 'no realignment'. $\mathrm{E}\pi_R$ is the average contribution of depreciations within the range of realignment to expected depreciation and $\mathrm{E}\pi_{NR}$ is the average contribution of depreciations within the band to expected depreciation. The first term is given by the summation of possible rates of depreciation in the realignment range weighted by their respective probability densities ($F(x)$ is the cumulative distribution of x)

$$\mathrm{E}\pi_R = \int_{\pi_m + d}^{\bar{x}} x\,dF(x) + (1-a)\int_{\pi_m}^{\pi_m + d} x\,dF(x). \tag{6a}$$

Similarly

$$\mathrm{E}\pi_{NR} = \int_{\bar{x}}^{\pi_m} x\,dF(x) + a\pi_m \int_{\pi_m}^{\pi_m + d} x\,dF(x) \tag{6b}$$

is the (density weighted) summation of rates of depreciation within the band. We refer to them as the contributions of expected realignments and of expected depreciations within the band to (overall) expected depreciation respectively.

The main empirical implication of this chapter is summarised in the following proposition.

Proposition

If all positive values of x have a nonzero probability and $a > 0$ the contribution of expected realignments to expected depreciation is larger the nearer the actual exchange rate at the end of period 1 to the upper limit of the band.

Proof

Differentiating equation (6a) with respect to π_m

$$\frac{\partial E\pi_R}{\partial \pi_m} = -\,[a(\pi_m + d)f(\pi_m + d) + (1-a)\pi_m f(\pi_m)] \tag{7}$$

where $f(\cdot)$ is the probability density of x. Since $\pi_m + d > 0$ and $\pi_m \geq 0$, $f(\pi_m + d)$ is positive and $f(\pi_m)$ is nonnegative. Since $a > 0$ it follows that the expression in equation (7) is negative. □

π_m is the maximum depreciation that policymakers can perform in period 2 subject to the constraint that they do not renege on the band. π_m obviously depends on the position of the exchange rate at the end of period 1. Hence another way of stating the proposition is that the contribution of expected realignments to expected depreciation is lower the further away is the exchange rate in period 1 from the upper limit of the band.

5 Empirical testing

In this section we provide simple tests of the hypothesis that the contribution of expected realignments to expected depreciation rises as the exchange rate increases toward the upper limit of the band. While the notion that expectations of realignments and depreciations are likely to depend on the position of the exchange rate within the band is not new, it is interesting that in the present model this relation is derived as a *result* of the underlying model of policymakers' decisions.

From equation (5) the contribution of expected realignments to expected depreciation is

$$E\pi_R = E\pi - E\pi_{NR}. \tag{8}$$

Under the assumption of uncovered interest parity, the unobservable (total) expected depreciation can be proxied by the (observable) interest rate differential δ. To obtain a measure of $E\pi_R$ we need an estimate of $E\pi_{NR}$. The *actual* rate of depreciation within the band, $E\pi_{NR}$, can be decomposed in the following manner

$$E\pi_{NR} \equiv E\pi_{NR} + u(x) \tag{9}$$

where $u(\cdot)$ is a random variable which depends on the realisation of the shock x. Let

$$NR \equiv \{x \leq \pi_m \text{ and policymaker is of type } W \text{ or } x \leq \pi_m + d \text{ and policymaker is of type } D\}. \tag{10}$$

It follows from (9) and (10) that

$$\int_{NR} \pi_{NR}(\cdot)du = \mathrm{E}\pi_{NR}, \qquad \int_{NR} u(\cdot)du = 0$$

so that $u(x)$ has an expected value of zero in the 'no realignment range'. Using the interest rate differential as a proxy for $\mathrm{E}\pi$, equation (8) can be rewritten as

$$\mathrm{E}\pi_R = \delta - \mathrm{E}\pi_{NR}. \tag{8a}$$

Subtracting $u(x)$ in the NR range from both sides of (8a)

$$\mathrm{E}\pi_R - u(x) = \delta - (\mathrm{E}\pi_{NR} + u(x)) = \delta - \pi_{NR}.^{13} \tag{8b}$$

The right-hand side of this equation therefore is a measurable proxy, up to a random noise term, of E_{NR}. To test the Proposition we have to regress this proxy on π_m and to examine whether the coefficient of π_m is negative. The fact that $\mathrm{E}\pi_R$ is measured up to a random error does not cause biases since the proxy $\delta - \pi_{NR}$ is the dependent variable of the regression. The estimated equation, including an explicit specification of periods, is

$$\rho_t \equiv \delta_t - \pi_{NR,t+1} = a + \beta\pi_{m,t}. \tag{11}$$

Since δ_t is a proxy for expected depreciation between t and $t+1$ the timing of the actual rate of depreciation within the band also refers to the same time interval. The Proposition implies that the left-hand side of equation (11) should be negatively related to π_m in period t. Because of this timing $u(x)$ also refers to period $t+1$ and is therefore orthogonal to π_{mt} and other period's t regressors.

We used monthly time-series data for five countries that maintained unilateral exchange rate bands in recent years: Finland, Norway, Sweden, Chile and Israel.[14] Since institutional details vary across countries, different periods are covered in each case. Interestingly, out of these five countries Chile is the only one to have set its central parity rate in relation to the US dollar (as opposed to a basket of foreign currencies) and to have a preannounced daily crawl in such a central parity rate (as opposed to a fixed central parity, as in most other cases). While the Nordic countries adopted bands of width of no more than ± 3% around the reference rate, Chile's band width gradually increased from ± 2% in 1985 to ± 10% in 1992, and Israel's band width increased from ± 3% in 1989 to ± 5% at the present time.

Table 6.1 reports the estimated equations. These were estimated by OLS and the standard errors are computed allowing for heteroscedasticity. Since the estimation is conditional upon no realignment, observations immediately before and after realignments are excluded; see Svensson

Table 6.1. *The contribution of expected realignment to expected depreciation*

$$E_t \pi_{R_t} = \sum_{j=1}^{n} \beta_{0j} d_j + \beta_1 \pi_{m_t}$$

	β_{01}	β_{02}	β_{03}	β_{04}	β_{05}	β_{06}	β_1	R^2	DW	N	σ
Israel	0.007 (0.003)	0.005 (0.002)	0.008 (0.005)	0.015 (0.006)	0.009 (0.004)	0.010 (0.005)	− 0.141 (0.061)	0.068	1.173	180	0.009
Finland	0.004 (0.001)	0.005 (0.002)	0.006 (0.002)	0.006 (0.001)	0.008 (0.002)	—	− 0.138 (0.041)	0.159	1.876	132	0.004
Norway	0.006 (0.003)	0.007 (0.003)	0.009 (0.002)	—	—	—	− 0.192 (0.069)	0.109	1.206	123	0.009
Sweden	0.007 (0.001)	0.007 (0.003)	0.008 (0.002)	—	—	—	− 0.262 (0.067)	0.103	1.543	134	0.005
Chile	0.001 (0.002)	0.011 (0.006)	0.006 (0.005)	—	—	—	− 0.272 (0.126)	0.108	1.588	55	0.011

Note: figures in parenthesis are standard errors.

(1991) for a similar procedure. The bands are assumed to differ in their constant terms and equation (11) is modified to include a variable d_j which is a dummy for 'regime j', that is, each period between realignments. For Chile, that has a 'crawling band' system, a change in the dummy variable signifies a change in the width of the band. In all cases the value of the constants β_{0j} has been estimated to be larger than zero. Notice that, as predicted by the model, for all cases there is a significant negative relation between $E\pi_R$ and π_m. That is, all estimated β_1 are negative and significant. Despite wide institutional differences across countries, it is interesting that estimated β_1s are of about the same orders of magnitude. Accordingly, we find that the contribution of expected realignments to expected depreciation rises with increases in the level of the exchange rate within the band. In the cases of Israel and Norway the estimates also reject the notion of perfectly credible bands, in that the joint hypothesis that $a = \beta = 0$ and that the residuals are white is rejected at standard significance levels. In the cases of Chile, Finland and Sweden, the estimates reject the hypothesis that $a = \beta = 0$, although for these countries the evidence regarding serially-correlated errors is inconclusive.

The actual and estimated negative relation between $E\pi_R$ and π_m is depicted in Figure 6.2. The time-path of the contribution of expected realignment to expected depreciation is shown in Figure 6.3. (For brevity we also refer to this concept as the 'expected rate of devaluation'.) Notice that in most cases shown in Figure 6.3 there is evidence of nonzero contribution of expected realignments to expected depreciation. There appears to be a buildup of expectations in anticipation of central parity changes. These expectations tend to decrease shortly after the devaluation. For Israel, these trends are evident in the first three bands. During these bands the average expected rate of devaluation differed significantly from zero. Accordingly, the average expected rates (expressed in weekly terms) were 0.06%, 0.11% and 0.19%. During the fourth band the exchange rate remained at the lower bound of the band throughout the entire period and Figure 6.3 suggests that the devaluation at the end of this band was unexpected. During the fifth band, strong devaluation expectations were temporarily subdued by the strict stance taken by the central bank in an attempt to defend the Shekel. The sixth band is the 'crawling band' in which the average expected rate of devaluation estimate was negative (– 0.01%), yet not significantly different from zero. In the case of Sweden the estimate of the average rate of expected depreciation is significantly larger than zero for all three bands (respectively, 0.24%, 0.18% and 0.17% per month). In the case of Norway, the expectations are estimated to be on average larger than zero in the second and third band (0.37% and 0.39%). In the case of Finland,

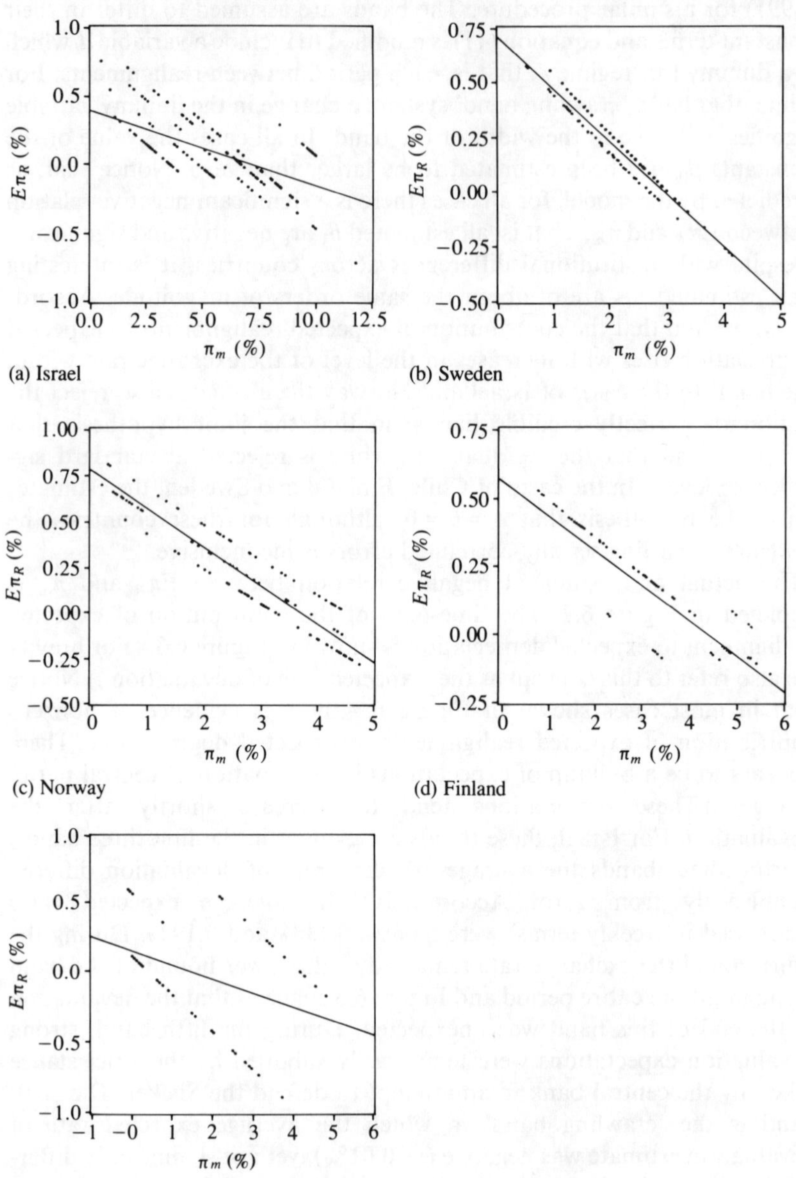

Figure 6.2 The contribution of expected realignment to expected depreciation and the position of the exchange rate within the band

The vertical axis is the contribution of expected realignment to expected depreciation. The horizontal axis measures the distance of the exchange rate from the upper bound of the band.

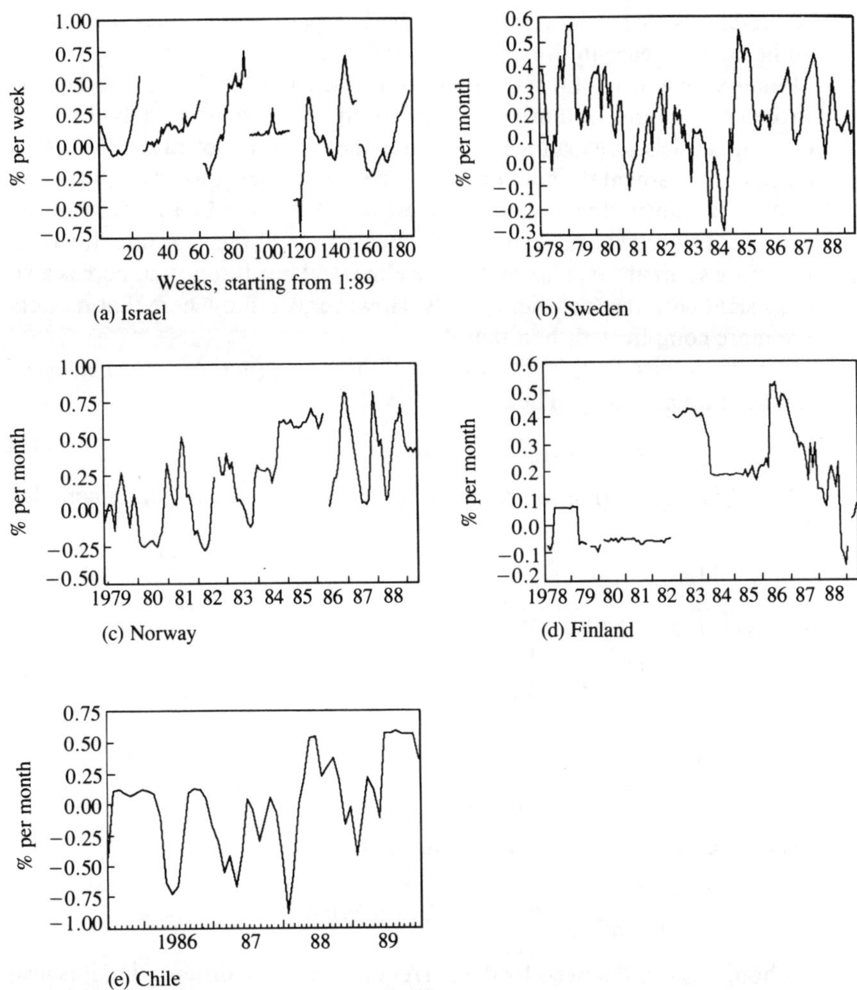

Figure 6.3 The time path of the contribution of expected realignment to expected depreciation
Breaks in data indicate a change in the central parity rate

downward adjustments of the central parity rate were preceded by significantly negative devaluation (i.e., revaluations) expectations. Notice in the case of Chile, that despite the upward crawling central band there were periods of significant devaluation expectations. On average, these expectations seem to strengthen over time. Throughout 1985:07–1988:04 the estimated average expected rate of devaluation was negative (– 0.2% per month), for the second period (1988:05–1989:05) the average is positive, 0.14% per month, and in the last period examined there is an additional increase in this average to 0.46%.

Finally, we address the issue of whether the empirical implication of the Proposition could obtain also in standard target zone models. In most existing models of exchange rate bands the current spot rate depends on current fundamentals and on the expected future spot rate. In these models causality runs from the interest rate differential (as a proxy of the expected future spot rate) to the current position of the spot rate. It would therefore seem at first glance that the empirical result reported here is also consistent with these earlier models. However, we show here that matters are more complicated than that.

In order to discuss this, it is useful to interpret equation (11) in terms of the traditional theory. The latter states that

$$e_t = f_t + a\mathrm{E}[e_{t+1}|I_t], \quad a > 0 \tag{12}$$

where I_t is the information set of period t and f stands for 'fundamentals'. But

$$\mathrm{E}[e_{t+1}|I_t] - e_t = \delta_t. \tag{13}$$

Using (13) in (12) and rearranging

$$e_t = \frac{1}{1-a}[f_t + a\delta_t]. \tag{14}$$

Equation (11) can be rewritten as

$$\rho_t = \delta_t - (e_{t+1} - e_t)|NR. \tag{11a}$$

Using (14) in (11a) and rearranging

$$\rho_t = \frac{1}{1-a}[\delta_t - a\delta_{t+1} - (f_{t+1} - f_t)]|NR. \tag{15}$$

Although ρ_t is influenced by the current interest rate differential, it is also affected by the next period's differential and by the first difference in fundamentals. Since those elements do not affect e_t (see equation (14)) the traditional model does not *necessarily* imply that ρ_t and e_t are positively related.

6 Concluding remarks

This chapter tested implications of a framework for the analysis of policymakers' choices regarding unilateral exchange rate bands. Such bands emerge here as the outcome of optimisation under a policy objective function that weighs the level of the real exchange rate against the level and variability of the nominal exchange rate. The determination of the band's key parameter involves the resolution of a tradeoff between credibility and flexibility in the presence of positive costs of reneging on the band. Simple tests based on data for Chile, Finland, Israel, Norway and Sweden provided evidence in support of the model's implication that the contribution of expected realignments to expected depreciation increases as the exchange rate increases toward the upper limit of the band.

In future work, it would be useful to determine whether observed differences in bands' width across countries can be accounted for by differences in the cost of reneging, in policymakers' reputation, and in the distribution of the x-shocks – factors which play a key role in the present model.

NOTES

The authors thank Giuseppe Bertola and Lars Svensson for their insightful comments and Gil Bufman for his efficient assistance with the data and estimations.

An earlier version of this chapter was presented at the Conference on 'International Capital Mobility and Development' sponsored by the Bank of Israel, the Centre for Economic Policy Research, and the Pinhas Sapir Center for Development, Tel-Aviv University (Tel-Aviv, 20–22 December 1992).

1 That this is the case for Chile is apparent from a recent statement by the president of the Banco Central de Chile; see Zahler (1992), who focuses his discussion on policy dilemmas that arise under high capital mobility.

2 Different rationales for the existence of exchange rate bands are provided in recent work by Krugman and Miller (1992) and Svensson (1992b). The former argue that the real world motivation for target zones is, to a large extent, the concern about irrational and unstable market behaviour. The latter stresses the role of exchange rate bands in increasing the independence and flexibility of monetary policy compared to fixed exchange rates.

3 See, for example, Williamson (1985), Frenkel and Goldstein (1986), and Williamson and Miller (1987).

4 For comprehensive surveys of recent work see Chapters 1 and 2 in Krugman and Miller (1991), and Svensson (1992a).

5 Such a way of modelling limited commitments is used in Chapter 6 of Cukierman (1992) to analyse the consequences of European monetary unification. See also Obstfeld (1991).

6 The presumption is that depreciations are inflationary.

7 The principles of a more general analysis in which x may be either positive or negative are discussed in Cukierman, Kiguel and Leiderman (1994).

8 This difference in costs may be thought of as reflecting a difference in rates of time-preference between the two types in a framework in which the cost of reneging arises from a reduction in future credibility. A fuller discussion of the nature of these costs appears in Cukierman and Liviatan (1991, 103).

9 Derivations and more details appear in Cukierman, Kiguel and Leiderman (1993).

10 The relationship between $\bar{e}$ and B is given by $\bar{e} \equiv (1 + B)e_c$.

11 This tradeoff has recently been investigated in Flood and Isard (1989), Lohmann (1992), Cukierman, Kiguel and Liviatan (1992) and Cukierman (1992). Here flexibility is valuable because it enables policymakers to devalue at a higher rate when the degree of misalignment as measured by x is higher.

12 But the government is still assumed to choose the band taking into consideration only its first period objective.

13 See Svensson (1991) and Rose and Svensson (1991) for a similar procedure to construct empirical proxies for expected realignments.

14 The data for the Nordic countries are the same as in Edin and Vredin (1991), who very kindly provided us with this information. The data for Chile and Israel are as in Helpman and Leiderman (1992). We thank Gil Bufman for his assistance with the data and computations in this section. Various aspects of the data are described in Cukierman, Kiguel and Leiderman (1993).

REFERENCES

Barro, Robert J. and David B. Gordon (1983) 'A Positive Theory of Monetary Policy in a Natural Rate Model', *Journal of Political Economy*, **91**, 589–610.

Cukierman, Alex (1992) *Central Bank Strategy, Credibility and Independence: Theory and Evidence*, Cambridge, MA: MIT Press.

Cukierman, Alex and Nissan Liviatan (1991) 'Optimal Accommodation by Strong Policymakers Under Incomplete Information', *Journal of Monetary Economics*, **27** (January), 99–127.

Cukierman, Alex, Miguel A. Kiguel and Leonardo Leiderman (1993) 'The Choice of Exchange Rate Bands: Balancing Credibility and Flexibility', *Working Paper*, **1993:1**, The Sackler Institute of Economic Studies, Tel-Aviv University.

Cukierman, Alex, Miguel A. Kiguel and Nissan Liviatan (1992) 'How Much to Commit to an Exchange Rate Rule? Balancing Credibility and Flexibility', *Revista de Analisis Economico*, **7**, 73–90.

Edin, Per-Anders and Anders Vredin (1991) 'Devaluation Risk in Target Zones: Evidence from the Nordic Countries', *Working Paper*, **1991:15**, Department of Economics, Uppsala University.

Flood, Robert P. and Peter Isard (1989) 'Monetary Policy Strategies', IMF, *Staff Papers*, **36** (September), 612–32.

Frenkel, Jacob A. and Morris Goldstein (1986) 'A Guide to Target Zones', *IMF Staff Papers*, **33**, 633–73.

Helpman, Elhanan and Leonardo Leiderman (1992) 'Israel's Exchange Rate Band', Study Series on Exchange Rate Policy, *Israeli International Institute for Applied Economic Policy Review* (August), Tel-Aviv.

Krugman, Paul and Marcus Miller (1991) (eds) *Exchange Rate Targets and Currency Bands*, Cambridge: Cambridge University Press.

(1992) 'Why Have a Target Zone?', Research Paper, **394** (August), Department of Economics, University of Warwick.

Lohmann, Susanne (1992) 'Optimal Commitment in Monetary Policy: Credibility Versus Flexibility', *American Economic Review*, **82** (March), 273–86.

Obstfeld, Maurice (1991) 'Destabilizing Effects of Exchange-Rate Escape Clauses', paper presented at the *Conference on Monetary Policy in Stage Two of EMU*, Milan (27–28 September).

Rose, Andrew K. and Lars E.O. Svensson (1991) 'Expected and Predicted Realignments: The FF/DM Exchange Rate During the EMS', Stockholm: Institute for International Economic Studies, *Seminar Paper*, **485**.

Svensson, Lars E.O. (1991) 'Assessing Target Zone Credibility: Mean Reversion and Devaluation Expectations in the EMS', Stockholm: Institute for International Economic Studies, *Seminar Paper*, **493**; (1993) *European Economic Review*, **37**.

(1992a) 'Recent Research on Exchange Rate Target Zones: An Interpretation', *Journal of Economic Perspectives*, **6** (Fall), 119–44.

(1992b) 'Monetary Independence and Optimal Intervention Policy in a Managed-Float Model of an Exchange Rate Target Zone', Institute for International Economic Studies, Stockholm University (April), unpublished paper.

Williamson, John (1985) *The Exchange Rate System*, Washington, DC: Institute for International Economics.

Williamson, John and Marcus Miller (1987) *Targets and Indicators: A Blueprint for the International Coordination of Economic Policy*, Washington, DC: Institute for International Economics.

Zahler, Robert M. (1992) 'Politica Monetaria en un Contexto de Apertura de la Cuenta de Capitales', *Boletin Mensual*, **771**, Banco Central de Chile (May).

Discussion

LARS E.O. SVENSSON

Most of the work about exchange rate target bands so far has been on positive issues (for instance, the dynamics of exchange rates, interest rates and interventions in exchange rate bands), and there is much less work on normative issues (for instance, what the optimal bandwidth is). Given that the understanding of how exchange rate bands function has improved considerably, it should now be appropriate to direct more of the work towards the normative issues. Chapter 6 by Cukierman, Kiguel and Leiderman (hereafter CKL) has the attractive property that it can be interpreted both as a positive theory of how a policymaker will determine the bandwidth for an exchange rate band and as a normative theory of how the bandwidth should be chosen given society's preferences. I therefore find the chapter a very welcome addition to the literature. It provides a nice application of a partial commitment idea to the choice of the bandwidth. Even though the basic setup is rather simple, the tradeoffs involved in the choice of bandwidth are complicated, and the authors do an admirable job in sorting out the comparative statics effects on the bandwidth of parameter changes. Specific results, however, require restrictions on the density function for the degree of misalignment. Under some restrictions the authors then show that a better reputation of the policymaker (the probability that the policymaker faces a cost when reneging) reduces the bandwidth and that a larger cost of reneging increases the bandwidth.

The model has the attractive feature that not only the bandwidth but also realignments are endogenous, and the endogenous expected rate of realignment is derived. The model predicts that the expected rate of realignment should be higher when the exchange rate is closer to the weak edge of the band. The authors test this prediction on data for a number of countries with exchange rate bands, and the empirical results are consistent with the prediction.

First I will use a convenient graph (Figure 6D.1) to illustrate the working of the authors' model. Then I will challenge the authors' view that the relevant tradeoff is best described as a tradeoff between flexibility and credibility. Finally I will comment upon the empirical test the authors' conduct and argue that it does not necessarily imply the same causal relation as in the model.

The policymaker's *ex post* utility function is

$$V(\pi - \pi^e, \pi, x) = x(\pi - \pi^e) - \pi^2/2, \tag{1}$$

where x, the degree of misalignment, is an exogenous i.i.d. stochastic variable with density function $f(x)$, π is the (domestic currency) depreciation chosen by the policymaker, and π^e is the (private sector's) expected (domestic currency) depreciation. Expectations are formed and the depreciation is chosen after the degree of misalignment is realised and observed. The private sector is uncertain about whether the policymaker is 'dependable' (that is, faces a fixed cost c when reneging) or 'weak' (that is, faces no cost when reneging). The private sector's subjective probability for a dependable government is given and denoted by a. In equilibrium the depreciation (the policy) and expected depreciation (the expected policy) can then *a priori* be considered functions of both x and a, $\pi(x,a)$ and $\pi^e(x,a)$. Whether the dependable policymaker reneges or not will also *a priori* depend on x and a. The *ex post* utility function for a dependable policymaker can then be written as a function of x and a according to

$$V(x,a) = x[\pi(x,a) - \pi^e(x,a)] - \pi(x,a)^2/2 - I(x,a)c, \tag{2}$$

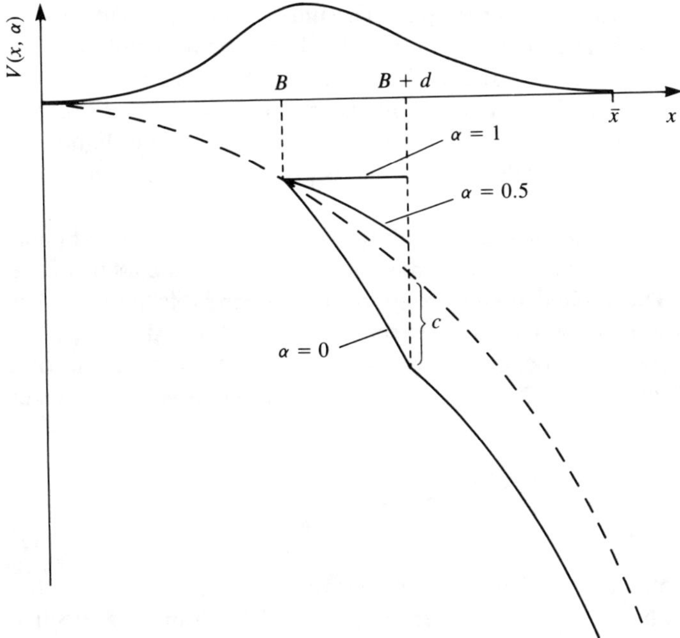

Figure 6D.1 ***Ex post*** **utility in the discretionary equilibrium**

where $I(x, a)$ denotes an indicator function that is unity when the dependable policymaker reneges and zero otherwise.

The *ex ante* utility function is

$$\mathrm{E}\,V(x,a) = \int V(x,a)\,f(x)dx. \tag{3}$$

First, we note that there is indeed a simple rules equilibrium in the model, namely zero depreciation, $\pi(x,a) \equiv 0$. Then expected depreciation is also zero, $\pi^e(x,a) \equiv 0$, and the *ex post* and *ex ante* utility is zero, $V(x,a) \equiv 0$ and $\mathrm{E}\,V(x,a) \equiv 0$. This is the first-best equilibrium in the model.

Second, if there is only a weak policymaker, and the private sector knows it ($a = 0$), there is a discretionary equilibrium with the depreciation and expected depreciation equal to the degree of misalignment, $\pi(x,0) \equiv \pi^e(x,0) \equiv x$. Then the *ex post* utility is

$$V(x,0) = x^2/2. \tag{4}$$

The *ex post* utility in the discretionary equilibrium is illustrated in Figure 6D.1. The degree of misalignment is plotted on the horizontal axis. The density function $f(x)$ is plotted along the vertical axis. Realisations of the degree of misalignment are for simplicity assumed to be nonnegative with an upper bound $\bar{x}$. The *ex post* utility in the discretionary equilibrium is also plotted along the vertical axis; it is given by the dashed downward-sloping concave curve. The *ex ante* utility is of course the integral over the *ex post* utility weighted with the density of the degree of misalignment. The *ex post* utility in the rules equilibrium is given by the horizontal axis itself.

Figure 6D.1 is useful for understanding the nature of the limited commitment equilibrium with an exchange rate band that is the focus of the CKL study. The limited commitment by the dependable policymaker consists of announcing a band between zero and B. As shown by the authors the dependable policymaker will then renege for realisations of x above $B + d$ where $d = \sqrt{2c}$. The policy for the dependable policymaker is then

$$\begin{aligned} \pi(x,a) &= x \quad \text{for } 0 \le x \le B \\ &= B \quad \text{for } B < x \le B + d \\ &= x \quad \text{for } B + d < x \le \bar{x}. \end{aligned} \tag{5}$$

The dependable policymaker chooses depreciation equal to B when the degree of misalignment falls between B and $B + d$, the 'range of effective commitment', otherwise he chooses depreciation equal to x.

The expected policy is then

$$\begin{aligned} \pi^e(x,a) = \pi(x,a) \qquad\qquad & \text{for } 0 \le x \le \bar{x} \\ + (1-a)[x - \pi(x,a)] \quad & \text{for } B < x \le B + d. \end{aligned} \tag{6}$$

That is, when the degree of misalignment falls in the range of effective commitment expectations include the possibility that the policymaker with probability $1 - a$ will be a weak policymaker and choose the depreciation equal to x instead of equal to B.

It follows that the *ex post* utility fulfils

$$\begin{aligned} V(x,a) = -x^2/2 \qquad\qquad & \text{for } 0 \le x \le \bar{x} \\ -(x^2 - B^2)/2 - (1-a)z(x-B) \quad & \text{for } B < x \le B + d \\ -c \qquad\qquad & \text{for } B + d < x \le \bar{x}. \end{aligned} \tag{7}$$

That is, the *ex post* utility coincides with that for the discretionary equilibrium for $x < B$ and it is c below that for the discretionary equilibrium for $x > B + d$. What it is in the region of effective commitment depends on the reputation of the policymaker, measured by a. The different possibilities are shown in Figure 6D.1. With perfect reputation

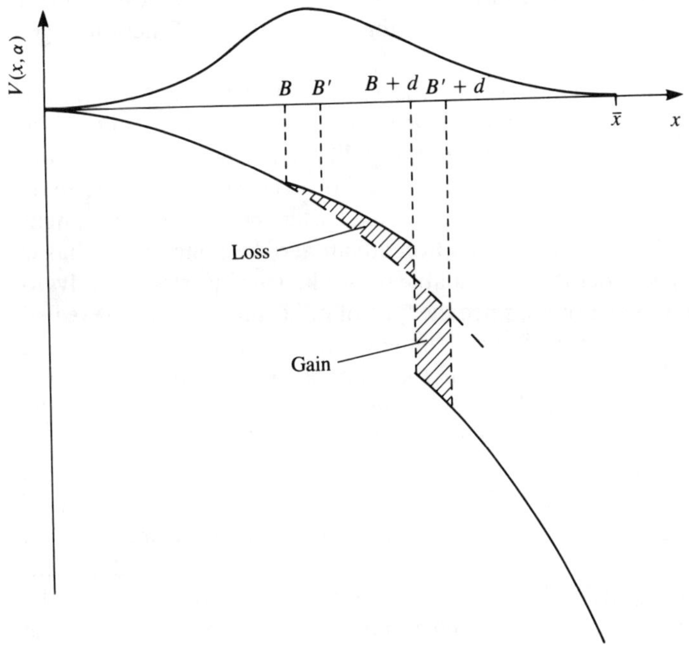

Figure 6D.2 The nature of the tradeoff in choosing the optimal bandwidth

($a = 1$) the *ex post* utility is constant and equal to $-B^2/2$. With perfect reputation the depreciation and expected depreciation coincide, so the first term on the right-hand side of (1) is zero and only the second term matters. With no reputation ($a = 0$) *ex post* utility is $-x^2/2 - (x - B)^2/2$ in the region of effective commitment. This is less than in the discretionary equilibrium. With no reputation, making a commitment only makes things worse. With intermediate reputation ($a = 0.5$) *ex post* utility is $-x^2/2 + B(x - B)/2$, which is better than the discretionary equilibrium but of course worse than with perfect reputation.

The nature of the tradeoff in choosing the optimal bandwidth is illustrated in Figure 6D.2, with intermediate reputation. Initially the bandwidth is B, and the *ex post* utility is given by the solid curve. Consider an increase of the bandwidth to B'. The new *ex post* utility is given by the dashed curve. The hatched areas show the gains and losses. These should be weighted with the density and integrated to get the net *ex ante* effect on *ex ante* utility of the change in bandwidth. The first-order condition for the optimal bandwidth is that the net *ex ante* effect on utility should be zero for marginal changes in the bandwidth. It is apparent from Figure

6D.1 and 6D.2 that this is a rather complicated tradeoff, and one realises why the authors have to impose conditions on the density function to get specific results.

Next, I would like to challenge the statement that the tradeoff the policymaker faces here is one between flexibility and credibility. The advantage of flexibility arises when the policymaker has an information advantage over the private sector. This is however hardly the case here, since private sector expectations are formed after the degree of misalignment is realised. The only information advantage the policymaker has is that he knows whether it is dependable or weak. This information advantage seems tenuous, though, since the type of policymaker will be revealed the first time the degree of misalignment falls in the region of effective commitment. I prefer to think of the tradeoff as involving, when the degree of misalignment falls in the range of effective commitment, the benefit (relative to the discretionary equilibrium) of low depreciation (the vertical distance between the horizontal line ($a = 1$) and the dashed curve in Figure 6D.1) and the cost of imperfect reputation (the vertical distance between the horizontal line ($a = 1$) and the curves corresponding to imperfect reputation ($a < 1$)) and, when the degree of misalignment exceeds the range of effective commitment, the cost of reneging (the vertical distance between the dashed and the solid curve to the right of the range of effective commitment).

Finally, let me comment on the empirical test in the chapter. Let s_t and $\bar{s}_t$ denote logs of the exchange rate and the central parity at time t, respectively, and let i_t and i_t^* denote (the logs of one plus) domestic and foreign currency interest rates of maturity $\tau > 0$, respectively. Under uncovered interest rate parity the interest rate differential equals the expected average rate of depreciation to maturity.

$$i_t - i_t^* = \mathrm{E}_t(s_{t+\tau} - s_t)/\tau. \tag{8}$$

This can be rewritten as

$$\mathrm{E}_t(\bar{s}_{t+\tau} - \bar{s}_t)/\tau = i_t - i_t^* - \mathrm{E}_t[(s_{t+\tau} - \bar{s}_{t+\tau}) - (s_t - \bar{s}_t)]/\tau, \tag{9}$$

which can be interpreted as stating that the expected rate of realignment ($\mathrm{E}\pi_R$ in CKL) equals the difference between the interest rate differential and the expected rate of depreciation within the band ($\mathrm{E}\pi_{NR}$ in CKL). The authors' method consists of regressing the difference between the interest rate differential and the *ex post* rate of depreciation within the band, $i_t - i_t^* - [(s_{t+\tau} - \bar{s}_{t+\tau}) - (s_t - \bar{s}_t)]/\tau$, on a constant and the maximum rate of depreciation within the band, $(\bar{s}_t - s_t)/\tau$. The model predicts that the coefficient on the maximum rate of depreciation within the band should be negative.

The method is similar to the so called drift-adjustment method to estimate expected rates of realignment, referred to in Svensson (1993b). In the latter the *ex post* rate of depreciation within the band, $[(s_{t+\tau} - \bar{s}_{t+\tau}) - (s_t - \bar{s}_t)]/\tau$, is regressed on variables in the current information set (the exchange rate within the band, interest rates, and possibly other variables). The fitted values of the regression, which are then estimates of the expected rate of depreciation within the band, are then subtracted from the interest rates, which gives estimates of the expected rates of realignment. The authors' test of their model would then involve regressing the estimated expected rates of realignment on a constant and the exchange rate within band, $s_t - \bar{s}_t$. The model then predicts that the coefficient on the exchange rate within the band should be positive.

Regressions of the *ex post* rate of depreciation within the band on variables in the current information set has revealed that interest rates sometimes help to predict the *ex post* rate of depreciation within the band (see for instance Svensson, 1993a). It might therefore be a good idea for the authors to include also interest rates, and possibly other variables, among their regressors. (Any effect of the domestic (foreign) interest rate on the *ex post* rate of depreciation would in the authors' regression show up as a coefficient different from unity (minus unity), since the interest rate differential in their case is part of the regressand.)

The empirical test of the authors shows that the expected rate of realignment indeed tends to be greater when the exchange rate is closer to the weak edge of the band. This is consistent with the authors' model. Let me end with a warning, though, namely that the correlation does not necessarily imply a causal relationship. In the authors' model it is true that the exchange rate causes the endogenous rate of realignment. In the model of Bertola and Svensson (1993), though, the expected rate of realignment is exogenous and the exchange rate endogenous, so the causality is reversed. Also in that model there may be a positive correlation between exchange rates and expected rates of realignment. The reason is that the exchange rate is determined in a forward-looking rational expectations equilibrium. An increase in the expected rate of realignment implies an increase in the expected rate of total depreciation, which immediately depreciates the currency and moves the exchange rate closer to the weak edge of the band. Without some identifying assumption the direction of the causality does not follow from the observation of a positive correlation between the exchange rate's position in the band and the expected rate of realignment.

REFERENCES

Bertola, Giuseppe and Lars E.O. Svensson (1993) 'Stochastic Devaluation Risk and the Empirical Fit of Target Zone Models', *Review of Economic Studies*, forthcoming.

Cukierman, Alex, Miguel A. Kiguel and Leonardo Leiderman (1993) 'Some Evidence on a Strategic Model of Exchange Rate Bands', Chapter 6 in this volume.

Svensson, Lars E.O. (1993a) 'Assessing Target Zone Credibility: Mean Reversion and Devaluation Expectations in the ERM 1973–1992', *European Economic Review*, **37**.

(1993b) 'An Interpretation of Recent Research on Exchange Rate Target Zones', Chapter 5 in this volume.

GIUSEPPE BERTOLA

I have some simple things to say on general issues facing research which, like that reported in Chapter 6, aims at motivating monetary policy rather than at simply describing its effects. My comments go on to discuss the relevance of such issues to work on exchange rate determination, and finally to interpret the empirical evidence of this chapter in light of recent theoretical work on so-called 'target zone' (TZ) models of exchange rate determination.

The authors take a well-travelled route assuming that output is demand-determined and that nominal prices are set before all uncertainty is resolved, leaving aside seigniorage, and taking for granted that nominal price stability is desirable *per se*. In this context, unconstrained monetary policy may well lead the economy to an inferior expectational equilibrium if the authorities' objectives differ from those which inform the public's price-setting decisions. In a Barro–Gordon (1983) 'discretionary' equilibrium, actual and expected inflation coincide at so high a level as to eliminate the authorities' incentives to exploit the *ex post* fixity of nominal prices. It is important to note that expectations are formed in a rather peculiar way in models of this type. The simplest such models feature no outside uncertainty, and no proper probability distribution on whose basis expectations may be formed: as is often the case in game-theoretic settings, events which have probability zero in equilibrium play a most important role in shaping both expectations and outcomes.

Dynamic uncertainty and unforeseen contingencies are very important in reality, of course, and monetary policy has a much more benign role when we account for the fact that nominal prices may be suboptimally rigid in the face of news. In theoretical models ranging from textbook Keynesian diagrams to Fischer–Taylor overlapping contract dynamics, 'discretionary' monetary policy works to both the public's and the authorities' advantage if the two share the same objective function, and the latter enjoy an informational advantage. When exogenous uncertainty and conflicting objectives coexist, a tension arises between flexibility (afforded by 'discretion') and anti-inflationary reputation (afforded by 'rules'). In even the most inflation-prone policy settings, a pure 'rules' equilibrium may not do as well as a regime which allows monetary flexibility in the face of dramatic (and verifiable) unforeseen contingencies.

Reality does feature odd mixtures of rules and discretion in nominal policies, and especially in exchange rate policies. Not only do the authorities typically 'commit' to a more or less wide range of possible values rather than to a unique nominal exchange rate, but such commitments are far from irrevocable. Can such complex institutional arrangements be rationalised in light of flexibility vs. reputation tradeoffs? A recent literature has focused on optimal contracts between the public and monetary authorities, showing how the tension between flexibility and reputation may be lessened or even eliminated by properly-specified contingent (on inflation) payment schedules for policymakers (see Walsh, 1992; Persson and Tabellini, 1992). Chapter 6 does not take this route. The authors take the structure of reputation-enforcing payments as exogenously given, and proceed to rationalise real-life arrangements in terms of the flexibility vs. reputation tradeoff sketched above.

As shown by Obstfeld (1991), realignments are not difficult to rationalise if the contract between the public and monetary authorities is (exogenously) taken to specify a lump-sum payment in the event of a realignment (see also the related work of De Kock and Grilli, 1993 on reputational equilibria of a seigniorage-based policy game). Under such 'escape clause' arrangements, the flexibility vs. reputation dilemma is addressed by a *real* exchange rate band of sorts: a commitment to fixed exchange rates (and no inflationary surprises) is reneged upon when *real* disturbances cause excessive misalignment of *ex post* price levels. A theoretical case of nominal exchange rate bands is much more difficult to make. Suppose the government is known (or suspected) to be weak in the face of inflationary temptations: then only the upper limit to depreciation or inflation should matter for the 'credibility' aspects of expectation formation; limits to nominal fluctuations in the opposite direction would have no such role in a one-shot policy game, or in the dynamic models of De Kock–Grilli and Obstfeld. As symmetric considerations would apply if the government were liable to implement deflationary surprises instead, it would appear impossible to derive an interior optimal *nominal* bandwidth: in Cukierman, Kiguel and Leiderman's work, however, the band (and the penalty for abandoning it) is declared before the realisation of a random variable which determines whether the government will *ex post* be prone to inflationary or deflationary temptations. Inasmuch as neither the authorities nor the public know whether the former will *ex post* want to climb up or down the Phillips curve, both margins of the band are relevant to expectation formation, so the width of the band can be endogenous to the problem's parameters. As in other work on 'escape clauses', declaring a band implies some expected losses for the policymaker (who knows that the announcement may *ex post* tie his hands or inflict the contractual lump-sum payment), but some expected gains as well (since expectation formation will be less adverse once x is realised). An interior optimal bandwidth may be formally derived under reasonable simplifying assumptions.

This formalisation of the problem quite neatly makes it possible to address real-life policy arrangements. The model is quite stylised, however, and in my view some important aspects deserve to be explored more fully in future work. First, I would like to see a more transparent discussion of the possible determinants of the exogenous shifts (indexed by 'x') in the authorities' *ex post* policy bias. The core of the Barro–Gordon 'credibility' problem lies in discrepancies between the authorities' and the public's objectives, and the model of Chapter 6 does not say much as to which of the two are supposed to (possibly) change between the time when the band is announced and the time when monetary policy is implemented. Second, the model works through imperfect commitment effects: since an (exogenous) finite penalty is imposed on realignment, the policymaker has only imperfect credibility when announcing exchange rate policy, and the full 'rules' equilibrium is unattainable. Prices are set after the realisation of all exogenous uncertainty: expectations are of the game-theoretic type at this stage, and the monetary authorities have no informational advantage. Recent work on optimal monetary policy contracts suggests that other types of ambiguous commitment, such as contingent crawling pegs, may yield better outcomes. Commitments to fixed nominal 'bands' are realistic, however, and may be more easily verifiable *ex post*.

Finally, I would like to comment briefly on the empirical portions of the paper, and on its relationship to the literature initiated by Krugman (1991). Some features of reality are exogenous to every tractable model, of course, and conditioning on such unmodelled features affords greater realism with respect to those aspects of reality which are modelled explicitly. TZ models choose to take the (probability distribution of) policy as given, and to analyse the theoretical and empirical effects of realistic policies rather than to rationalise their motivations. In TZ models, expectations have a very different role from that assumed in Chapter 6. The exchange rate is realistically modelled as a forward-looking asset price, hence its value *today* depends on expectations of future policy. In Chapter 6, conversely, economic interactions are essentially static, with one exception: prices are *ex post* fixed and backward-looking, and today's realisations of economic variables and policy depend on yesterday's expectations of today's events.

The timing of intertemporal linkages in this model is so different from that of TZ models of exchange rate dynamics that theoretical results are not easy to compare. As acknowledged by the authors, however, the empirical evidence of this chapter is not inconsistent with what would be predicted by the forward-looking models I am more familiar with. The authors find that devaluations are more likely to occur when the exchange rate is already depreciated 'within the band', and interpret this empirical result from the perspective of their backward-looking model of exchange rate policy. The finding can be easily interpreted from the forward-looking perspective of TZ models, where a higher likelihood (or larger expected size) of devaluation tends to depreciate the exchange rate (see, e.g., Bertola and Svensson, 1993, or Bertola and Caballero, 1992). It would indeed be hard to concoct a forward-looking model where devaluations are more likely at times when the exchange rate is strong within its fluctuation band: in terms of the chapter's equation (15), where $a < 1$, it would have to be the case that changes in fundamentals are strongly and negatively correlated to that component of interest rate differentials which is driven by realignment expectations. Reassuringly, neither the data nor this paper's nice theoretical arguments suggest that strenuous efforts need to be undertaken in that direction.

REFERENCES

Barro, Robert J. and David B. Gordon (1983) 'A Positive Theory of Monetary Policy in a Natural Rate Model', *Journal of Political Economy*, **91,** 589–610.

Bertola, Giuseppe and Ricardo Caballero (1992) 'Target Zones and Realignments', *American Economic Review*, **82** (June), 520–36.

Bertola, Giuseppe and Lars E.O. Svensson (1993) 'Stochastic Devaluation Risk and the Empirical Fit of Target Zone Models', *Review of Economic Studies*, forthcoming.

De Kock, Gabriel and Vittorio Grilli (1993) 'Endogenous Exchange Rate Regime Switches', *The Economic Journal*, forthcoming.

Krugman, Paul (1991) 'Target Zones and Exchange Rate Dynamics', *Quarterly Journal of Economics*, **106** (August), 669–82.

Obstfeld, M. (1991) 'Destabilizing effects of exchange-rate escape clauses', paper presented at the *Conference on Monetary Policy in Stage Two of EMU*, Milan (27–28 September).

Persson, T. and G. Tabellini (1992) 'Designing institutions for monetary stability', paper presented at Carnegie–Rochester Conference on Public Policy.

Walsh, C. (1992) 'Optimal contracts for central bankers', *Working Paper*, University of California, Santa Cruz.

7 Exchange rate volatility, uncertainty, and investment: an empirical investigation

JOHN HUIZINGA

1 Introduction

The move to flexible exchange rates nearly twenty years ago brought with it an explosion in the volatility of nominal exchange rate changes. Combined with the fact that these changes have been largely unpredictable, the current environment is one with substantial exchange rate uncertainty. This chapter provides empirical evidence which hopefully will be useful in determining whether this uncertainty has had an economically important impact on the investment and productivity performance of firms open to international competition.

The motivation for the chapter comes from two sources. The first is the observation that, given that the volatility of the exchange rate far exceeds the volatility of prices in the goods and labour markets, nominal exchange rate uncertainty is likely to be correlated with uncertainty about important real economic variables. The second is the recent theoretical literature on investment which highlights the potentially negative impact of uncertainty on those capital expenditures which are postponable and entail a substantial fixed cost. This literature, nicely summarised by Pindyck (1991), emphasises the relevance of option pricing theory for investment.

Section 2 provides a more detailed explanation of this motivation. The real economic variables whose uncertainty will be linked with investment are identified, and the potential connection between their uncertainty and nominal exchange rate volatility discussed. A numerical example is considered to illustrate that the negative impact of uncertainty on investment may be sufficiently large to be empirically detectable and that the availability of standard hedging instruments in the financial markets does not eliminate this impact.

Section 3 provides empirical evidence on the connection between exchange rate volatility and uncertainty. A comparison of uncertainty during the fixed-rate period with uncertainty during the flexible-rate period is made for both relative price and quantity variables in a sample of several hundred four-digit 1972 SIC code manufacturing industries in the United States. Noticeable increases in uncertainty are shown to have accompanied the move to flexible exchange rates for all variables. Furthermore, the disparity of changes in uncertainty across industries suggests that exchange rate volatility may have played an important causal role in increasing this uncertainty.

Section 3 also provides empirical evidence on how the measured changes in uncertainty are related to changes in the amount of investment, changes in the composition of the capital stock, and changes in the growth rate of productivity. The results which best support the conclusion that the ideas discussed in this chapter are empirically important are that higher uncertainty about real output price is negatively correlated with the investment rate and productivity growth, and positively correlated with equipment's share in the capital stock. In contrast, however, higher uncertainty about the real price of materials inputs is shown to be positively correlated with the investment rate, but positively correlated with productivity growth and negatively correlated with equipment's share in the capital stock.

Section 4 contains brief summary remarks and conclusions.

2 Background

2.1 Uncertainty and capital expenditures

The theoretical literature on the determinants of investment has demonstrated that increased uncertainty may increase, decrease, or have no effect on capital expenditures, depending on the particular type of uncertainty being considered and the specific formulation of the model being used.[1] Recently, however, there has been increasing attention given to the negative impact that uncertainty about the net present value of a capital expenditure can have on a firm's willingness to undertake an expenditure which is postponable and entails large fixed costs. In this subsection, a simple example is discussed in order to illustrate (1) that the potential effects of this uncertainty on investment may be sufficiently large to be empirically detectable, (2) how this uncertainty may be linked to uncertainty about observable economic variables, and (3) that the availability of standard hedging instruments in the financial markets does not eliminate this impact.

Suppose a firm is contemplating making a capital expenditure of $400,000 to update and modernise its production facility.[2] Operating the

Table 7.1. *Uncertainty and the hesitancy to invest*

Basic facts	
	$
Initial capital expenditure	400,000
Annual ongoing operating expense	100,000
Discount rate	2.5%
Invest today	
	$
Net present value with revenue certainty ($120,000, known for sure)	400,000
Net present value with revenue uncertainty ($120,000 expected, ± 10% either $132,000 or $108,000, resolved in 1 year)	400,000
Net present value with revenue uncertainty ($122,000 expected, ± 10% either $134,200 or $109,800, resolved in 1 year)	480,000
Wait for one year to decide	
	$
Net present value with revenue certainty ($120,000, known for sure)	390,244
Net present value with revenue uncertainty ($120,000 expected, ± 10% either $132,000 or $108,000, resolved in 1 year)	429,268
Net present value with revenue uncertainty ($122,000 expected, ± 10% either $134,200 or $109,800, resolved in 1 year)	472,195

new, improved facility will add $100,000 to the annual cost of operation and add a projected $120,000 of additional revenue. These costs and revenues will begin in one year, will continue into the foreseeable future, and will occur only if the project is undertaken. this project can be undertaken now or later. The firm uses a discount rate of 2.5%.

Should the firm make the capital expenditures? The relevant details are listed in Table 7.1. If the increased future revenues can be predicted with perfect certainty, the project should be undertaken. Any revenue above the level of $110,000 would yield a positive net present value and justify the investment. With a known additional revenue of $120,000, the present discounted value of the cost is $4,400,000 while the present discounted value of the revenue is $4,800,000, so that making the capital expenditure increases the value of the firm by $400,000.

Suppose, however, that revenues are uncertain.[3] Specifically, suppose that with probability 0.5 additional annual revenues will be $132,000 and with probability 0.5 additional annual revenues will be $108,000. This makes expected additional revenues equal to $120,000, the same as in the case of revenue certainty. To make this example as simple as possible, suppose also that it is known that all uncertainty will be resolved after one year, with revenues at that time to be fixed at one of these two levels.

In this case, the expected net present value of the capital expenditure if made today is still $400,000, but the investment should not be undertaken! The reason is that even though it is profitable to invest today, it is more profitable to wait a year and then make a decision. By assumption, the choice that faces the firm is not, as economists often suggest, invest now or never invest. The option of delay is a possibility.

Delay is ill advised, of course, when there is certainty about future revenues. There is no incentive to delay undertaking a project with a certain positive net present value. Delaying this investment will reduce the net present value of the project to $400,000/1.025 = $390,244.

The wait and delay strategy can become the optimal one when there is uncertainty, however. Consider the two possible outcomes. If one year from now the additional annual revenues become known to be $108,000, then the capital expenditures will not be undertaken. At this point there is no uncertainty and revenue is not above the required revenue level of $110,000. The net revenue to the firm in this case is zero. In contrast, if one year from now the additional annual revenues become known to be $132,000, then the expenditures will be made. There will be a one-year delay in the update and modernisation and an additional one-year delay in the added revenues. The net revenue to the firm of this possibility is $880,000/1.025 = $858,536. Weighing each possible outcome by its probability of 0.5 give an expected net present value of $429,268 to the firm with the optimal wait and see strategy, which exceeds by $29,268 the net present value of starting the project today.

The important lesson here is that increased uncertainty can cause a prudent firm to delay and not take a positive expected net present value project. What is the reason for this delay? Primarily, that a firm which makes a decision to undertake a postponable project with a fixed, irreversible cost gives up the option of waiting to obtain relevant new information and using that information to its advantage. As a result, firms should undertake projects only if the perceived profit, measured as the project's expected net present value, is sufficiently large that it compensates the firm for giving up this option. Furthermore, since it is well known from financial theory that options are worth more when there is increased uncertainty, the effect of increased uncertainty is to raise the level of perceived profit necessary to undertake a project.

This interpretation of the current example suggests that if the expected net revenues were high enough, the uncertainty would fail to matter and delay would be a mistake. This is correct. Suppose that instead of projected revenues being $132,000 with probability 0.5 and $108,000 with probability 0.5 (which is expected revenues of $120,000 ± 10%) projected revenues were $134,200 with probability 0.5 and $109,800 with probability 0.5 (which is expected revenues of $122,000 ± 10%). In this case the incentive to wait is eliminated. Investing now yields an expected net present vaue of $480,000 while the optimal delay and decide in one year strategy yields $472,195. Given the higher expected revenues, the cost of delay outweighs the value of the additional information that will arrive. Note this is true even though all uncertainty will be resolved in one year and it is possible that the project will turn out *ex post* to be a mistake. In the current example there is a fifty-fifty chance that the revenues will be less than $110,000 and hence that the firm will, *ex post*, regret having made the expenditures.

Although this example is overly simplistic as a description of the type of uncertainty which firms face, it is informative.[4] It illustrates that one way to measure the impact of increased uncertainty is to determine the additional expected revenues necessary to offset the increased uncertainty and leave a firm willing to invest. It also suggests that uncertainty might exert a significant influence on investment. In the current example, revenues above $110,000 would be sufficient to induce a firm to invest when there is no uncertainty. With revenues which can rise or fall 10%, expected revenues need to be above $121,579 to induce a firm to invest.[5] This is an increase of over 10% in expected revenues, sufficiently large to be economically important.

The current example also makes clear that the presence of actuarial fair forward markets does not eliminate the negative impact of increased uncertainty on investment decisions. For the case where the firm faces net revenues of $120,000 ± 10%, it would not be desirable to lock in a fixed net revenue of $120,000. This gives a net present value of $400,000, which is less than the $429,268 available with the wait and see strategy. Intuitively, the ability to buy and/or sell a forward contract does not change the fact that the firm gives up its option when it decides to invest, and must be sufficiently compensated for doing so.

The final benefit of the current example is to focus attention on several measurable sources of uncertainty that might be associated with uncertainty about the real net present value of a capital expenditure. The uncertainty about real revenues highlighted in the example can be decomposed into uncertainty about the real price of output (i.e., product price deflated by the price of consumption) and uncertainty about the quantity of output which can be sold at that real price (i.e., the size of the market for the output produced by the capital expenditure). In addition, since a firm is fundamentally interested in the real net revenues which a capital expenditure generates, uncertainty about the real cost of alternative factors of production should also be relevant. Thus, uncertainty about the real wage and real price of materials inputs may be measurable sources of uncertainty associated with uncertainty about the real net present value of a capital expenditure.

2.2 Exchange rate volatility and uncertainty

In this subsection the potential link between nominal exchange rate volatility and uncertainty about the real net present value of a capital expenditure is discussed. It is argued that both domestic firms which compete in the domestic market with foreign producers, import-competing firms, and domestic firms which compete in foreign markets with foreign producers, export-competing firms, will face a more uncertain real net present value for capital expenditures when the nominal exchange rate is more volatile.

Consider a US firm competing with a Japanese firm in the US market, where prices are set in US dollars. I assume that nominal variable costs are fixed in dollar terms for the US firm and fixed in yen terms for the Japanese firm. An appreciation of the US dollar vis-à-vis the Japanese yen will lower the Japanese firm's dollar costs, giving rise to the three possibilities listed in the top panel of Table 7.2. First, the Japanese firm can leave prices unchanged and take higher profits. In this case, no response by the US firm would appear warranted and there would be no effect on the US firm. The second possibility is for the Japanese firm to at least partially pass these lower dollar costs on in terms of lower dollar prices and have the US firm respond by matching the price decrease. In this case, real variable costs for the US firm will rise (nominal variable costs being fixed in dollar terms) and real output price fall (nontraded goods firms do not have this price pressure). The third possibility is for the Japanese firm to at least partially pass these lower dollar costs on in terms of lower dollar prices and have the US firm not match the price decrease. In this case, the US firm should face a drop in demand due to a shift in its relevant price.

Given these three possibilities, and the uncertainty that may surround which possibility will be relevant for any particular exchange rate change, uncertainty about where the exchange rate will go is translated into

Table 7.2. *Potential effects of domestic currency appreciation*

Foreign firm action	Domestic firm action	Outcome for domestic firm
Import-competing firms		
None	None	No effect
Lower price	Match lower price	Higher real wage Lower real price
Lower price	Do not match lower price	Lose market share Lower demand
Export-competing firms		
Foreign firm action	Domestic firm action	Outcome for domestic firm
Fully raise price	Fully raise price	No effect
Fully raise price	Partially raise price	Lose market share Lower demand
Partially raise price		Higher real wage Lower real price

uncertainty about a firm's real output price, real variable costs, and/or product demand. These are the types of uncertainty described in subsection 2.1 as being related to uncertainty about the net present value of capital expenditures.

A similar situation arises for US firms competing with German firms in the German market, where prices are set in marks. An appreciation of the US dollar vis-à-vis the German mark will raise the US firm's costs measured in marks and put the US firm at a cost disadvantage, giving rise to three possibilities. First, the US firm could raise the mark price by the amount of the appreciation and have the German firm respond by matching the price increase. In this case, there is no effect on the US firm. A second possibility is for the US firm to raise the mark price by the amount of the appreciation and have the German firm respond by not matching the price increase. In this case, the US firm should face a drop in demand due to a shift in its relative price. The third possibility is for the US firm to not raise the mark price by the amount of the appreciation. In this case, real variable costs for the US firm will rise and real output price fall.

Just as with the case for import-competing firms, exchange rate uncertainty gets translated into uncertainty about a firm's real output price, real variable costs, and/or product demand, and can be expected to

Table 7.3. *Key to variables used in the empirical analysis*

Economic variables	
VCA	Variable cost index which treats real materials prices and the real wage of all employees as variable costs
VCP	Variable cost index which treats real materials prices and the real wage of production workers as variable costs
RWA	Log of the real wage of all employees (in terms of product price)
RWP	Log of the real wage of production workers (in terms of product price)
RMP	Log of the real materials prices (in terms of product price)
ROP	Log of the output price (in terms of the consumer price index)
RS	Log of real shipments
IPR	Import penetration ratio, imports divided by the sum of imports and domestic shipments
ESR	Export sales ratio, exports divided by total shipments
IRAT	Investment rate, ratio of real investment to the capital stock
EQSHR	Share of equipment (as opposed to plant) in the capital stock
VAPE	Value added per employee
VAPH	Value added per production worker hour
Time-series moments	
CSD	Conditional standard deviation, formed as the standard deviation of the residuals in a second-order, univariate, autoregression with a linear time trend
MN	Unconditional mean
TG	Trend growth rate, formed as the coefficient on the linear time trend in a second-order, univariate, autoregression with a linear time trend
Time period	
FX	The period of fixed exchange rates, 1958–72
FL	The period of floating exchange rates, 1973–86
CH	The change in the moment from the fixed to the flexible rate period

increase the uncertainty about the net present value of capital expenditures.

3 Empirical results

3.1 Data

Section 2 described why there might be a link between nominal exchange rate volatility, uncertainty about the real net value of a capital expenditure and the amount of capital expenditures undertaken. Uncertainty about real variable costs, real output prices, and output demand were identified as types of measurable uncertainty that could be important indicators of uncertainty about the real net present value of capital expenditures.

In order to investigate these issues, annual data for the period 1958 to 1986 was obtained for several hundred, four-digit 1972 SIC code, US manufacturing industries.[6] Data was available on produce price, wages, employment, price of materials inputs, shipments, imports, exports, investment, and the capital stock. The variables to be used in the empirical analysis are described in Table 7.3.

Two measures of the real price of variable factors of production were constructed, one which treats all labour as a variable factor of production and one which treats only production workers as a variable factor. *VCA* is a weighted average of the log of the real price of materials inputs (*RMP*) and the log of real compensation per employee (*RWA*), with the time-varying weights determined by the ratio of employee compensation to the sum of employee compensation and the cost of materials inputs. *VCP* is a weighted average of the log of the real price of materials inputs (*RMP*) and the log of the real wage per hour for production workers (*RWP*), with the time-varying weights determined by the ratio of production worker compensation to the sum of production worker compensation and the cost of materials inputs. In order to allow uncertainty about the different components of the variable cost to both respond to exchange rate volatility differently and influence investment differently, the component terms *RWA*, *RWP*, and *RMP* are also used separately.

Real output price is measured by *ROP*, the log of the ratio of product price to the consumer price index.

Three variables are used to capture demand effects. *RS* is the log of real shipments. *IPR* is the import penetration ratio, the fraction of domestic sales filled by imported goods. *ESR* is the export sales ratio, the fraction of domestic production which is exported.

Investment performance is measured by *IRAT*, the ratio of gross investment to the capital stock and *EQSHR*, the share of the capital stock which is equipment (as opposed to plant). Productivity is measured by *VAPE* and *VAPH*, value added per employee and value added per production worker hour.

For each of these economic variables, time-series moments are constructed over different time periods. Uncertainty is measured as the conditional standard deviation (denoted *CSD*) and is formed as the sample standard deviation of the residuals in a second-order, univariate, autoregression with a linear time trend. With several hundred industries to analyse, a simple, standardised, easily implemented, forecasting equation seemed necessary.[7] Average performance is measured as the unconditional mean (denoted *MN*) and is formed as the sample mean. Trend growth rates (denoted *TG*) are formed as the estimated coefficient on a linear time trend in a second-order, univariate, autoregression.

Two time periods are utilised for computing the time-series moments. The fixed exchange rate period (denoted *FX*) is 1958–72. The floating rate period (denoted *FL*) is 1973–86. *CH* indicates the change in a given moment from the fixed-rate to the flexible-rate period.

3.2 Exchange rate volatility and uncertainty

To see if higher nominal exchange rate volatility has an impact on the type of uncertainty which may affect investment it is useful to identify periods of high and low nominal exchange rate volatility and determine if there is a significant difference in uncertainty across the two periods. This is done in Table 7.4 for nine variables using the period of fixed and flexible exchange rates.

Beginning with *VCA*, the variable cost index which includes all labour, it can be seen that in the fixed exchange rate period the mean value of uncertainty in the cross-section of industries was 3.78%, with a low value 0.97% in one industry and a high value of 13.49% in another. After the move to flexible exchange rates the mean value of uncertainty rose to 4.49%. For those industries where uncertainty can be measured in both time periods, the mean increase in uncertainty was 0.73% percentage points. The increase in uncertainty about this measure of real variable costs is thus just under 20% (0.73/3.78 = 0.19) following the move to flexible exchange rates.

There are other ways to measure the change in uncertainty, of course. Table 7.4 also reports information about the median amount of uncertainty in the cross-section of industries. The benefit of using the median is that it will be less sensitive to the potential problem of having the experience of one industry derive the results. For *VCA*, this potential problem is not apparent. Its median uncertainty rose from 3.27% to 3.72% following the move to flexible exchange rates, an increase of 0.45 percentage points, which is slightly less than a 15% increase.

A third way of measuring the change in uncertainty is the percentage of industries whose uncertainty increased. For *VCA* this was 61.0%. A value so close to 50% clearly indicates the presence of other factors affecting the uncertainty of *VCA*, and raises the obvious question of whether the increase in uncertainty across periods is due to increased nominal exchange rate volatility or is due to some other difference between the periods 1958–72 and 1973–86. Evidence related to this question will be presented below.

A comparison of the results in Table 7.4 for *VCP* and *VCA* indicate that

Table 7.4. *Distribution of measures of uncertainty*

Variable	Mean	Std dev.	% > 0	Low	Q1	Med	Q3	High
VCA_CSD_FX	3.78	2.16		0.97	2.34	3.27	4.47	13.49
VCA_CSD_FL	4.49	2.98		1.05	2.55	3.72	5.35	21.06
VCA_CSD_CH	0.73	2.88	61.0	− 9.88	− 0.57	0.45	1.68	16.71
VCP_CSD_FX	3.16	1.61		0.96	2.00	2.82	3.80	13.15
VCP_CSD_FL	4.10	2.85		0.87	2.32	3.41	4.78	22.49
VCP_CSD_CH	0.98	2.56	66.2	− 5.13	− 0.36	0.52	1.74	18.32
RWA_CSD_FX	3.78	1.88		1.02	2.49	3.36	4.48	18.73
RWA_CSD_FL	5.31	3.40		1.40	3.27	4.48	6.08	25.35
RWA_CSD_CH	1.47	3.22	72.3	− 15.91	− 0.12	1.12	2.60	20.03
RWP_CSD_FX	3.82	1.84		0.79	2.39	3.47	4.61	13.17
RWP_CSD_FL	5.57	3.76		0.95	3.29	4.58	6.46	33.18
RWP_CSD_CH	1.74	3.40	73.6	− 8.67	− 0.11	1.22	2.90	25.01
RMP_CSD_FX	2.10	1.36		0.40	1.18	1.71	2.57	11.55
RMP_CSD_FL	3.20	2.49		0.47	1.73	2.47	3.64	20.62
RMP_CSD_CH	1.08	2.26	73.4	− 4.56	− 0.01	0.67	1.59	17.85
ROP_CSD_FX	2.23	1.73		0.31	1.18	1.71	2.60	12.58
ROP_CSD_FL	3.39	2.95		0.61	1.68	2.34	4.03	22.94
ROP_CSD_CH	1.21	2.37	74.4	− 4.37	− 0.02	0.64	1.87	17.10
RS_CSD_FX	8.34	4.71		1.67	5.14	7.25	9.84	37.98
RS_CSD_FL	9.38	4.92		1.61	6.14	8.51	11.25	43.91
RS_CSD_CH	1.01	5.78	61.6	− 25.70	− 1.47	0.93	5.78	10.13
IPR_CSD_FX	0.73	1.00		0.00	0.17	0.39	0.89	8.82
IPR_CSD_FL	1.50	1.88		0.01	0.42	1.00	1.89	16.19
IPR_CSD_CH	0.70	1.47	85.8	− 3.70	0.07	0.40	0.90	14.08
ESR_CSD_FX	0.93	1.39		0.01	0.18	0.45	1.10	9.96
ESR_CSD_FL	1.52	1.68		0.01	0.50	1.03	1.96	14.62
ESR_CSD_CH	0.59	1.24	83.6	− 5.93	− 0.10	0.40	0.94	10.26

The columns on this page report the mean, standard deviation, percentage of observations which are positive, low value, first quartile, median, third quartile, and high value for variables in a cross-section of US manufacturing industries. Industries are disaggregated to their 1972 four-digit SIC code. Each variable name has the form *A_B_C* where *A* signifies the economic variable, *B* signifies the time-series moment of the variable, and *C* signifies either the time period over which the moment was estimated or the change in the time-series moment across time periods. The values for *A*, *B*, and *C* are given in Table 7.3.

VCP shows an even larger increase in uncertainty than does *VCA*. Nearly two-thirds (65.2%) of the industries experienced more uncertainty in *VCP* in the floating-rate than in the fixed-rate period. The mean amount of uncertainty rose from 3.16% to 4.10%. The mean increase of 0.98 percentage points was an increase of over 30%. The median increase of 0.52 percentage points is just under 20% of the median uncertainty in the fixed-rate period.

The difference between the results for *VCA* and *VCP* is mirrored, not surprisingly, by the difference between the results for *RWA* and *RWP*. Uncertainty about the real hourly wage of production workers rose more than uncertainty about the real compensation per employee in both absolute and relative terms. It is not the difference in the results between *RWA* and *RWP*, but rather their similarity, that is most important for the analysis of this chapter, however. There was a widespread and dramatic increase in uncertainty for both measures of real labour cost with the move to flexible exchange rates.

Evidence presented for *RMP* and *ROP* shows that uncertainty about the real price of materials inputs and the real output price also showed widespread and significant increases when nominal exchange rate volatility increased. The magnitude of the changes is slightly larger than, but roughly in line with, the changes recorded for uncertainty about real labour costs. The mean increase in uncertainty for both *RMP* and *ROP* was over 50% of the mean level in the fixed-rate period.

Evidence presented for *RS* shows that uncertainty about the quantity of output also rose with increased nominal exchange rate volatility, but that the rise was substantially smaller than was evident for uncertainty about relative prices. The mean (median) increase in uncertainty was 1.01 (0.93) percentage points, which is 12 (13) % of the mean (median) level in the fixed-rate period. Slightly over 60% of the industries experienced an increase in output uncertainty.

Turning to uncertainty about import and export penetration, over 85% of the industries experienced an increase in uncertainty about *IPR* and over 80% experienced an increase in uncertainty about *ESR* after the switch to flexible exchange rates. These increases were substantial in relative terms, with the median level of uncertainty more than doubling in both cases.

The evidence presented in Table 7.4 is certainly consistent with the proposition that higher nominal exchange rate volatility increases uncertainty about important relative prices and quantities. However, it may be that factors other than nominal exchange rate volatility also changed from the fixed- to the flexible-rate periods and that these other factors are the ones responsible for the documented increase in uncertainty.

In order to address this possibility, the distribution of the computed changes in uncertainty was calculated conditional on an industry's exposure to international competition. This exposure is calculated two ways, the mean value during the floating-rate period of an industry's import penetration ratio and the mean value during the floating-rate period of its export sales ratio. If increased nominal exchange rate volatility is the relevant factor behind the increased uncertainty, the observed increases in uncertainty should be larger for industries with larger import penetration and export sales ratios.

Table 7.5 reports the results for conditioning on the import penetration ratio. Three categories of the conditioning variable are considered; missing value, greater than the cross-sectional mean, and less than or equal to the cross-sectional mean. The results support the proposition that changes in nominal exchange rate volatility are an important contributing factor in explaining the observed increases in uncertainty.

For *VCA* the average increase in uncertainty is over three times as large for industries with import penetration ratios above the mean as for industries with import penetration levels below the mean; 1.41 vs. 0.44 for the mean increase in uncertainty and 0.86 vs. 0.27 for the median increase. Similar results are reported for *VCP*. The results are slightly weaker for individual components of the variable cost indices, though for *RWP* the average increase in uncertainty is still over $2\frac{1}{2}$ times as large for the industries with the higher import penetration ratios. For uncertainty about relative output price and shipments, the average increase is about 50% larger for the industries with the higher import penetration ratios.

Table 7.6 reports results for conditioning on the export sales ratio. For the increases in uncertainty about the relative prices of inputs, the results are weaker than those in Table 7.5, while for increases in uncertainty about shipments and the relative price of output the results are virtually the same. Table 7.6 thus provides additional support for identifying nominal exchange rate volatility as an important source for creating uncertainty.

3.3 Uncertainty, investment, and productivity growth

Subsection 3.2 presented evidence that the move to a system of more highly volatile nominal exchange rate changes was accompanied by a significant increase in uncertainty about many variables which may be associated with uncertainty about the net present value of capital expenditures. The focus was on the average increase, on the overall behaviour of the manufacturing sector. Attention is now given to the wide disparity across industries of the changes in uncertainty. The results in Table 7.4

Table 7.5. *Distribution of changes in uncertainty conditional on import penetration ratio*

Uncertainty variable	Conditioning variable	Condition	Mean	Med
VCA_CSD_CH	*IPR*	Missing	0.70	0.50
VCA_CSD_CH	*IPR*	> *IPR_MN_FL*	0.44	0.27
VCA_CSD_CH	*IPR*	≤ *IPR_MN_FL*	1.41	0.86
VCP_CSD_CH	*IPR*	Missing	0.89	0.35
VCP_CSD_CH	*IPR*	> *IPR_MN_FL*	0.67	0.43
VCP_CSD_CH	*IPR*	≤ *IPR_MN_FL*	1.74	1.06
RWA_CSD_CH	*IPR*	Missing	1.53	1.11
RWA_CSD_CH	*IPR*	> *IPR_MN_FL*	1.23	1.11
RWA_CSD_CH	*IPR*	≤ *IPR_MN_FL*	1.85	1.15
RWP_CSD_CH	*IPR*	Missing	1.80	1.13
RWP_CSD_CH	*IPR*	> *IPR_MN_FL*	1.14	0.85
RWP_CSD_CH	*IPR*	≤ *IPR_MN_FL*	2.80	2.04
RMP_CSD_CH	*IPR*	Missing	1.06	0.71
RMP_CSD_CH	*IPR*	> *IPR_MN_FL*	0.97	0.53
RMP_CSD_CH	*IPR*	≤ *IPR_MN_FL*	1.35	0.66
ROP_CSD_CH	*IPR*	Missing	1.37	0.74
ROP_CSD_CH	*IPR*	> *IPR_MN_FL*	0.97	0.50
ROP_CSD_CH	*IPR*	≤ *IPR_MN_FL*	1.45	0.97
RS_CSD_CH	*IPR*	Missing	0.70	0.56
RS_CSD_CH	*IPR*	> *IPR_MN_FL*	1.01	1.20
RS_CSD_CH	*IPR*	≤ *IPR_MN_FL*	1.52	1.68
IPR_CSD_CH	*IPR*	Missing	n.a	n.a.
IPR_CSD_CH	*IPR*	> *IPR_MN_FL*	0.41	0.22
IPR_CSD_CH	*IPR*	≤ *IPR_MN_FL*	1.31	0.90

The columns on this page report the mean and median for variables in a cross-section of US manufacturing industries, conditional on whether an industry's value of *IPR* is missing, is above the cross-sectional mean for *IPR*, or is less than or equal to the cross-sectional mean for *IPR*. Industries are disaggregated to their 1972 four-digit SIC code. Each variable name has the form *A_B_C* where *A* signifies the economic variable, *B* signifies the time-series moment of the variable, and *C* signifies either the time period over which the moment was estimated or the change in the time-series moment across time periods. The values for *A*, *B*, and *C* are given in Table 7.3.

Table 7.6. *Distribution of changes in uncertainty conditional on export penetration sales ratio*

Uncertainty variable	Conditioning variable	Condition	Mean	Med
VCA_CSD_CH	*ESR*	Missing	0.70	0.50
VCA_CSD_CH	*ESR*	> *ESR_MN_FL*	0.72	0.32
VCA_CSD_CH	*ESR*	≤ *ESR_MN_FL*	0.83	0.74
VCP_CSD_CH	*ESR*	Missing	0.89	0.35
VCP_CSD_CH	*ESR*	> *ESR_MN_FL*	0.89	0.44
VCP_CSD_CH	*ESR*	≤ *ESR_MN_FL*	1.28	0.88
RWA_CSD_CH	*ESR*	Missing	1.53	1.11
RWA_CSD_CH	*ESR*	> *ESR_MN_FL*	1.35	1.12
RWA_CSD_CH	*ESR*	≤ *ESR_MN_FL*	1.60	1.12
RWP_CSD_CH	*ESR*	Missing	1.80	1.13
RWP_CSD_CH	*ESR*	> *ESR_MN_FL*	1.65	1.21
RWP_CSD_CH	*ESR*	≤ *ESR_MN_FL*	2.68	1.40
RMP_CSD_CH	*ESR*	Missing	1.06	0.71
RMP_CSD_CH	*ESR*	> *ESR_MN_FL*	0.97	0.53
RMP_CSD_CH	*ESR*	≤ *ESR_MN_FL*	1.33	0.67
ROP_CSD_CH	*ESR*	Missing	1.37	0.74
ROP_CSD_CH	*ESR*	> *ESR_MN_FL*	0.96	0.54
ROP_CSD_CH	*ESR*	≤ *ESR_MN_FL*	1.44	0.72
RS_CSD_CH	*ESR*	Missing	0.70	0.56
RS_CSD_CH	*ESR*	> *ESR_MN_FL*	1.05	1.29
RS_CSD_CH	*ESR*	≤ *ESR_MN_FL*	1.43	1.40
ESR_CSD_CH	*ESR*	Missing	n.a	n.a.
ESR_CSD_CH	*ESR*	> *ESR_MN_FL*	0.45	0.31
ESR_CSD_CH	*ESR*	≤ *ESR_MN_FL*	0.86	0.71

The columns on this page report the mean and median for variables in a cross-section of US manufacturing industries, conditional on whether an industry's value of *ESR* is missing, is above the cross-sectional mean for *ESR*, or is less than or equal to the cross-sectional mean for *ESR*. Industries are disaggregated to their 1972 four-digit SIC code. Each variable name has the form *A_B_C* where *A* signifies the economic variable, *B* signifies the time-series moment of the variable, and *C* signifies either the time period over which the moment was estimated or the change in the time-series moment across time periods. The values for *A*, *B*, and *C* are given in Table 7.3.

show, for example, that while nearly 75% of industries experienced an increase in uncertainty about their real price of output, uncertainty fell by over 4 percentage points for one industry and rose by over 17 percentage points for another.

More specifically, in this subsection the diversity of the experiences across industries is used to test for an effect of increased uncertainty on investment and productivity growth. Regressions are run to see if those industries whose uncertainty changed by an amount different from the average change exhibited investment or productivity growth behaviour which was different from the average. If uncertainty has an important impact on investment, the large cross-sectional variation in the changes in uncertainty documented in Table 7.4 should be associated with large, predictable, cross-sectional variation in investment performance.

Before proceeding to the results, it is appropriate to explain the expansion of the analysis to include productivity growth. This decision is based on two factors. First, interest in investment is often derived from an interest in the productivity of labour and the resulting real wage that labour can earn. Second, it is possible that investment behaviour and productivity are affected differently by uncertainty. An example of this phenomenon would be a change in uncertainty which left the amount of investment unchanged but caused the composition of the capital stock to change in a way that was productive *ex ante* but unproductive *ex post*.

Table 7.7 contains summary statistics for measures of investment performance and productivity growth. During the period of fixed exchange rates, the cross-sectional mean of the industries' investment rate (their mean ratio of investment to the capital stock) was 8.48%. After the move to flexible exchange rates, the mean investment rate dropped to 8.01%. The cross-sectional mean of the change in the investment rate was a drop of 0.48 percentage points and the cross-sectional median value of the change was a drop of 0.32 percentage points.

While this reduction of investment (when combined with the previously documented increases in uncertainty) supports the proposition that there is a negative impact of uncertainty on capital expenditures, it would be unwise to view this as very strong support. Factors such as the move from low real interest rates in the 1970s to high real interest rates in the early 1980s and changes in investment tax law are reasonable alternative explanations for the drop in the investment rate and have not been accounted for. As described above, in this subsection detecting an impact of uncertainty will be concentrated on explaining the cross-sectional differences of changes in investment and productivity, not changes across time in the average behaviour. The results in Table 7.7 shows the cross-sectional differences in investment rate changes to be substantial, with a

Table 7.7. *Distribution of investment and productivity variables*

Variable	Mean	Std dev.	% < 0	Low	Q1	Med	Q3	High
IRAT_MN_FX	8.48	2.81		2.47	6.72	8.15	9.64	23.74
IRAT_MN_FL	8.01	2.74		0.31	6.42	7.71	9.36	23.88
IRAT_MN_CH	− 0.48	3.32	54.9	− 15.92	− 2.06	− 0.32	1.45	15.36
EQSHR_MN_FX	60.44	8.46		24.92	55.05	61.42	66.32	78.13
EQSHR_MN_FL	64.00	7.05		33.63	59.97	64.85	68.85	80.47
EQSHR_MN_CH	3.56	5.69	16.4	− 19.41	0.30	3.39	7.00	25.11
VAPE_TG_FX	2.78	2.93		− 3.94	0.88	2.03	4.10	18.48
VAPE_TG_FL	2.42	3.44		− 8.89	0.49	1.73	3.84	42.30
VAPE_TG_CH	− 0.38	4.72	56.2	− 16.26	− 2.93	− 0.47	1.37	37.98
VAPH_TG_FX	3.12	3.02		− 3.20	1.21	2.55	4.34	19.46
VAPH_TG_FL	2.72	4.19		− 9.49	0.67	2.00	4.11	40.45
VAPH_TG_CH	− 0.40	4.73	57.4	− 18.53	− 2.76	− 0.53	1.47	34.47

The columns on this page report the mean, standard deviation, percentage of observations which are negative, low value, first quartile, median, third quartile, and high value for variables in a cross-section of US manufacturing industries. Industries are disaggregated to their 1972 four-digit SIC code. Each variable name has the form *A_B_C* where *A* signifies the economic variable, *B* signifies the time-series moment of the variable, and *C* signifies either the time period over which the moment was estimated or the change in the time-series moment across time periods. The values for *A*, *B*, and *C* are given in Table 7.3.

fall of over 15 percentage points in one industry and a rise of over 15 percentage points in another.

Equipment's share of the capital stock is the other measure of investment performance examined here. If the effects described in section 2 are important, the two types of capital on which data are available, plant and equipment, may respond differently to uncertainty. This results from the possibilities that (1) one type of capital expenditure is more easily postponable than the other, (2) one type of capital involves a higher irretrievable fixed cost than the other, and (3) one type of capital is longer lived than the other.

The results in Table 7.7 show a noticeable shift away from plant and toward equipment in US manufacturing's capital stock. Of primary importance for the analysis of this chapter, however, is the wide disparity of experiences across industries. The mean level of equipment's share of the capital stock fell by over 19 percentage points in one industry after the move to flexible exchange rates and rose by over 25 percentage points in another.

Two measures of productivity are examined in this section, the growth rate of value added per employee and the growth rate of value added per production worker hour. Both show the famous slowdown post-1973. The variation across industries is again substantial. Despite a drop in the mean of the growth rate of value added per employee, over a quarter of the industries showed an increase of more than 1.3 percentage points and another quarter of the industries showed a decrease of more than 2.9 percentage points.

Tables 7.8a and 7.8b contain the results of attempting to explain the cross-sectional variation in the change in an industry's investment rate following the move to flexible exchange rates. The independent variables used in the regression have been standardised by first subtracting the cross-sectional mean of that variable and then dividing by the cross-sectional standard deviation of that variable. This has no effect on t-statistics or R^2 and allows a simple and informative interpretation of the estimated coefficients. An estimated slope coefficient of -1.00 indicates that an industry which experienced an increase in uncertainty that is 1 standard deviation above the mean increase in uncertainty had its investment rate drop by 1 percentage point more than the average drop in the investment rate. The constant term estimates the change in the investment rate of an industry which experienced the average increase in all the types of uncertainty included in the regression.

Columns (1) and (4) of Table 7.8a report the results for a regression which includes the change in uncertainty about real variable costs, real output price, and real shipments.[8] This specification allows the largest data set to be used and thus provides the broadest description of the data.

Table 7.8. *Effect of uncertainty on investment rates*

(a) Independent variables	(1)	(2)	(3)	(4)	(5)	(6)
Intercept	− 0.57*	− 0.49*	− 0.54*	− 0.51*	− 0.51*	− 0.51*
	(0.16)	(0.22)	(0.22)	(0.17)	(0.24)	(0.24)
VCA_CSD_CH	− 0.04	0.12	0.13			
	(0.21)	(0.27)	(0.30)			
VCP_CSD_CH				0.00	0.26	0.25
				(0.25)	(0.36)	(0.37)
ROP_CSD_CH	− 0.33	− 0.52	− 0.62*	− 0.33	− 0.59	− 0.73
	(0.19)	(0.28)	(0.28)	(0.24)	(0.37)	(0.37)
IPR_CSD_CH		− 0.35	− 0.28		− 0.27	− 0.23
		(0.21)	(0.22)		(0.23)	(0.23)
ESR_CSD_CH		0.01	− 0.13		0.15	0.03
		(0.21)	(0.26)		(0.22)	(0.22)
RS_CSD_CH	− 0.11		0.05	− 0.17		0.08
	(0.18)		(0.29)	(0.18)		(0.31)
R^2	0.016	0.031	0.037	0.015	0.021	0.028
NOBS	369	200	193	362	196	188

Each column on this page presents the estimated coefficients from an OLS regression of *IRAT_MN_CH* on the indicated independent variables. Numbers in parentheses are standard errors and a * indicates a coefficient which has a t-statistic greater than 1.96 in absolute value. R^2 is the R-squared and NOBS is the number of observations in the regression. NOBS varies across regressions due to data availability.

When using the *VCA* measure of variable costs, higher uncertainty is associated with lower investment for each type of uncertainty. Industries whose increase in uncertainty about their real output price was 1 standard deviation above the average increase are estimated to have a drop in their investment rate of 0.33 percentage points more than the average drop of 0.57 percentage points. Industries whose increase in uncertainty about their real variable costs (shipments) was 1 standard deviation above the average increase are estimated to have a drop in their investment rate of 0.04 (0.11) percentage points more than the average drop of 0.57 percentage points. When *VCP* is used instead of *VCA* the estimated effect of uncertainty about the real variable costs diminishes slightly, while the estimated effect of uncertainty about shipments increases somewhat and

Table 7.8. *Effect of uncertainty on investment rates*

(b) Independent variables	(1)	(2)	(3)	(4)	(5)	(6)
Intercept	− 0.48*	− 0.39	− 0.36	− 0.47*	− 0.39	− 0.35
	(0.17)	(0.23)	(0.23)	(0.17)	(0.24)	(0.24)
RWA_CSD_CH	− 0.44	− 0.27	− 0.31			
	(0.23)	(0.35)	(0.36)			
RWP_CSD_CH				− 0.43	− 0.10	− 0.19
				(0.22)	(0.36)	(0.36)
RMP_CSD_CH	0.45	0.39	0.39	0.32	0.34	0.34
	(0.29)	(0.38)	(0.28)	(0.29)	(0.38)	(0.37)
ROP_CSD_CH	− 0.48	− 0.67	− 0.75	− 0.33	− 0.74	− 0.79
	(0.32)	(0.42)	(0.42)	(0.31)	(0.43)	(0.43)
IPR_CSD_CH		− 0.25	− 0.23		− 0.23	− 0.19
		(0.23)	(0.22)		(0.24)	(0.24)
ESR_CSD_CH		0.20	0.16		0.20	0.15
		(0.22)	(0.28)		(0.22)	(0.22)
RS_CSD_CH	0.03		0.04	− 0.03		0.10
	(0.18)		(0.29)	(0.18)		(0.29)
R^2	0.032	0.033	0.040	0.027	0.030	0.038
NOBS	350	197	190	344	189	182

Each column on this page presents the estimated coefficients from an OLS regression of *IRAT_MN_CH* on the indicated independent variables. Numbers in parentheses are standard errors and a * indicates a coefficient which has a *t*-statistic greater than 1.96 in absolute value. R^2 is the *R*-squared adjusted for degrees of freedom and NOBS is the number of observations in the regression. NOBS varies across regressions due to data availability.

the estimated effect of uncertainty about the real output price is unaffected.

The standard errors reported below the estimated coefficients do not allow for the fact that the errors in the regression may be correlated across observation, nor for the fact that both the dependent and independent variables have been constructed in a previous step and are therefore undoubtedly measured with error. As a result, the reported standard errors must be interpreted with caution. This errors-in-variables problem may also bias the estimated coefficients toward zero.

If one wishes to push the coefficient estimates in Table 7.8a further, it is possible to combine them with the results presented in Table 7.4 to obtain an upper bound estimate of the effect that the higher nominal exchange rate volatility which accompanied the move to flexible exchange rates had on the mean investment rate of the manufacturing sector, decomposed by the separate sources of increased uncertainty that the increased volatility may have created. For example, operating through its impact on higher uncertainty about the real price of output, higher nominal exchange rate volatility is estimated to have lowered the mean investment rate by 0.33, divided by 2.37 (the cross-sectional standard deviation of the change in uncertainty about real output price), times 1.21 (the cross-sectional mean of the change in uncertainty about real output price), which equals 0.17 percentage points.[9] The estimated effects arising from higher uncertainty about real shipments and real variable costs are 0.02 and 0.01 percentage points, respectively,

The columns (2), (3), (5) and (6) of Table 7.8a report results when uncertainty about the import penetration ratio and export sales ratio are included in the regression. These measures of uncertainty are included both with and without the measure of output uncertainty in an attempt to determine if they matter through their impact on product demand. If uncertainty about the import penetration ratio and export sales ratio affect investment because they represent uncertainty about product demand, they would show an effect when entered into the regression by themselves but not when uncertainty about product demand is also entered. If uncertainty about the import penetration ratio and export sales ratio affect investment for some other reason, they would show an effect regardless of whether or not a measure of uncertainty about product demand was included.

The inclusion of uncertainty about import penetration and export sales into the regression strengthens the estimated impact of real output price uncertainty and eliminates any estimated negative impact of uncertainty about real variable costs. Uncertainty about import penetration is consistently estimated to lower the investment rate, but this is not true for uncertainty about export sales. The estimated effect of uncertainty about import penetration is essentially unaffected by the inclusion of the measure of product demand uncertainty. This suggests that either the effect on investment of uncertainty about import penetration is through a channel different from uncertainty about product demand or the measure of product demand uncertainty used here is so poor that the measure of uncertainty about import penetration continues to capture the effect of product demand uncertainty.

Table 7.8b repeats the regressions of Table 7.8a, with uncertainty about the components of the variable cost index entering separately. Interest-

Table 7.9. *Effect of uncertainty on equipment's share in the capital stock*

(a) Independent variables	(1)	(2)	(3)	(4)	(5)	(6)
Intercept	3.34*	3.98*	3.91*	3.30*	4.01*	3.99*
	(0.29)	(0.38)	(0.38)	(0.29)	(0.37)	(0.38)
VCA_CSD_CH	− 1.76*	− 1.62*	− 1.72*			
	(0.37)	(0.48)	(0.51)			
VCP_CSD_CH				− 1.37*	− 1.37*	− 1.32*
				(0.25)	(0.56)	(0.59)
ROP_CSD_CH	1.20*	1.18*	1.03*	1.26*	1.47*	1.30*
	(0.34)	(0.48)	(0.49)	(0.41)	(0.58)	(0.58)
IPR_CSD_CH		− 0.68	− 0.68		− 0.35	− 0.34
		(0.36)	(0.37)		(0.35)	(0.36)
ESR_CSD_CH		− 0.15	− 0.50		− 0.19	− 0.50
		(0.35)	(0.44)		(0.34)	(0.43)
RS_CSD_CH	− 0.26		0.59	− 0.59		0.26
	(0.32)		(0.49)	(0.30)		(0.48)
R^2	0.080	0.075	0.081	0.054	0.046	0.047
NOBS	369	200	193	363	196	188

Each column on this page presents the estimated coefficients from an OLS regression of *EQSHR_MN_CH* on the indicated independent variables. Numbers in parentheses are standard errors and a * indicates a coefficient which has a t-statistic greater than 1.96 in absolute value. R^2 is the R-squared adjusted for degrees of freedom and NOBS is the number of observations in the regression. NOBS varies across regressions due to data availability.

ingly, increased uncertainty about real wages is estimated to reduce investment but increased uncertainty about the real price of materials inputs is estimated to increase it. The estimated effects on investment of increases in other types of uncertainty do not differ significantly from those in Table 7.8a.

When the results of column (3) in Table 7.8b are used to repeat the exercise of obtaining an upper bound estimate of the effect that the move to flexible exchange rates had on the mean investment rate of the manufacturing sector, decomposed by the separate sources of increased uncertainty, the results are: − 0.14 percentage points for of increased real wage uncertainty, 0.19 percentage points for increased real price of

Table 7.9. *Effect of uncertainty on equipment's share in the capital stock*

(b) Independent variables	(1)	(2)	(3)	(4)	(5)	(6)
Intercept	3.46*	4.10*	4.14*	3.43*	4.18*	4.23*
	(0.30)	(0.38)	(0.39)	(0.30)	(0.39)	(0.41)
RWA_CSD_CH	− 1.21*	− 0.21	− 0.16			
	(0.40)	(0.57)	(0.60)			
RWP_CSD_CH				− 1.31*	− 0.39	− 0.36
				(0.38)	(0.58)	(0.60)
RMP_CSD_CH	0.31	− 0.24	− 0.28	0.44	− 0.19	− 0.24
	(0.51)	(0.38)	(0.64)	(0.51)	(0.63)	(0.65)
ROP_CSD_CH	0.97	0.66	0.68	0.77	0.65	0.60
	(0.55)	(0.69)	(0.70)	(0.54)	(0.70)	(0.72)
IPR_CSD_CH		− 0.38	− 0.41		− 0.33	− 0.37
		(0.38)	(0.40)		(0.39)	(0.41)
ESR_CSD_CH		0.06	− 0.04		0.03	− 0.08
		(0.36)	(0.46)		(0.36)	(0.47)
RS_CSD_CH	− 0.51		− 0.13	− 0.54		− 0.08
	(0.32)		(0.48)	(0.31)		(0.49)
R^2	0.053	0.011	0.014	0.058	0.012	0.014
NOBS	350	197	190	344	189	182

Each column on this page presents the estimated coefficients from an OLS regression of *EQSHR_MN_CH* on the indicated independent variables. Numbers in parentheses are standard errors and a * indicates a coefficient which has a *t*-statistic greater than 1.96 in absolute value. R^2 is the *R*-squared adjusted for degrees of freedom and NOBS is the number of observations in the regression. NOBS varies across regressions due to data availability.

materials inputs uncertainty, − 0.38 percentage points for increased real output price uncertainty, − 0.11 percentage points for increased import penetration uncertainty, 0.08 percentage points for increased export sales uncertainty, and 0.01 percentage points for increased shipments uncertainty, for a total of − 0.35 percentage points.

Tables 7.9a and 7.9b report the estimated effects of the various types of uncertainty on equipment's share in the capital stock. The R^2 are much higher than in Tables 7.8a and 7.8b, indicating that changes in uncertainty do a better job of predicting changes in the composition of the capital stock than they do of predicting changes in the investment rate. The bulk of the predictive power comes from uncertainty about the relative prices. Increased uncertainty about real variable costs, and primarily uncertainty about real wages, is estimated to shift an industry away from equipment towards plant, while increased uncertainty about the real price of output is estimated to do the reverse. Based on the estimates from column (1) of Table 7.9a, industries which experienced an increase in uncertainty about real variable costs which was 1 standard deviation above the average increase raised equipment's share in the capital stock by 1.76 percentage points less than the average increase of 3.34 percentage points. Industries which experienced an increase in uncertainty about real output price which was 1 standard deviation above the average increase raised equipment's share in the capital stock by 1.20 percentage points more than the average increase of 3.34 percentage points.

The finding that increased uncertainty about the real price of output shifts an industry to the more short-lived form of capital, equipment, appears consistent with the discussion of section 2. The option value of waiting to receive additional information should be less for shorter-lived investments and thus they may be less sensitive to increased uncertainty. This presumes, of course, that the critical factor of irretrievable fixed cost is not an important difference between the two types of capital.

The finding that increased uncertainty about the real price of variable inputs has the opposite effect on the composition of the capital stock than does increased uncertainty about the real price of output is hard to reconcile with the discussion of section 2. It appears that the substitutability of labour, materials inputs, and different forms of capital in the production process, which was omitted from the discussion, may be an important issue.

Tables 7.10a and 7.10b report the estimated effects of the various types of uncertainty on productivity growth, measured by the trend growth rate of value added per production worker hour.[10] In general, changes in uncertainty do a very poor job of predicting changes in productivity growth, worse even than predicting changes in investment rates. Nonetheless, some interesting facts emerge.

The consistent pattern of increased uncertainty about the real output price lowering the investment rate reported in Tables 7.8a and 7.8b is matched in Table 7.10b by an estimated negative impact of uncertainty about the real output price on productivity growth. Based on the estimates from column (1) of Table 7.10b, industries which experienced an increase in uncertainty about real output price which was 1 standard deviation above the average increase experienced a fall in the annual growth rate of value added per production worker hour which was 0.43 percentage points more than the average fall of 0.43 percentage points.

Table 7.10. *Effect of uncertainty on growth rate of value added*

(a)

Independent variables	(1)	(2)	(3)	(4)	(5)	(6)
Intercept	− 0.41	0.17	0.31	− 0.32	0.29	0.22
	(0.23)	(0.41)	(0.37)	(0.24)	(0.41)	(0.38)
VCA_CSD_CH	0.15	0.49	0.51			
	(0.31)	(0.52)	(0.50)			
VCP_CSD_CH				0.21	0.41	0.46
				(0.36)	(0.62)	(0.58)
ROP_CSD_CH	0.29	0.22	− 0.08	0.15	0.11	− 0.25
	(0.28)	(0.52)	(0.48)	(0.34)	(0.63)	(0.58)
IPR_CSD_CH		− 0.06	0.07		− 0.12	0.01
		(0.38)	(0.36)		(0.39)	(0.36)
ESR_CSD_CH		0.39	0.59		0.37	0.53
		(0.38)	(0.43)		(0.38)	(0.42)
RS_CSD_CH	− 0.06		− 0.14	0.01		0.03
	(0.28)		(0.48)	(0.27)		(0.49)
R^2	0.008	0.016	0.018	0.006	0.012	0.015
NOBS	360	195	188	355	192	184

Each column on this page presents the estimated coefficients from an OLS regression of *VAPH_MN_CH* on the indicated independent variables. Numbers in parentheses are standard errors. R^2 is the R-squared adjusted for degrees of freedom and NOBS is the number of observations in the regression. NOBS varies across regressions due to data availability.

This result is not found in Table 7.10a, however, where uncertainty about real wages and the real price of materials inputs are constrained to affect productivity growth in the same way.

Likewise, the consistent pattern of increased uncertainty about the real price of materials inputs increasing the investment rate reported in Table 7.8b is matched in Table 7.10b by an estimated positive impact of uncertainty on productivity growth. Based on the estimates from column (1) of Table 7.10b, industries which experienced an increase in uncertainty about the real price of materials inputs which was 1 standard deviation above the average increase experienced a rise in the annual growth rate of value added per production worker hour of 0.81 percentage points more than the average.

Table 7.10. *Effect of uncertainty on growth rate of value added*

(b) Independent variables	(1)	(2)	(3)	(4)	(5)	(6)
Intercept	− 0.43	− 0.14	− 0.04	− 0.43	− 0.07	0.04
	(0.24)	(0.37)	(0.38)	(0.25)	(0.38)	(0.39)
RWA_CSD_CH	0.30	0.68	0.77			
	(0.33)	(0.57)	(0.60)			
RWP_CSD_CH				0.39	0.46	0.37
				(0.31)	(0.56)	(0.58)
RMP_CSD_CH	0.81	0.57	0.50	0.65	0.46	0.40
	(0.42)	(0.61)	(0.64)	(0.41)	(0.61)	(0.62)
ROP_CSD_CH	− 0.43	− 0.82	− 0.81	− 0.40	− 0.52	− 0.43
	(0.45)	(0.67)	(0.68)	(0.44)	(0.68)	(0.69)
IPR_CSD_CH		− 0.07	− 0.02		− 0.16	− 0.10
		(0.37)	(0.38)		(0.37)	(0.39)
ESR_CSD_CH		0.13	0.49		0.16	0.49
		(0.35)	(0.44)		(0.35)	(0.45)
RS_CSD_CH	− 0.28		− 0.12	− 0.09		0.00
	(0.28)		(0.47)	(0.26)		(0.48)
R^2	0.023	0.017	0.023	0.019	0.010	0.014
NOBS	342	192	185	336	185	178

Each column on this page presents the estimated coefficients from an OLS regression of *VAPH_MN_CH* on the indicated independent variables. Numbers in parentheses are standard errors. R^2 is the *R*-squared adjusted for degrees of freedom and NOBS is the number of observations in the regression. NOBS varies across regressions due to data availability.

With regards to the effects of increased uncertainty about real wages, there is no consistency across the results of Tables 7.8b and 7.10b. Increased uncertainty about real wages is estimated to lower the investment rate but raise the productivity growth rate.

4 Summary remarks and conclusions

This chapter has presented a discussion of why an increase in nominal exchange rate volatility might be expected to increase uncertainty about real wages, the real price of materials inputs, the real output price, and/or product demand, thereby increasing uncertainty about the real net present value of capital expenditures, and thereby reducing investment. Evidence has been presented that for US manufacturing industries the move to flexible exchange rates was in fact accompanied by significant and widespread increases in uncertainty about real wages, the real price of materials inputs, the real output price, import penetration, export sales, and the quantity of shipments. Furthermore, these increases in uncertainty were shown to be more pronounced in industries which are more open to international trade and are therefore more likely to be affected by exchange rate volatility.

The diversity of changes in uncertainty across industries was used to determine if there was a detectable link between uncertainty on the one hand and the ratio of investment to the capital stock, equipment's share in the capital stock, and/or the trend growth rate of value added per production worker hour on the other. Higher uncertainty about real output price was shown to be negatively correlated with the investment rate and productivity growth, and positively correlated with equipment's share in the capital stock. Higher uncertainty about real wages was also shown to be negatively correlated with the investment rate, but was positively correlated with productivity growth and negatively correlated with equipment's share in the capital stock. Higher uncertainty about the real price of materials inputs was shown to be positively correlated with the investment rate and productivity growth.

The correlations of various types of uncertainty with the investment rate, composition of the capital stock, and productivity growth were shown to be sufficiently large to be economically interesting. Unfortunately, they appear to be rather imprecisely estimated. The need to estimate uncertainty in a preliminary first step and then link it with investment and productivity growth creates problems for accurately measuring the precision of the estimate presented here, and may well bias the estimates towards zero.

In conclusion, a connection between nominal exchange rate volatility and uncertainty about key economic variables relevant for the investment decision appears to be present in the data. A connection between uncertainty about these variables and either investment or productivity growth seems more tenuous. The tenuousness of these connections could arise for many reasons, several of which warrant mention here.

The relation between uncertainty and investment described in this chapter is well known to be highly nonlinear. It may be that the amount of uncertainty which existed prior to the move to flexible exchange rates was sufficiently high that the additional uncertainty was inconsequential. It is also possible that the horizon over which uncertainty matters has not been appropriately chosen or that the conditional expectations used to form the measures of uncertainty are unreliable.

It should also be noted that the discussion of how uncertainty may affect investment was decidedly partial equilibrium, and should be interpreted as indicating a change in desired investment at existing interest rates. In a general equilibrium where savings is relatively insensitive to real interest rates, changes in desired investment may show up more in interest rates than in investment quantities.

Finally, the discussion of this chapter ignored the ability of, and incentives for, firms to diversify their capital stock internationally in times of nominal exchange rate volatility. This diversification may bring with it an increase in investment and offset the forces highlighted here.

NOTES

I would like to thank conference participants, and especially my discussants, for useful comments. Helpful conversations with Bob Pindyck and Guiseppe Bertola are also gratefully acknowledged.

1 See, for example, early work by Hartman (1972) and Abel (1983, 1984) in comparison to more recent work by Zeira (1990). Caballero (1991) presents a useful summary.

2 This example is similar to one used in Pindyck (1991).

3 For purposes of exposition, all uncertainty in this example is put into the revenues which the investment project generates and none into the costs associated with the investment. It should be obvious from examination of the example that it is uncertainty about the net revenues of the project which is crucial. This point is discussed in more detail later in the section.

4 The uncertainty considered in this example is unrealistic in large part because it is totally resolved after one period. Work by Dixit (1989) and others shows that the implications of the example are quite robust to changing the nature of the uncertainty. One can allow uncertainty that is never totally resolved and is greater for the distant future than it is for the near future, and still obtain results similar to those in the example.

5 In this case the expected net present value of the investment is $463,156 under both the invest now and the wait and decide strategy.

6 I would like to thank Eric Bartlesman and Steve Davis for providing me with the data.

7 When the univariate autoregression failed to capture stationary movement around the linear trend (i.e., the sum of the autoregressive coefficients exceeded 1 in absolute value), the industry was assigned a missing value.

8 The use of real shipments is a proxy for product demand. It would be preferable, but unfortunately it is not feasible in this chapter, to fit individual demand curves for each of the over 300 industries and measure uncertainty about demand as residual variance in these demand curves.

9 This is an upper bound estimate in the sense that it attributes all the average increase in uncertainty to the increased volatility of nominal exchange rates. It is not an upper bound estimate in the sense that it allows for sampling error.

10 Regressions have also been estimated using the change in the growth rate of value added per employee as the dependent variable. Results for these regressions are essentially the same as those reported here, and are omitted to save space.

REFERENCES

Abel, A. (1983) 'Optimal Investment Under Uncertainty', *American Economic Review*, **73**, 228–33.

(1984) 'The Effects of Uncertainty on Investment and the Expected Long-Run Capital Stock', *Journal of Economic Dynamics and Control*, **7**, 39–53.

Caballero, R. (1991) 'On the Sign of the Investment–Uncertainty Relationship', *American Economic Review*, **81**, 279–88.

Dixit, A. (1989) 'Entry and Exit Decisions Under Uncertainty', *Journal of Political Economy*, **97**, 620–38.

Hartman, R. (1972) 'The Effects of Price and Cost Uncertainty on Investment', *Journal of Economic Theory*, **5**, 258–66.

Pindyck, R. (1991) 'Irreversibility, Uncertainty, and Investment', *Journal of Economic Theory*, **29**, 1110–48.

Zeira, J. (1990) 'Cost Uncertainty and the Rate of Investment', *Journal of Economic Dynamics and Control*, **14**, 53–63.

Discussion

RAFI MELNICK

The purpose of Chapter 7 is to evaluate the impact of the rise in exchange rate uncertainty on investment and on the productivity of firms open to international competition. The main empirical findings, although statistically quite weak, are the negative correlation between real output price variability and investment, the negative correlation between real output price variability and productivity growth, and the positive correlation between real output price variability and the share of equipment in capital stock.

The research strategy was to identify two periods, one when exchange rate variability was high and the other when it was low. This was done using a sample of firms for a fixed-exchange rate period (1958–72) and for a flexible-exchange rate period (1973–86). The data show that the variance of a variety of variables rose as the exchange rate period moved from fixed to flexible. They also show that the rise in variance was greater for firms with a larger exposure to foreign markets.

The main issue for the interpretation of the findings is whether the initial exogenous shock is the rise in exchange rate variability or whether the latter reflects more fundamental shocks (oil-shock) that affected both exchange rates and relative prices. If the joint rise in variability is accepted, the decline in investment should be attributed to the initial shock rather than to its reflection. This is an important policy issue, since the question whether exchange rate variability is solely a result of the exchange rate regime is still open.

A more technical comment is related to the operational measure of uncertainty. Uncertainty is measured as the standard deviation of the residuals of a two-lag autoregressive model incorporating a deterministic trend. This measure is appropriate under the assumption that the stochastic processes of all the series are stationary around a deterministic trend. If this is not the case then this measure may include spurious variability. An alternative measure of variability, that is appropriate if the processes contain unit roots (as many economic series do), is the standard deviation of the rate of growth of the different series. To test for the robustness of the results it is recommended that both measures be presented.

Part Three
Investment and growth

8 Foreign finance and economic growth: an empirical analysis

DANIEL COHEN

1 Introduction

Can the world financial markets help a poor country to get richer? The answer obviously depends on why the country is 'poor'. Take – for the sake of exposition – the Solow view that countries are converging towards a steady state which depends on the country's propensity to save and upon its long-run productivity. The country may be poor either because it is far off its steady state or because its steady state itself is low. First take the view that the country is poor because of poor initial conditions. This is a case when the access to the world financial markets can be very useful. By speeding up the transitional dynamics of the country to its steady state, the financial markets could bring the country to a point which is eventually self-sustainable. Where do we stand empirically? A simple way to answer the question is to calculate the stock of capital that the countries are converging to – when holding constant their saving rate and their productivity – and to compare that 'steady-state' value to the current value of the stock of capital (a more subtle approach is presented in section 3 below). The results are shown in Table 8A.1 (in Appendix 1). Although the developing countries were further off their steady state than the OECD countries in the mid-1960s, one finds that this was no longer the case as early as the mid-1970s. From that perspective, one should not expect the financial markets to do much to help the developing countries (see also Cohen, 1992).

Let us now focus on the reason why the developing countries' steady state appears to be low. Again it may be for two reasons. The steady state may be low because the developing countries have a low propensity to accumulate capital, or because their 'intrinsic' productivity is low. Each of these two factors can be characterised as a shortage of domestic investment: towards physical capital or towards what it takes to raise productivity (human capital or technologies). Leaving aside the sovereign risk constraint, is there room for foreign finance to supplement the domestic accumulation of physical capital? One simple way to answer this question is to calculate the marginal productivity of capital in poor and rich countries. This calculation is shown in Table 8A.2 (p. 228). One does find that the social return to capital accumulation is higher in the poor countries. From that perspective, there is room for foreign finance to raise growth.

What about productivity? We go here into lesser-known territories. For one thing the empirical theory of the law of motion of productivity is still a hot topic of controversy. It is obviously even harder to tell the extent to which foreign finance may influence it. Although the answer is theoretically ambiguous, we now want to argue that, empirically, there are reasons to believe that it is essentially through this channel that the effect of foreign finance on growth has been operating.

2 A framework of analysis

2.1 *Structural form of the model*

In order to investigate the origin of the 'poverty of nations', we shall build on the 'augmented' Solow model analysed in Mankiw, Romer and Weil (1992) (henceforth MRW), and assume that production can be written as:

$$Q_t = K_t^{\alpha} H_t^{\beta}(A_t L_t)^{1-\alpha-\beta} \tag{1}$$

in which K_t is physical capital, H_t is 'human' capital, L_t is raw labour and A_t is an exogenous productivity term.

Let us then write the law of motion of physical capital as:

$$K_{t+1} = K_t(1-d) + s_1 K_t^{\alpha} H_t^{\beta}(A_t L_t)^{1-\alpha-\beta} \tag{2}$$

in which s_1 is the share of GDP which is invested in physical capital.

We now depart from MRW in the following important way. While they take investment in human capital to be proportional to output, we postulate instead that it is proportional to an aggregate measure of 'knowledge' in which both physical and human capital enter, but not necessarily with the same weights as in GDP. Specifically, let us assume that

$$H_{t+1} = H_t(1-\delta) + s_2^{\epsilon} K_t^{\nu} H_t^{\lambda}(A_t L_t)^{1-\nu-\lambda} \tag{3}$$

in which s_2 is secondary school enrolment (taken as in MRW as a proxy for the training efforts of the country), ϵ (<1) is a measure of the decreasing returns associated to training and $K_t^{\nu} H_t^{\lambda}(A_t L_t)^{1-\nu-\lambda}$ can be thought of as the stock of 'knowledge' on top of which training can take place (see, e.g., Rosen, 1989 for a similar formulation). The reason why the stock of capital enters the training technology can be interpreted as a learning-by-doing effect.

2.2 *Empirical analysis*

Getting estimates of the stock of physical capital is a precarious exercise, but at least one that is conceptually easy (details on physical capital are provided in Appendix 2; I use capital stock data for the period 1966–87).

Getting estimates of the stock of human capital is an impossible task both conceptually and empirically. In order to obviate the difficulty, let us accept MRW's prescription that $Q_t = K_t^{1/3} H_t^{\beta} L_t^{\gamma}$ (with $1/3 + \beta + \gamma = 1$) so that one can define human capital (in log of per capita terms) up to a multiplicative constant. More specifically, we can define:

$$z_t = 3y_t - k_t$$

in which:

$$z_t = \zeta h_t, \qquad \zeta = 3\beta.$$

z is computable, ζ is an unknown parameter. With these definitions, we can log-linearise equations (2) and (3) above as follows:

$$\frac{d}{dt} k_t = C_1 + \theta_1 \log s_1 - \theta_1(2/3)k_t + \theta_1(1/3)z_t \tag{4}$$

$$\frac{d}{dt} z_t = C_2 + \epsilon\zeta\theta_2 \log s_2 - \theta_2\zeta v k_t - \theta_2(1+\lambda)z_t \tag{5}$$

in which:

$$\begin{cases} \theta_1 = d + n + \mu & \text{(6a)} \\ \theta_2 = \delta + n + \mu & \text{(6b)} \end{cases}$$

We have estimated the system (4) and (5) by pooling cross-section and time-series data over the following three subperiods: 1966–73, 1973–80, 1980–7. We get the following results (see also Appendix 3 for details):

$$dk = -0.381 + \underset{(30.2)}{0.129}\, linv - \underset{(-46.5)}{0.795}\, k_0 + \underset{(30.7)}{0.0483}\, h_0; \; R^2 = 0.89 \tag{7}$$

$$dh = -0.0691 + \underset{(3.61)}{0.0270}\, lenr2 + \underset{(7.86)}{0.0307}\, k_0 - \underset{(-7.50)}{0.0261}\, h_0; \; R^2 = 0.47 \tag{8}$$

Period of estimation: 1966–76; Sur estimator; (t-statistics in parentheses).

The first equation is an overidentified quasi-identity which leads us to reconstruct $\theta_1 = 0.129$. (None of the coefficients of k_0 and h_0 are significantly different from what they are supposed to be, namely $-2/3\theta_1$ and $1/3\theta_1$.)

The second equation is an underidentified equation. In order to reconstruct the values of the coefficients, we need two identifying restrictions. We choose the two restrictions which are closer to MRW's model, namely: $\theta_2 = \theta_1$ and $\zeta = 1$ (which amounts to accepting their result on the production function). With these identifying restrictions, we find:

$$\epsilon = 0.21, \quad \lambda = 0.24 \quad \text{and} \quad \nu = 0.80.$$

We can then write the law of motion of human capital as:

$$H_{t+1} = H_t(1-\delta) + s_2^{\epsilon}\Omega_t \tag{9}$$

in which

$$\Omega_t = K_t^{0.24} H_t^{0.80} \tag{10}$$

which has an appealing feature. It displays constant returns to scale with respect to physical and human capital, and decreasing returns with respect to school enrolment.

2.3 *Dynamics of the model*

Since there are constant returns to scale with respect to physical and human capital, there is *potentially* room for endogenous growth. To the extent, however, that physical capital (whose supply exhibits decreasing returns) enters the production function of human capital, endogenous growth is not a sure thing. A Wald Test leads us to *reject* the hypothesis that the system is either exploding or endogenously growing. The value of the test however is equal to 1.79 and only on the margin of 95% confidence.

Since the point estimate of the system shows that there is convergence to a steady state, we can reconstruct such a long-run target out of equations (4) and (5). Up to a constant, we can write this steady state as:

$$\left(\begin{aligned} k_\infty &= \frac{1}{\Delta}[(1-\lambda)\log s_1 + \beta\epsilon\log s_2] \\ h_\infty &= \frac{1}{\Delta}[\nu\log s_1 + (1-\alpha)\epsilon\log s_2] \end{aligned}\right. \tag{11}$$

with $\Delta = (1-\alpha)(1-\lambda) - \beta\nu$ (see Appendix 4 for details).

In practice, obviously, neither of these saving rates are exogenous: they depend upon the wealth of the country, and they depend (as far as s_1 is concerned) upon the access to the world financial markets. We consequently refer to the solution to (11) as a pseudo-steady state 'PSS', i.e., as a steady state to prevail, *ceteris paribus* how far the developing countries stand with respect to their pseudo-'steady-state' targets, and compare them to the OECD countries.

The results are shown in Tables 8A.3 and 8A.4 (in Appendix 4). They amplify those which were shown in Table 8A.1. In all points in time, the developing countries appear to be closer to their pseudo-steady-state targets than the OECD countries are.

2.4 *One-dimensional dynamics*

When adding together equations (4) and (5), we can get back to the analysis of the dynamics of per capita GDP. To the extent, however, that the law of motion of human capital is not collinear to the law of motion of physical capital, we cannot simplify the pattern of growth of a country to being proportional to the distance between initial income and the steady state. An additional term steps in: the Knowledge-to-GDP ratio. With the identifying restrictions that we made above, one can write:

$$g_t = C + (1/3)\theta_1 \log s_1 + (1/3)\epsilon\theta_1 \log s_2 - (1/3)\theta_1\, y_0 + (1/3)\theta_1 \omega_t$$

in which $\omega_t = \log(\Omega_t/Q_t)$.

With this formulation, growth can be viewed as the sum of two terms: the transitional dynamics of the Solow model, plus the productivity wedge, which corresponds to the 'endogenous' part of the model. We re-estimated such an equation directly and got the following result (see Appendix 5 for details):

$$g_t = -0.10 + \underset{(11.0)}{0.0410}\, linv + \underset{(3.57)}{0.00973}\, lenr2 - \underset{(-8.26)}{0.0321}\, y_0 + \underset{(8.75)}{0.0359}\, \omega_t \qquad (12)$$

With such an equation, we are led to reconstruct that $\epsilon = 0.24$ which is not significantly different from the value (= 0.21) found above and we cannot reject either that the coefficients of $linv_t$, y_0 and ω_t are identical.

3 Patterns of growth of the debtor countries

We are now able to analyse the channels through which external debt has influenced the pattern of growth of developing countries. It can be either through the law of motion of physical capital, or through the law of motion of productivity. Let us examine each of these channels in turn and then move on to analyse their overall effect on growth itself.

3.1 *Effect on investment*

The most straightforward channel through which foreign finance can lift up the growth rate of a country is to supplement domestic saving and correspondingly to raise capital accumulation. In view of the opening remarks made in section 1, one might expect that domestic investment would be lifted up more spectacularly in those places where the countries stand far off their steady state or far off the world return on capital. This does not appear to be the case, and all attempts to correlate the inflows of foreign finance to either one of these determinants failed. On the other hand, one does find a positive effect of foreign finance on investment (see Cohen, 1992, 1993 for a more thorough analysis of investment):

$$\begin{array}{l} linv = 0.311 \underset{(-0.78)}{-0.095\, D7380} \underset{(-2.40)}{-0.257\, D8087} \underset{(3.13)}{+0.212\, lenr2} \underset{(2.85)}{+0.204\, y_0} \\ \qquad \underset{(1.59)}{+0.330^{*} vt} \end{array} \tag{13}$$

In order to get a measure of the quantitative effects of foreign finance on investment over the 1970s and the 1980s, we decomposed the magnitude involved into three effects: the structural effects which account for income and education (terms of trade are not significant when time dummies are introduced), foreign finance (which simply measures the direct effect of foreign finance on investment) and the unexplained residual. The decomposition is offered for two categories of debtors: the severely indebted low-income countries (group 1) and the severely indebted middle-income countries (group 2). The results are shown in Table 8.1 below. One finds that the investment ratio rose in the 1970s by about 5% (in log terms from 2.33 to 2.45 in the low-income group and from 2.60 to 2.80 in the middle-income group) and that foreign finance does account for a substantial part of it. On the other hand, in the 1980s, foreign finance is essentially neutral in the middle-income debtors. In the low-income group, one sees that the fall of the investment rate can be accounted for its structural determinants, while the positive effect of foreign finance seems to have been dissipated.

3.2 *Productivity*

Let us now proceed to analyse the effect of foreign finance on productivity. *A priori*, one wants to think of 'human capital' in terms of a non-traded asset, and it is not obvious that foreign finance should have any effect at all on its law of motion. In practice, obviously, productivity involves many other items and it may simply be that the countries which

Table 8.1. *The determinants of investment*

Low-income debtors	
1960s	
Average	2.33
Structural determinants	2.20
1970s	
Average	2.45
Structural determinants	2.25
Foreign finance	0.15
1980s	
Average	2.19
Structural determinants	2.09
Foreign finance	0.08
Middle-income debtors	
1960s	
Average	2.60
Structural determinants	2.68
1970s	
Average	2.80
Structural determinants	2.70
Foreign finance	0.14
1980s	
Average	2.60
Structural determinants	2.65
Foreign finance	0.01

managed to borrow, by being able to spend more, succeeded in raising the productivity of their factors of production through a demand-induced boom (and perhaps only temporarily). But it may also be that foreign finance allowed debtor countries to raise their imports of new technological items that helped them to raise the efficiency of their production process.

Let us then turn to equation (3) and see through which channels foreign finance may operate. For one thing, it may lift up the stock of 'knowledge' on which the country builds its productivity. It may also help to improve the efficiency of the 'training' technology by raising (for a given level of school enrolment) the ability of a country to raise its productivity; finally, it may work directly on productivity through (perhaps) the demand-induced effects of foreign finance on growth. In order to investigate which channel played a role, we tested the significance of the correlation of productivity with the net transfers themselves, the net transfers multiplied by the knowledge factor, and finally, the net transfers multiplied by the school enrolment figure. When analysing these channels separately, it appears that both the second and the last channels are significant. However, when put together, only the training factor ends up significant. We finally converge to the following regression in which time dummies and a terms of trade factor were also added.

$$\begin{aligned} dh = 0.0353 &+ \underset{(2.25)}{0.0185\,lenr2} + \underset{(6.04)}{0.0312k_0} - \underset{(-5.50)}{0.0234h_0} + \underset{(1.86)}{0.0157\,vt^*lenr2} \qquad (14) \\ &\underset{(1.80)}{0.0285\,D7380} + \underset{(0.12)}{0.002\,D8087} + \underset{(3.24)}{0.43\,TOT} \end{aligned}$$

$R^2 = 0.48$ (t-statistics in parentheses).

Taken at face value, this equation implies that foreign finance raised the efficiency of the underlying process through which a country raises its productivity. We shall get back to the intuition behind this result after having spelled out the empirical magnitude that it involves for analysing growth.

3.3 Dynamics of per capita income

We can now get back to the analysis of the dynamics of per capita income. Specifically we re-estimated the following growth equation:

$$\begin{aligned} g = -0.830 &+ \underset{(1.91)}{0.006\,lenr2} + \underset{(9.09)}{0.0364\,linv} - \underset{(-5.65)}{0.0284\,y_0} \\ &+ \underset{(7.03)}{0.0318\,omeg} + \underset{(3.66)}{0.0184\,tot} + \underset{(3.40)}{0.00890\,vt^*lenr2} \qquad (15) \end{aligned}$$

$R^2 = 0.40$ (t-statistics in parentheses).

Splitting, as for the investment equation, the influence of each of these items onto growth, we get the decomposition in Table 8.2.

Table 8.2 shows the remarkable magnitude of foreign finance on growth during the 1970s. About a quarter of a percentage point was achieved through its effect on investment, and almost a full percentage point was obtained through increased productivity. It would be obviously naive to believe that the whole of this later increase amounts to an improvement in the technological performance of the debtor countries. As I pointed out above, a country which gains a new access to the world financial markets uses an important part of these resources to spend more, and this alone creates a demand-led boom which raises the productivity of the country. However, against this demand-induced view of the productivity puzzle, it

Table 8.2. *The determinants of economic growth*

Low-income debtors	
	1960s
Average growth rate	1.55
Structural determinants	− 1.74
(other than investment)	
Investment	3.50
	1970s
Average growth rate	− 0.31
Structural determinants	− 3.09
(other than investment)	
Investment	3.79
(due to foreign finance)	0.24
Foreign finance	0.96
Terms of trade	− 0.09
	1980s
Average growth rate	− 2.2
Structural determinants	− 4.79
(other than investment)	
Investment	3.39
(due to foreign finance)	0.13
Terms of trade	− 0.49
Foreign finance	0.51
Residual	
Middle-income debtors	
	1960s
Average growth rate	2.70
Structural determinants	− 1.47
(other than investment)	
Investment	4.19
	1970s
Average growth rate	2.54
Structural determinants	− 2.96
(other than investment)	
Investment	4.43
(due to foreign finance)	0.22
Foreign finance	1.25
Terms of trade	− 0.04
	1980s
Average growth rate	− 1.4
Structural determinants	− 4.79
(other than investment)	
Investment	4.02
(due to foreign finance)	0.02
Terms of trade	− 0.61
Foreign finance	0.08

is interesting to note that the influence of foreign finance on growth appears to be better explained by its mediated effect through school enrolment rather than directly through the overall productivity of the factors of production.

4 Summary of the results

We have introduced a new notion in this chapter: the 'productivity wedge', which measures the stock of 'knowledge' that a country can count on to raise its prospect of growth. We have argued that in a two-dimensional world in which output must be raised through the accumulation of physical capital *and* through the accumulation of human capital, the productivity wedge is a significant determinant of economic growth. When analysing the pattern of growth of the debtor countries, we have found that foreign finance appeared to have raised the efficiency of the process through which the debtor countries turn their productivity wedge into growth.

Appendix 1: convergence in the closed and in the open economy

In order to put some structure on the discussion sketched in the introduction, consider for instance a simple Solow model in which production is

$$Q_t = A K_t^a L_t^{1-a}$$

and let $Y_t = A(K_t/L_t)^{1-a}$ be per capita income.

Consider first the closed economy and take saving as a fixed proportion of income so that the law of motion of capital can be written as:

$$\dot{K}_t = -dK_t + sQ_t.$$

Income follows a law of motion which can be log-linearised as:

$$\frac{d}{dt} y_t = d(1-a)(\hat{y}_c - y_t)$$

in which: $\hat{y}_c = \frac{1}{1-a} a + \frac{a}{1-a} \theta_c$, with $\theta_c = \log \frac{a}{d}$

(in which the small letters are the log of the capital letters). Consider now what happens when the country gains a free access to the world financial markets, in which a constant interest rate r prevails. The stock of capital immediately jumps to a level K_0 such that

$$aAK_0^{a-1} = r + d$$

Table 8A.1. *Closed-economy benchmark*

	1966	1973	1980	1987
Average				
OECD	1.2885	1.0625	0.8403	0.49
LDC	2.1244	0.64855	0.415	0.1048
Debtors 1		0.6879	0.50315	0.1495
Debtors 2		0.97033	0.877	0.2664
Standard error				
OECD	0.43095	0.1494	0.1586	0.9058
LDC	0.4347	0:39658	0.6135	0.5801

so that the level of income is now (in log terms):

$$\hat{y}_0 = \frac{1}{1-a}a + \frac{a}{1-a}\theta_0, \quad \text{with } \theta_0 = \log\frac{a}{r+d}.$$

One can define a 'closed economy target' as the value of the stock of capital that the closed economy is converging to. In log terms, it is simply determined as:

$$k^c = \frac{1}{1-a}(a + \log s)$$

in which s is the share of GDP that goes to investment and a is calculated as the log of the Solow residual. (The way the capital stock data are constructed is shown in Appendix 2). (See also Barro, Mankiw and Sala-i-Martin, 1992 for a similar exercise.)

We can then calculate the difference between this target and the current value of the stock of capital as:

$$\omega^c = k^c - k.$$

Such a value is shown in Table 8A.1.

We next define the open economy target as the level of the stock of capital whose marginal product is equal to the corresponding averages in the OECD countries. It is then defined as:

$$k^0 = \frac{1}{1-a}(a + \theta_0)$$

in which θ_0 is the corresponding average for the OECD countries. We then calculate

$$\omega^0 = k^0 - k.$$

The results are shown in Table 8A.2.

Table 8A.2. *Open-economy benchmark*

	1966	1973	1980	1987
Average				
OECD	0	0	0	0
LDC	2.546	1.138	0.794	0.82059
Debtors 1		0.7756	0.757	0.759
Debtors 2		0.7934	0.4955	0.5408
Standard error				
OECD	0.7025	0.376	0.265	0.94
LDC	1.577	1.003	0.89	0.82059

Appendix 2: capital stock data

The Summers–Heston (1991) latest estimates include data on the capital stock for a subgroup of 29 countries for the years 1980–8 (in most cases, see the list in Appendix 5). We took an aggregate measure of capital (inclusive of residential capital, because of lack of data on the decomposition of investment), and we reconstructed capital stock data for the period 1966–1987–1988 by an inventory formula:

$$K_t = \sum_{s=0}^{t} I_s(1-\delta)^{(t-s)} + K_0(1-\delta)^t.$$

We took $\delta = 10\%$, which was the value that best fitted Summers–Heston's (1991) capital stock series after 1980. We had to drop 10 countries, however (Zimbabwe, Korea, Philippines, Thailand, Guatemala, Chile, Greece, the United Kingdom, Australia, Austria) for which the 1966 data made no sense.

In order to extrapolate these data to the larger subgroup (consisting of nonoil-producing countries), we have run the following regression:

$$\log(K65) = a + b\log(Z65) + c\log(Y60)$$

in which: $Z65 = \sum_{s=1960}^{1965} I_s(1-\delta)^{(1965-s)}$.

Method of estimation = Ordinary Least Squares

Dependent variable: *LK*10
Current sample: 1 to 29
No. of observations: 19

Mean of dependent var.	= 24.9719
Std dev. of dependent var.	= 2.69353
Sum of squared residuals	= 30.5813
Variance of residuals	= 1.91133
Std error of regression	= 1.38251
R^2	= 0.76
Adjusted R^2	= 0.73
F-statistic (zero slopes)	= 26.0
Schwarz Bayes. Info. Crit.	= 0.94
Log of likelihood function	= − 31

Variable	*Estimated coefficient*	*Standard error*	t-*statistic*
C	− 6.99522	4.98658	− 1.40281
*LZ*10	2.13330	0.762928	2.79620
*LY*60	− 0.859129	0.810336	− 1.06021

Appendix 3: The dynamics of human and physical capital

Estimation of:

$$dk = A0 + A1\,linv + A2k_0 + A3h_0. \tag{4}$$

$$dh = B0 + B1\,lenr2 + B2k_0 + B3h_0. \tag{5}$$

Period of estimation: 1966–87. Sur estimator.

Seemingly unrelated regression

Residual covariance matrix

	PHYSIC	*HUMAN*
PHYSIC	0.00081074	
HUMAN	0.000015872	0.0046656

Weighting matrix

	PHYSIC	*HUMAN*
PHYSIC	35.12041	− 0.28662
HUMAN		14.64065

Covariance matrix of transformed residuals

	PHYSIC	*HUMAN*
PHYSIC	269.0000	
HUMAN	4.65475*D*-15	269.00000

Trace of matrix = 538.000
No. of observations = 269

Parameter	*Estimate*	*Standard error*	t-*statistic*
*A*0	– 0.380770	0.020332	– 18.7276
*A*1	0.129003	0.427340*E*-02	30.1875
*A*2	– 0.079479	0.171021*E*-02	– 46.4734
*A*3	0.043816	0.142719*E*-02	30.7009
*B*0	0.069081	0.046491	1.48589
*B*1	0.026960	0.746065*E*-02	3.61368
*B*2	0.030676	0.390261*E*-02	7.86039
*B*3	– 0.026125	0.348471*E*-02	– 7.49692

Standard errors computed from quadratic form of analytic first derivatives (Gauss)

Equation PHYSIC

*Dependent variable: DK*10

Mean of dependent var. = 0.078385
Std dev. of dependent var. = 0.086745
Sum of squared residuals = 0.218089
Variance of residuals = 0.810739*E*-03

Equation HUMAN

*Dependent variable: DH*10

Mean of dependent var. = – 0.030375
Std dev. of dependent var. = 0.093723
Sum of squared residuals = 1.25505
Variance of residuals = 0.466461*E*-02
Std error of regression = 0.06830
R^2 = 0.46686
Durbin–Watson statistic = 1.4534

Covariance matrix

	1	*2*	*3*	*4*
1	0.00041339			
2	– 0.000035909	0.000018262		
3	0.000014835	– 5.42602*D*-06	2.92483*D*-06	
4	– 0.000026688	1.66153*D*-06	– 1.36584*D*-06	2.03688*D*-06
5	6.66963*D*-03	2.08911*D*-08	7.53429*D*-08	– 4.56609*D*-07
6	– 2.23032*D*-08	1.13426*D*-08	– 3.37013*D*-09	1.03198*D*-09
7	8.98327*D*-08	– 4.21224*D*-09	2.69494*D*-04	– 1.74578*D*-08
8	– 4.55113*D*-07	– 1.72771*D*-09	– 1.65613*D*-08	3.67597*D*-08

	5	*6*	*7*	*8*
5	0.0021614			
6	0.00010252	0.000055661		
7	– 0.000014100	– 0.000020671	0.000015230	
8	– 0.00015040	– 8.47838*D*-06	– 1.87052*D*-06	0.000012143

Appendix 4: transitional dynamics and the productivity wedge

1 Transitional dynamics

So as to simplify the analysis of the dynamics of the system (3), assume, here, that $d = \delta = 1$ (so that, say, one speaks of a generation) and let us simply take population and exogenous productivity to be constant. In log terms one can then write:

$$k_{t+1} = \log s_1 + ak_t + \beta h_t$$

$$h_{t+1} = \epsilon \log s_2 + vk_t + \lambda h_t.$$

We assume that $\lambda \leq 1$ so that the system is convergent if and only if:

$$\Delta \equiv (1-a)(1-\lambda) - \beta v > 0.$$

In order to go from this system to the analysis of the growth of output, we simply add these two equations. To the extent, however, that v and λ are different from a and β, one cannot proceed to a one-dimensional analysis of the law of motion of GDP. Instead, we can write:

$$g_{t+1} = (1 - a - \beta)(y_\infty - y_t) + \omega_t$$

in which $y_\infty = \log s_1 + \beta\epsilon \log s_2$ is the standard steady state that the country would converge to in the one-dimensional version of MRW and in which:

Table 8A.3. *Steady-state targets of capital*

	1966	1973	1980	1987
Average				
OECD	4.769	4.955	4.64	4.089
LDC	0.672	0.7606	1.627	1.259
Debtors 1		2.456	2.494	1.887
Debtors 2		2.6382	3.496	2.617
Standard error				
OECD	1.058	1.073	0.968	0.962
LDC	3.155	3.279	3.092	2.9427

Table 8A.4. *Steady-state targets of human capital*

	1966	1973	1980	1987
Average				
OECD	5.559	6.275	6.14	5.811
LDC	− 2.3457	0.1967	1.95	2.10035
Debtors 1		2.8587	3.216	2.8303
Debtors 2		2.693	4.2288	3.798
Standard error				
OECD	1.78	1.59	1.385	1.305
LDC	5.514	4.803	4.299	2.1003

$$\omega_t = (v - a)k_t + (\lambda - \beta)h_t.$$

ω_t is a (new) crucial parameter. It amounts to the log of the Knowledge-to-GDP ratio. With this formulation, growth is the sum of two components: one is a version of the transitional dynamics to be found in the Solow model (which measures how poor the country is with respect to its steady state); the other one is a productivity 'wedge' which measures how much additional growth a country (with similar per capita income and similar saving rates than another) can generate because of a larger aggregate 'knowledge'.

2 *Steady-state targets*

Table 8A.3 and 8A.4 present the 'steady-state' targets which are presented in equation (11).

Appendix 5: the estimation of equations (13) and (15)

Method of estimation = Ordinary Least Squares

Dependent variable: *DY*
No. of observations: 190

Mean of dependent var.	=	0.013058
Std dev. of dependent var.	=	0.031599
Sum of squared residuals	=	0.114816
Variance of residuals	=	0.630858*E*-03
Std error of regression	=	0.025117
R^2	=	0.391593
Durbin–Watson statistic	=	0.368193
F-statistic (zero slopes)	=	16.7345
Schwarz Bayes. Info. Crit.	=	– 7.19052
Log of likelihood function	=	434.489

Variable	*Estimated coefficient*	*Standard error*	t-*statistic*
C	0.426037*E*-03	0.21776	0.19565
*D*7380	– 0.015759	0.555529*E*-02	– 2.83669
*D*8087	– 0.033349	0.502533*E*-02	– 6.63609
*LENR*2	0.477216*E*-02	0.315296*E*-02	1.51355
LINV	0.16102	0.333528*E*-02	4.82791
LYPCI	– 0.398563*E*-02	0.382135*E*-02	– 1.04299
*TT*7387	0.157448		3.03536
VTENR	0.913301*E*-02		2.77413

Method of estimation = Ordinary Least Squares

Dependent variable: *LINV*
No. of observations: 194

Mean of dependent var.	=	2.51459
Std dev. of dependent var.	=	0.629036
Sum of squared residuals	=	57.6067
Variance of residuals	=	0.306419
Std error of regression	=	0.5534551
R^2	=	0.245663
Adjusted R^2	=	0.225601
F-statistic (zero slopes)	=	12.2451
Schwarz Bayes. Info. Crit.	=	– 1.0513
Log of likelihood function	=	– 157.49

Variable	*Estimated coefficient*	*Standard error*	t-*statistic*
C	0.310595	0.471789	0.658335
*D*7380	− 0.095252	0.122109	− 0.780053
*D*8087	− 0.257372	0.107044	− 2.40436
*LENR*2	0.204016	0.065243	3.12701
LYPCI	− 0.228813	0.080169	2.85415
VT	0.330220	0.207837	1.58884

NOTE

I thank Laurence Rioux for her excellent research assistance. This work was undertaken while I was a consultant to the Debt and International Finance Division of the World Bank. It does not necessarily reflect the views of the World Bank.

REFERENCES

Barro, R. and X. Sala-i-Martin (1991) 'Convergence across states and regions', *Brookings Papers on Economic Activity*, **1**.

Barro, R., G. Mankiw and X. Sala-i-Martin (1992) 'Capital mobility in neo-classical models of growth' NBER, *Working Paper*, **4206**.

Cohen, D. (1991) *Private Lending to Sovereign States: A Theoretical Autopsy*, Cambridge, MA: MIT Press.

(1992) 'The debt crisis' A post mortem', in O. Blanchard and S. Fischer (eds), *NBER Macroeconomics Annual*, vol. 7, Cambridge, MA: MIT Press.

(1993) 'Low investment and large LDC debt in the Eighties', *American Economic Review* (June).

Mankiw, G., D. Romer and P. Weil (1992) 'A contribution to the empirics of economic growth', *Quarterly Journal of Economics*, **107** (May), 407–37.

Rosen, S. (1978) 'A theory of life earnings', *Journal of Political Economy*, **94(5)**.

Summers, R. and A. Heston (1991) 'A new set of international comparisons of real product and price levels estimates for 130 countries, 1950–1985', *Review of Income and Wealth*, **35** (March), 1–25.

Discussion

ELHANAN HELPMAN

Daniel Cohen in Chapter 8 challenges the specification employed by Mankiw, Romer and Weil (1992) (hereafter MRW), while focusing on their treatment of the accumulation of human capital. Under Cohen's formulation of the null hypothesis MRW specify a stock of knowledge that is proportional to aggregate output. He suggests a more flexible specification, whereby the functional form of the stock of knowledge is the same as the production function (i.e., Cobb–Douglas) except that it has potentially different coefficients. In this way he obtains a nested model. Instead of performing a direct test of the null hypothesis, however, Cohen uses a roundabout method, which I find less convincing than a direct test. Nevertheless, Cohen's findings leave a strong impression that these data reject the MRW specification. Cohen's estimates suggest that these data also reject a simple form of the Solow model, which is in contrast to the main thrust of MRW's argument.

One may interpret these findings as a challenge to MRW's main argument using their own terms of reference. But there is, of course, no need to employ these terms of reference. Take for example, the fact that MRW's equations of cross-country variations of income per capita explain about 80% of the variance in the large sample of 98 countries and only 25% in the smaller sample of OECD countries. One interpretation of this finding is that input accumulation explains a large fraction of the variation of income per capita in non-OECD countries and only a small fraction in the advanced economies, and that therefore differences in the level of technological know-how are more important in advanced countries than in less developed and semi-industrial countries. Is this interpretation unreasonable? Not if there exists corroborative evidence. There exist, in fact, two independent pieces of evidence that support this interpretation. First, Syrquin (1992) reports that calculations of total factor productivity (TFP) for a large sample of countries show that the fraction of output growth explained by TFP growth rather than by factor accumulation rises with income per capita. It follows that factor accumulation is more important in the growth experience of poor countries while technical progress is more important in the growth experience of rich ones. Second, Lichtenberg (1992) finds that, controlling for all the variables that were used by MRW, R&D investment has a significant impact on output per capita in the MRW data. Productivity is therefore related to R&D investment and countries that invest larger fractions of output in R&D attain a higher productivity level.

Is the secondary school enrolment rate a good proxy for the growth rate of human capital? One may argue that in a cross-country comparison it proxies at least as well the available stock of human capital. Think about the finite lives of individuals and the fact that their human capital passes away with them. In a stationary environment with constant population a constant secondary school enrolment rate leads to a constant long-run stock of human capital. Countries with higher school enrolment rates end up with higher stocks of human capital. This shows that the secondary school enrolment rate may well proxy the stock of human capital. In this even MRW's regressions that explain the rate of output growth show that the growth *rate* is positively related to the *stock* of human capital (in line with Barro, 1991). This finding is not in line with a neoclassical model, but it is in line with models that were developed by Romer (1990), Grossman and Helpman (1991), and Aghion and Howitt (1992).

Finally, conditional convergence, reflected in the fact that the rate of growth depends negatively on the initial level of income per capita, can be interpreted as saying that countries that have initially low capital–labour ratios accumulate capital faster than countries that have initially higher capital–labour ratios. This is in line with Solow, but is also is in line with the newer-type models when allowing for capital accumulation. This piece of evidence therefore in no way contradicts the implications of new growth models.

All this suggests that the strong claim made by MRW that the neoclassical growth model is sufficient for explaining the data is not warranted.

REFERENCES

Aghion, P. and P. Howitt (1992) 'A model of growth through creative destruction', *Econometrica*, **60**, 323–51.

Barro, R. (1991) 'Economic growth in a cross-section of countries', *Quarterly Journal of Economics*, **106**, 407–43.

Grossman, G.M. and E. Helpman (1991) *Innovation and Growth in the Global Economy*, Cambridge, MA: MIT Press.

Lichtenberg, F.R. (1992) 'R&D investment and international productivity differences', NBER, *Working Paper*, **4161** (September).

Mankiw, G., D. Romer and P. Weil (1992) 'A contribution to the empirics of economic growth', *Quarterly Journal of Economics*, **107** (May), 407–37.

Romer, P. (1990) 'Endogenous technical change', *Journal of Political Economy*, **98**, S1002–37.

Syrquin, M. (1992) 'Structural transformation and the new growth theory' (September), mimeo.

9 Convergence in growth rates: a quantitative assessment of the role of capital mobility and international taxation

ASSAF RAZIN and CHI-WA YUEN

1 Introduction

The objective of this chapter is to provide a quantitative assessment of the role of two factors (often overlooked in the growth literature) – capital mobility and international taxation – in explaining the observed diversity in the long-run rates of growth of per capita and total incomes as well as the population growth rates across countries. In so doing, we hope to shed some light on the problem of economic development posed by Lucas (1988), i.e., accounting for the observed diversity across countries.

The idea that government policy can induce *growth* effects and thus diversity in growth rates can be traced to asymmetry in tax policies has been explored quite extensively.[1] With a few exceptions, however, such analysis has been conducted for closed economies without taking account of the growing interaction among countries in the world in terms of commodity trade and capital flows. When capital is internationally mobile, the foreign-source capital income becomes an additional tax base from which the fiscal authorities in both the home and foreign countries can generate tax revenues. As we show in a companion paper (Razin and Yuen, 1992), the tax treatment of this income by the two governments and the degree of capital mobility will determine whether tax-driven growth differences can be preserved in an open economy. *Inter alia*, we find that:

Proposition 1

> Under perfect capital mobility, long-term rates of growth of total (but not necessarily per capita) GDPs will be equal across countries. (P1)

Proposition 2

> Under asymmetric capital income tax rates, the *source* (or *territorial*) principle of international income taxation is growth-

equalising whereas the *residence* (or *worldwide*) principle is growth-diverging. (P2)

Here, we shall take these two propositions more seriously by confronting their empirical implications with data and/or observed facts and performing some exploratory quantitative analysis. To examine the allocative and growth effects of capital mobility and international taxation quantitatively, we shall also calibrate the open-economy growth model in Razin and Yuen (1992) to the Group of Seven (G-7) data over the period 1965–87 by splitting them into a 'two-country world': the United States (US) versus the other G-6 countries (G-6). Assuming that fundamental parameters remain the same across global tax and capital mobility regimes, we simulate the effects of various tax reforms and restrictions on capital flows on long-term resource allocation and growth rates.

The paper is organised as follows. Sections 2 and 3 provide the intention behind (P1) and (P2) and explore the growth rates implications of capital mobility (P1) and international taxation of capital income (P2) respectively. Section 4 describes the parametric version of the Razin and Yuen (1992) model used in the calibration and simulation exercises, and reports the numerical results. Section 5 draws the main conclusions.

2 The role of capital mobility

Under free capital mobility, the law of diminishing returns implies that capital will move from capital-rich (low marginal product of capital, henceforth, MPK) countries to capital-poor (high MPK) countries.[2] Over time, such cross-border capital flows will equalise the MPKs prevailing in all countries.[3] Absent dynamic inefficiency in the sense of capital overaccumulation, the short-run effect of such capital movement is to shorten the transition path of the capital-importing country and lengthen that of the capital-exporting country.[4] Without further restrictions, three situations are possible in the long run:

(a) all capital in the world resides in one single country
(b) no cross-border capital flows (i.e., back to autarky)
(c) positive net capital flows from some countries to some other countries.

Both (a) and (b) are unrealistic cases; only (c) is empirically relevant. What, then, does it take to eliminate (a) and (b) even as theoretical possibilities? Case (a) will not occur if the MPK becomes infinitely high when the capital remaining in any capital-exporting country gets sufficiently small (i.e., the Inada conditions can rule out this corner solution).

Case (b) will not occur as long as the countries are heterogeneous in some key fundamentals. If they were homogeneous, capital flows would not have taken place in the first place. Since we also want to investigate the role of taxes on growth, let us assume that asymmetry in capital income tax rates is the factor that first induced cross-border capital flows. Suppose further that these countries were travelling along their steady-state growth paths initially. Should these taxes remain different, the driving force that initiated capital movement to begin with will again be active when the countries return to their long-run autarky growth paths. As such, (b) can also be ruled out. The only interesting case that remains is therefore (c).

To understand how capital mobility may affect the convergence in long-term growth rates across countries, we have to be more specific about what we mean by the long run. We shall follow the convention in the growth literature and identify *long-run growth* with *balanced* or *steady-state growth*: the particular solution such that the rates of growth of all growing variables are constant (so that ratios among these variables defined in certain ways will also be time-invariant). Granted this definition, it is then not difficult to see that, for growth to be *balanced* in all countries the net capital flow of each country must be growing at the same rate as its total income. But since the capital inflow of one country is equal to the capital outflow of another country, the balanced growth restriction forces the total income growth rates to be uniform across countries in the long run, i.e., Proposition 1 of Razin and Yuen (1992).

Recall that per capita income equals total income divided by the size of the population. We can thus decompose the *total* income growth rate into the *per capita* income growth rates and *population* growth rates: $(1 + g_Y) = (1 + g_N)(1 + g_y)$. Here, g_x denotes the growth rate of variable x between two periods, Y the total GDP, N the population, and y the per capita GDP (so $y = Y/N$). Together with (P1), this decomposition implies that $(1 + g_N^A)(1 + g_y^A) = (1 + g_N^B)(1 + g_y^B)$. Two empirical implications follow:

(1) Long-term rates of growth of population and per capita incomes should be negatively correlated across countries;
(2) Total income growth rates should exhibit less variation than per capita income growth rates across countries.

Implication (1) says that countries with higher population growth rates will have, on average, slower growth in per capita income. While the negative correlation between population growth rates and the levels of per capita income has been fairly well accepted as a stylised fact,[5] similar correlation between population growth and per capita income growth is not as clear. The time-series counterpart of these correlations is more a

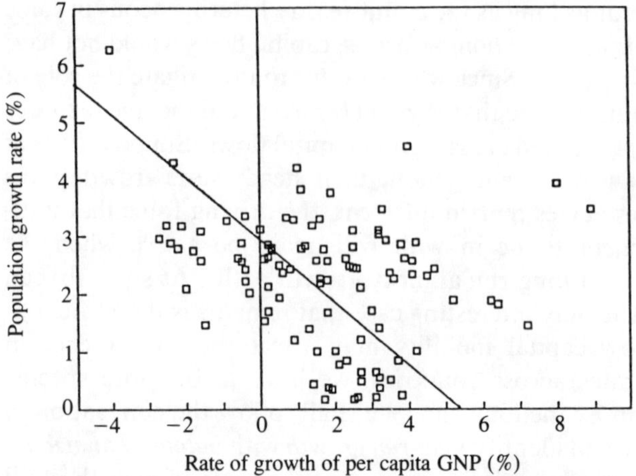

Figure 9.1 Correlation between population growth and *per capita* income growth
1965–87 data for the 120 countries (excluding those with missing data) listed in *World Development Report* (1989), Tables 1 and 26.

question of demographic transition – a transition from high rates of fertility and mortality rates to relatively low rates during the development process – and thus varies with the stage of development of the various countries.[6] Actually, both of these correlations tend to be negative during the more advanced phase of development. But since implication (1) refers to long-run average growth rates irrespective of whether the countries are DCs or LDCs, we show in Figure 9.1 the correlation between g_N and g_y, incorporating countries at all stages of development. The downward-sloping regression line fitted through the points 'roughly' confirms the negative correlation.[7] As a further confirmation, we find that the correlation coefficient between g_N and g_y is -0.27.

Implication (2) does not follow directly from, and is actually a weaker form of, (P1). It takes account of the fact that, in the real world, countries – being bombarded by all kinds of shocks from time to time – will not be operating on their steady-state growth paths most of the time. Given such short-term disturbances, we should not expect to find support for the strong version of (P1) as stated above. However, if we average the growth rates in every country over longer time periods, these fluctuations will be smoothed out so they will be closer to being in the long run. Then, the weak version of (P2) says that the average total income growth rates should be less variable than the average per capita income growth rates.

Figure 9.2 plots these two income growth rates for the various countries (averaged over the period 1965–87) against their per capita income levels in 1987. The horizontal straight line (at a GNP growth rate of 3.94%)

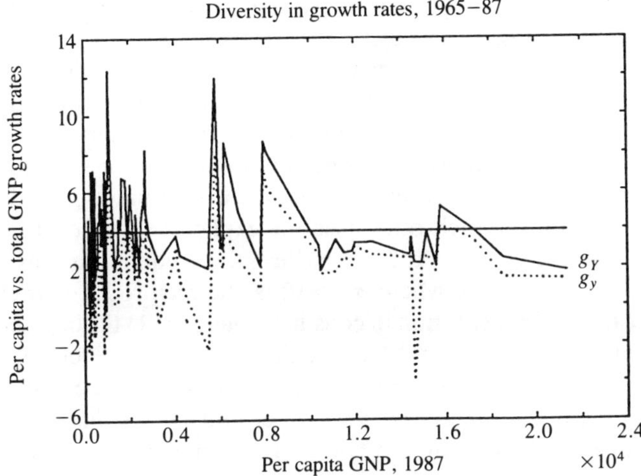

Figure 9.2 Relative variability of total and *per capita* income growth rates
As figure 9.1.

portrays the ideal situation where (P1) holds exactly. Simple eyeball observation seems to indicate that there is less variability in the total GNP growth rates across countries than in their per capita counterpart. To check our eyesight, we compute the coefficients of variation (CVs) in these two growth rates from the data described in Figures 9.1 and 9.2, and find that the CV in the total income growth rates [$=0.58$ for $g_Y \equiv \ln((1+g_N)(1+g_y))$, and 1.28 for $g_Y \equiv \ln((1+g_N)(1+g_y)-1)$ indeed falls short of the CV in the per capita income growth rates [$=1.35$]. Implication (2) is therefore supported by the data.

With capital market imperfections in the real world, it is not surprising to find that the data provide only a 'rough' confirmation of implications (1) and (2), and hence (P1). Since perfect capital mobility is a precondition for (P1), we should expect these implications to find stronger support from a sample of countries with less restrictions on capital flows. This hypothesis is, nonetheless, difficult to test due to the data problem. The IMF *Restrictions on Payments on Capital Transactions*, say, that one may want to use as proxies for capital controls do not take into account the degrees of intensity of such restrictions.

3 The role of international taxation

When capital is mobile, the choice of international tax principle and tax rates levied on capital incomes earned by residents and non-residents at home and abroad will affect (i) the after-tax rates of return on capital ($\bar{r}$)

and, indirectly, (ii) the rates of growth of per capita consumption and population (g_c and g_N) across countries.

The relation between (i) and (ii) can be obtained from the familiar marginal condition for the intertemporal choice of consumption adjusted for capital taxes: $\text{IMRS}_{t-1,t} = 1 + \bar{r}_t$ where $\text{IMRS}_{t-1,t}$ is the intertemporal marginal rate of substitution between consumption in period $t-1$ and consumption in period t. If preferences are isoelastic in consumption and people are altruistic towards each other (see the explicit expression for preferences on p. 245), we can rewrite the condition as: $(1 + g_{ct})^{\sigma}(1 + g_{Nt})^{1-\xi} = \beta(1 + \bar{r}_t)$, where σ (> 0) is the reciprocal of the intertemporal elasticity of substitution in consumption, ξ (≤ 1) the degree of interpersonal altruism, and β the subjective discount factor. Focusing on the balanced growth path where growth rates are constant, (per capita) consumption and output grow at the same rate, and (P1) holds, and taking the ratio of growth rates in two countries (A and B) after some rearrangement, we get:

$$\frac{1 + \bar{r}^A}{1 + \bar{r}^B} = \left(\frac{1 + g_B^A}{1 + g_Y^B}\right)^{\xi - (1 - \sigma)}$$

This holds for $\xi \neq 1 - \sigma$. The special case where $\xi = 1 - \sigma$ will not be considered in this chapter.

The above formula shows how capital income taxes can affect the relative income growth rates via the after-tax rates of return on capital ($\bar{r}$s). At this point, the reader may be tempted to think that no-arbitrage restrictions will force the $\bar{r}$s to be equalised across countries under perfect capital mobility, implying convergence in both the per capita and total income growth rates. In fact, this reasoning is true only under the *source* or *territorial* tax principle, whereby all types of income originating in the country are taxed uniformly regardless of the place of residence of the income recipients. Under the alternative *residence* or *worldwide* principle, residents are taxed on their worldwide income uniformly regardless of the source of income, while nonresidents are not taxed on income originating in the country. In that case, domestic-source and foreign-source incomes receive identical tax treatment for residents within each country, but asymmetric treatment across countries if different countries impose different capital income tax rates. Asymmetry in $\bar{r}$s implies, in turn, asymmetry in growth rates.[8]

The formula also indicates that under residence-based taxation, when

$\xi \neq 1 - \sigma$, asymmetric tax rates may have differential effects on the growth of per capita income and population. In particular, when people are more individualistic or selfish ($\xi < 1 - \sigma$), the country with a higher capital tax rate will exhibit faster growth in per capita income and slower growth in population. The reverse is true when people are more altruistic towards each other ($\xi > 1 - \sigma$). Although the link is not that direct, one can relate this discussion to the tradeoff between the quantity and quality of children *à la* Becker and Lewis (1973). $\xi > 1 - \sigma$ then corresponds to the case where people care more about quantity than quality. Hence, the population growth rate is higher, but per capita income growth lower, when capital taxes are relatively high (so investment in physical capital becomes less attractive relative to investment in either the quality or quantity of children), and vice versa.

Everything seems to be possible under (P2). In order to determine whether growth rates will more likely be converging or diverging in the face of differential capital tax rates, we display in Table 9.1 data extracted from Table 2.1 of Frenkel, Razin and Sadka (1991) to see which international income tax principle is more popular (at the individual and corporate levels) among major industrial countries. R in Table 9.1 stands for the residence principle, and S for the source principle.

Evidently, the residence principle is the dominant tax principle among countries in the world. The production efficiency, Ramsey (second-best) efficiency, and capital export neutrality implications of residence-based taxation may explain its popularity.[9] From (P2), we can thus conclude that asymmetry in cross-country capital taxes is a plausible explanation of diversity in growth rates. A closer examination of the relation between capital taxes on the one hand and income and population growth rates on the other suggests that $\xi > 1 - \sigma$ seems to conform to the situation in these countries. In other words, low capital tax rates tend to be associated with faster growth in per capita income and slower growth in population. This phenomenon is also revealed by the calibration result below.

4 The parametric model: calibration and simulations

In this section, we shall briefly review the analytical framework in Razin and Yuen (1992), parameterise and calibrate the model to real-world data, and simulate the effects of different tax structures and restrictions on capital flows on long-term growth rates across countries.

We consider a two-country dynastic world with N_t^i identical, rational agents in each country i in each period t ($i = A, B$; $t = 0, 1, 2, \ldots$), with two engines of growth (human capital and population) and capital

Table 9.1. *Taxation of foreign-source capital income, selected countries*

Country	Individual		Corporate	
	Top tax rate (%)	Dominant principle	Top tax rate (%)	Dominant principle
Belgium	55	R	43	S
Denmark	68	R	50	R (with credit)
France	53	R	39	S
Germany	56	R	56	R (with deduction)[a]
Greece	50	R	35	R (with credit)
Ireland	58	R	43	R (with credit or deduction)
Italy	50	R	46	R (with credit)[b]
Luxembourg	56	R	36	R (with credit)
Netherlands	72	R	36	R (with credit or deduction)[a]
Portugal	40	R	36	R (with credit)
Spain	56	R	35	R (with credit)
United Kingdom	60	R	35	R (with credit)
Canada	42–49[c]		38	
Japan	50		42	
United States	28–38[d]	R	34	R (with credit)

Sources: Lans Bovenberg and George Kopits, 'Harmonization of Taxes on Capital Income and Commodities in the European Community', IMF (October 1989) and *Individual Taxes: A Worldwide Summary*, Price Waterhouse (1989).

[a] The source principle applies under treaties and for substantial participation in foreign companies.

[b] With refund for excess foreign tax credit.

[c] Including provincial taxes.

[d] Including state taxes.

mobility, with frictionless and competitive markets, and without international policy coordination. The typical agent cares about his own consumption c_t^i and the population in his country N_t^i. His preferences are given by:

$$\sum_{t=0}^{\infty} \beta^t (N_t^i)^{\xi} \left[\frac{(c_t^i)^{1-\sigma}}{1-\sigma} \right]$$

where β is the subjective discount factor, ξ the degree of altruism towards people, and σ the inverse of the intertemporal elasticity of substitution in consumption.

Each household member is endowed with 1 unit of time, possesses h_t^i of human capital and S_t^i/N_t^i of physical capital carried over from period $t-1$ (given S_0^i/N_0^i at $t=0$), and receives a lump-sum transfer of T_t^i/N_t^i from its government, in each period t. S/he can split the unit time among work (n_t^i), learning in schools (e_t^i), and child-rearing (v_t^i), and allocate the physical capital as inputs to final goods production ($\eta_t^i S_t^{ii}/N_t^i$) and human capital formation ($k_{ht}^i = (1-\eta_t^i)S_t^{ii}/N_t^i$). S/he also has to decide how much capital (S_{t+1}^i) to be carried forward to the ensuing period, and where to locate such investment – at home (S_{t+1}^{ii}) or abroad (S_{t+1}^{ij}).

The dynamics of the two growth engines are determined as follows. The child-rearing activity gives rise to population growth:

$$N_{t+1}^i = D(v_t^i)^a N_t^i + (1-\delta_N)N_t^i$$

where D and a are the fertility coefficient and productivity parameter respectively, and δ_N is the mortality rate. The schooling activity contributes to human capital growth:

$$h_{t+1}^i = B(k_{ht}^i)^{\gamma}(e_t^i h_t^i)^{1-\gamma} + (1-\delta_h)h_t^i$$

where B is the knowledge-production coefficient, γ the share of the physical capital input, and δ_h the rate of depreciation of human capital.

Each national government levies five kinds of distortionary taxes – on domestic consumption (τ_{ct}^i),[10] on domestic labour income (τ_{wt}^i), on residents' domestic-source capital income (τ_{rDt}^i), on residents' foreign-source capital income net of taxes paid to the foreign government (τ_{rFt}^i), and on capital income earned by nonresidents in its country (τ_{rNt}^i) – to finance its exogenous spending (G_t^i) and transfers (T_t^i). Depreciation allowances are deductible from capital taxes. Without deficit finance, the fiscal budget is balanced in every period.

Final output is produced with physical capital (K_{yt}^i) – supplied domestically ($\eta_t^i S_t^{ii}/N_t^i$) and, if there exists capital inflow, imported from abroad (S_t^{ji}) – and total effective labour ($H_t^i = N_t^i n_t^i h_t^i$) via a Cobb–Douglas technology. Accordingly, gross domestic product is given by:

$$Y_t^i = A(K_{yt}^i)^{\epsilon}(H_t^i)^{1-\epsilon}$$

where A is the production coefficient, and ϵ the output share of capital. Since total resources can be spent on private and government consumption and investment, the resource constraint in country i can be stated as:

$$N_t^i c_t^i + S_{t+1}^i - (1-\delta_k)S_t^i + G_t^i = GNP_t^i$$

where GNP_t^i is the sum of Y_t^i and the net capital income from abroad, $[(1-\tau_{rNt}^i)(r_t^i - \delta_k) + \delta_k]S_t^{ij} - [(1-\tau_{rNt}^i)(r_t^i - \delta_k)\delta_k]S_t^{ji}$, and r_t^i is the rate of return on, and δ_k the rate of depreciation of, physical capital.

We lay out in the Appendix on p. 254 the set of equations that describes the global steady-state growth equilibrium. These equations are used to calibrate and simulate the model along the lines of Lucas (1990a). Imagine that the US and the G-6 were growing along their balanced growth paths in the period 1965–87, we choose benchmark values for the parameters (β, σ, ξ, a, ϵ, γ, δ_k, δ_h, δ_N, A, B, D), allocations (c^i, n^i, e^i, η^i, S^{ii}, S^{ij}, $N^B h^B / N^A h^A$), growth rates (g_h^i, g_N^i), and policy variables (g^i, T^i, τ_c^i, τ_w^i, τ_{rD}^i, τ_{rF}^i, τ_{rN}^i) so that the theoretical equilibrium values of these variables 'match' as closely as possible their long-run average values from the data. Long-run levels and growth rates data are drawn largely from the 1989 *World Development Report*, and tax rates data from Mendoza, Razin and Tesar (1992). Some of the parameter values are borrowed from previous empirical studies. Others whose values are less well documented, together with some of the variables which do not have direct empirical counterparts, are treated as unknowns and 'estimated' from the steady-state equations. In our benchmark case, we assume perfect capital mobility and the international income tax principle is residence-based (given that most of the G-7 countries follow the residence principle). In Table 9.2, we summarise the benchmark parameter and initial values.

We will skip the details about our choice of parameter and initial values because after prolonged experimentation we have achieved only partial success in calibrating our model to data. As is evident from comparing the numbers in Table 9.2 with actual data, there are at least three aspects of the data that our model values fail to mimic: (a) the per capita income should be lower in the G-6 than in the US, (b) the output shares of both private and public consumption should be lower in the G-6 than in the US, and (c) the consumption tax rate should be much higher in the G-6 than in the US.[11] The reason for these discrepancies is obvious: capital movement between the US and the G-6 is *not* 100% free. In what follows, the reader is welcomed, if s/he so wishes, to interpret what we label as the US and G-6 simply as two artificial economies. The hypothetical experiments described below will then serve as an illustration of the potential quantitative effects of capital mobility and tax changes in an artificial (but hopefully close enough to real) environment.

Table 9.2. *Summary of benchmark values*

Initial steady-state values			
Per capita output (US)	y^A	1.000	(1.000)
Per capita output (G-6)	y^B	1.050	(0.725)
Consumption–output (US)	C^A/Y^A	0.650	(0.660)
Consumption–output (G-6)	C^B/Y^B	0.660	(0.588)
Capital–output (US)	K^A/Y^A	1.795	
Capital–output (G-6)	K^B/Y^B	1.751	
Ratio of net capital flow from G-6 to US (= US current account deficits) to US output	S^{AB}/Y^A	– 0.035	(– 0.035)
Fraction of capital allocated to goods production (US)	η^A	0.690	
Fraction of capital allocated to goods production (G-6)	η^B	0.714	
Fraction of time allocated to goods production (US)	n^A	0.409	
Fraction of time allocated to goods production (G-6)	n^B	0.430	
Fraction of time allocated to human capital formation (US)	e^A	0.376	
Fraction of time allocated to human capital formation (G-6)	e^B	0.401	
Population growth rate (US)	g_N^A	0.013	(0.010)
Population growth rate (G-6)	g_N^B	0.008	(0.006)
Per capita income rate (US)	g_y^A	0.018	(0.015)
Per capita income rate (G-6)	g_y^B	0.023	(0.028)
Initial values of policy variables			
Output share of government spending (US)	G^A/Y^A	0.200	(0.210)
Output share of government spending (G-6)	G^B/Y^B	0.200	(0.176)
Ratio of lump-sum transfers to output (US)	T^A/Y^A	0.243	
Ratio of lump-sum transfers to output (G-6)	T^B/Y^B	0.168	
Consumption tax rate (US)	τ_c^A	0.320	(0.050)
Consumption tax rate (G-6)	τ_c^B	0.130	(0.014)

Table 9.2 (*cont.*)

Labour income tax rate (US)	τ_w^A	0.240	(0.240)
Labour income tax rate (G-6)	τ_w^B	0.303	(0.300)
Tax rate on domestic-source capital income (US residents)	τ_{rD}^A	0.300	(0.300)
Tax rate on domestic-source capital income (G-6 residents)	τ_{rD}^B	0.290	(0.290)
Tax rate on foreign-source capital income (US residents)	τ_{rF}^A	0.300	(0.300)
Tax rate on foreign-source capital income (G-6 residents)	τ_{rF}^B	0.290	(0.290)
US tax rate on G-6 residents' capital income earned (US)	τ_{rN}^A	0.000	(0.000)
G-6 tax rate on US residents' capital income earned (G-6)	τ_{rN}^B	0.000	(0.000)
Production parameter values			
Capital's share in goods production	ϵ	0.250	
Capital's share in human capital production	γ	0.165	
Fertility productivity parameter	a	1.000	
Rate of depreciation of physical capital	δ_k	0.050	
Rate of depreciation of human capital	δ_h	0.080	
Mortality rate	δ_N	0.009	
Output production coefficient	A	1.848	
Human capital production coefficient	B	0.245	
Fertility coefficient	D	0.104	
Preference parameter values			
Subjective discount factor	β	0.912	
Inverse of intertemporal elasticity of substitution	σ	0.398	
Altruism parameter	ξ	0.956	

Numbers in brackets are actual long-run average (1965–87) data for the G-7, whereas all other numbers are calibrated to match closely the data while satisfying all the steady-state equations.

Our first experiment examines the role of capital mobility. It involves switching from a state where cross-country capital flows are perfectly mobile to a state where capital movements are shut down altogether. The autarky equilibria are computed for the two countries separately under the same parameter and policy settings as in the free mobility case, assuming that lump-sum taxes or subsidies are used to re-balance the fiscal budgets in the absence of foreign-source capital income tax proceeds.

The effects of capital control on growth rate and MPK differentials are intuitively clear. As the numbers on the first rows of the four panels in Table 9.3 indicate, shutting down capital mobility leads to bigger diversity in cross-country growth rates and rates of return on physical capital. Without capital flows, the pre-tax returns rs, which are equalised under capital mobility and the residence principle, are now different across countries ($\Delta r > 0$), let alone the post-tax returns $\bar{r}$s. Not surprisingly, the diversity in both the population and per capita income growth rates widens. The population growth rate rises from 1.30% to 1.37% in the US, and falls from 0.83% to 0.79% in the G-6, leading to an increase in the population growth rate differential from 0.47% to 0.58%. On the other hand, the per capita income growth rate drops from 1.80% to 1.66% in the US, and rises from 2.28% to 2.35% in the G-6. The per capita income growth differential therefore grows from 0.48% to 0.69%. Under capital controls, (P1) need not hold. The total income growth rates diverge from the uniform rate of 3.12% under capital mobility to 3.05% in the US and 3.16% in the G-6. Losing the opportunity to channel savings abroad, the G-6 devotes them back to domestic production, causing a rise in both the long-run level and rate of growth of per capita GDP. The reverse is true in the US, the capital-importing country before the imposition of capital controls. The steady-state welfare levels under the two capital-mobility regimes, and hence the welfare loss from shutting down capital flows, depend on the steady-state levels of the normalising variables (stocks of human capital in the two countries), which cannot be determined uniquely in models of endogenous growth such as ours without tracing out the transitional dynamics. Without carrying out this exercise, we can nonetheless be sure that such capital restrictions will give rise to welfare losses for both countries simply by observing that autarky is feasible but not chosen by agents in the two countries under the global free-capital-mobility equilibrium.

The second experiment demonstrates the effects of changes in the capital income taxes. By capital income tax reform, we mean altering the tax rate on capital income with compensating changes in lump-sum taxes to balance the fiscal budgets. We continue to assume the residence principle

Table 9.3. *Capital income tax reforms with and without capital mobility*

g_N^A	g_N^B	Δg_N	g_y^A	g_y^B	Δg_y	g_Y^A	g_Y^B	Δg_Y	Δr	$\Delta \bar{r}$	τ_r^A
Perfect capital mobility: (a) reform in the US											
1.300	0.830	− 0.470	1.800	2.275	0.475	3.123	3.123	0.000	0.000	0.1820	30.000
1.305	0.835	− 0.469	1.791	2.265	0.474	3.119	3.119	0.000	0.000	0.1818	29.999
1.309	0.840	− 0.469	1.781	2.255	0.473	3.114	3.114	0.000	0.000	0.1816	29.998
1.314	0.845	− 0.468	1.772	2.245	0.473	3.109	3.109	0.000	0.000	0.1814	29.997
1.318	0.850	− 0.468	1.762	2.235	0.472	3.104	3.104	0.000	0.000	0.1812	29.996
Perfect capital mobility: (b) reform in the G-6											
g_N^A	g_N^B	Δg_N	g_y^A	g_y^B	Δg_y	g_Y^A	g_Y^B	Δg_Y	Δr	$\Delta \bar{r}$	τ_r^B
1.300	0.830	− 0.470	1.800	2.275	0.475	3.123	3.123	0.000	0.000	0.1820	28.786
1.294	0.823	− 0.471	1.813	2.288	0.475	3.130	3.130	0.000	0.000	0.1823	28.785
1.389	0.818	− 0.471	1.822	2.298	0.476	3.135	3.135	0.000	0.000	0.1826	28.784
1.285	0.813	− 0.472	1.831	2.308	0.477	3.140	3.140	0.000	0.000	0.1828	28.783
1.289	0.817	− 0.471	1.823	2.299	0.476	3.136	3.136	0.000	0.000	0.1829	28.782
No capital mobility: (a) reform in the US											
g_N^A	g_N^B	Δg_N	g_y^A	g_y^B	Δg_y	g_Y^A	g_Y^B	Δg_Y	Δr	$\Delta \bar{r}$	τ_r^A
1.370	0.793	− 0.577	1.655	2.348	0.693	3.048	3.159	0.111	0.127	0.271	30.000
1.353	0.793	− 0.560	1.696	2.348	0.652	3.072	3.159	0.087	0.313	0.254	29.000
1.335	0.793	− 0.542	1.737	2.348	0.611	3.096	3.159	0.063	0.494	0.237	28.000
1.317	0.793	− 0.524	1.778	2.348	0.570	3.119	3.159	0.040	0.670	0.221	27.000
1.300	0.793	− 0.507	1.818	2.348	0.530	3.142	3.159	0.017	0.842	0.204	26.000

No capital mobility: (b) reform in the G-6

g_N^A	g_N^B	Δg_N	g_y^A	g_y^B	Δg_y	g_Y^A	g_Y^B	Δg_Y	Δr	$\Delta \bar{r}$	τ_r^B
1.300	0.793	−0.577	1.655	2.348	0.693	3.048	3.159	0.111	0.127	0.271	28.786
1.370	0.779	−0.591	1.655	2.379	0.724	3.048	3.177	0.129	−0.020	0.284	28.000
1.370	0.761	−0.609	1.655	2.419	0.764	3.048	3.198	0.150	−0.202	0.300	27.000
1.370	0.743	−0.627	1.655	2.458	0.803	3.048	3.220	0.172	−0.379	0.316	26.000
1.370	0.726	−0.644	1.655	2.497	0.842	3.048	3.241	0.193	−0.552	0.332	25.000

(i) All entries in the table are in percentage terms (i.e., multiplied by 100).
(ii) $\Delta x \equiv x^B - x^A$ for variable x.

under capital mobility so that τ_r^i $(i = A, B)$ in the first two panels of Table 9.3 refers to both τ_{rD}^i and τ_{rF}^i (with $\tau_{rN}^i = 0$). Only very small tax changes are considered in the perfect-capital-mobility (PCM) case because, given the complexity and nonlinearity of the equations, the Gauss equation-solver we use for our simulations breaks down easily for larger deviations from the initial steady state. Relatively bigger tax changes are considered, however, in the no-capital-mobility (NCM) case, for two reasons. Computationally, the lower dimensionality of the autarky equilibrium allows us to examine bigger changes. Besides, the growth rate changes resulting from a change in the capital tax of the same order of magnitude as in the PCM case are negligible, almost totally unnoticeable. This suggests that the *growth* effects of capital taxes are much bigger with than without capital mobility: 0.004 of a 1% change in τ_r under PCM approximates the growth effect of a 1% change in τ_r under NCM. Note also that there exist cross-country spillovers of growth effects under PCM, but tax changes in one country will have no effect on the growth rates in the other country under NCM. Without opening the economy, the recent growth literature may thus have substantially underestimated the potentially large growth effects due to tax changes and cross-border policy spillovers.

A few remarks on the implications of capital tax reforms in the two countries for population and income growth and the diversity in these growth rates are now in order.

1. The effects of lowering capital taxes on the growth of population, per capita and total incomes are asymmetric and non-monotonic in the US (the high-τ_r country) and the G-6 (the low-τ_r country) under PCM, but symmetric and monotonic under NCM. In the PCM case, while a reduction in τ_r^A may stimulate an increase in g_N^A and a fall in g_y^A and g_Y^A initially, these changes can be reversed for further tax reduction. Opposite changes in g_N^B, g_y^B, and g_Y^B occur in response to a fall in τ_r^B. In the NCM case, g_N will fall and g_y and g_Y rise following a decrease in τ_r. These seemingly weird results can be understood in terms of the response of $\bar{r}$ to changes in τ_r. Recall that $\bar{r} = (1 - \tau_r)(\text{MPK} - \delta_k)$. Since $1 - \tau_r$ rises and MPK falls – due to the stimulative effect of tax reduction on capital accumulation and diminishing marginal productivity – when τ_r is lowered, the effect on $\bar{r}$ is in general unclear. This is reminiscent of the Laffer Curve, which can be multimodal in our setup. The differential effects of tax rate changes on the growth of population (g_N) and per capita income (g_y) are a consequence of our benchmark parameter restriction: $\xi > 1 - \sigma$.

2. There is positive comovement of the various growth rates in the US and G-6 under PCM. This is because both countries are exposed to the same (physical capital) investment opportunities under capital mobility

and the residence principle. In the absence of policy spillovers, no such comovement exists in the NCM case.

3. The growth rate differentials Δg_N, Δg_y and Δg_Y may not necessarily be narrowed as the capital tax rates in the two countries get closer. This is not a violation of (P2) because (P2) only predicts the signs, but not also the sizes, of these gaps. In fact, these growth rate gaps will not be closed even if the two countries have identical capital tax rates because what really matter are the after-tax rates of return on capital $\bar{r}$s (not the tax rates themselves), and these $\bar{r}$s will not be equalised because the consumption and labour income taxes are different across countries.

In yet another experiment (not shown), we switch the international income tax rule from the residence principle to the source principle. The theoretical results in Razin and Yuen (1992) are confirmed numerically. In particular, the population, per capita and total income growth rates are symmetric across countries despite capital tax asymmetries. So are the post-tax returns $\bar{r}$s, implying efficiency in the allocation of world savings. The Ramsey (and production) inefficiency of the source principle, however, results in welfare losses relative to the residence principle.

5 Conclusion

In this chapter, we have found some supportive evidence for the theoretical results on the convergence in long-term population, per capita and total income growth rates under capital mobility and global taxation obtained in Razin and Yuen (1992). In particular, we find that (1) population growth and per capita income growth are negatively correlated across countries, (2) the total income growth rates are less variable across countries than the per capita income growth rates across countries, and (3) asymmetry in capital income tax rates, coupled with the residence principle, can be an important source of cross-country differences in per capita income growth. Computer simulations are run to assess the quantitative effects of varying the degree of capital mobility and the rates of capital income taxes. Our numerical results show that although the effect of liberalising capital flows in long-run growth may not be all that sizable, the growth effects of policy changes can be tremendously magnified by cross-border capital flows and policy spillovers.

Having stated the good news, let us also caution the reader by admitting that our analysis is preliminary – largely exploratory in nature – and incomplete. We have not been successful in matching all relevant aspects of our model to real-world data. Incorporating some forms of capital controls into the theoretical framework may help. Econometric estimation of the unknown parameters can reduce the degree of arbitrariness that calibration entails. If one's purpose of conducting such experiments is to understand better the effects of various factors affecting growth and development, one may also want to expand the sample and consider perhaps the LDCs versus the DCs (less similar economies) rather than the US versus the G-6 (more similar economies). Regarding the policy experiments, other kinds of changes such as the consumption tax reform, labour income tax reform, population control, with and without international policy coordination are of interest. It will also be important to compute the transitional dynamics for the evaluation of policy effects in both the short and long run and for welfare calculations. We hope our work serves as a fruitful first step for more serious research in the area of growth and policy in open economies.

Appendix: steady-state growth equilibrium

Since we want to analyse the long-run effects of changes in taxes and capital mobility, we shall focus only on steady-state behaviour. Along the balanced growth path, the time allocations (n, e, v), capital sector-allocation factor η^i, tax rates (τ_c^i, τ_w^i, τ_{rD}^i, τ_{rF}^i, τ_{rN}^i) and growth rates (g_h^i, g_N^i) are constant. The following 'ratio' variables will also be time-invariant:

$$c^i = \frac{c_t^i}{h_t^i},\ S^{ii} = \frac{S_t^{ii}}{N_t^i h_t^i},\ S^{ij} = \frac{S_t^{ij}}{N_t^i h_t^i},\ k_y^i = \frac{K_{yt}^i}{N_t^i h_t^i},\ k_h^i = \frac{k_{ht}^i}{h_t^i},$$

$$G^i = \frac{G_t^i}{N_t^i h_t^i},\ T^i = \frac{T_t^i}{N_t^i h_t^i},\ y^i = \frac{y_t^i}{N_t^i h_t^i}.$$

We can then obtain the following equations as steady state analogues of equations (7)–(10), (2), (3), (4)′, and (5) in Razin and Yuen (1992).

$$\frac{(1-\tau_w^i)(1-\epsilon)y^i/n^i}{(1-\tau_{rD}^i)\epsilon y^i/k_y^i + \delta_k} = \left(\frac{1-\gamma}{\gamma}\right)\left(\frac{k_h^i}{e^i}\right),$$

$$\frac{n^i}{e^i} = \frac{1-\beta^i(1-\gamma R_h^i)}{\beta^i(1-\gamma)R_h^i},$$

$$\beta^i(1+\tau_c^i)c^i\left(\frac{\xi}{1-\sigma}-1\right)\left(\frac{aR_N^i}{1-n^i-e^i}\right)$$
$$= (1-\tau_w^i)(1-\epsilon)\left(\frac{y^i}{n^i}\right)\left\{1-\beta^i\left[1+\frac{aR_N^i[(1-\gamma)n^i-\gamma e^i]}{(1-\gamma)(1-n^i-e^i)}\right]\right\},$$

$$(1-\tau_{rD}^i)\left(\frac{\epsilon y^i}{k_y^i}-\delta_k\right) = \frac{(1+g_N^i)(1+g_h^i)}{\beta^i}-1$$
$$= (1-\tau_{rF}^i)(1-\tau_{rN}^j)\left(\frac{\epsilon y^j}{k_y^j}-\delta_k\right),$$

$$g_h^i = B(k_h^i)^\gamma (e^i)^{1-\gamma} - \delta_h,$$

$$g_N^i = D(N^i)^a - \delta_N,$$

$$c^i + [(1+g_N^i)(1+g_h^i) - (1-\delta_k)]S^i + G^i$$

$$= y^i + \left[(1-\tau_{rN}^j)\left(\frac{\epsilon y^j}{k_y^j} - \delta_k\right) + \delta_k\right] S^{ij}$$

$$- \left[(1-\tau_{rN}^j)\left(\frac{\epsilon y^i}{k_y^i} - \delta_k\right) + \delta_k\right] S^{ji}\left(\frac{N^j h^j}{N^i h^i}\right),$$

$$\tau_c^i c^i + \tau_w^i (1-\epsilon) y^i + \left[\tau_{rD}^i S^{ii}\eta^i + \tau_{rN}^i S^{ji}\left(\frac{N^j h^j}{N^i h^i}\right)\right]\left(\frac{\epsilon y^i}{k_y^i} - \delta_k\right)$$

$$+ \tau_{rF}^i (1-\tau_{rN}^j) S^{ij}\left(\frac{\epsilon y^j}{k_y^j} - \delta_k\right) = g^i + T^i,$$

where

$$y^i = A(k_y^i)(n^i)^{1-\epsilon},\ k_y^i = \eta^i S^{ii} + S^{ji},\ k_h^i = (1-\eta^i)S^{ii},$$

$$\beta^i = \beta(1+g_N^i)^\xi (1+g_h^i)^{1-\sigma},\ R_h^i = \frac{g_h^i + \delta_h}{1+g_h^i},\ R_N^i = \frac{g_N^i + \delta_N}{1+g_N^i}.$$

Proposition 1 introduces one additional equation that should hold in the long run, i.e.,

$$(1+g_N^A)(1+g_h^A) = (1+g_N^B)(1+g_h^B).$$

Together, they constitute 19 equations in 19 unknowns – $(c^i, n^i, e^i, \eta^i, S^{ii}, S^{ij}, g_h^i, g_N^i)$ $(i = A, B; j = B, A)$ – plus the steady-state ratio of 'total' human capitals $N^B h^B / N^A h^A$ and two policy variables, one for each country. (Each policy variable acts as the compensating factor to balance the fiscal budget in its country, given the values of the other policy variables.)

NOTES

This chapter was originally prepared for the conference on 'International Capital Mobility and Development', sponsored by the Bank of Israel, the Centre for Economic Policy Research, and the Pinhas Sapir Center for Development, Tel-Aviv University (Tel-Aviv, 20–22 December 1992). For helpful discussions, we thank Willem Buiter, Isaac Ehrlich, Nouriel Roubini, T.N. Srinivasan, Oren Sussman, and Philippe Weil. The usual disclaimer applies.

1 See, e.g., Rebelo (1991) and Jones and Manuelli (1990) for a qualitative analysis, and King and Rebelo (1990), Lucas (1990a) and Kim (1991) for a quantitative assessment, of the *level* and *growth* effects of various tax structures.

2 See Lucas (1990b) for why, in practice, we may not see huge flows of capital from rich to poor countries.
3 Post-tax MPKs if taxes are levied on capital incomes (domestic or foreign). Note, however, that equalisation of after-tax MPKs through capital movement will, in general, not obtain under the *residence* principle (see section 3 below).
4 Barro, Mankiw and Sala-i-Martin (1992) address exactly this issue, i.e., how capital mobility affects the speed of converging from the transition path to the steady-state growth path.
5 This negative correlation is referred to by Romer (1989) as stylised fact 9 in his survey paper.
6 See Ehrlich and Lui (1991) for a theory of the demographic transition linking longevity, fertility, and economic growth.
7 Had we plotted $1 + g^i_N$ against $1 + g^i_y$ instead, these points should line up along a rectangular hyperbola if implication (1) holds.
8 Note from the lower half of the formula, though, that existence of balanced growth requires symmetry in $\bar{r}$s, and hence the capital income tax rates, under the residence principle if $\xi = 1 - \sigma$ (since the right-hand side equals unity by (P1)).
9 See Frenkel, Razin and Sadka (1991) or Razin and Yuen (1992) for a discussion of these implications of the residence principle.
10 The consumption taxes were absent in Razin and Yuen (1992). We incorporate them here because the US and the G-6 differ prominently in their VAT (value added tax) rates. Taking account of these taxes can help us better calibrate our model.
11 The output shares of capital and transfer payments may not match the data very well either. The reported K/Y and T/Y numbers in Table 9.2 are chosen to satisfy the resource and government budget constraints respectively.

REFERENCES

Barro, Robert J., N. Gregory Mankiw and Xavier Sala-i-Martin (1992) 'Capital Mobility in Neo-classical Models of Growth', NBER, *Working Paper*, **4206**.

Becker, Gary S. and H. Gregg Lewis (1973) 'On the Interaction between the Quantity and Quality of Children', *Journal of Political Economy*, **81**, S279–88.

Ehrlich, Isaac and Francis T. Lui (1991) 'Intergenerational Trade, Longevity, and Economic Growth', *Journal of Political Economy*, **99**, 1029–59.

Frenkel, Jacob, Assaf Razin and Efraim Sadka (1991) *International Taxation in an Integrated World*, Cambridge, MA: MIT Press.

Jones, Larry E and Rodolfo E. Manuelli (1990) 'A Convex Model of Equilibrium Growth', *Journal of Political Economy*, **98**, 1008–38.

Kim, Se-Jik (1991) 'How Much Difference do Tax Structures Make to Economic Growth?', *Working Paper*, University of Chicago.

King, Robert G. and Sergio T. Rebelo (1990) 'Public Policy and Economic Growth: Developing Neoclassical Implications', *Journal of Political Economy*, **98**, S126–49

Lucas, Robert E., Jr (1988) 'On the Mechanics of Economic Development', *Journal of Monetary Economics*, **22**, 3–42.

(1990a) 'Supply Side Economics: An Analytical Review', *Oxford Economic Papers*, **42**, 293–316.

(1990b) 'Why Doesn't Capital Flow from Rich to Poor Countries?', *American Economic Review Papers and Proceedings*, **80**, 92–6.

Mendoza, Enrique G., Assaf Razin and Linda L. Tesar (1992) 'Average Marginal Tax Rates on Consumption and Capital and Labor Income in Industrial Countries', IMF, *Working Paper*.

Razin, Assaf and Chi-Wa Yuen (1992) 'Convergence in Growth Rates: The Role of Capital Mobility and International Taxation', NBER, *Working Paper*, **4214**; see also Chapter 9 in this volume.

Rebelo, Sergio T. (1991) 'Long Run Policy Analysis and Long Run Growth', *Journal of Political Economy*, **99**, 500–21.

Romer, Paul M. (1989) 'Capital Accumulation in the Theory of Long-Run Growth', in Robert J. Barro (ed.), *Modern Business Cycle Theory*, Cambridge, MA: Harvard University Press.

World Bank (1989) *World Development Report*, Oxford: Oxford University Press.

Discussion

PHILIPPE WEIL

1 Issues discussed in the chapter

Chapter 9 asks a simple question: under free capital mobility, are long-run growth rates equalised in a multi-country model when taxation is distortionary? This is an important and legitimate question, as most of the literature on convergence takes as its departure point the *island model* – i.e., the closed economy model.

2 Characteristics of the model

The model's main ingredients are the following:

(1) Endogenous quantity (fertility) and quality (human capital) of children. As we shall see, many of the model's results still obtain without this assumption.

(2) Multi-period model (a two-period framework would however be sufficient since the chapter's analysis is confined to steady states).

A weakness of the chapter is that it sweeps time-consistency issues under the rug. This is, alas, traditional in the optimal taxation literature.

3 Basic insights – 1: tax principles and convergence

(1) *Source (territorial) principle*: thus homogenises investment opportunity sets worldwide. Hence it leads to a worldwide equalisation of marginal rates of substitution, and to a convergence of consumption growth rates if all countries have the same utility function. According to this taxation principle, 'countries do not matter'.
(2) *Residence (worldwide) principle*: thus introduces heterogeneity in investment opportunity sets across countries and thus leads to a divergence of growth rates. Thus, according to this taxation principle, 'countries do matter'.

4 Basic insights – 2: tax principles and efficiency

(1) The *source (territorial) taxation* is consumption efficient (MRSs are equalised across countries), but is production inefficient (tax rates do distort the allocation of capital across different countries).
(2) The *residence (worldwide) taxation* is consumption inefficient (MRSs are not equalised across countries) but is production efficient (tax rates do not distort the allocation of capital across different countries).

5 A simpler model

I now show that some of the results of the chapter are easily replicated in a two-country linear production AK model with constant population and free capital mobility:

Home country: $y_h = a_h k_h$, $k_h(0)$ given. Foreign country: $y_f = a_f k_f$, $k_f(0)$ given. $a_h > a_f$. Logarithmic utility: $U = \int_0^\infty e^{-\delta t} \ln c_t \, dt$.

The linear nature of the model allows for a computation of world equilibria as corner solutions in which the production function of only one country can be active at any given date. The bang-bang nature of the solution makes for its simplicity. In the Razin–Yuen chapter, by contrast, both countries produce at the same time.

5.1 *Free trade, no taxes equilibrium*

Under free trade and in the absence of taxes on capital, only the home production function (the most productive one) is active, and:

$$c_h(0) = \delta k_h(0), \qquad c_f(0) = \delta k_f(0),$$
$$\dot{c}_h/c_h = \dot{c}_f/c_f = a_h - \delta.$$

This competitive equilibrium is obviously both consumption efficient (consumption grows at the same rate in both countries) and production efficient (only the most active technology is active).

5.2 *Tax rates and convergence*

5.2.1 Source principle

Only the technology with the highest after-tax rate of return on capital is active and

$$c_h(0) = \delta k_h(0), \qquad c_f(0) = \delta k_f(0),$$
$$\dot{c}_h/c_h = \dot{c}_f/c_f = \max_h\{(1 - \tau^h)a_h - \delta\}.$$

Note, however, that the technology with the highest after-tax rate of return on capital is not necessarily the most productive one: convergence in consumption growth rates (consumption efficiency) is attained under the source principle, but it might well be at the cost of productive inefficiency.

5.2.2 Residence principle

Only the most productive technology is active, and

$$c_h(0) = \delta k_h(0), \qquad c_f(0) = \delta k_f(0),$$
$$\dot{c}_h/c_h = (1 - \tau_h)a_h - \delta, \qquad \dot{c}_f/c_f = (1 - \tau^f)a_h - \delta.$$

Under the residence principle, convergence in consumption growth rates will not in general be achieved (consumption inefficiency), but productive efficiency will be guaranteed.

These results mimic, to a large extent, the theoretical insights of Chapter 9.

6 What have we learned?

(1) The residence (worldwide) principle has centrifugal effects on growth rates, but is good from the point of view of productive efficiency. The reverse is true for source taxation. This is a very interesting result which sheds new light on the debate between residence and source taxation, as it establishes the existence of a

tradeoff, when taxes are not set optimally, between consumption and production efficiency.

(2) The endogenisation of the quality and quantity of children is not required to establish the existence of this tradeoff. The authors' more complex model is however required for a richer and more realistic simulation exercise.

OREN SUSSMAN

It is a matter of fact (documented in Table 9.1) that there are some substantial differences in capital income tax rates even across the industrialised states. While the top tax rate a Dutch resident has to pay on capital income (from either a local or foreign source) is 72%, an American resident would pay at most 38%. The objective of Razin and Yuen's interesting Chapter 9 is to assess the effect of this phenomenon on capital accumulation and economic growth within the G-7 group. Since the analytical framework is of an endogenous growth model, taxes can affect the steady-state growth rate of the economies considered, not just the level of capital accumulation.

A fundamental distinction is made between the *residence* and the *source* principles of capital income taxation. In a two-state world where (free) capital flows are taxed by both states, agents in each state equate the after-tax rate of return on domestic and foreign investment. Thus, the following arbitrage condition (stated in continuous time) should hold in country A

$$\bar{r}^A = \mathrm{MPK}^A - \tau^A_{rD} = \mathrm{MPK}^B - \tau^B_{rN} - \tau^A_{rF}$$

where MPK^i is the marginal product of capital in state i, τ^A_{rD} and τ^A_{rF} the capital income tax collected by state A on investments made by its own residents at home and abroad respectively; in addition, residents of state A may have to pay capital income tax of τ^B_{rN} to state B on investments made there (a similar arbitrage condition exists for state B). Under the residence principle, each agent is taxed at home on his world income so $\tau^A_{rD} = \tau^A_{rF}$ and $\tau^B_{rN} = 0$. Under the source principle, each agent is taxed at source by the state where the investment is located so $\tau_{rF}^{A} = 0$, but τ_{rD}^{A} and τ_{rN}^{B} may be different. It is obvious that under the residence principle the marginal product of capital in both states is equalised, but the after-tax interest rate is different (unless capital income tax is symmetric). Under the source principle, the after-tax interest rate in both states is equalised but the marginal product of capital may be different. Most countries adopt the residence principle. The reason may be related to its properties: it is efficient in production (since it equates the marginal product of capital across states) and it is capital-export neutral.

So how do cross-country differences in capital income tax rate affect their respective growth rates? The authors restrict the discussion to balanced-growth steady states where free capital flows must equate the growth rate of total GDP (P1 in the chapter). Still, differences in after-tax interest rates may affect the growth rate of population and per capita consumption. The authors construct an endogenous growth model where agents allocate resources (labour and savings) among production, schooling and child-rearing, so that the growth rate of population, human capital and physical capital are endogenously determined. The parameters of the model are chosen so that lower after-tax interest rates (i.e., higher capital income tax) result in higher population growth rate.

The model is calibrated in an attempt to explain growth-rates, differences among the US and the rest of the G-7 (i.e., the G-6). Total income-growth rates are similar: 2.5% in the US and 2.9% in the G-6, in line with the theoretical analysis. Population, however, grows at 1.3% in the US, but only 0.8% in the G-6. So income per capita in the US grows at a slower 1.8% pace compared with 2.3% in the G-6. The model is calibrated with the same behavioural parameters for both economies, but different initial conditions and tax rates.

In the authors' own words, 'prolonged experimentation' with the model led to only 'partial success'. In their view, the problem is caused by the fact that in the real world capital flows are '*not* 100% free'. While it is hard to debate this statement, I would like to point out an additional source of potential trouble.

The model is constructed for linear taxes. So some aggregate tax rate must be computed for the actual tax system of the economies under consideration (which are non-linear). A capital income tax of 30% is substituted for the US, and 29% for the G-6. The induced difference in after-tax interest rates are very small (0.1% for a marginal product of capital of, say, 10%). This seems to be a severe under-statement of actual differences in tax patterns. As mentioned above, the differences in *marginal* capital income tax are much higher. Moreover, Table 9.1 suggests that marginal capital income tax rates in the US are lower than in the G-6.

This means that aggregate and marginal tax rates reverse their order: aggregate rates are higher in the US, but marginal rates are lower. It is possible that some vital information is lost in the aggregation process, which ultimately has crippled the authors' approach.

It is important to stress that the results do not indicate that real-world differences in capital income tax are insignificant, or that they cannot account for growth rate differences.

10 Will government policy magnify capital flow volatility?

GIUSEPPE BERTOLA and ALLAN DRAZEN

1 Motivation and overview

In 1991–2 there has been a significant change in capital inflows into Latin America. In the mid-1980s capital flows into the 10 countries that make up South America averaged 8 billion dollars a year; they rose to 20 billion dollars in 1990 and to 40 billion dollars in 1991. Furthermore, capital inflow into Latin America has been highly volatile over this period. What lies behind these changes?

One line of argument relates recent capital inflows into Latin America to what has been happening in the United States, specifically the sharp drop in interest rates and the sluggish level of economic activity. This point of view is well represented in a recent paper by Calvo, Leiderman, and Reinhart (1992). Taking the change in officially-held foreign exchange reserves as a proxy for capital flows, they show, first of all, that the inflow was spread across several countries in Latin America. Using principal-components analysis, they demonstrate that there has been a common factor in the inflow into all of these countries, and that the first principal component of various United States macroeconomic time series (including a measure of economic activity, various interest rates, and financial returns data) is correlated to Latin American capital inflows and real exchange rates. Put in simple terms, the drop in short-term interest rates in the United States since mid-1991 combined with the slowdown in economic activity led investors to shift their focus Southward.

Though this line of argument has much merit, two types of criticisms can be levelled against it. First, given the nature of investment decisions, a perspective of longer than a year or two is needed. Second, external factors are clearly important, but factors internal to the region (such as the sharp change in government attitudes with increased reliance on free markets) have played a role as well, and perhaps a crucial one.

First, consider the nature of investment decisions. It is generally agreed that a long-run perspective is needed to understand investment dynamics in a macroeconomic context. Accumulation of physical capital and financial capital flows need to be analysed in terms of their driving processes' stochastic properties rather than in terms of current events only. One must consider the interactions of stochastic shocks that exhibit persistence, as well as irreversibility of investment and adjustment costs that imply that investment decisions should be forward-looking. Such features should characterise any model of investment, and suggest that modelling fluctuations require a view of longer that a year or two.

In terms of capital flows, explaining the volatility of returns to country-specific investment is the key to understanding the dynamic features of capital flows, leading one to ask what macroeconomic features may underlie such volatility. In so doing, we are motivated by recent Latin American experience. There is widespread agreement that the capital inflow is a regional phenomenon, rather than being limited to a few countries (the Calvo–Leiderman–Reinhart paper makes a strong case for this). There is far less agreement, however, on the view that economic developments in the United States were the primary motivating factor. There is mixed evidence on whether inflows of similar magnitude have taken place into other regions of the world, as the Calvo–Leiderman–Reinhart hypothesis would suggest. Moreover, if low US interest rates were a key factor, why did we observe a similar massive inflow into Latin America in the late 1970s and early 1980s, when US interest rates were very high? (We return below to an explanation of these episodes in terms of interest rate differentials.)

An alternative point of view is that the capital inflow represents the response to events within Latin America, rather than outside the region. More specifically, we suggest that variability of government policies may be responsible for the volatility of capital inflows. In viewing the inflow as a regional phenomenon, we think of the 'country' under consideration as a Latin American aggregate, meaning that investment flows are highly correlated across neighbouring countries in a region. There are a number of reasons why this is likely to be the case. Foremost in our minds is the view that outsiders perceive there to be unobserved shocks which are common to neighbouring countries. That is, if there is a positive shock to economic activity and the profitability of investment in one country, it is believed there is a component to the shock which is common to the region, though not to countries outside the region. Secondly, there will be spillovers of observed activity across borders, both on the supply and on the demand side. Finally, competition for funds in the world capital markets will lead countries to adopt similar policies with respect to foreign investment. That is, in order to remain attractive to foreign investors who believe there are regional factors, a country will be led to liberalise when its neighbours do.

We are currently involved in a research project whose aim is to study investment behaviour in a dynamic optimising model in which supply and demand shocks interact with government policies. In a framework where primitive productivity shocks can induce persistent effects on investment and capital flows, we argue that expected government policies and other institutional characteristics of the economy can *magnify* the effects of these shocks. The mathematical development of these points is somewhat complex. We eschew formalities in this chapter, and simply outline some of our perspective's main insights in a non-technical, but nonetheless rigorous way.

When technological productivity shocks are the primary cause of volatility, they may of course be magnified by market structure and increasing returns at the local level (due to strategic complementarities, infrastructure, thick markets, threshold effects, etc.). Such effects are not unique to Latin America, however, and technological shocks, even when magnified by these effects, may not explain why the volatility of capital flows is so high in Latin America relative to other regions.

The focus of our research is therefore on how government policy can magnify the effects of technology shocks. There are a number of possible mechanisms. First, the expectation that the government may 'waffle' between the imposition and liberalisation of capital account restrictions will mean that realisable returns to investment will similarly fluctuate. If capital controls are tightened in bad times and relaxed in good times, as would seem to characterise the policy of many Latin American governments, the effect of productivity shocks will be magnified. Second, there may be a positive feedback between capital movements and fiscal policy, a sort of 'dynamic Laffer curve'. Specifically, a given level of expenditure implies higher tax rates in bad times for a given tax base; these higher tax rates, however, discourage capital inflow, thus lowering the tax base and magnifying the tax consequences of an adverse shock. Finally, government expenditures and transfers can also have a magnifying effect in at least two ways. On the one hand, public investment in infrastructure is often procyclical; to the extent that private investment and public infrastructure investment are complements in production, magnification of productivity shocks will result. On the other hand, bad times may increase political pressure for redistribution of income flows towards domestic residents with no access to the international capital market. Such redistributive policies appear especially descriptive of many Latin American governments, and need to be financed by increased taxes on capital, the *ex ante* internationally mobile factor of production.

The plan of the chapter is as follows. In section 2 we discuss our basic approach, which is focused on a stochastic production structure (but with no 'magnification' effects from government policy), and illustrate it with a simple model. We show how the stochastic nature of production leads to variability in asset returns, asset prices, and capital inflows. In section 3, we consider what determines the extent of fluctuations in private investment incentives and hence fluctuations in asset prices and capital inflows. We then proceed to sketch ways in which such volatility might be endogenous to the country's economic structure. In section 4, we consider the mechanisms set out above by which government policy will *magnify* fluctuations due to stochastic productivity shocks. Section 5 presents conclusions.

2 A basic model

Our goal is to show how fluctuations in underlying determinants of productivity (or of any other stochastic fundamental, such as demand conditions) can induce variability in patterns of investment and capital flows which looks quite different from the underlying driving process. Magnification of underlying variability through government intervention is our primary, though not our only, interest. Our research strategy is to begin with a very basic stochastic model. Of course, such a model should be viewed as representative of a much wider class of models. We analyse how capital flows into a country are affected by uncertainty as to local investment profitability. Our modelling of uncertainty is kept as simple as possible (a two-state Markov chain) to focus on the economics of the interaction between international supply of funds and local technological, market, and policy developments.

Consider an economy that produces a single good, where production is represented by a Cobb–Douglas production function,

$$Y(t) = A(t)L(t)^{a}K(t)^{1-a}, \tag{1}$$

where $Y(t)$ is output at time t; $A(t)$ is a productivity indicator; $L(t)$ denotes labour (or land), which is internationally immobile; and $K(t)$ is the installed stock of capital.

The economy's productivity grows exponentially (and exogenously) over time, but is also subject to equally exogenous fluctuations. Specifically, we write

$$A(t) = a(t)e^{\theta t}, \tag{2}$$

where the trend parameter θ indexes technological progress. To model stochastic productivity fluctuations, we let the scale parameter a follow a two-state Markov process: $a(t) = a_g$ in a (country-specific) good state, but

$a(t) = a_b < a_g$ in a (country-specific) bad state at time t, and transitions between the two states occur with constant probability intensity δ in continuous time.

The economy is open to international trade, but we abstract from issues of exchange rate determination by letting the single produced good be identical to what is produced abroad. Thus, only intertemporal trade has a role in our model, and we focus on the consumption and investment choices of domestic and foreign residents. The production flow can be either consumed (locally or abroad), or invested. Physical investment translates one-to-one into an increase of the installed capital stock[1] and is irreversible: when local business conditions deteriorate, the physical capital stock installed in the country cannot decrease. We assume perfect mobility of financial capital, however, and consider a simple characterisation of capital market equilibrium relationships.

Ruling out irrational bubbles, asset values depend on the current value and expected dynamics of dividends accruing to each unit of homogeneous capital. We denote by γ the share of the country's production which is paid as compensation for the services of the installed capital stock and, for simplicity, we take it to be constant within each productivity state. Denoting capital's income share in good times and bad times by γ_g and γ_b respectively and employment by L_g and L_b,[2] the dividend flow accruing to each unit of capital is

$$\gamma_i \frac{Y(t)}{K(t)} = \gamma_i e^{\theta t} a_i L_i^a K(t)^{-a} \tag{3}$$

in state i, $i = g, b$. To simplify notation, we define the profitability indicator

$$\eta_i(t) \equiv \gamma_i a_i L_i^a, \tag{4}$$

and rewrite the dividends expression in (3) as

$$\gamma_i \frac{Y(t)}{K(t)} = \eta_i e^{\theta t} K(t)^{-a}. \tag{5}$$

For the purpose of interpreting the results of this section, it may be useful to consider as a baseline the case of competitive decentralisation (with no taxes or subsidies), and constant employment. Under Cobb–Douglas production, the competitive factor share of capital would be state-independent and equal to $(1 - a)$. The dividends process thus responds one-for-one to changes in the productivity indicator in (2) and is a decreasing function of the installed capital stock with elasticity a. In (3), however, both capital's income share γ and employment L are indexed by state i. Inasmuch as they vary across states, the dynamics of the profitability index η in (5) differ from those of the primitive technological index a. In our working paper (1993), we consider how such state-dependency may magnify the volatility of capital income, and of capital-flows' responses to the primitive shocks as indexed by a. We do not develop such insights formally in this chapter, but simply discuss the qualitative insights afforded by this and similar models.

To examine how stochastic productivity affects macroeconomic variables, we want to relate realisations of the profitability indices η_g and η_b to investment decisions, asset prices, and capital flows. To do so, consider the no-arbitrage relationships required by financial market equilibrium. They require that the asset value of capital in each state at each point in time (which we denote $q_g(t)$ and $q_b(t)$) must be such that current dividends and expected capital gains per unit time yield a return r on the asset's value, where r is the rate of discount applied by well-diversified global investors to income flows from the country under consideration. (A formal, mathematical derivation of these equations, and of the results that follow, can be found in our working paper.) These equations may be thought of as yielding relations from the productivity indicators η_g and η_b to the asset prices in the two states and the stock of capital $K(t)$.

We assume that parameters are such that investment is positive in this country in good times, that is, when profitability is indexed by η_g. Thus, the good-time value of capital is fixed at the unitary output and consumption price of investment in our single-output-good model, for any discrepancy between the value of installed capital and the unit cost of investment would allow arbitrage opportunities between installation of new capital on the one hand, and financial claims to the existing stock on the other. We further assume that investment is irreversible. Hence when bad times (as indexed by η_b) first hit, the irreversibility constraint is binding and the currently installed capital stock $K(t)$ will be constant.

These assumptions imply the following characteristics of the paths. In bad times (that is, times during which $\eta = \eta_b$) the irreversibility constraint may bite, to imply that the unit value of capital will be strictly less than the current cost of installation ($q_b(t) \leq 1$). As dividends grow exponentially while the bad state persists, the unit value will not be constant over time, but will be rising monotonically to unity. If bad times persist long enough, productivity growth at rate θ will eventually make investment profitable even when $\eta = \eta_b$. Whenever there is positive investment, the value of installed capital must equal its installation cost ($q_b(t) \leq 1$).

In good times ($\eta = \eta_g$), the value of installed capital equals its installation cost ($q_g(t) = 1$), and capital grows exponentially. If the good state were perceived as permanent ($\delta = 0$), the equation determining the rate of growth of capital would reflect the equality of capital's current marginal revenue product to its user cost r. With $\delta > 0$ and $\eta_b < \eta_g$, investors realise that times will eventually turn bad, and that the downturn may in fact occur in the immediate future. With investment irreversibility, capital accumulation in good times must then reflect the fact that if and when a negative productivity shock hits the economy it will be impossible to recoup the installation cost of existing units of capital.

3 Capital accumulation and capital flows

The solution of the model has been a straightforward logical structure (see our working paper for derivations and details). The equations of the model determine $K(t)$ (and $q(t) = 1$) when the irreversibility constraint is not binding, and determine $q(t)$ when binding irreversibility constraints yield a constant K. The top panel of Figure 10.1 displays a realisation of the η Markov chain; the other panels illustrate the dynamics of the capital stock, of output, of the unit value of the country's capital stock, and of realised returns on holdings of country-specific capital.

Whenever the irreversibility constraint is not binding, the country's capital stock increases so as to keep the value of capital at unity in the face of productivity growth: as in the steady state of a Solow (1956) model, capital grows at rate θ/a if θ is the exponential rate of growth of disembodied productivity and/or population. If the country is hit by a negative profitability shock, however, the value of installed capital drops below unity, the irreversibility constraint bites, and the stock of capital ceases to grow. If 'bad times' persist long enough that $q_b(t)$ reaches unity, the irreversibility constraint ceases to bind and investment resumes, again at rate θ/a. As soon as profitability conditions are improved by the next Poisson shock, the capital level jumps to prevent q_g from exceeding unity, and investment proceeds at rate θ whether or not it was ongoing in the bad state. The 'good-' and 'bad'-time behaviour of the various series plotted in Figure 10.1 is not as sharply defined in real life as it is in the model, but the latter's implications appear qualitatively realistic. Output growth is slower when investment is not taking place, though positive within each state (explicit treatment of depreciation would of course imply slower and possibly negative output growth in bad times). When good news arrives and profitability improves, both output growth and investment spike upwards. The value of the country's installed capital stock, or its stock market's value, jumps upwards as the quantity of capital increases; a spike in the unit value of installed capital may or may not accompany the investment boom, depending on how long the previous depression lasted.

To discuss the *financial* capital-flow counterpart to the capital-accumu-

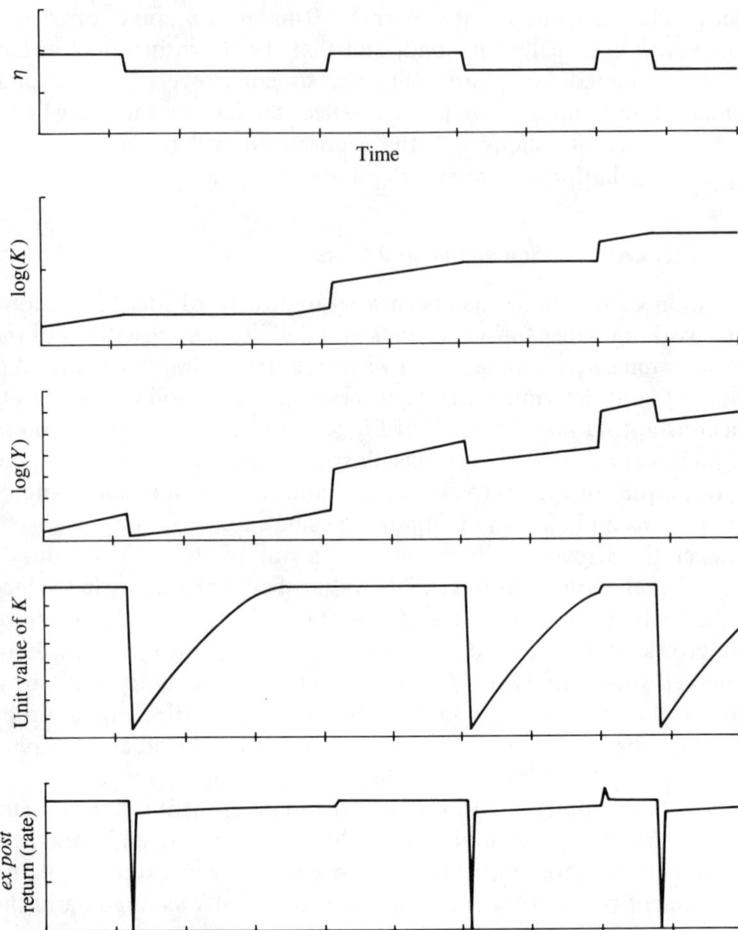

Figure 10.1 Sample paths of irreversible capital accumulation

lation dynamics, one can combine the essentially microeconomic aspects of our investment model with equally simple models of saving and consumption decisions in a small open-economy setting. When individuals can borrow and lend at the world risk-free rate and the income stream is subject to stochastic fluctuations, consumption–saving decisions are not easy to model, since they will depend on the specific stochastic process followed by income. Some special cases, however, may provide some insight. Consider the extreme case in which domestic residents have no access to world capital markets, so that they would simply consume their current income at each point in time.[3] In this case, domestic consumption responds one-for-one to GNP. Since the investment model above is solved under the assumption that financial capital is internationally mobile, we should think of all claims to the installed capital stock as being owned by non-residents. Income flows from this capital, which would appear as a deficit item in the current account, would equal $\gamma Y(t)$. Periods of high investment would correspond to capital inflows and balance of payments surpluses, periods of low or zero investment as balance of payments deficits.

However, standard residency-based definitions of capital flows may be quite misleading for interpreting accounting data from LDCs, and especially Latin American countries. When some or all capital flows take the form of unrecorded and often illegal 'capital flight', official data measure only very imperfectly the amount and dynamics of local residents' net foreign assets. Even at a theoretical level, it is not quite clear that those Latin American citizens who hold much of their wealth in the United States are 'resident' in any economic sense. It may then be useful to consider a less standard definition of capital flows, defined in terms of resource flows in and out of the country regardless of their owners' domestic of foreign residency. We can say that a country experiences positive capital inflows whenever the sum of domestic consumption and domestic investment exceeds domestic production in (1). We could then consider the dynamics of capital flows $F(t)$ defined by

$$F(t) = C(t) + \dot{K}(t) - Y(t). \tag{6}$$

In the extreme case where all local residents are liquidity constrained, domestic consumption coincides with GNP, and capital flows correspond to investment by foreigners. More realistically, in a typical Latin American country, some local residents may consume current income, while others smooth consumption through access to the world capital market. When the relevant transactions occur via overinvoicing of exports and other unofficial channels, recorded capital flows will reflect only imperfectly the investment decisions of local and foreign residents. They might instead be closely related to $F(t)$ in (6), with domestic consumption a weighted average of that of consumption-'smoothers' and 'rule-of-thumb' consumers. In any case, capital flows would be closely related to the capital accumulation process illustrated in Figure 10.1.

Figure 10.1 also plots a series of realised returns on holdings of country-specific capital (returns per infinitesimal unit of time spike to plus or minus infinity upon a state transition, and Figure 10.1 plots their counterpart over finite intervals of time). It is important to note that the relationship between stock market rates of return and investment flows is consistent with the evidence in Calvo, Leiderman and Reinhart (1992). First, the country is the recipient of ongoing positive capital flows in 'good times', when the realised rate of return is inclusive of a 'crash' premium which realises upon state transition. Second, upon a transition from bad to good times there is a step capital inflow, and the return on the country's asset includes the realisation of step capital gains on q. Such relationships follow immediately from the assumption of capital market equilibrium in a stochastic context, of course, and there is no sense in which high rates of return *cause* capital flows. The two phenomena are jointly and endogenously derived from underlying profitability dynamics.

The caution against taking high rate of return differentials as causing a capital inflow when both reflect underlying shocks is strengthened when one realises that large flows of capital into the stock market may induce a run-up of stock prices. Such autonomous capital inflows would show up as a rate-of-return differential if rates of return are measured inclusive of realised capital gains, so that causation would run from capital flows to return differentials, not vice versa. This may be descriptive of the Latin American experience in the late 1970s.

The above model illustrates the role of a primitive stochastic component in the production process in inducing fluctuations in key variables. We purposely kept the stochastic specification as simple as possible, by focusing on a two-state process for the country's productivity and capital's profitability. The key characteristics of the model are: forward-looking behaviour in physical investment (which we rationalise in terms of irreversibility but, of course, may reflect a variety of other realistic adjustment costs); and perfect flows of financial capital in the presence of local sources of uncertainty. Other features are admittedly simple, but more sophisticated modelling would not change the basic message.

The point that future expected business conditions matter for current investment is familiar from, e.g., Bernanke (1983), Dixit (1991), and much other recent work on investment dynamics under irreversibility. Of course, very similar if less dramatic insights could be obtained from any model where investment and disinvestment entail adjustment costs (with irreversibility representing the extreme case of prohibitive 'adjustment' costs for disinvestment). An explicitly dynamic framework makes it possible to go beyond consideration of currently unconstrained investment decision, however. Quite clearly, the counterpart of restrained investment in good times is an excess of installed capital in bad times, when the irreversibility constraint bites. Rational investors behave so as to keep realised returns on country-specific investment as close as possible to the required rate of return (r in the model). A supernormal return in good times (and the attendant restrained investment, given decreasing returns to capital) has a counterpart in lower-than-normal returns in bad times, and irreversibility *per se* deters capital accumulation in an average sense. Rather, realistic irreversibilities and other adjustment costs affect the *dynamics* of capital accumulation, which are reflected in the dynamics of (unconstrained) flows of financial capital.

The model could be extended in several ways. We could consider demand-side shocks, for example in an analogous two-state framework. There could also be magnification from endogenous labour supply decisions or 'thick-market' externalities. It would be hard, however, to argue that technological uncertainty or 'thick-market phenomena' are especially important for capital profitability in specific countries, or indeed in LDCs as a whole. Even a simple look at the data makes it apparent that Latin American countries feature much more drastic swings in savings, investment, and capital flows than East Asian or sub-Saharan LDCs. Though the level of technological uncertainty, for example, may differ across countries, it is difficult to believe that it is sufficiently higher in Latin America than in the rest of the world to explain the high volatility of capital flows relative to other countries. One must therefore look at something other than primitive technological uncertainty to see what may distinguish Latin America from other regions in the world. As indicated in the introduction, our focus is on the role of government policy in magnifying technological shocks. In section 4, we go on to highlight the role of government policy variables, and argue that they should be regarded as crucial in the Latin American context.

4 The role of government policy

Frequent changes in political regime and significant shifts in government policy are an often-noted characteristic of the economic policymaking environment in Latin America. Argentina and Brazil, for example, are often given as examples of countries which have been hampered by frequent sharp policy shifts (for example in inflation stabilisation or balance of payments policy). The East Asian 'dragons', by contrast, are notable for a high degree of policy stability (Larrain and Vergara, 1991). The mid- and late 1980s have witnessed another significant shift in policy in Latin America. Several countries in the region have moved sharply towards a much less interventionist stance and far greater reliance on the market; others have taken less drastic steps but have still moved along with the trend to free-market economics. The purpose of this section is informally to investigate the extent to which government policy decisions may help explain volatility of capital flows. More specifically, we are interested in how volatility in policy can *magnify* the volatility of fluctuations in investment profitability and investment, and we will discuss a number of possible mechanisms.

In arguing that variability in government policy may be what distinguishes Latin America from other regions in accounting for the variability of investment, we are *not* arguing that no other country exhibits similar instability of policy. The crucial point here is *magnification*: government policy can magnify the ups and downs due to technological shocks, but cannot induce a significant and sustained investment boom and capital inflow if the technological conditions are not right. That is, a region characterised by political instability need not experience volatility in investment opportunities and capital inflows if the underlying technological developments are uniformly unfavourable. As indicated in the introduction, our goal is to explain volatility of capital flows and not a uniformly low level. It is now well known that expectations of future economic conditions become especially important in investment decisions when investment is irreversible (see, e.g., Bernanke, 1983). In the case of foreign investment, this especially means conditions under which profits may be repatriated. Hence expectations of future restrictions are crucial. In countries with a history of capital controls, foreign investors will not automatically assume that the capital account will be open in the future simply because it is open today. (Van Wijnbergen, 1985 and Rodrik, 1989, discuss how uncertainty about capital account policy will affect investment incentives from abroad. Drazen, 1992, discusses how expectations of possible future trade restrictions induced low volatility in importation of consumer durables in Israel in the 1980s.) The link we see to primitive technological uncertainty is via the response of policy to economic conditions. Unlike East Asia, in Latin America a deterioration of economic conditions often leads to a major change in the direction of economic policy (see, for example, Kiguel, 1989). The imposition of restrictions on both current and capital account transactions is a common response to the balance of payments problems that often accompany an economic slowdown. Hence, a drop in productivity could bring with it the expectation that capital account policy will soon become less favourable to foreign investment, especially if the lower level of economic activity is expected to persist. Similarly, an increase of productivity may bring with it the expectation of liberalisation if the high-activity state is similarly viewed as persistent. This policy response would itself further dampen capital inflow when times turn bad and further increase capital inflow when times turn good. Hence the sort of endogenous trade policy response to economic fluctuations which often characterises Latin American governments may magnify underlying volatility of production.

The second mechanism we consider concerns how the tax system may magnify the effect of technological shocks. Our basic idea is that fiscal systems in Latin America are often characterised by a positive feedback between the tax base and the tax rate. More specifically, there is a positive feedback loop between capital inflows and the tax rate on capital. A technological shock which lowers the tax base will induce an increase in the tax rate on capital, thus reducing capital inflows and further eroding the tax base and inducing a further increase in the tax rate. We term this effect the 'dynamic Laffer curve'. For such a feedback loop to be present, shocks to productivity must be met by tax changes rather than by changes in government expenditure or by changes in the deficit (as a tax-smoothing model would suggest).[4]

The failure of governments to respond to supply shocks by cutting government expenditure so as to keep tax rates and the deficit unchanged is a realistic description of how the world works. Certain aspects of IMF stabilisation programmes may also work in this direction: their primary focus on restraining public sector borrowing requirements may sometimes generate swings in tax rates of the type we consider. It certainly seems descriptive of many Latin American countries in which expenditure programmes are extremely difficult to cut. The difficulty in cutting government expenditures when the size of the pie has decreased may reflect a war of attrition over how to divide the burden of the cut, as in Alesina and Drazen (1991).

It is harder to argue that supply shocks which are perceived as not being permanent are *not* fully absorbed in the deficit, that is, that full smoothing of tax rates does not occur. Latin American countries in general have been far from averse to deficits. One argument concerns the implications of tax smoothing in a stochastic framework. Since η is stochastic and could stay low or high for a long period of time, keeping tax rates constant and meeting fiscal requirements (higher expenditures or shrinkage of the tax base) by issuing debt would require state-contingent instruments. In their absence, the intertemporal budget constraint would risk being violated by perfect smoothing of tax rates.

An empirically more relevant argument for the dynamic Laffer effect in Latin America may be the change in the composition of taxes in response to an adverse supply shock. An Alesina–Drazen-type argument suggests that it may also be difficult to get agreement on changing *certain* types of taxes in an economy, namely those falling on domestic interest groups with significant political clout. This suggests that other types of taxes, those falling more heavily on nonresidents, would be disproportionately affected by a productivity shock. That is, if the political system is such that fiscal decisions heavily reflect interest group pressure, tax rates on foreign-source capital might be expected to rise sharply in response to a negative productivity shock, even when overall government spending is fixed over the cycle.

Finally, we consider how variable government expenditure and transfers can induce a similar magnification of primitive technological uncertainty to that discussed in section 3. We discuss two specific mechanisms: public investment and redistribution of income towards domestic residents. The public investment channel is straightforward and flows from the provision of infrastructure discussed by Barro (1990), among others, leading to public and private investment being complementary. That the correlation between public and private investment is strong and positive is quite apparent from both Latin American and East Asian data. If publicly supplied infrastructure makes private investment more profitable, an increase in public investment will encourage capital inflow. The link to production volatility comes from the sensitivity of public investment expenditure to economic activity.

The possibility that income redistribution policies may magnify technological uncertainty may be especially relevant to Latin America, where governments seem to be prone to intervene in the income-distribution process. Intervention to smooth consumption of domestic residents over the cycle seems quite benign, but we will show that it can have the effect of magnifying productivity shocks. To see why, suppose there exists a class of agents who do not have access to international capital markets and therefore simply consume a state-dependent fraction of domestic production. In the absence of redistributive activity, the consumption of 'local' factors of production would be procyclical, responding one-for-one to technological shocks. If the government wishes to smooth the consumption of such factors' owners over the cycle, it will intervene with *countercyclical* transfers, financed by taxes on agents with access to international capital markets. Hence, to the extent that the tax-transfer programme smooths consumption of the first class of agents, it must *unsmooth* income flows of the second-class, that is, makes its income flows more procyclical. In other words, it must magnify the effect of variability in a on capital's profitability as indexed by η.

5 Conclusions

The phenomenon of high volatility of capital flows into Latin America has rightfully generated a good deal of attention and interest. One line of explanation is that it reflects developments outside the region; a second, that it reflects developments within the region. We hold with those who favour the second line of argument. More specifically, we believe that the volatility of capital flows into Latin America reflects the vagaries of government policies. Moreover, we argue that the nature of investment decisions requires focusing on horizons of longer than 1 year, as some explanations of the recent Latin American experience have done.

Our discussion of the specific application to Latin America was simply meant to support in a way we think is empirically relevant the basic argument that imperfect smoothing of taxes may generate magnifying effects of fiscal policy. We do not claim to have proved the crucial role of government policy. Instead, our methodology has been to examine a simple representative model in which stochastic swings in the underlying profitability of local investment interact with forward-looking investment behaviour (due to irreversibilities) to yield volatility of capital inflows. We take the model to be representative in that any model of investment under uncertainty should have these two features, and any model with these two features will yield the basic patterns our model exhibited. Many substantive issues can be addressed by our formal model, and we have focused our analysis on realistic mechanisms by which government policy responses would *magnify* the effects of underlying technological uncertainty. All of these mechanisms need to be explored in greater detail. This chapter is meant to suggest how fruitful such an exploration may possibly be in explaining the volatility of capital flows.

NOTES

We thank the discussants and other conference participants for helpful comments. Giuseppe Bertola gratefully acknowledges support from the National Science Foundation. Allan Drazen gratefully acknowledges support from the IRIS Project, University of Maryland.

1 We disregard depreciation, but its role would be quite similar to that of technical progress, as indexed by θ.
2 A constant growth rate of labour supply could be included in the exponential term, since technical progress could be seen as labour-augmenting.
3 Similar, though less extreme, assumptions are considered and rationalised by Gertler and Rogoff (1990) and by Barro, Mankiw and Sala-i-Martin (1992).
4 It may seem strange that an income-based tax system would magnify rather than dampen fluctuations, given the basic textbook story of the tax system as an automatic stabiliser. In the automatic stabiliser story, tax rates stay constant (or even fall in a progressive tax system) in response to a shock, with the deficit taking up the slack. Here, if the deficit stays constant, tax rates must 'take up the slack', with tax rates moving *countercyclically*.

REFERENCES

Alesina, Alberto and Allan Drazen (1991) 'Why are Stabilizations Delayed?', *American Economic Review*, **81** (December), 1170–88.

Barro, Robert J. (1990) 'Government Spending in a Simple Model of Endogenous Growth', *Journal of Political Economy*, **98**, S103–25.

Barro, Robert J, N. Gregory Mankiw and Xavier Sala-i-Martin (1992) 'Capital Mobility in Neo-classical Models of Growth', NBER, *Working Paper*, **4206**.

Bernanke, Ben (1983) 'Irreversibility, Uncertainty, and Cyclical Investment', *Quarterly Journal of Economics*, **98**, 85–106.

Bertola, Giuseppe and Allan Drazen (1993), 'Capital-Flow Volatility and Expected Government Policy', *Working Paper*, Princeton University.

Calvo, Guillermo A., Leonardo Leiderman and Carmen M. Reinhart (1992) 'Capital Inflows and Real Exchange Rate Appreciation in Latin America: The role of external factors', IMF, *Staff Papers*, **40** (March).

Dixit, Avinash (1991) 'The Art of Smooth Pasting', *Working Paper*, Princeton University.

Drazen, Allan (1992) 'Uncertain Trade Policy and Import Booms', *Working Paper*, University of Maryland.

Gertler, Mark and Kenneth Rogoff (1990) 'North–South Lending and Endogenous Domestic Capital Market Inefficiencies', *Journal of Monetary Economics*, **26**, 245–66.

Kiguel, Miguel (1989) 'Inflation in Argentina: Stop and Go Since the Austral Plan', *PPR Working Paper*, Washington, DC: World Bank.

Larrain, Felipe, and Rodrigo Vergara (1991) 'Investment and Macroeconomic Adjustment: The Case of East Asia', *Working Paper*, Pontificia Universidad Catolica de Chile and Central Bank of Chile.

Rodrik, Dani (1989) 'Policy Uncertainty and Private Investment in Developing Countries', NBER, *Working Paper*, **2999**.

Solow, Robert M. (1956) 'A Contribution to the Theory of Economic Growth', *Quarterly Journal of Economics*, **70**, 65–94.

Van Wijnbergen, Sweder (1985) 'Trade Reform, Aggregate Investment, and Capital Flight', *Economics Letters*, **17**.

Discussion

GIAN MARIA MILESI-FERRETTI

The analysis of capital flows and investment incentives should take into account the irreversible nature of investment in physical capital. Starting from this consideration, Bertola and Drazen provide in Chapter 10 a first 'building block' towards the construction of a fully-fledged model that would allow one to analyse the interaction between irreversible investment decisions, government policy and exogenous productivity shocks.

I think the chapter addresses very interesting issues in a clear and systematic way, although much work remains to be done before the authors' claims can be confronted with empirical data. The model sketched in this chapter derives the dynamic behaviour of investment in the presence of productivity growth and stochastic shocks, for a given distribution of returns between labour and capital, but it does not 'endogenise' these shares analytically nor does it formally relate them to policy variables. The discussion the authors provide is very stimulating, and it highlights many potential insights one could derive from a fuller model specification. My comments include a brief summary of the chapter and a discussion of some of the policy issues it raises.

1 The structure of the model

A small open economy produces a single good, that can either be consumed or invested in physical capital. Investment is irreversible (although the model could easily accommodate capital depreciation). The factors of production are labour and capital, and the production function is Cobb–Douglas. There is deterministic productivity growth and two possible states of the world, 'good' and 'bad', that alternate stochastically. The *share* of capital in total output is assumed to be state-dependent and exogenous; labour is inelastically supplied and constant. When the economy is in a good state, investment is always positive, so that the price of investment (present discounted value of future income streams) equals the unit consumption price of the single good. When the economy is facing bad times the irreversibility constraint may be binding, so that a unit of investment may have a value smaller than 1. In this case, there is no investment. However, even if bad times persist, the exogenous productivity growth rate will eventually stimulate resumption of investment. Of course, investment would be stimulated should times change from bad to good.

Once the pattern of investment returns is determined as a function of the stochastic structure (productivity shocks) and the exogenous state-dependent shares accruing to capital and labour, the authors proceed to relate the volatility of returns to the cyclical behaviour of income distribution. In order to derive implications for the behaviour of capital flows, they redefine the latter as the difference between income and absorption, regardless of the ownership pattern of capital.

2 Regional factors and policy issues

A first observation concerns the modelling strategy. The framework used by the authors assumes that capital inflows finance investment in the form of physical capital. One would also need to account for the possibility that some of the volatility in capital flows is due to 'hot money' that can be 'disinvested' more easily.

Bertola and Drazen argue that it is necessary to understand the volatility of returns to country-specific investment in order to explain capital flows. They are in favour of a 'regional' explanation for the capital inflows in Latin America. However, they do not provide any supporting evidence and, from a theoretical standpoint, their 'regional explanation' is assumed rather than derived. For both these reasons, the comparison with the empirical paper of Calvo, Leiderman and Reinhart (1992) is, in my opinion, misplaced. Three factors are cited in support of the authors' view that capital inflows are primarily motivated by 'region-specific' events:

(1) outsiders perceive that there are unobserved shocks common to neighbouring countries
(2) there are spillover effects, both on the demand and on the supply side, between countries
(3) competition for funds leads countries to adopt similar policies.

Of course, all these points are debatable: for example, some productivity shocks (like oil-shocks) have obviously asymmetric effects on different countries in Latin America. However, I will focus on the main point of the chapter: namely, that government policy can magnify the fluctuations in profitability and investment generated by productivity shocks. Bertola and Drazen mentions some features of the political system in Latin American countries, such as high policy volatility, that support their main thesis. Although I do not question the importance of political instability in explaining macro policies and investment incentives in Latin America – stressed, for example, in the NBER volume edited by Dornbusch and Edwards (1991) – it cannot be claimed that the model does indeed support the conjecture that government policy magnifies the volatility of capital flows to and from Latin American countries. Instead, the model *assumes* this view: namely, it argues that *if* government policy has certain characteristics, specified below, *then* this 'magnification' can occur. The authors' argument relies on four types of policy measures that enhance the volatility of capital flows:

(1) volatility of capital controls: in bad times the imposition of capital controls may be more likely, and this further discourages capital inflows
(2) positive feedback between capital movements and fiscal policy through the size of the tax base and through the composition of taxes (dynamic Laffer curve)

(3) procyclical government investment expenditure (a complement in production)
(4) stronger redistribution pressures in bad times.

I find argument (1) convincing. However, I have some doubt on (2), the 'dynamic Laffer curve' story. Even though cuts in government spending are difficult to achieve, I am not convinced by the (implicit) description of Latin American countries as less deficit-prone than other developing countries because of IMF-prescribed policies. Furthermore, significant cuts in spending have been achieved in stabilising Latin American countries, such as Mexico. The authors mention a 'war of attrition' situation in which spending cuts are the source of conflict. They also recognise that the source of disagreement behind a 'war of attrition' situation may be tax policy: namely, who will bear the tax burden of a stabilisation. If taxes falling on domestic interest groups are difficult to change, the *composition* of taxes may shift towards those falling more heavily on nonresidents when a negative productivity shock occurs. I am not sure, however, that taxes on foreign-source capital may be the 'residual' in a war of attrition situation. First of all, inflation seems to be a more likely candidate.[1] Second, it is not clear how much revenue the government can raise through this channel, taking into account the size of the tax base, the relative inefficiency of the tax system in several Latin American countries and the ease with which capital can be channelled abroad. Moreover, the price in terms of scaring foreign investors may be higher than the potential benefits.

Argument (3) relies on the procyclical pattern of public investment, where the latter is viewed as a complement to private investment. This seems *prima facie* reasonable: it would be interesting to study why governments cut investment to infrastructure in bad times while other forms of spending are not cut. Why would Latin American countries be more likely than others to cut public investment in 'bad' times? Government 'myopia' caused by political instability is a common explanation, justified by the fact that the political situation has been more unstable in Latin America than, say, in East Asian countries. Clearly, more research is needed to establish the relevance of this proposition.

Explanation (4) relies on income redistribution, in the form of policies that 'insure' labour income by redistributing resources towards labour in bad times. If the labour share is countercyclical, then the capital share is procyclical, implying a lower share for capital in bad times. These two effects (bad times and falling capital share) reduce investment incentives. While intuitively appealing, this explanation needs in my opinion to be grounded in some empirical evidence.

When one moves towards a fuller discussion of fiscal policy decisions, several interesting issues arise. Do these redistributive features depend on who is in power? Are 'populist' governments more likely to win elections in bad times? I find these questions to be worthwhile research topics in their own right. From a theoretical point of view, an effort in modelling endogenous fiscal policy formation under political constraints such as those stressed by Bertola and Drazen would complement their effort on modelling the private investment side. Of course, the authors' case would be strengthened if they could provide some tangible evidence on some of their claims: for example, if they could show that Latin American governments in bad times tend to tax capital more heavily.

Summing up, I believe that the research project initiated by Bertola and Drazen is interesting and important. I also find some of their insights concerning the role of government policy volatility in shaping investment incentives to be on the mark. However, a project that intends to address the issues raised by the authors should model explicitly policy decisions as carefully as investment decisions. Even more importantly, these insights cannot be meaningfully applied to the experience of Latin American countries without considering any empirical evidence.

NOTES

The first draft of these comments were written while I was affiliated with the Centre for Economic Performance of the London School of Economics. I am grateful to José De Gregorio and Enrique Mendoza for comments and suggestions.

1 However, one could argue that inflation may act as a deterrent to investment for a variety of reasons (reduction in the informational content of prices; optimality of waiting for the resolution of uncertainty, etc.). For a discussion and some evidence (based on Summers–Heston data) see, for example, Fischer (1993).

REFERENCES

Calvo, G.A., L. Leiderman and C.M. Reinhart (1992) 'Capital inflows and real exchange rate appreciation in Latin America: The role of external factors', *IMF Staff Papers*, **40** (March).

Dornbusch, R. and S. Edwards (eds) (1991) *The Macroeconomics of Populism in Latin America*, Chicago: University of Chicago Press for NBER.

Fischer, S. (1993) 'Macroeconomics Factors in Growth', paper presented at the World Bank conference 'How Do National Policies Affect Long-Run Growth'; Washington, DC (February).

NATHAN SUSSMAN

The volatile nature of capital flows to and from lesser developed countries is well documented. Early manifestations of this phenomenon can be found in the primitive international capital markets of late medieval Europe, where developed nations, such as Florence, invested in lesser developed countries, such as England. The most intensively-studied cases are those related to Latin America and associated with the emergence of modern capital markets in the 1870s. Indeed, as Bertola and Drazen themselves point out, they are addressing a widespread empirical phenomenon that merits a theoretical treatment.

As an economic historian I must welcome a model that claims to offer a theoretical treatment of such an important phenomenon: it allows the historian to structure his analysis, focus on the relevant historical data, relate the various variables in a consistent and logical manner and test alternative hypotheses. On the other hand, before embracing any new theoretical development, I must question the relevance of the model for the study of historical episodes, its level of generality and whether it provides any additional insights, not already offered by existing models or discussions. In this Discussion I shall try to carry out an initial assessment of this new model from the perspective of an economic historian.

Before turning to the discussion of the model in historical perspective I shall briefly outline its major arguments. The model assumes a stochastic Cobb–Douglas production function whereby productivity is the stochastic element which in each period can take on one of two possible states – a good state and a bad state. The profitability of investment can therefore belong to either of the two states. Using a no-arbitrage equation for both states and assuming nonreversibility the model can be used to derive an implicit definition of the capital stock. The authors use a simple consumption function. They define net capital flows according to standard national accounting conventions, as the difference between aggregate domestic expenditure and output. This definition allows them to argue that given their characterisation of the production function, all capital flow fluctuations around their mean would be driven by productivity developments. In the concluding sections of the chapter the authors discuss how government policies in unstable regimes can *magnify* technology shocks by resorting to higher tax rates on capital or to the taxing of foreigners rather than of domestic interest groups. To do justice to the chapter, it also offers additional insights into issues such as the volatility of returns to investment and capital flows, simulations of the model and much more.

The main points an economic historian or any policy-minded economist can draw from this chapter are (1) that capital flows are driven by supply-side productivity shocks, and (2), which follows from (1), that government's role is secondary to that of the supply side and serves mainly, in the Latin American case, to exacerbate the already adverse effects of the technology shock. How do these main points compare with previous explanations of the capital flow phenomenon? I will not even attempt to provide an exhaustive list of these cases but merely give examples that, I hope, will serve to highlight the strengths and weaknesses of this new approach.

The foreign debt crisis of the 1980s generated – apart from discussions on solutions and remedies and other theoretical issues related to creditor–debtor mechanisms' design – a large measure of discussion on the roots of the problem. How are debt defaults related to the issue at hand? First, even though Bertola and Drazen focus on the relationship between capital flows and the stock of capital, an equally important relationship seems to be tucked under the carpet. Chapter 10 ignores the short- and long-run relationships between capital flows and the foreign debt (the stock). Second, the defaults literature emphasises the role of liquidity crises initiated by a decline in capital flows.

This literature (such as Cardoso and Dornbusch, 1989) points to three main culprits who are responsible for the drying up of capital flows, (1) domestic fiscal crisis that undermines confidence of international investors, (2) a deterioration of the terms of trade, and (3) a decline in available savings in the investing countries. Out of these three causes only (2), the terms of trade, could be considered a supply-side shock that is similar to a technological shock, albeit more appropriate for discussing primary rather than manufactured goods. Bertola and Drazen argue quite convincingly that external reasons emanating in the investing country are of secondary importance, so that leaves us with argument (1) – domestic fiscal crisis.

The discussion of Latin American foreign investment crises, namely those of Argentina and Brazil, focus primarily on the underlying political and fiscal chaos prevailing in these countries at the time capital flows dried up. Contemporary accounts emanating from the lending country – England – are concerned more with the inflationary finance (money creation) of fiscal deficit than with falling coffee prices or the terms of trade. The restructuring of the repayment schedule and the resumption of foreign investment are almost always linked to austerity plans and fiscal responsibility. It thus seems that in historical perspective, what could be termed as demand-side causes have figured prominently as explanations for the variability of capital flows.

Another equally important set of models is invoked to explain yet other episodes of capital-flow variability. The models I am referring to are the portfolio capital flows theories that invoke the same no-arbitrage arguments used in this chapter. In these models exchange rate uncertainty figures prominently as a source affecting the profitability of foreign investment. In a study of tsarist Russia, Gregory (1979) established that the adoption of the gold standard by Russia in 1896 was correlated with positive and large (three times pre-gold standard levels) capital flows. One can easily relate the Russian experience with that of Brazil or Argentina by arguing that fiscal stability is a necessary condition for a successful commitment to an external constraint such as the gold standard imposed. The fiscal crisis and political weakness of Latin American countries imposed, at times, great exchange rates risks which affected the profitability of foreign investment.

In fairness, I must add that those papers dealing with Argentina seem to include sentences such as the decline in net profits from railroads and other investments prior to the deterioration in the balance of payments and collapse of foreign lending. However, these assertions are not fully developed as the discussion then heads toward budget deficits and balance of payments crisis.

A brief and incomplete survey of some episodes that exhibited capital-flow volatility has shown that existing treatments emphasise domestic demand-side arguments as an explanation for capital flow volatility – fiscal crisis and exchange rate uncertainty are the driving forces behind reduced expected profitability of foreign investment. There is a way to resolve the apparent dichotomy between this and existing treatments of the sources of capital flow. The authors should try to incorporate exchange rate risks explicitly in the no-arbitrage equation and to explicitly incorporate the government deficit in the resources flow equation.

In the current version of the model the authors use the equation:

$$F = \dot{K} + C - Y \tag{1}$$

to define net capital flows as equal to domestic resources minus domstic uses.

Since $Y = C + S$ we can write the equation as:

$$F = \dot{K} - S$$

or in a more standard notation:

$$IM - EX = I - S. \tag{2}$$

The last equation ignores the government sector. We should write domestic savings as the sum of private and public sector savings:

$$S = Sp + Sg. \quad \text{where} \quad Sg = G - T.$$

Substituting S in (2) we get:

$$IM - EX = I - Sp - (G - T) \text{ or} \tag{3}$$

$$F = \dot{K} + C + G - Y. \tag{4}$$

The current absence of government deficit from the model has to be defended, because its exclusion both assumes *ex ante* the results the authors would like to establish and plays down the role of government policy that is, after all, the underlying motivation for the chapter. Once both elements are included, a fair horse-race can be run between the supply-side and demand-side theories.

To conclude, I found two problems with the chapter: (1) It ignores, *ex ante*, demand-side explanations that figure prominently in the literature, and (2) it ignores the feedback between the flows and the stock (the foreign debt). Nevertheless, I have benefited from reading this chapter. In particular, it directs the attention of the economic historian and policy-oriented economist to the fundamentals, i.e., the supply-side shocks that could have initiated the capital flow crisis faced by lesser developing countries. The role of political instability and fiscal crisis would then be indeed in magnifying the effects of this initial shocks. This assertion has to be tested against the alternative which puts the blame on the demand side. I am sure that the debate that this chapter will generate would help us better to understand the process and to describe better remedies for those countries faced with capital-flow volatility.

REFERENCES

Cardoso, E.A. and R. Dornbusch (1989) 'Brazilian debt crises: Past and present', in B. Eichengreen and P. Lindert (eds), *The International Debt Crisis in Historical Perspective*, Cambridge, MA: MIT Press.

Gregory, P.R. (1979) 'The Russian balance of payments, the gold standard, and monetary policy: A historical example of foreign capital movements', *Journal of Economic History* (June), 379–95.

Part Four
Policy perspectives

11 The political economy of capital controls

ALBERTO ALESINA, VITTORIO GRILLI
and GIAN MARIA MILESI-FERRETTI

1 Introduction

This chapter studies the institutional and political determinants of capital controls. On the one hand, recent work relating economic policy decisions to political and institutional factors has helped to shed light on several important observations, such as large budget deficits in representative democracies and low inflation in countries with an independent central bank, that are difficult to explain with models using the assumptions of social planner and representative agent.[1] On the other hand, capital controls have not been examined from this political–institutional perspective. Capital controls and other forms of foreign exchange restrictions are the rule rather than the exception, warranting a closer look at their determinants and effects: data from the IMF for 1990 show that only 30 countries (9 industrialised countries and 21 developing countries) had no limitations on capital flows (Mathieson and Rojas-Suarez, 1992).

Numerous theoretical studies have examined how capital controls affect economic policy conduct (optimality and sustainability of different policies), the possible motivations for the introduction of capital controls, their welfare implications, the importance of 'sequencing' in a process of reform leading to a removal of foreign exchange restrictions, etc.[2] The empirical literature has addressed such important issues as the actual degree of capital mobility, the impact of capital controls and political risk on interest differentials, and the effectiveness of capital controls in 'segmenting' domestic and foreign financial markets.[3] However, little attention has been devoted to investigating empirically the relation between the presence or removal of capital controls in various countries on the one side, and the structural economic and political features of these countries on the other. Such an empirical investigation is the object of this chapter. We believe this investigation is useful because the motivations for the introduction of capital controls appear to be closely related to political and institutional factors. For example, one motivation for introducing capital controls is the maintenance of a larger tax base for a capital levy or for the inflation tax. The importance of this argument is likely to depend on the government's preferences over the distribution of the tax burden (reflecting political factors) and on the costs of alternative forms of taxation (reflecting structural and institutional factors). Another motivation, the prevention of speculative attacks on the foreign exchange reserves of the central bank, clearly depends on a structural factor such as the exchange rate regime.

More specifically, we address two questions. First, we examine whether the presence of capital controls can be related to a number of economic, political and institutional variables. Second, we investigate whether the presence of capital controls, along with other political and institutional variables, helps to explain the evolution of macroeconomic variables such as inflation and seigniorage, government debt, real interest rates and growth. Our sample consists of 20 OECD countries in the period between 1950 and 1989. Although there is no shortage of theoretical models of capital controls, this chapter is not based on a single formal model. Rather, it looks at the empirical support for existing theories. One reason for this choice is that we want to look at a broad set of issues which can hardly be encompassed in a single theoretical framework. Because our sample is composed by OECD countries, there are few references to the literature on capital controls in developing countries.

Even though the data set has shortcomings, which we will discuss, our results show several interesting regularities. The evidence is consistent with an inflation-tax explanation for capital controls: by reducing the possibility of portfolio diversification into foreign currency assets, capital controls limit the ability of individuals to avoid the inflation tax and facilitate the imposition of administrative measures designed to keep domestic interest rates artificially low. Indeed, we find that inflation and seigniorage revenue are significantly higher in the presence of capital controls. Capital controls are also associated with lower domestic real interest rates, after controlling for the level of domestic debt. Furthermore, capital controls are more likely to be in place when the central bank is not independent, when the exchange rate is managed and when there is a majority government: other political variables seem to have more limited explanatory power. The rest of the chapter is organised as follows. Section 2 briefly reviews the vast theoretical literature on the effects of foreign exchange restrictions on economic performance. In particular, it looks at monetary policy and tax policy under capital controls. Section 3 considers possible motivations for the introduction of capital controls, and highlights the role of institutional and political factors in determining the relative importance of these motivations. Section 4 presents the data and discusses the empirical results. Section 5 summarises the main conclusions.

2 The effects of capital controls

2.1 General issues

The impact of different degrees of capital mobility on the effectiveness of monetary and fiscal policy is discussed in the early Mundell–Fleming models in the context of different exchange rate regimes. For example, under fixed exchange rates, starting from a position of trade balance monetary policy has only a short-run impact on output: an expansionary monetary policy increases output and imports, generating a loss of foreign exchange reserves and therefore a monetary contraction. With perfect capital mobility, the same policy induces an immediate loss of reserves and no effects on output. Under flexible exchange rates, a fiscal expansion generates an increase in output and an exchange rate depreciation to maintain the trade balance. The same policy under full capital mobility would generate an exchange rate appreciation by putting upward pressure on domestic interest rates. Output would remain constant, as increased government expenditure 'crowds out' net exports.

More recent work has reconsidered the macroeconomic effects of capital controls in a flexible-price, utility-maximising framework. For example, Adams and Greenwood (1985) argue that in a small open economy dual exchange rates and capital controls are equivalent (in the same sense that tariffs and quotas are) and that they represent a tax (subsidy) on capital account transactions. In the absence of other distortions, it follows that capital controls and dual exchange rates in a small open economy are welfare-decreasing. By contrast, if the economy is large, both can increase welfare, by an optimum tariff argument. The presence of capital controls also modifies the transmission of monetary and fiscal disturbances across countries (Greenwood and Kimbrough, 1985; Guidotti and Végh, 1992). The effectiveness of a devaluation under capital controls and the impact of the latter on the level of the real exchange rate are other widely debated questions: the latter question is particularly important in the study of trade and financial liberalisation in developing countries.[4] Both are, however, outside the scope of this chapter.

2.2 Capital controls and monetary policy with a managed exchange rate

Effective capital controls can provide some degree of monetary policy autonomy under a fixed exchange rate system or a crawling peg. For example, the early years of the EMS, with large (albeit shrinking) inflation differentials across countries, were characterised by widespread capital controls.[5] Wyplosz (1986), Park and Sachs (1987) and Bacchetta (1990) investigated whether capital controls can prevent runs on the currency and balance of payments crises when the government is pursuing monetary and credit policies that are inconsistent with the exchange rate peg. These studies pointed out that effective capital controls can prevent speculative attacks on foreign exchange reserves, but that in the long run reserve depletion takes place anyway through the current account channel. A shortcoming of these studies is the failure to provide a justification for the 'inconsistency' between monetary policy and the exchange rate peg, since government behaviour is taken as exogenous. However, Obstfeld (1986a) showed that self-fulfilling balance of payments crises can occur even when government policies are consistent with the exchange rate peg, implicitly providing a rationale for the imposition of capital controls.[6]

Empirical studies have used high-frequency data to examine whether capital controls are effective in de-linking domestic and foreign financial markets, especially in the wake of expected realignments (Giavazzi and Pagano, 1988; Giavazzi and Giovannini, 1989, Chapters 5 and 6). Overall, these studies find a significant impact of capital controls on onshore–offshore interest differentials in periods of turbulence near realignments, but a modest impact in other periods.

2.3 A public finance perspective

Another important question is how the presence of capital controls affects optimal taxation decisions on the part of the government. This question is particularly important in the study of inflation from a public finance perspective. Capital controls limit the ability of individuals to avoid the inflation tax on domestic money holdings by holding foreign currency assets and deposits: hence they have a direct impact on the 'tax base' of the inflation tax. Drazen (1989) emphasises that capital controls allow the imposition of measures such as high reserve requirements that raise the demand for money and therefore the inflation tax base. He also argues that these measures may be detrimental in the long run, because they may discourage capital accumulation by raising the interest rates that banks charge on loans.[7] In order to maintain seigniorage revenue following the dismantling of barriers to trade and capital flows, Brock (1984) argues that the central bank can impose a reserve requirement on foreign capital inflows and a prior import deposit.

Capital controls are often accompanied by various types of financial market restrictions, such as controls on interest rates. Giovannini and de

Melo (1991) focus on a sample of developing countries and relate capital controls to government revenue from financial repression, measured by comparing the government's domestic and foreign cost of borrowing. Recent work by Roubini and Sala-i-Martin (1991, 1992) relates financial repression to macroeconomic performance. The argument is that an underdeveloped and repressed financial system allows the government to finance public expenditure more easily when the tax system is inefficient, but may constitute an obstacle to growth.

Similarly, when tax distortions are high and domestic debt is large, capital controls may be justified, since they allow the government to reduce the cost of financing its debt (Aizenman and Guidotti, 1993).[8] This is equivalent to a form of seigniorage on government liabilities. An interesting question, which we address in our empirical analysis, is whether the reduction in the cost of servicing the public debt, together with the easier access to seigniorage revenue, can actually *reduce* public debt accumulation in the presence of capital controls.

To our knowledge, the only theoretical paper explicitly building a link between the political determinants of tax policy and capital controls is Alesina and Tabellini (1989). The authors view capital controls as a form of limiting holdings of foreign assets that are nontaxable. Individuals would accumulate foreign assets to avoid the risk of future taxation. In their model there are two social groups, 'workers' and 'capitalists', and two parties, each representing a social group. The workers' source of income is labour (they cannot own domestic capital), while the capitalists' income comes from capital holdings. Under reasonable assumptions about initial endowments and distribution it is shown that fear of a future workers' government may induce capitalists to export capital. Among other things, the chapter shows that once homogeneity between private agents is removed, distributional reasons become an important consideration in the evaluation of foreign exchange restrictions.

We turn now more directly to the justifications for imposing capital controls and to the degree to which political and institutional factors may shape these motivations.

3 Why capital controls?

In a recent study, Mathieson and Rojas-Suarez (1992) identify four reasons for the imposition of capital controls, which we will examine in turn:

(1) Limiting volatile short-run capital flows (avoiding balance of payments crises, etc.)
(2) Maintenance of the domestic tax base

(3) Retention of domestic savings
(4) Help the stabilisation and structural reform programmes.

3.1 Limiting volatile short-term capital flows (stability of foreign exchange markets)

A case for limiting capital mobility under floating exchange rates relies on the differential speed of adjustment between the financial and the real sector. While the nominal exchange rate reacts instantaneously to clear asset markets, the real economy undergoes slower adjustment, for example, because of stickiness in real wages and irreversibilities in investment decisions. Authors such as Tobin (1978) and Dornbusch (1986) argue that this differential speed of adjustment, together with exogenous 'excess volatility' in financial markets, may induce excess exchange rate volatility (overshooting; bubbles, etc.), with negative effects on real economic activity. Tobin proposed to 'throw sand in the wheels' of short-run capital flows through a uniform tax on all foreign exchange transactions, thereby discouraging very short-term capital flows, but with negligible effects on long-run ones.[9] Dornbusch (1986) suggests the adoption of measures such as dual exchange rate systems, that are able to shield the real economy, at least partially, from the vagaries of short-term financial markets' behaviour.

When exchange rates are pegged, unrestricted short-term capital flows may cause large variations in foreign exchange reserves, the collapse of the peg or high interest rate variability. The recent turbulence experienced in the European Monetary System (EMS) and in countries that unilaterally pegged their rate to the ECU or the D-Mark proves this point very effectively.[10] Effective capital controls can at least mitigate these undesirable effects in the short run. Obviously crises can occur because fundamentals are out of line, as is the case when two macroeconomic policy objectives (say, domestic credit expansion and fixed exchange rates) are mutually inconsistent. This is shown in the literature on speculative attacks and balance of payments crises briefly discussed in section 2.3 above. In the absence of capital controls, sustainability of an adjustable-peg mechanism requires large interest rate changes before realignments, to compensate asset-holders for capital losses. This interest rate variability is particularly damaging in countries where the government has a large short-term public debt, or when longer-term debt instruments are indexed to short-term interest rates, as in Italy.[11] Although one would need to motivate explicitly the adoption of policy measures that are inconsistent with the exchange rate peg in the long run, the incentive to introduce capital controls is obviously greater when the exchange rate is managed. The possibility of self-fulfilling speculative attacks against a fixed exchange rate, not motivated by market fundamentals, would provide an additional justification for the imposition of capital controls: the exchange rate peg can collapse even when current fundamentals are consistent with the peg (Obstfeld, 1986a, 1988, and his comments to Giovannini, 1988). This line of analysis would suggest that governments with stronger 'credibility problems' would be more likely targets of speculative attacks and may therefore be more likely to impose capital controls.[12]

3.2 Maintenance of the domestic tax base

As discussed in section 2.3, capital controls may allow the government to tax money and asset holdings more effectively. The presence of capital controls also allows the imposition of administrative measures designed to reduce the value of domestic interest rates and hence to facilitate the financing of government expenditure needs.[13] For example, the literature on the inflation tax in an open economy (section 2.3) suggests that capital controls may reduce the real cost of domestic debt (Aizenman and Guidotti, 1993; Sussman, 1991) and increase seigniorage revenue.[14] Of course, one needs to justify capital controls with the existence of distortions that prevent the fiscal system from operating effectively under free capital mobility.

Giovannini (1988) and Razin and Sadka (1991) focus instead on the taxation of capital. They argue that capital controls may be justified by the difficulty of taxing foreign-source income. Giovannini suggests that the distortions introduced by capital controls may be smaller than those implied by the impossibility of taxing foreign-source income. Razin and Sadka show that when taxing foreign-source income is impossible, it may be optimal to impose a restriction on capital exports in order to generate 'over-investment' domestically.

Abandoning a representative agent framework, one can analyse the impact of political and distributional considerations on the choice of tax instruments. Capital controls affect the amount of revenue that can be raised from different taxes: hence one can relate the decision to impose capital controls to taxation and distributional issues reflecting the political preferences of the government, as in Alesina and Tabellini (1989). For example, governments that are closer to 'workers' may have a bigger incentive to impose a capital levy, and may therefore impose capital controls in order to avoid capital flight.[15] Section 4 explores this point further.

3.3 Retention of domestic savings

The idea is that the private return from holding domestic instruments may be below the social return. Countries may also wish to limit foreign ownership of domestic factors of production. The incentive to impose capital controls for this purpose would depend on the actual degree of capital mobility. As pointed out by Marco Pagano in his Discussion, the government may be willing to adopt measures that stimulate savings if the latter are prevented from flowing abroad by low capital mobility or by capital controls. This is consistent with results presented in a panel study of OECD countries by Jappelli and Pagano (1992).

3.4 Help for stabilisation and structural reform programmes

Free capital flows can be destabilising when a country implements a stabilisation or a structural reform plan. For example, lack of credibility of the stabilisation plan may cause capital flight and a balance of payments crisis, making plan failure more likely. Also, if the plan is (partially) credible, the high real interest rates typically associated with a stabilisation programme may cause (temporary) large capital inflows and an appreciation of the real exchange rate: the latter may hamper a trade reform aiming at lower barriers to imports. From a political economy point of view, one should consider the relation between political stability, government preferences and credibility. Again, governments with lower initial credibility may be those with stronger incentives to introduce capital controls (see 3.1 above). This motivation for the introduction of capital controls may also have larger relevance for developing countries.

We believe that the first two motivations for the imposition of capital controls are the most important ones for industrialised countries; they also provide a clearer set of variables that may matter in the decision to impose or remove capital controls. The relevance of all these motivations depends on the ability of the government to impose effective capital controls. This ability has probably weakened over time, for two reasons. The first is the endogenous 'erosion' of existing barriers, as agents find ways to avoid official restrictions. The second has to do with structural change and technological progress in financial markets that facilitate international capital movements and make them harder to monitor. Because of the nature of our data,[16] we are currently unable to account for these factors.

4 Empirical evidence

In this section we investigate the empirical relevance of some of the theory discussed in sections 2 and 3. We analyse a panel composed of 20 OECD countries in the period between 1950 and 1989. The countries are Australia, Austria, Belgium, Canada, Denmark, Finland, France, Germany, Greece, Ireland, Italy, Japan, the Netherlands, Norway, Portugal, Spain, Sweden, Turkey, the United Kingdom and the United States.[17] Not all variables are available over the whole period in all countries: thus the actual sample is smaller than the full 800 observations implied by the panel size. The Appendix lists and briefly describes all the variables we use.

Our analysis proceeds in two stages. First, we want to understand which political and institutional factors make the decision to introduce capital controls more likely. In this stage, therefore, we use capital controls as the dependent variable and regress it on a set of political and institutional variables. Second, we trace the effect of capital controls on economic performance. In this stage, we thus follow previous analysis by Grilli, Masciandaro and Tabellini (1991) by including capital controls in a group of institutional variables which are used to explain the behaviour of macroeconomic aggregates.

The problem is to find a proper definition of foreign exchange restrictions. In practice, the latter can take several different forms: strict capital controls, dual exchange rates, limitations on current account transactions such as compulsory surrendering of export receipts, prior import deposits, etc. We employ a concept of capital controls defined in *Restrictions on Payments on Capital Transactions* by the International Monetary Fund.[18] As in Grilli (1989), this information is used to construct a dummy variable taking the value of 1 when capital controls are in place and 0 otherwise. A shortcoming of this measure is that we have no way to account for different degrees of intensity of capital controls. One should also note that the effectiveness of controls on capital account transactions may be enhanced by controls on current account transactions, such as trade financing, since the latter transactions provide a channel through which 'unofficial' capital movements can take place (leads and lags in the settlement of commercial transactions).[19] In that case, current account restrictions may be a proxy for the intensity of capital controls.

Isolating the impact of capital controls is also difficult, since they are typically adopted (or removed) together with other policy measures. Indeed, since many studies have stressed the impact of capital controls on the optimal policy mix, it is not surprising that their imposition or removal is rarely undertaken in isolation, without any change in policy course. In the empirical analysis, we try to control for variables whose effects may interact with those of capital controls.

Most of the political variables used in our analysis have been constructed and employed in previous research. In particular, we make use of variables described in Alesina (1989), Grilli, Masciandaro and Tabellini

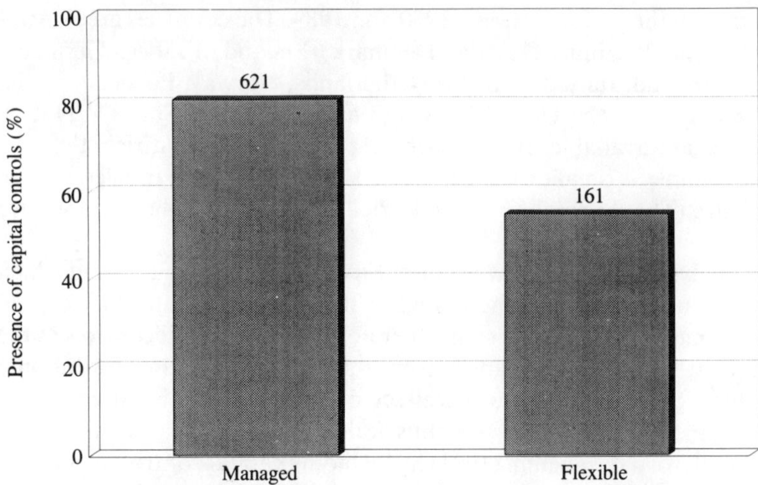

Figure 11.1 Capital controls and institutions: exchange rate regime

(1991), Cukierman, Edwards and Tabellini (1992) and Alesina, Ozler, Roubini and Swagel (1992). All of these papers demonstrate the importance of political and institutional factors in economic policy decisions and their effects on the business cycle, inflation performance, the size of budget deficits and debt.

4.1 Effect of institutional and political factors on capital controls

The main arguments in favour of capital controls in developed countries that we surveyed in section 3 can be classified into two broad categories. The first (case 3.1) relates capital controls to foreign exchange market stability. The second (case 3.2) views capital controls as an integral part of governments' taxation strategies.

4.1.1 Capital controls and exchange rate regime

As we have discussed above, the introduction of capital controls should be more likely during fixed and managed exchange rate regimes. They help prevent or mitigate speculative attacks and, therefore, facilitate the defence of a fixed exchange rate parity or of an exchange rate band. We constructed a dummy variable (*EXR*) taking value of 1 during periods of fixed or managed exchange rates and 0 during periods of free floating exchange rates. Figure 11.1 contrasts the use of capital controls during periods of managed and fixed exchange rates with that during periods of floating exchange rates. Capital controls were in place 80% of the times when a managed or fixed exchange rate policy was followed and only 54% of the times when the exchange rate was floating.

4.1.2 Capital controls and taxation

From a public finance point of view, capital controls can allow the preservation of a large tax base despite the imposition of high tax rates. Various theories summarised in section 3 point to two different tax instruments for which capital controls may be particularly useful: capital levy and inflation tax. To understand which political and institutional factors can be crucial for the introduction of capital controls, it is useful to distinguish between theories based on social conflict and theories based on representative agent frameworks, i.e. where social conflicts are absent.

(a) Social conflict theories: capital levy vs. income tax

Since left-wing governments tend to favour the taxation of capital income over that of labour income, they may be tempted to introduce capital controls to prevent capital export and thus maintain a large tax base for capital levies. This theory was formally modelled by Alesina and Tabellini (1989).

(b) Social conflict theories: inflation tax vs. other taxes

The inflation tax can be viewed as a form of capital levy. Instead of taxing savings held in the form of real assets, it taxes savings held in nominal assets, like cash holdings, bank deposits or nominal bonds.[20] If nominal assets are not held in similar proportions across the population, the inflation tax will affect some social groups more than others. The decision of using the inflation tax can therefore be influenced by political considerations in ways similar to the decision of using capital levies. Unlike a capital levy, however, it is not immediately clear which type of governments would support the inflation tax, whether left-wing or right-wing governments. On the one hand, inflation might be a regressive form of taxation and right-wing governments might therefore favour it more than left-wing governments for distributional reasons. Capital controls, by isolating domestic financial intermediaries from foreign competition, allow the imposition of high bank reserve requirements. This maintains a high demand for monetary base and thus assures a large tax base for the inflation tax. On the other hand, a left-wing government may be more unemployment averse than a right-wing government, and thus the former may attempt to exploit the Phillips curve by creating inflation (Alesina, 1989; Alesina and Roubini, 1992). Furthermore, if a left-wing government prefers higher public spending than a right-wing one, it may need more seigniorage.

To test whether the political leaning of governments has any impact on the decision of imposing capital controls, we use a dummy variable

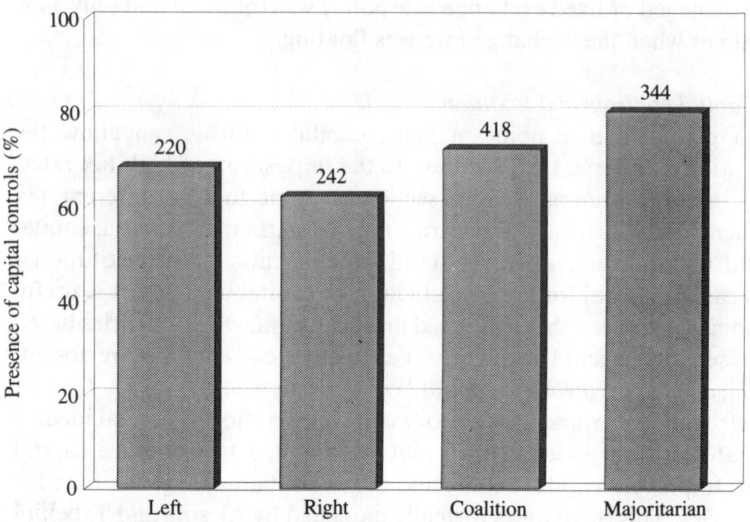

Figure 11.2 Capital controls and institutions: type of government

(*RADM*) which equals −1 in case of left-wing governments and +1 in case of right-wing governments.[21] Figure 11.2 shows that left-wing governments have been slightly more prone to impose capital controls than right-wing governments. Capital controls were present in 69% of the cases in which left-wing governments were in power, compared to 63% of the cases in which right-wing governments were in power. This difference is so small that it is clearly insignificant in any statistical sense.

Underlying the capital levy explanation of capital controls is the assumption that the executive has sufficient political power to impose a higher burden of taxes on some groups: in other words, the government must have sufficiently wide support. For the case of inflation, however, one could also argue that governments without wide support may be unable to finance expenditure using 'other taxes', and may therefore be more likely to resort to capital controls and use the inflation tax. As suggested in Grilli, Masciandaro and Tabellini (1991), an indicator of government strength is whether the executive is a one-party government enjoying a parliamentary majority or, instead, is a coalition of parties and/or a minority government. In order to control for the degree of support of the government we use a dummy variable (*MAJOR*) which takes value of 1 in case of majority governments and 0 in case of a coalition and/or minority governments. Figure 11.2 shows that majority governments have been more likely to impose capital controls (81% of the cases) than coalition and minority governments (72% of the cases). It should be pointed out that, in our definition, dictatorships have been classified as majority governments; however, even if we were to eliminate dictatorship from the sample, majority governments still have a higher occurrence of capital controls (76% of the cases) than coalition and minority governments.[22]

(*c*) *Social conflict theories: inflation tax as the residual tax in a war of attrition situation*

In unstable political systems, where there exist unresolved social conflicts concerning the distribution of the burden of taxation, inflation may well be the only viable tax instrument for financing (at least part of) the budget deficit. This idea is modelled by Alesina and Drazen (1991) and Drazen and Grilli (1993). Unlike the argument in point (*b*) above, here inflation is not the deliberate choice of a right- or left-wing government intending to impose the burden of taxation on holders of nominal assets. Instead, it is viewed as the only option for a weak government which does not have sufficient authority to introduce a fiscal reform in one direction (capital levy) or the other (income tax). In this case minority or coalition governments should be more likely to resort to capital controls than majority governments. As suggested by Grilli, Masciandaro and Tabellini (1991), potential indicators of social conflicts and political instability are the durability of governments, i.e. the average number of years in power of the executive, and the stability of the political system, measured by the frequency with which 'significant changes' in the executive take place. 'Significant changes' in the executive refer to changes in the government involving the transfer of power from a political group to another, as opposed to changes within the same party or within the same coalition of parties. To measure government durability we use a dummy variable (*DURA*), taking a constant value for each country equal to the average number of years in power of the executive between 1950 and 1990. To measure political stability we use another variable (*STAB*) taking a constant value for each country equal to the average number of years between significant government changes. Figure 11.3 shows that capital controls were much more common under short-lived governments (79% of the cases) than under long-lived governments (53% of the cases); it also shows that capital controls were marginally more common in highly stable political systems (72% of the cases) than in unstable political systems (68% of the cases).[23]

(*d*) *Optimal taxation theories*

The inflation tax or capital levies do not need to be used only in social conflict situations. In fact, the inflation tax or capital levies can be socially accepted as part of a portfolio of tax instruments, set according to

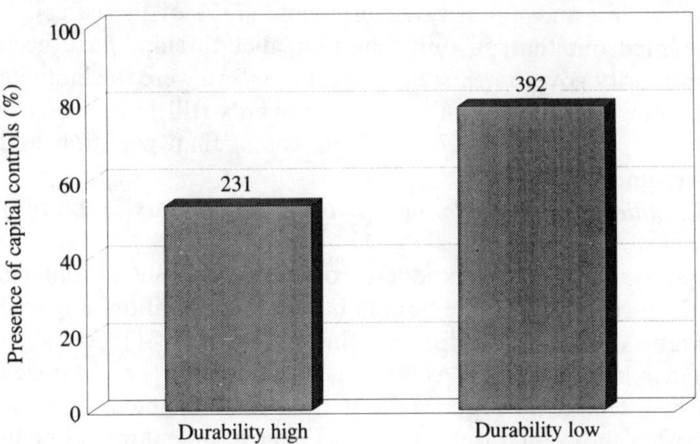

Figure 11.3 Capital controls and institutions: government durability

Ramsey's principles which are common to all governments, independently of their political leaning. In this case, the use of inflation tax need not be associated with situations of political instability, low government durability or with any particular political leaning of the executive. For example, theories of optimal seigniorage based on perfect government credibility, as in Mankiw (1987) and Grilli (1989), suggest that the inflation tax could be part of a global taxation plan of an infinitely-lived government, and thus in a situation of perfect political stability and government durability.

The inflation tax, however, may not be a choice variable for the government if monetary policy conduct is delegated to an independent central bank, with preferences that do not exactly coincide with those of the government. Structural factors, such as, for example, level and composition of GDP, are also going to influence optimal tax decisions. Besides the political variables discussed above, we therefore consider two other sets of institutional and structural indicators, reflecting the above considerations. The first is the degree of independence of the national central bank. As shown in Grilli, Masciandaro and Tabellini (1991) and Alesina and Summers (1993), the degree of independence of the central bank is an essential factor in explaining a country's inflation performance. These authors show that the scope for using inflation to finance budget deficits is greatly reduced in the presence of an independent central bank. If the inflation-tax motivation is correct, we would therefore expect that the introduction of capital controls would be less likely in the presence of an independent central bank. Here we employ the classification developed

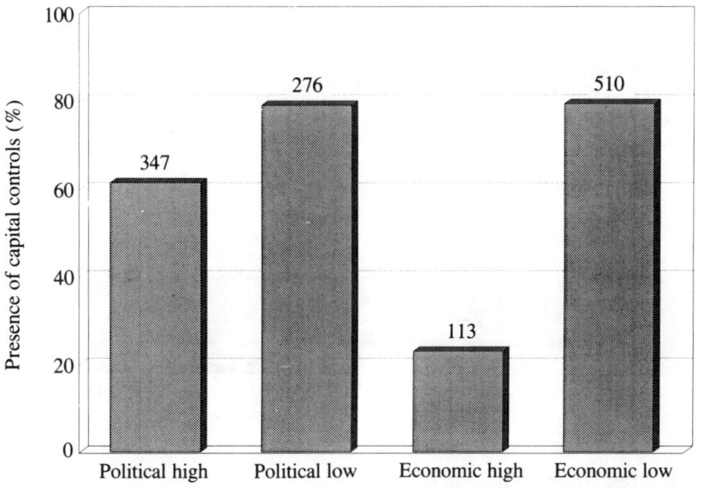

Figure 11.4 Capital controls and institutions: central bank independence

in Grilli, Masciandaro and Tabellini (1991) which distinguishes between political independence (*CBPN*) and economic independence (*CBEN*) of a central bank. The first refers to the appointment procedure and the duration in office of the governing body of the central bank. The less control the government has over the appointments of the governor and the composition of the board of the central bank, and the longer the duration in office of central bank officials, the higher is the degree of political independence of the central bank. The second refers to the obligations of the central bank regarding the financing of the budget deficit through money creation and/or interest rates manipulation. The freer is the central bank from the Treasury from this point of view, the more economic independence it enjoys. Both variables are constant for each country. Figure 11.4 shows that capital controls are more likely to be in place when the degree of central bank independence is low. Capital controls were present in 79% of the cases in which the central bank had a low degree of political independence and in 61% of the cases where a high degree of political independence was present. Economic independence appears to be even more important since capital controls were present in 79% of the cases of low economic independence but in only 23% of the cases of high economic independence.[24] Figure 11.5 summarises the relationship between capital controls and central bank independence. The reader can certainly detect a downward-sloping relationship between the frequency of capital controls and the degree of central bank indepen-

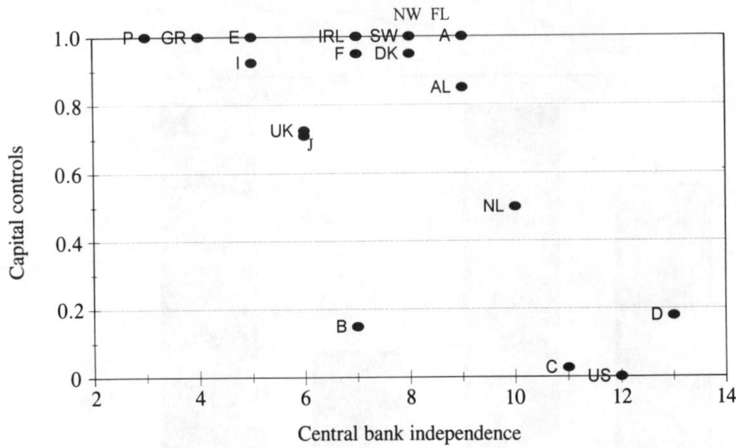

Figure 11.5 Capital controls and the central bank

dence. This curve is reminiscent of the downward-sloping relationship between inflation and independence described in Grilli, Masciandaro and Tabellini (1991) and Alesina and Summers (1993). Our curve in Figure 11.5 appears perhaps a bit less striking because so many countries have the same value (i.e., 1) for capital controls.

The other variable which we consider is an indicator of the structure of the economy. The use of the inflation tax is more attractive in the presence of a large tax base, i.e. when the demand for base money is high. This is more likely in economies where a large amount of transactions take place with the use of cash, and where banks have large amounts of reserves. Economies of this type are usually characterised by large black economies and underdeveloped financial markets. We use as an indicator of this situation the relative importance of the agricultural sector compared to the service sector. The variable *AGRSER* is the ratio between the value added produced by the agricultural sector and the value added produced by the service sector.[25] Figure 11.6 shows that capital controls are more common when the agricultural sector is relatively large (100% of the cases) than when it is small (50% of the cases).

In Table 11.1 we present the result of probit estimations where the capital control dummy was regressed on all the variables described above. The sample size is substantially reduced in this case, mainly because of the scarcity of data on the sectoral value added (*AGRSER*) and the political leaning of the government (*RADM*). In order to increase the number of observations, we next eliminate from the set of independent variables

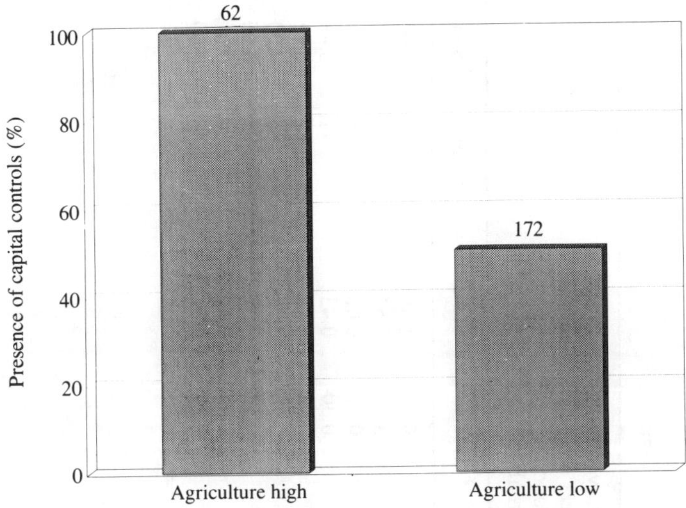

Figure 11.6 Capital controls and institutions: importance of agriculture vs. services

AGRSER, in Table 11.2, and both *AGRSER* and *RADM*, in Table 11.3. Table 11.3, therefore, contains the most reliable results, but the effects of *AGRSER* and *RADM* can only be assessed within the more limited samples of Tables 11.1 and 11.2. On the one hand, Table 11.1 and 11.2 suggest that the political leaning of the government has no significant effecty on the decision of whether to introduce capital controls. However, strong (majority) governments are more likely to impose capital controls. On the other hand, Table 11.1 provides evidence that the structure of the economy is important. The larger the agricultural sector with respect to the service sector, the higher is the probability that capital controls will be in place. Turning now to the indications of Table 11.3, the evidence suggests that stable political systems characterised by majoritarian and long-lived governments are more likely to adopt capital controls measures. The evidence also strongly supports the conjecture that countries with highly independent central banks are less likely to resort to capital controls. Finally, the exchange rate regime is important; as expected, capital controls are more likely to be in place during periods of managed exchange rates than during free floating. As reported in Table 11.3, the results are quite robust to different model specifications, for example if we were to assume a logit instead of a probit structure, and to the introduction of random effects. The results of this simple statistical exercise are perfectly consistent with our previous graphical analysis.

Table 11.1. *Political and institutional determinants of capital controls, all variables*

Dependent variable: Capital Controls

Estimation by probit					Estimation by logit				
Usable observations	170				Usable observations	170			
Cases correct	144				Cases correct	144			
Log likelihood	− 60.74				Log likelihood	− 60.81			
Average likelihood	0.70				Average likelihood	0.70			
Variable	Coeff.	Std error	*t*-stat.	Signif.	Variable	Coeff.	Std error	*t*-stat.	Signif.
Constant	5.48	1.10	5.01	0.00	Constant	9.35	1.96	4.77	0.00
MAJOR	1.88	0.33	5.61	0.00	*MAJOR*	3.30	0.64	5.13	0.00
STAB	0.01	0.01	0.78	0.44	*STAB*	0.02	0.02	1.06	0.29
DURA	0.14	0.23	0.62	0.54	*DURA*	0.30	0.43	0.71	0.48
RADM	0.02	0.14	0.13	0.90	*RADM*	0.04	0.26	0.17	0.87
CBEN	− 0.48	0.16	− 2.98	0.00	*CBEN*	− 0.93	0.32	− 2.86	0.00
CBPN	− 0.28	0.14	− 1.94	0.05	*CBPN*	− 0.52	0.27	− 1.93	0.05
EXR	0.92	0.34	2.69	0.01	*EXR*	1.65	0.62	2.64	0.01
AGRSER	1.42	0.38	3.79	0.00	*AGRSER*	2.29	0.67	3.43	0.00

Table 11.2. *Political and institutional determinants of capital controls, excluding* AGSER

Dependent variable: Capital Controls									
Estimation by probit					Estimation by logit				
Usable observations		375			Usable observations		375		
Cases correct		322			Cases correct		322		
Log likelihood		− 145.99			Log likelihood		− 145.96		
Average likelihood		0.67			Average likelihood		0.67		
Variable	Coeff.	Std error	*t*-stat.	Signif.	Variable	Coeff.	Std error	*t*-stat.	Signif.
Constant	2.69	0.44	6.18	0.00	Constant	5.61	0.94	6.00	0.00
MAJOR	1.03	0.20	5.26	0.00	*MAJOR*	1.89	0.37	5.15	0.00
STAB	0.03	0.01	3.47	0.00	*STAB*	0.05	0.01	3.66	0.00
DURA	0.37	0.11	3.44	0.00	*DURA*	0.71	0.20	3.54	0.00
RADM	− 0.05	0.09	− 0.56	0.57	*RADM*	− 0.15	0.15	− 0.96	0.34
CBEN	− 0.80	0.09	− 8.53	0.00	*CBEN*	− 1.60	0.21	− 7.55	0.00
CBPN	− 0.39	0.08	− 5.12	0.00	*CBPN*	− 0.72	0.15	− 4.87	0.00
EXR	1.58	0.25	6.35	0.00	*EXR*	2.91	0.50	5.86	0.00

Table 11.3. *Political and institutional determinants of capital controls, excluding* AGSER *and* RADM

Dependent variable: Capital Controls
Estimation by probit

Usable observations	607
Cases correct	516
Log likelihood	– 213.26
Average likelihood	0.70

Variable	Coeff.	Std error	*t*-stat.	Signif.
Constant	2.66	0.31	8.68	0.00
MAJOR	0.66	0.16	4.05	0.00
STAB	0.03	0.01	4.10	0.00
DURA	0.16	0.07	2.26	0.02
CBEN	– 0.67	0.06	– 10.97	0.00
CBPN	– 0.24	0.05	– 5.02	0.00
EXR	1.32	0.19	6.92	0.00

Dependent variable: Capital Controls
Estimation by logit

Usable observations	607
Cases correct	516
Log likelihood	– 211.06
Average likelihood	0.70

Variable	Coeff.	Std error	*t*-stat.	Signif.
Constant	5.08	0.61	8.29	0.00
MAJOR	1.23	0.30	4.12	0.00
STAB	0.05	0.01	4.17	0.00
DURA	0.30	0.13	2.33	0.02
CBEN	– 1.30	0.13	– 9.95	0.00
CBPN	– 0.39	0.09	– 4.28	0.00
EXR	2.40	0.37	6.56	0.00

Dependent variable: Capital Controls
Estimation by probit with random effects

Usable observations	607

Variable	Coeff.	Std error	*t*-stat.	Signif.
Constant	1.18	0.11	10.96	0.00
MAJOR	0.11	0.03	3.65	0.00
STAB	0.01	0.00	2.01	0.04
DURA	0.03	0.04	0.84	0.40
CBEN	– 0.14	0.02	– 5.52	0.00
CBPN	– 0.06	0.02	– 2.55	0.01
EXR	1.17	0.03	5.44	0.00

Our results can be summarised as follows. One of the strongest and most interesting findings is that independent central banks are less likely to impose capital controls than more dependent ones. This suggests, indirectly, that capital controls are probably used by governments that, by controlling monetary policy more directly, can impose a higher inflation levy when capital controls are in place. A second strong result is that 'strong' majoritarian governments are much more likely to impose capital controls than weak, short-lived coalition governments. This finding suggests that the imposition of capital controls is a conscious policy decision, rather than the result of a deadlocked political system. This evidence is, therefore, not consistent with a 'war of attrition' explanation of inflation for these countries; that is, capital controls do not appear to be the last resort to raise revenue of deadlocked and/or weak governments. Probably the 'war of attrition' explanation of inflation is more appropriate for less developed countries and for historical periods with a very high degree of social conflict (see Alesina and Drazen, 1991).

Finally, the political orientation of the government does not appear to be a good predictor of capital controls. This inconclusive finding is, however, consistent with our discussion which has highlighted several arguments pointing in different and opposing directions on this issue.

4.2 Effects of capital controls on macroeconomic variables

Roubini and Sachs (1989) and Grilli, Masciandaro and Tabellini (1991) relate the behaviour of several economic aggregates to institutional and political indicators. In this section we extend these analyses to include capital controls in the set of potential institutional indicators. In so doing, we want to answer two basic questions. First, after we control for other aspects of the political and institutional environment, like government type, political stability, central bank independence and exchange rate regime, do capital controls have any additional explanatory power? Second, if there are independent effects from capital controls, are these effects compatible with an inflation-tax interpretation of the type discussed in sections 2 and 3 above?

The first variable we analyse is public debt. Grilli, Masciandaro and Tabellini (1991) showed that debt accumulation is greater in unstable political systems, characterised by low durability of the executive and by coalition or minority governments. Table 11.4 reports the results of running a linear regression of gross debt to GDP ratio on *MAJOR*, *STAB*, *DURA* and *CONTROLS*. The relationship between political instability and coalition governments on the one side and a large public debt on the other is confirmed by our analysis: stable and majority

Table 11.4. *Capital controls and public debt*

Dependent variable: GROSS DEBT (% of GDP)
Least squares, White consistent estimate of standard errors

Usable observations	324
Adjusted R^2	0.17

Variable	Coeff.	Std error	*t*-stat.	Signif.
Constant	0.67	0.55	13.94	0.00
CONTROLS	− 0.11	0.03	− 3.25	0.00
MAJOR	− 0.11	0.02	− 4.67	0.00
STAB	− 0.01	0.00	− 5.85	0.00
DURA	− 0.01	0.01	− 1.06	0.29

governments accumulate less public debt. More importantly, capital controls appear to have a significant, *negative* impact on debt accumulation. Our interpretation is that the use of capital controls provides the governments with two channels that help prevent a large debt accumulation, both of which can be viewed as different effects of the inflation tax. First, by allowing substantial seigniorage revenues, capital controls make it easier to finance primary deficits. Second, in line with the literature on 'financial repression', we conjecture that capital controls can keep real interest rates on government debt artificially low by preventing international arbitrage in the asset market. This reduces the size of interest payments on the public debt. Table 11.5 and 11.6 explore the validity of these two claims.

Table 11.5 presents the results for the rate of inflation and a measure of inflation-tax revenues, computed as the product between the rate of money growth and real monetary base (as a percentage of total revenues and as a percentage of GDP). All three regressions confirm the negative effect of central bank independence (particularly economic independence) and of managed exchange rates on the inflation rate and on seigniorage. Consistently with our conjecture, capital controls are associated with both higher inflation rates and higher levels of seigniorage. The results for the political variables are less clear-cut. With the inflation rate as the dependent variable, the variables capturing government stability (*STAB*) and majority governments (*MAJOR*) are significant and with the expected sign: more stable and majority governments are associated with lower inflation. In the seigniorage regressions, however, the *MAJOR* variable is not significant, and the *STAB* variable is significant and with the wrong sign (albeit with a very small coefficient).

Table 11.5. *Capital controls, inflation and seigniorage*

Dependent variable: INFLATION RATE
Least squares, White consistent estimate of standard errors

Usable observations	597
Adjusted R^2	0.28

Variable	Coeff.	Std error	*t*-stat.	Signif.
Constant	0.132	0.011	11.751	0.000
CONTROLS	0.028	0.005	5.641	0.000
MAJOR	– 0.012	0.004	– 2.635	0.008
STAB	– 0.001	0.000	– 2.872	0.004
DURA	– 0.003	0.002	– 1.593	0.111
CBEN	– 0.003	0.002	– 2.037	0.042
CBPN	– 0.002	0.001	– 1.373	0.170
EXR	– 0.059	0.005	– 11.120	0.000

Dependent variable: INFLATION TAX (% of total revenues)
Least squares, White consistent estimate of standard errors

Usable observations	506
Adjusted R^2	0.31

Variable	Coeff.	Std error	*t*-stat.	Signif.
Constant	0.109	0.011	9.997	0.000
CONTROLS	0.007	0.003	2.034	0.042
MAJOR	– 0.003	0.004	– 0.867	0.386
STAB	0.0003	0.000	2.224	0.026
DURA	– 0.003	0.002	– 1.853	0.064
CBEN	– 0.009	0.001	– 6.844	0.000
CBPN	– 0.002	0.001	– 2.569	0.010
EXR	– 0.030	0.005	– 5.842	0.000

Dependent variable: INFLATION TAX (% of GDP)
Least squares, White consistent estimate of standard errors

Usable observations	506
Adjusted R^2	0.31

Variable	Coeff.	Std error	*t*-stat.	Signif.
Constant	0.0291	0.0032	9.0017	0.0000
CONTROLS	0.0027	0.0013	2.1120	0.0347
MAJOR	– 0.0003	0.0014	– 0.2323	0.8163
STAB	0.0001	0.0000	1.9626	0.0497
DURA	– 0.0017	0.0006	– 2.7967	0.0052
CBEN	– 0.0027	0.0004	– 6.7046	0.0000
CBPN	0.0001	0.0003	0.3555	0.7223
EXR	– 0.0054	0.0017	– 3.1837	0.0015

Table 11.6. *Capital controls and interest rates*

Dependent variable: REAL INTEREST RATE
Least squares, White consistent estimate of standard errors

Usable observations	523
Adjusted R^2	0.12

Variable	Coeff.	Std error	*t*-stat.	Signif.
Constant	0.02	0.01	3.12	0.00
CONTROLS	– 0.02	0.003	– 6.86	0.00
MAJOR	– 0.01	0.003	– 2.09	0.04
STAB	0.0003	0.0001	2.12	0.03
DURA	0.0013	0.0014	0.92	0.36
EXR	0.02	0.00	3.82	0.00

Dependent variable: REAL INTEREST RATE
Least squares, White consistent estimate of standard errors

Usable observations	295
Adjusted R^2	0.21

Variable	Coeff.	Std error	*t*-stat.	Signif.
Constant	– 0.001	0.009	– 0.071	0.944
CONTROLS	– 0.014	0.004	– 3.252	0.001
MAJOR	– 0.0178	0.0047	– 3.751	0.000
STAB	0.0003	0.0001	2.101	0.036
DURA	0.005	0.002	2.521	0.012
EXR	0.016	0.004	3.679	0.000
DEBT{1}	0.03	0.01	3.58	0.00

Table 11.6 analyses the relationship between (*ex post*) real interest rates and institutional and political indicators. Majoritarian (strong) governments are associated with lower real interest rates than coalition and minority governments. Also the stability of the executive and that of the political system do appear to have a significant effect on interest rates. Fixed exchange rate regimes are characterised by higher real interest rates than floating regimes. Crucially, as expected, capital controls have a significant negative effect on real interest rates. As argued in previous sections, capital controls facilitate the imposition of administrative measures designed to keep domestic interest rates artificially low, so we might be capturing the effect of these measures.

Finally, in Table 11.7, we investigate the relationship between

Table 11.7. *Capital controls and growth rates*

Dependent variable: REAL GDP GROWTH RATE
Least squares, White consistent estimate of standard errors

Usable observations 583
Adjusted R^2 0.06

Variable	Coeff.	Std error	*t*-stat.	Signif.
Constant	0.021	0.008	2.746	0.006
CONTROLS	0.009	0.004	2.200	0.028
MAJOR	– 0.003	0.004	0.871	0.383
STAB	0.001	0.0002	3.026	0.002
DURA	– 0.001	0.002	– 0.483	0.629
EXR	0.016	0.005	3.506	0.000

Dependent variable: REAL PER CAPITA GDP GROWTH RATE
Least squares, White consistent estimate of standard errors

Usable observations 549
Adjusted R^2 0.11

Variable	Coeff.	Std error	*t*-stat.	Signif.
Constant	0.024	0.005	4.459	0.000
CONTROLS	0.004	0.003	1.246	0.213
MAJOR	0.003	0.004	2.838	0.005
STAB	0.001	0.000	4.510	0.000
DURA	– 0.005	0.001	– 4.421	0.000
EXR	0.012	0.004	3.107	0.002

Dependent variable: REAL PER CAPITAL GDP GROWTH RATE
Least squares, White consistent estimate of standard errors

Usable observations 549
Adjusted R^2 0.12

Variable	Coeff.	Std error	*t*-stat.	Signif.
Constant	0.092	0.033	2.785	0.005
CONTROLS	0.001	0.003	0.469	0.639
MAJOR	0.007	0.003	2.150	0.032
STAB	0.000	0.0000	2.964	0.003
DURA	– 0.002	0.002	– 1.308	0.191
EXR	0.014	0.004	3.534	0.000
RGDPP0	– 0.009	0.004	– 2.147	0.032

institutional variable and rate of growth of real GDP. In the first regression, the dependent variable is the growth rate of GDP, in the last two it is the growth rate of GDP per capita. The last regression includes initial income per capita as an independent variable. The latter variable is significant and with the right sign. The results also indicate that fixed exchange rate regimes and stable political systems have been associated with higher growth rates. The impact of capital controls does not appear to be significant (it is significant only in the first regression, and with a positive sign).[26] We therefore do not find a negative impact of capital controls on economic growth in our OECD sample.

5 Conclusions

Our results highlight an intriguing hypothesis. Capital controls are more likely to be imposed by strong governments which have a relatively 'free' hand over monetary policy, because the central bank is not very independent. By imposing capital controls, these governments raise more seigniorage revenue and keep interest rates artificially low. As a result, public debt accumulates at a slower rate than otherwise. This suggests that an institutional reform which makes the central bank more independent makes it more difficult for the government to finance its budget. The tightening of the fiscal constraint may force the government to adjust towards a more sound fiscal policy.

We also found that, as expected and in accordance with the theory, capital controls are more likely to be introduced when the exchange rate is pegged or managed. On the contrary, we found no effects of capital controls on growth: we reject rather strongly the hypothesis that capital controls reduce growth.

Extending this analysis to a larger sample of countries, including developing countries, is a task for future research. We conjecture that this extension may yield some different results, concerning in particular the relation between social conflict and the imposition of capital controls. The analysis can also be extended by looking at other measures of foreign exchange restrictions that we ignored in this study.

Appendix

1 Variables used in the first set of regressions of section 4

Dependent variable

CONTROLS: Dummy variable taking the value of 1 when capital controls are in place, 0 otherwise. Capital controls defined in *Restrictions on*

Payments on Capital Transactions by the International Monetary Fund.
Source: elaborations on IMF, *Exchange Rate and Monetary Arrangements*, various issues.

Independent variables
EXR: Dummy variable taking the value of 1 during periods of fixed or managed exchange rates and 0 during periods of freely floating exchange rates.
Source: elaboration on IMF, *Exchange Rate and Monetary Arrangements*, various issues.
RADM: Dummy variable taking the value of −1 when a left-wing government is in power and +1 when a right-wing government is in power.
Source: Alesina, Ozler, Roubini and Swagel (1992) and references therein.
MAJOR: Dummy variable taking the value of 1 when a majority government is in power, and 0 in the case of a coalition or minority government.
Source: Grilli, Masciandaro and Tabellini (1991) and references therein.
DURA: Country-specific variable taking values equal to the average number of years in power of the executive between 1950 and 1990.
Source: Grilli, Masciandaro and Tabellini (1991) and references therein.
STAB: Country-specific constant variable taking values equal to the average number of years between 'significant' government changes.
Source: Grilli, Masciandaro and Tabellini (1991) and references therein.
CBPN: Country-specific dummy variable measuring the political independence of the central bank. This measure depends on the length of appointment of the governor and board of the central bank and on the government's degree of control over these appointments. Higher values correspond to a more politically independent central bank.
Source: Grilli, Masciandaro and Tabellini (1991).
CBEN: Country-specific dummy variable measuring the economic independence of the central bank from the Treasury with regard to deficit financing, interest rate manipulation, etc.. Higher values correspond to a more economically independent central bank.
Source: Grilli, Masciandaro and Tabellini (1991).
AGRSER: Ratio between value added in the agricultural sector and value added in the service sector.
Source: World Bank, *World Tables*.

2 *Variables used in the second set of regressions in Section 4*

Dependent variable(s)
GROSS DEBT (% of GDP): gross government debt as a percentage of GDP.

Source: OECD, *National Income Accounts.*
INFLATION RATE: Annual rate of change of the Consumer Price Index.
Source: Cukierman, Edwards and Tabellini (1992).
INFLATION TAX (% of total revenue): the inflation tax is measured as the inflation rate times the lagged value of high-powered money.
Source: Cukierman, Edwards and Tabellini (1992).
INFLATION TAX (% of GDP): See above.
Source: Cukierman, Edwards and Tabellini (1992).
REAL INTEREST RATE: Short-term nominal interest rate on government debt minus actual inflation.
Source: OECD, *Main Economic Indicators*, various issues.
REAL GDP GROWTH RATE Source: OECD, *National Income Accounts*, various issues.
REAL PER CAPITA GDP GROWTH RATE Source: OECD, *National Income Accounts*, various issues.

Independent variables (not included above)
DEBT {1}: lagged value of gross government debt as a percentage of GDP.
Source: OECD, *National Income Accounts*, various issues.
RGDPPO: level of GDP per capita in 1950 (or first available).
Source: OECD, *National Income Accounts*, various levels.

NOTES

This chapter was originally prepared for the conference on 'International Capital Motility and Development', sponsored by the Bank of Israel, the Centre for Economic Policy Research and the Pinhas Sapir Center for Development, Tel-Aviv University (Tel-Aviv, 20–22 December 1992). We are grateful to Phillip Swagel for providing some data, to our discussants Ron Shachar and Marco Pagano and to other conference participants for useful comments. Gian Maria Milesi-Ferretti was affiliated to the Centre for Economic Performance of the London School of Economics when this chapter was written.

1 For example, see Alesina (1989), Roubini and Sachs (1989), Grilli, Masciandaro and Tabellini (1991) and Cukierman, Edwards and Tabellini (1992).
2 See section 2 and the references therein.
3 On the first topic, see for example Feldstein and Horioka (1980), Feldstein (1983), Obstfeld (1986c, 1989), Frankel (1991) and Tesar (1992). On the second, see Dooley and Isard (1980). On the third, see Claassen and Wyplosz (1982) and Giavazzi and Pagano (1988).
4 On the former, see Obstfeld (1986a); on the latter, see Edwards (1989), Stockman and Hernandez (1988) and Van Wijnbergen (1990).
5 Indeed many authors (for example Rogoff, 1985) stressed that capital controls were the reason behind the sustainability of the system. In the wake of the decision to dismantle all remaining foreign exchange restrictions in several EC countries, the issue of sustainability of the ERM of the EMS after the abolition

of controls was widely debated: see for example *European Economy* (May 1988).

6 See also Obstfeld (1988). This is discussed further in section 3 below.

7 On the relation between reserve requirements and the inflation tax, see also Brock (1989).

8 Using an overlapping-generations framework, Sussman (1991) also suggests that capital controls (in the form of a tax on interest-bearing foreign assets, accompanied by a tax on domestic assets) reduce debt service and increase the demand for money.

9 This type of measure should be adopted by all countries to avoid capital flows to 'tax-haven' countries. Of course, this raises serious coordination problems.

10 Indeed, the recent turmoil in currency markets has renewed interest on the issue of capital controls. Tobin's proposal is mentioned in an article in *The Economist*, discussing the pros and cons of capital controls ('The way we were', 3 October 1992, p. 65).

11 Giavazzi and Giovannini (1989) underline the asymmetry between strong- and weak-currency countries: as long as the burden of adjustment falls on the weak-currency countries, the other countries are 'isolated' from the effects of interest rate variability. Giavazzi and Pagano (1990) relate the likelihood of a 'confidence crisis' to public debt management.

12 However, it is necessary to take into account the impact of imposing capital controls on the credibility of the policy itself. Suppose, for example, that the imposition of capital controls allows the government to pursue 'inconsistent' policies for a while. Then private agents, if they do not fully know the government's intentions, may raise the probability that the government will indeed behave inconsistently, implying a worsening of credibility rather than an improvement. Lane and Rojas-Suarez (1992) analyse the impact of capital controls on the credibility of a commitment to keep the exchange rate within pre-specified bands.

13 However, a few countries (Switzerland, Japan and Germany in the 1970s; Spain in the late 1980s) used capital controls in order to limit capital *inflows*, rather than outflows, and were therefore trying to keep interest rates *high*.

14 Bruni *et al.* (1989) examine public debt and the revenue from financial repression in Italy, Braga de Macedo and Sebastiao (1989) in Portugal.

15 On the other side, capital flight may be induced by expectations of future capital controls and capital levies.

16 See section 4 below.

17 The unavailability of data on political and institutional variables forced us to drop New Zealand and Switzerland from the sample.

18 The IMF defines capital controls as: 'Restrictions (i.e., official actions directly affecting the availability or cost of exchange, or involving undue delay) on payments concerning resident-owned funds to member countries, other than restrictions imposed for security reasons under Executive Board Decision no. 114-(52/51), adopted August 14, 1952.' This measure includes restrictions on capital flows and/or outflows.

19 Giovannini and Park (1992) study the interaction between capital controls and international trade finance.

20 Interest and noninterest-bearing assets are affected by inflation in different ways. In particular, interest-bearing assets are affected only by unexpected inflation, unless interest rates are prevented from adjusting fully to expected inflation, perhaps through the use of capital controls.

21 This variable was constructed by Alesina and Roubini (1992)

22 Notice that the results of the probit analysis which we present later on do not depend on this classification. The analysis was also conducted eliminating dictatorship periods from the sample: this did not affect the results.

23 The distinction between high and low government durability and political stability is a simplistic one, based on the average value of *DURA* and *STAB*. Values below the mean are classified as low, and values above the mean are classified as high.

24 As for government durability and political stability, the distinction between high and low independence is based on the average value of *CBPN* and *CBEN*. Values below the mean are classified as low, and values above the mean are classified as high.

25 Marco Pagano in his Discussion has suggested the use of more direct proxies for the magnitude of the inflation tax base, such as the number of bank branches scaled by population or data on required reserves. Data availability makes use of the first variable difficult; as for the second, the ability of countries to impose different reserve requirements depends itself on capital controls. In their absence, higher reserve requirements would hamper domestic banks on international markets. Drazen (1989) and Pagano (1989) further explore the relation between reserve requirements and the inflation tax.

26 We also tried to identify a possible link between capital controls and the growth rate through the effects of the former on savings, along the lines suggested by Marco Pagano (see section 3.3). The results (not reported) showed no relation between capital controls and the savings rate.

REFERENCES

Adams, C. and J. Greenwood (1985) 'Dual Exchange Rate Systems and Capital Controls: An Investigation', *Journal of International Economics*, **18** (February), 43–63.

Aizenman, J. and P.E. Guidotti (1993) 'Capital Controls, Collection Costs, and Domestic Public Debt', *Journal of International Money and Finance*, forthcoming.

Alesina, A. (1989) 'Politics and Business Cycles in Industrial Democracies', *Economic Policy*, **4**, 55–98.

Alesina, A. and A. Drazen (1991) 'Why Are Stabilizations Delayed?', *American Economic Review*, **81** (December), 1170–88.

Alesina, A. and N. Roubini (1992) 'Political Cycles in OECD Economies', *Review of Economic Studies*, **59** (October), 663–88.

Alesina, A. and L. Summers (1993) 'Central Bank Independence and Economic Performance: Some Comparative Evidence', *Journal of Money, Credit and Banking* (May).

Alesina, A. and G. Tabellini (1989) 'External Debt, Capital Flight and Political Risk', *Journal of International Economics*, **27** (November), 199–220.

Alesina, A., S. Ozler, N. Roubini and P. Swagel (1992) 'Political Instability and Economic Growth', NBER, *Working Paper*, **4173** (September).

Bacchetta, P. (1990) 'Temporary Capital Controls in a Balance-of-Payments Crisis', *Journal of International Money and Finance*, **9**, 246–57.

Braga de Macedo, J. and M. Sebastiao (1989) 'Public Debt and Implicit Taxes: The Portuguese Experience', *European Economic Review*, **33** (March), 573–79.

Brock, P. (1984) 'Inflationary Finance in an Open Economy', *Journal of Monetary Economics*, **14** (July), 37–53.

(1989) 'Reserve Requirements and the Inflation Tax', *Journal of Money, Credit and Banking*, **21** (July), 106–21.

Bruni, F., A. Penati and A. Porta (1989) 'Financial Regulation, Implicit Taxes and Fiscal Adjustment in Italy', in M. Monti (ed.), *Fiscal Policy, Economic Adjustment and Financial Markets*, Washington, DC: IMF, 197–230.

Claassen, E.M. and C. Wyplosz (1982) 'Capital Controls: Some Principles and the French Experience', *Annales de l'Insée*, reprinted in J. Mélitz and C. Wyplosz (eds), *The French Economy: Theory and Policy*, Boulder: Westview Press (1985).

Cukierman, A., S. Edwards and G. Tabellini (1992) 'Seigniorage and Political Instability', *American Economic Review*, **82** (June), 537–55.

Dooley, M. and P. Isard (1980) 'Capital Controls, Political Risk and Deviations from Interest-Rate Parity', *Journal of Political Economy*, **88** (April), 370–84.

Dornbusch, R. (1986) 'Special Exchange Rates for Capital Account Transactions', *The World Bank Economic Review*, **1**, 1–33.

Drazen, A. (1989) 'Monetary Policy, Capital Controls and Seigniorage in an Open Economy', in M. De Cecco and A. Giovannini (eds), *A European Central Bank?*, Cambridge: Cambridge University Press, 13–32.

Drazen, A. and V. Grilli (1993) 'The Benefits of Crises for Economic Reforms', *American Economic Review*, forthcoming.

Edwards, S. (1989) *Real Exchange Rates, Devaluation and Adjustment*, Cambridge, MA: MIT Press.

Feldstein, M. (1983) 'Domestic Saving and International Capital Movements in the Long Run and the Short Run', *European Economic Review*, **21** (June), 129–51.

Feldstein, M. and C. Horioka (1980) 'Domestic Savings and International Capital Flows', *Economic Journal*, **90** (June), 314–29.

Frankel, J.A. (1991) 'Quantifying International Capital Mobility in the 1990s', in B.D. Bernheim and J. Shoven (eds), *National Saving and Economic Performance*, Chicago: University of Chicago Press and NBER, 227–60.

Giavazzi, F. and A. Giovannini (1989) *Limiting Exchange Rate Flexibility: The European Monetary System*, Cambridge, MA: MIT Press.

Giavazzi, F. and M. Pagano (1988) 'Capital Controls in the EMS', in D.E. Fair and C. de Boissieu (eds), *International Monetary and Financial Integration: the European Dimension*, Dordrecht: Martinus Nijhoff, 261–89.

(1990) 'Confidence Crises and Public Debt Management', in R. Dornbusch and M. Draghi (eds), *Public Debt Management: Theory and History*, Cambridge: Cambridge University Press.

Giovannini, A. (1988) 'Capital Controls and Public Finance: The Experience of Italy', in F. Giavazzi and L. Spaventa (eds), *High Public Debt: The Italian Experience*, Cambridge: Cambridge University Press, 177–211.

Giovannini, A. and M. de Melo (1991) 'Government Revenue from Financial Repression', NBER, *Working Paper*, **3604** (January).

Giovannini, A. and J.W. Park (1992) 'Capital Controls and International Trade Finance', *Journal of International Economics*, **33** (November), 285–304.

Greenwood, J. and K. Kimbrough (1985) 'Capital Controls and Fiscal Policy in the World Economy', *Canadian Journal of Economics*, **18**, 743–65.

Grilli, V. (1989) 'Seigniorage in Europe', in M. de Cecco and A. Giovannini (eds), *A European Central Bank?*, Cambridge: Cambridge University Press, 53–79.

Grilli, V. and N. Roubini (1993) 'Liquidity, Capital Controls and Exchange Rates', *Journal of International Money and Finance*, forthcoming.

Grilli, V., D. Masciandaro and G. Tabellini (1991) 'Political and Monetary Institutions and Public Financial Policies in the Industrial Countries', *Economic Policy*, **13** (Fall), 341–92.

Guidotti, P.E. and C.A. Végh (1992) 'Macroeconomic Interdependence under Capital Controls', *Journal of International Economics*, **32** (May), 353–67.

Jappelli, T. and M. Pagano (1992) 'Savings, Growth and Liquidity Constraints', Centre for Economic Policy Research, *Discussion Paper*, **662**.

Lane, T. and L. Rojas-Suarez (1992) 'Credibility, Capital Controls and the EMS', *Journal of International Economics*, **32** (May), 321–37.

Mankiw, N.G. (1987) 'The Optimal Collection of Seigniorage: Theory and Evidence', *Journal of Monetary Economics*, **20**, 327–41.

Mathieson, D.J. and L. Rojas-Suarez (1993) 'Liberalization of the Capital Account: Experiences and Issues', IMF, *Working Paper*, **92/46** (June). See Chapter 12 in this volume.

Obstfeld, M. (1986a) 'Capital Controls, the Dual Exchange Rate, and Devaluation', *Journal of International Econmics* (February), 1–20.

(1986b) 'Rational and Self-Fulfilling Balance-of-Payments Crises', *American Economic Review*, **76** (March), 72–81.

(1986c) 'Capital Mobility in the World Economy: Theory and Measurement', *Carnegie–Rochester Conference Series on Public Policy*, **24** (Spring), 55–104.

(1988) 'Comments to Giovannini', in F. Giavazzi and L. Spaventa (eds), *High Public Debt: The Italian Experience*, Cambridge: Cambridge University Press, 212–16.

(1989) 'How Integrated Are World Capital Markets? Some New Tests', in G. Calvo, R. Findlay and J. Braga de Macedo (eds), *Debt, Stabilization and Development: Essays in Memory of Carlos Diaz-Alejandro*, Oxford: Basil Blackwell, 134–55.

Pagano, M. (1989) 'Comments to Drazen', in M. de Cecco and A. Giovannini (eds), *A European Central Bank?*, Cambridge: Cambridge University Press, 37–52.

Park, D. and J. Sachs (1987) 'Capital Controls and the Timing of Exchange Regime Collapse', NBER, *Working Paper*, **2250** (May).

Razin, A. and E. Sadka (1991) 'Efficient Investment Incentives in the Presence of Capital Flight', *Journal of International Economics*, **31** (1–2) (August), 171–81.

Rogoff, K. (1985) 'Can Exchange-Rate Predictability Be Achieved without Monetary Convergence? Evidence from the EMS', *European Economic Review*, **28** (June–July).

Roubini, N. and J. Sachs (1989) 'Political and Economic Determinants of Budget Deficits in Industrial Democracies', *European Economic Review*, **33** (June), 903–33.

Roubini, N. and X. Sala-i-Matin (1991) 'Financial Development, the Trade Regime, and Economic Growth', NBER, *Working Paper*, **3876** (October).

(1992) 'Financial Repression and Economic Growth', *Journal of Development Economics*, **39**, 5–30.

Stockman, A. and A. Hernandez (1988) 'Exchange Controls, Capital Controls and International Financial Markets', *American Economic Review*, **78** (June), 362–74.

Sussman, O. (1991) 'Macroeconomic Effects of a Tax on Bond Interest Rates', *Journal of Money, Credit and Banking*, **23** (August), 352–66.

Tesar, L. (1992) 'Savings, Investment and International Capital Flow', *Journal of International Economics*, **31** (August), 55–78.
Tobin, J. (1978) 'A Proposal for International Monetary Reform', *Eastern Economic Journal*, **4**.
Van Wijnbergen, S. (1990) 'Capital Controls and the Real Exchange Rate', *Economica*, **57** (February), 15–28.
Wyplosz, C. (1986) 'Capital Controls and Balance of Payments Crises', *Journal of International Money and Finance*, **5** (June), 167–79.
(1988) 'Capital Flows and the EMS: A French Perspective', *European Economy*, **36** (May).

Discussion

RON SHACHAR

Chapter 11 is within the line of research that examines the two-sided relationship between political motivations and economic decisions. Moreover, this chapter continues a line of empirical studies which analyse the data without commitment to a single model or theory. Previous studies in this group deal, for example, with the political business cycle and with the relations between political instability and growth. This method has its limitations, but it may sometimes take us on a fascinating guided tour of the data. This is also the case with respect to this chapter.

The chapter studies the motivation behind capital controls (hereafter CC). This is done in two ways: (a) study of the economic implications of CC and (b) study of dependence of CC on political and institutional motivations that the economic implications create. The empirical study begins with (b).

There are supposed to be two main reasons to create CC: (a) to defend the exchange rate regime and (b) to finance government expenditures. The study focuses on three financing channels of such expenditures that are possibly related to CC: (1) taxation of capital, (2) inflation tax and (3) reducing the interest payments on government domestic debt.

CC can allow the maintenance of a relatively high capital stock despite the burden of a high tax rate. This is especially attractive to (1) governments that are closer to the 'workers' and to (2) the executive who has 'sufficient political power to impose a higher burden of taxes on some social groups'.

CC may allow the government to tax money more effectively. This is especially attractive when there are (1) 'unstable political systems, where there exist unresolved social conflicts concerning the distribution of the burden of taxation', when (2) the degree of independence of the central bank is small and when (3) the demand for monetary base is high and 'this is more likely in economy where the relative importance of the agriculture sector compared to the service sector is high'.

CC also allow the government to reduce the cost of financing its debt.

Estimation results support most of the hypotheses. The data do not support the dependence of CC on the political leaning of the government. The effect of unstable political system is the inverse of that predicted – which means that the more stable systems tend to adopt CC. There was no indirect test whether governments tend to choose CC in order to reduce the cost of financing their debt.

Another interesting implication of the data is that under CC the gross debt is smaller, the inflation rate is higher, the inflation tax is higher, the real interest rate is lower.

The meaning of these results is that the most important factor in motivating governments to execute CC is financing their expenditures trough: (a) taxation on capital, (b) inflation tax and (c) low interest payment on the government debt.

* * *

This chapter raises an important issue. I would therefore suggest extending the study in the following directions:

(1) As the authors say: 'Isolating the impact of capital controls is also difficult, since they are typically adopted (or removed) together with other policy measures'. Therefore, using policy decisions as independent variables – as is done with the exchange rate regime and the degree of independence of the central bank[1] – may create bias in the estimation results. It is not unreasonable to think, for example, that under CC the tendency of governments to choose a fixed or managed exchange rate regime instead of a flexible one is higher. This means that causality may work the other way around, and that the exchange rate regime is endogenous in this model.

The solution to this problem is *estimating a simultaneous system, where all the policy decisions are endogenously determined.*

(2) As the authors say: '[foreign exchange restrictions] can take several different forms: strict capital controls, dual exchange rates, limitations on current account transactions such as compulsory surrendering of export receipts, prior import deposits, etc'. The choice of a

dummy variable taking value of 1 when capital controls are in place according to the IMF definition is therefore not appropriate.

The proper solution is *using a multinomial-logit model, where each kind of CC has a special category.*

This may be important with respect to some of the arguments discussed in the chapter. Some of the theories that the authors present suggest, for example, that under a flexible exchange rate regime governments may tend to choose a dual exchange rate policy, while under a fixed or managed exchange rate regime, they tend to choose other CC policies. Estimating a multinomial-logit model enables us to distinguish between the two effects. Estimation using probit or logit compels the authors to test the hypothesis that CC appears only when the government conducts a fixed or managed exchange rate regime.

(3) We may consider adding some economic variables in the estimation in order to correct for the bias that their absence may create.

Since the most important factor in motivating governments to execute CC is financing their expenditures, *government consumption and the budget deficit should be also taken into account.* For example, we would like to know the correlations between these variables and CC.

Adams and Greenwood (1985) argue that in the absence of other distortions CC and dual exchange rates in a small open economy are welfare-decreasing, while in a large economy both can increase welfare. We may thus consider *adding the size of the economy as an explanatory variable in the probit CC model.*

Another interesting independent variable is the *timing of a stabilisation reform programmes.* Governments may also use CC to help stabilisation reform programmes in developed economies.

We may also consider adding variables to the set of equations that account for the effect of CC on economic variables. Alesina and Sachs (1988) showed that Democratic administrations tended to choose a higher money growth rate than Republican administrations. *Therefore, adding the type of the government to the inflation equation may help.*

(4) While 'figure 11.3 shows that capital controls were much more common under short-lived governments (79% of the cases) than under long-lived governments (53% of the cases)', the evidence in table 11.3 suggests that 'stable political systems characterised by majoritarian and long-lived governments are more likely to adopt capital controls measures'. This means that while the unconditional correlation between the stability of the political system and CC is

negative, the conditional correlation is positive. Future research should try to reveal which of the conditioning variables switch the correlation, and to understand the reason.

(5) Another interesting result concerning the stability of the political system variable appears in table 11.6. According to this table, the real interest rate is higher in the more stable countries. Future research should try to understand the reason for this counter-intuitive result.

(6) I think that the concept of *protection*, in the way it has been presented by Grossman and Helpman (1992), may also suit the issue of CC. A formulation and estimation of such a model is thus an important task and another interesting extension of this study.

NOTE

1 The degree of independence of the central bank is a policy decision in the long run, even if it is given to the government in the short run.

REFERENCES

Adams, C. and J. Greenwood (1985) 'Dual Exchange Rate Systems and Capital Controls: An Investigation', *Journal of International Economics*, **18** (February), 43–63.

Alesina, A. and J. Sachs (1988) 'Political Parties and the Business Cycle in the United States, 1948–1984', *Journal of Money, Credit and Banking*, **20**, 63–82.

Grossman, G. and E. Helpman (1992) 'Protection for Sale', *Woodrow Wilson School Discussion Paper in Economics*, **162**, Princeton University.

MARCO PAGANO

Chapter 11 takes a fresh look at the causes and effects of capital controls by drawing on the political economy approach developed by Alesina, Drazen, Grilli, Tabellini and others. After summarising the implications of this literature for the issues at hand, the authors test them using panel data for the OECD economies. The empirical tests try to throw light on two distinct issues. First, what are the institutional and political features that make policymakers more likely to impose capital controls? Second, what are the effects of capital controls on the rate of inflation, the accumulation of public debt and the growth rate, once one controls for other institutional variables?

The empirical investigation conducted in this chapter is not only novel but also quite welcome, as it goes towards redressing the present imbalance between theoretical analysis and empirical research in this area. Amidst the recent proliferation of political economy models, empirical studies such as this are badly needed to assess which of the existing models are relevant and to provide guidance for further theoretical analysis. The payoff of empirical work is particularly high when existing models offer sharply different predictions. This appears to be the case for political economy models insofar as it concerns their predictions about the types of government that favour capital controls: in contrast, their implications for the relationship between central bank independence and capital controls are unambiguous.

1 Type of government and capital controls

Insofar as imposing capital controls enlarges the inflation tax base, the issue of which governments are more likely to impose capital controls boils down to deciding which type of government is more prone to rely on inflation to finance public spending. As the authors explain in section 4.1.2, existing models offer little guidance on whether the inflation tax should be more favoured by left-wing or by right-wing governments, by strong (majority) or rather by weak (minority or coalition) governments. Right-wing governments may like the inflation tax because it is regressive, left-wing ones because they are more averse to unemployment than inflation, and because they may need more seigniorage revenue to expand public spending. Similarly, strong governments may rely more on seigniorage because they can better withstand the turmoil caused by the distributional effects of inflation; but weak governments may resort to the inflation tax as a residual source of revenue, being unable to finance spending with direct or indirect taxes. In addition, the inflation tax may be used as a residual tax in a war-of-attrition situation, again implying that it should be favoured by minority or coalition rather than by majority governments.

The evidence produced in the chapter suggests that indeed capital controls are not clearly correlated with the political colour of the government. On the other hand, it consistently suggests that capital controls are more often associated with strong governments than with weak ones, and – according to some of the estimates – they correlate also with the stability and durability of governments. If the main reason for capital controls is to raise more revenue via the inflation tax, this would logically imply that high inflation should be associated with strong, durable and stable governments, other things being equal. I regard this claim as puzzling, especially considering that, using a similar data set, Grilli, Masciandaro and Tabellini (1991) find that inflation holds little relationship to government characteristics, once one controls for the independence of the central bank – and in fact, if anything, inflation bears a weak positive correlation with *unstable* governments. If the findings of the present chapter are taken at face value on this point, they seriously question the empirical relevance of the models which predict that social conflict and weak governments lead to the imposition of capital controls and to high inflation rates – at least insofar as the OECD countries are concerned.

2 Central bank independence and capital controls

As far as the independence of the central bank from the government is concerned, the predictions of political economy models are more straightforward and the empirical results more convincing. Capital controls are more frequent and inflation tends to be higher where the central bank is less independent from the government. Moreover, capital controls correlate with lower ratios of public debt to GDP and with lower real interest rates. As the authors point out, these results square with the idea that when a government has a strong control over monetary policy, it has the incentive to introduce capital controls to increase its revenue from the inflation tax. Capital controls then contribute to slowing down debt accumulation, both by generating higher seigniorage revenue and by keeping real interest rates below the world level.

While this story appears both internally consistent and supported by the evidence, the authors' conclusion that greater central bank independence, stripping the executive of its control over seigniorage, 'may force the government to adjust towards a more sound fiscal policy' (section 5) is far less convincing. First, the very interpretation of the evidence proposed by the authors suggests that central bank independence is unlikely to have such an incentive effect: according to that story, central bank independence and free capital mobility are associated not only with low seigniorage but also with high debt–GDP ratios. Second, one of the conclusions of the paper by Grilli, Masciandaro and Tabellini (1991, p. 375) was that 'monetary independence does not discourage budget deficits. Monetary and fiscal discipline thus seem to be orthogonal to each other'. The evolution of fiscal policy in Italy over the last decade provides, if it were needed, a strong endorsement of that conclusion: increased central bank independence and removal of capital controls have severely limited government control over seigniorage revenue, but this appears to have provided little incentive for the government to pursue 'a more sound fiscal policy'.

3 Growth and capital controls

My final comments concern the relationship between capital controls and the growth rate, a point briefly touched upon at the end of the chapter. The authors find that capital controls, other things being equal, have no effect on the growth rate of per capita GDP. This may reflect the fact that capital controls affect growth in many different and contradictory ways, so that their net effect is on average zero.

On the one hand, if capital controls are used in conjunction with other policy measures aimed at stimulating saving, countries with capital controls should have a higher saving rate than other countries, which in an endogenous growth framework translates into a higher growth rate. Note that if the government wants to raise growth, it will stimulate domestic saving *only if* it is confident the extra saving will be funnelled into extra domestic investment. So capital controls are a natural complement of policy packages designed to stimulate saving. In a recent study, also based on an OECD panel, Tullio Jappelli and I have found that restrictions on household borrowing raise the saving and the growth rate – a result that can be explained only if capital controls are prevalent in the sample (Jappelli and Pagano, 1992). It would be interesting to know if indeed measures designed to stimulate saving (such as restrictions on household borrowing) have a larger impact on national saving and growth in countries with capital controls.

On the other hand, capital controls can affect the saving rate and the growth rate by preventing international risk sharing. Devereux and Smith (1991) have shown that in autarky the saving and growth rates can be higher than with international capital mobility. But Obstfeld (1992) has extended their analysis to the case where the world asset portfolio accommodates endogenously the asset demand shifts implied by the transition from autarky to international economic integration, and finds that in general opening up the capital market is beneficial for growth.

In closing, I would like to point to another aspect of the relationship between capital controls and growth that could be analysed empirically with the data set employed here. In the context of endogenous growth models, capital controls are crucial in determining cross-country differences in growth rates: as pointed out by Rebelo (1992, p. 5) 'with free international capital mobility [these models] imply that the growth rate of consumption and GNP would be quickly equalized all over the world'. Thus a potentially testable prediction of these models is whether the growth rates of countries with no capital controls are closer to, or converge faster to a common value, than those of countries with capital controls.

REFERENCES

Devereux, M.B. and G.W. Smith (1991) 'International risk sharing and economic growth', *Discussion Paper*, **829**, Department of Economics, Queen's University (August).

Grilli, V., D. Masciandaro and G. Tabellini (1991) 'Political and monetary institutions and public financial policies in the industrial countries', *Economic Policy*, **13** (Fall), 341–92.

Jappelli, T. and M. Pagano (1992) 'Savings, growth and liquidity constraints', Centre for Economic Policy Research, *Discussion Paper* **662**.

Obstfeld, M. (1992) 'Risk-taking, global diversification, and growth', NBER, *Working Paper* **4092** (June).

Rebelo, S.T. (1992) 'Growth in Open Economies', *Carnegie–Rochester Conference Series on Public Policy*, **36** (July), 5–46.

12 Capital controls and capital account liberalisation in industrial countries

DONALD J. MATHIESON and LILIANA ROJAS-SUAREZ

1 Introduction

A fundamental structural change in the world economy during the past two decades has been the growing integration of financial markets located in the industrial countries and in major offshore centres. This increased integration has reflected the relaxation of capital controls and broader financial liberalisation in the industrial countries, as well as new telecommunications and computer technologies that have facilitated the cross-border transfer of funds.

This chapter reviews the experience with capital controls in industrial countries, considers some of the key policy issues raised by the diminished effectiveness of capital controls, examines the potential medium-term benefits and costs of an open capital account, and analyses the policy measures that helped sustain capital account convertibility.

2 Restrictions on capital account transactions

Most industrial and developing countries imposed some restrictions on capital account transactions throughout the post-World War II period. As analysed in the International Monetary Fund's 1990 *Annual Report of Exchange Arrangements and Exchange Restrictions*, at the end of 1989, 123 out of the 153 territories and member countries of the IMF were reported as using restrictions on payments for capital transactions and/or separate exchange rates for some or all capital account transactions (Table 12.1). However, industrial countries with capital account convertibility rose from 3 in 1975 to 9 in 1990.

2.1 Types of capital controls

In the industrial countries in the 1960s and 1970s, the most common restrictions on capital account convertibility encompassed exchange

Table 12.1. *Restrictions on capital account transactions, 1975, 1980, 1985 and 1990*[1]

	1975	1980	1985	1990
Number of countries[2]	128	140	148	153
Separate exchange rate(s) for some capital transactions and/or some or all invisibles *and* restrictions on payments for capital transactions	22	26	32	32
Industrial countries[3]	2	2	—	—
Developing countries	20	24	32	32
Restrictions on payments for capital transactions *only*[4,5]	102	107[6]	116	120
Industrial countries	17	14	11	11
Developing countries	85	91	105	109
Separate exchange rate(s) for some capital transactions and/or some or all invisibles *only*	25	31	34	35
Industrial countries	3	3	1	1
Developing countries	22	28	33	34
Neither separate exchange rate(s) for some capital transactions and/or some or all invisibles *nor* restrictions on payments for capital transactions	23	28	30	30
Industrial countries	3	6	9	9
Developing countries	20	22	21	21

[1] The years indicate the publication year of the Reports from which data are collected.
[2] Belgium and Luxembourg have been treated as one country – Belgium–Luxembourg.
[3] Grouping definition is based on the existing grouping presented in the latest issue of the *International Financial Statistics* and the *World Economic Outlook*.
[4] 'Restrictions (i.e., official actions directly affecting the availability or cost of exchange, or involving undue delay) on payments concerning resident-owned funds to member countries, other than restrictions imposed for security reasons under Executive Board Decision, no. 144-(52/51) adopted August 14, 1952.'
[5] Resident-owned funds.
[6] Numbers for industrial and developing countries do not sum up to the total because the position of two developing countries – Botswana and Haiti – is undetermined.
Sources: IMF (1975) *Twenty-Sixth Annual Report on Exchange Restrictions*, 544–48 (for 1975); IMF (1980) *Annual Report on Exchange Arrangements and Exchange Restrictions*, 456–60 (for 1980); IMF (1985) *Exchange Arrangements and Exchange Restrictions, Annual Report*, 552–57 (for 1985); and IMF (1990) *Exchange Arrangements and Exchange Restrictions, Annual Report*, 576–81 (for 1990).

controls or quantitative restrictions on capital movements, dual or multiple exchange arrangements, and taxes on external financial transactions. Quantitative restrictions typically involved limitations on the external asset and liability positions of domestic financial institutions (especially banks), on the domestic operations of foreign financial institutions, and on the external portfolio, real estate, and direct investments of nonbank residents.

At a minimum, dual or multiple exchange rate systems involved separate exchange rates for commercial and financial transactions. In most dual exchange rate systems, the commercial exchange rate was controlled by the authorities while the financial exchange rate was allowed to float. A key element determining the effectiveness of these systems was the degree to which current and capital account transactions could be kept separate. In order to achieve this separation, there were often complex sets of rules that both defined what constituted current and capital account transactions, and attempted to establish control over the foreign exchange transactions of residents and the domestic currency transactions of non-residents. Enforcement of these rules implied that dual (or multiple) exchange rate systems shared much, if not most, of the costs of administering a system of quantitative restrictions on capital flows.

Explicit and implicit taxes on external financial transactions and income also were used to discourage or control capital flows. For example, interest equalisation taxes were designed to eliminate the higher yield that domestic (foreign) residents might see on holding foreign (domestic) financial instruments.

2.2 Rationales for capital controls

In the industrial countries, the use of capital controls was often justified on three grounds: (1) to help manage balance of payments crises or unstable exchange rates generated by excessively volatile short-run capital flows, (2) to ensure that domestic savings were used to finance domestic investment and to limit foreign ownership of domestic factors of production and (3) to maintain the authorities' ability to tax domestic financial activities, income and wealth.

2.2.1 Limiting volatile short-term capital flows

Transaction taxes on short-term financial transactions have often been viewed as a means of limiting short-term capital flows which were driven by investors who ignored fundamentals and transacted on the basis of rumour, trading strategies, or uncertainties about the sustainability of macroeconomic or exchange rate policies. In some cases, such capital flows have been seen as leading to speculative 'bubbles' in which asset prices, especially exchange rates, depart systematically from underlying fundamentals. It has therefore been argued that the authorities should limit speculative capital flows rather than alter financial and macroeconomic policies designed to achieve medium-term objectives. Nonetheless, it has proven difficult to identify both the fundamentals driving exchange rates and the extent to which exchange rates have departed from these fundamentals.[1] Moreover, even if such bubbles occur periodically, it is not clear that capital controls or taxes would be preferable to occasional central bank foreign exchange market intervention.

Doubts about the sustainability of a country's policy stance can potentially lead investors to alter their holdings of domestic and external assets in order to protect the value of their portfolios. While capital controls could be used to prevent these adjustments from occurring, this may not address the fundamental problem of building credibility for authorities' policies. Moreover, conflicting macroeconomic policies in different major countries can generate capital flows as well as exchange rate changes; and adjustments in macroeconomic policies rather than the imposition of capital controls would then be the appropriate policy response.

2.2.2 Retention of domestic savings

A second rationale for the capital controls has been to ensure that domestic savings are used to finance domestic investment and to limit foreign ownership of domestic factors of production. The uncertainties created by an unstable macroeconomic and political environment can lead savers to hold a significant portion of their wealth in foreign assets that are perceived to yield higher or more certain real returns. It has been argued that capital controls can be used to help retain domestic savings by reducing the return on foreign assets (e.g., through an interest equalisation tax or by raising the implicit cost of moving funds abroad) and by limiting access to foreign assets.

2.2.3 Maintenance of the domestic tax base

Another rationale was that capital controls were needed to maintain the authorities' ability to tax financial activities, income and wealth. Stamp duties and taxes on securities transactions have often been important sources of government revenues in countries with large securities markets (e.g., Switzerland), and income taxes on interest and dividend income are key components of most tax systems. In addition to such explicit taxes, effective capital controls – by increasing holdings of domestic assets – can allow the authorities to impose an 'inflation tax' on holding domestic monetary instruments.[2] Adams and Greenwood (1985) have argued that there is an equivalence between capital controls, taxes on capital flows and dual exchange rates; and this suggests that capital controls could be justified from an optimal taxation perspective when the government minimises the welfare losses induced by various distortionary taxes.[3]

However, these discussions implicitly assume that capital controls can 'effectively' restrict capital flows even if current account convertibility is established. However, as discussed in section 3, there is empirical evidence that residents of industrial countries often found ways around capital controls whenever there were large differentials between the yields on domestic and foreign instruments.

3 The effectiveness of capital controls

The incentives for and costs of evading capital controls played a key role in determining the channels that were used to evade capital controls and to arbitrage between the official and financial exchange markets under dual exchange rate systems. One of the most frequently used channels was underinvoicing and overinvoicing of export and import contracts. To shift funds abroad, for example, an exporter (importer) would underinvoice (overinvoice) a foreign customer and then use the unreported funds to invest in external assets. Such overinvoicing and underinvoicing was often an efficient means of shifting funds across national borders, since it exploited one of the fundamental tensions in most capital control and/or dual exchange rate systems, namely the need to control unauthorised capital flows while at the same time not interfering unduly with either normal trade financing for imports and exports or with the typical transfer operations between a parent firm and its subsidiary for permitted foreign direct investment.

Giddy (1979) also argued that the transfer pricing policies of multinational companies provided a similar means of evading capital controls. Prior to an anticipated exchange rate adjustment, change in transfer prices and the leading and lagging of intra-company transfers provide a means of shifting funds.

Another trade-related channel for unrecorded capital flows has been the leads and lags in the settlement of commercial transactions or variations in the terms on short-term trade credits. During the collapse of the Bretton Woods system in the early 1970s, for example, some industrial countries with extensive capital controls nonetheless experienced significant capital inflows as a result of the prepayment of exports by foreign entities (often the foreign subsidiaries of domestic corporations).

The balances in nonresidents' 'commercial' accounts in the domestic financial system, especially in countries with dual exchange rate arrangements, were often drawn down sharply prior to a devaluation and then rebuilt relatively quickly in the period following the devaluation. Remittances of savings by foreign workers in the domestic economy and by domestic nationals working abroad, family remittances, and tourist expenditures, while traditionally regarded as current account transactions, were also used to acquire or remit foreign assets.

During the 1960s and 1970s, forward foreign exchange operations in industrial countries with capital controls and/or dual exchange rates provided residents with another channel for moving capital. When a major exchange rate depreciation was anticipated, the forward net foreign asset position of domestic residents often changed dramatically as many exporters responded by hedging a much smaller (or zero) proportion of their anticipated foreign exchange receipts, whereas importers would try to obtain more cover.

While there are clearly a variety of channels for evading capital controls, there are still the empirical questions of just how important these channels have been and under what conditions they may be instrumental in undermining the effectiveness of capital controls. During the immediate post-World War II period, most industrial countries used exchange, trade and capital controls to limit both current and capital account convertibility and their residents' net foreign asset and liability positions.[4] However, since current account controls created a variety of distortions, current account convertibility was formally restored (by acceptance of the obligations of the IMF's Article of Agreement VIII) by the industrial countries in Western Europe by 1961 and by Japan in 1964. Nonetheless, many major industrial countries continued to maintain capital controls (including dual exchange rates) throughout the 1960s and 1970s with some (such as France and Italy) abolishing the last of their major capital controls only during the late 1980s.

The conclusions that have typically emerged from the many studies of the use of capital controls by industrial countries in the post-World War II period[5] can be illustrated by first considering the experience of Japan in the period 1945–80 and then that of Ireland in the early 1980s. Since it has been argued that Japan had the most effective and efficiently administered system of capital controls in the period up to the late 1970s,[6] Japan's experience can be used to identify some of the factors that contributed to the effectiveness as well as the breakdown of capital controls. Ireland's experience in turn illustrates the difficulties encountered by countries attempting to reimpose capital controls on previously integrated financial markets.

The legal basis for Japan's post-World War II capital controls was initially provided by the Foreign Exchange and Foreign Trade Control law, passed in 1949, under which foreign exchange transactions were prohibited in principle and permitted only in exceptional cases according to the directives and notifications from government ministries. Initially, private holdings of foreign exchange were restricted and export receipts had to be sold to authorised foreign exchange banks. The authorities also specified a standard settlement period and required approval of prepayments or acceptance of advance receipts. Holdings of yen by nonresidents were subject to controls.[7]

In 1960, the authorities announced a trade and exchange liberalisation plan which had as one of its goals achieving Article VIII status. This programme included abolition of foreign exchange controls on current account transactions, creation of 'free' yen accounts for nonresidents, liberalised use of foreign exchange for tourist travel and some relaxation of the controls on capital account transactions related to exports and imports. With this partial liberalisation, the scale of capital flows in the 1960s expanded relative to those in the 1950s, and periods of monetary tightening in the summers of 1961 and 1967 were accompanied by capital inflows which required the imposition or tightening of capital controls.

Following the floating of the Deutsche mark in May 1971, Japan initially attempted to maintain a fixed US dollar/yen exchange rate and, as a result, experienced large capital inflows.[8] The foreign subsidiaries of Japanese firms were an important source of inflows as they used US dollar-denominated loans to make prepayments on exports from the parent company or to purchase yen-denominated securities. The authorities responded initially with a severe tightening of capital controls, which disrupted trade financing, and eventually a floating of the exchange rate. A system of capital controls, which had been highly effective when the exchange rate was viewed as stable and interest rate differentials were limited,[9] was thus unable to stem a large-scale inflow once the expectation of a large exchange rate adjustment took hold.

Japan shifted from a fixed to a floating exchange rate in the spring of 1973, and Fukao argued that the degree of short-term capital mobility declined because of strict capital controls and the elimination of the prospect of a near-certain capital gain when a large discrete exchange rate adjustment took place. Moreover, the differentials between domestic and offshore money market interest rates in the period after 1974 were much smaller, even during the first and second oil price shocks, than in the period surrounding the collapse of the Bretton Woods system.[10]

While there were relatively few official restrictions limiting transactions between financial markets in Ireland and the United Kingdom prior to December 1978, the Irish authorities then imposed a set of exchange controls that included: (1) limitations on the accounts of UK residents in Irish bank and nonbank financial institutions, (2) prohibition of Irish residents holding accounts with financial institutions in the United Kingdom, (3) prior approval for all foreign borrowing, (4) prior approval for portfolio investment inflows and outflows and (5) limitations on provision of forward cover by authorised banks to nonbank residents except for trade related transactions.

Browne and McNelis (1990) (hereafter BM) have recently examined the effectiveness of the Irish capital controls in terms of their ability to restore the authorities' control over domestic interest rates. Their analysis was based on an empirical model which related quarterly changes in various domestic Irish interest rates to (1) the differential between the sum of the comparable world interest rate, the expected rate of depreciation of the Irish pound and a risk premium and the previous quarter's domestic interest rate and (2) the current and lagged values of the domestic excess demand for money. To see if economic agents learned how to evade capital controls over time, BM allowed the influence of external financial market conditions on domestic interest rates to grow over time relative to that of domestic money market conditions.

BM's empirical analysis employed data on interest rates on financial instruments of various expected degrees of international tradability.[11] One empirical result was that the interbank market continued to be highly integrated with the external market;[12] and the degree of integration in the mortgage market, which initially declined with the imposition of capital controls, eventually recovered and exceeded its initial level. Exchange controls drove a permanent wedge in the interest rate parity relationship only in the markets for small deposits in clearing banks and share accounts in the building societies.

The author's empirical results suggest that, even when capital controls drive a wedge between the *levels* of domestic and external interest rates, they may only temporarily break the correlation between *movements* in domestic and international interest rates over time. BM argued that significant interest rate differentials between domestic and external markets made it profitable for some firms and individuals to incur the costs of establishing new channels for moving funds abroad; and, over time, the controls became increasingly less effective.[13]

Moreover, since quantitative capital controls which restrict capital outflows are in many respects equivalent to a tax on the ownership of foreign assets, the incidence of this tax depends crucially on the ability of different groups of residents to evade the controls. BM's results imply that such a tax falls most heavily on those residents who have the least market power in domestic financial markets and have the weakest links or access to international markets (often due to high transactions costs). In a public finance sense, capital controls are thus likely to be a regressive tax.

4 The implications of the reduced effectiveness of capital controls

As structural changes in the international financial system and other factors reduced the ability of capital controls to insulate domestic financial market conditions from those in external markets during the 1970s and 1980s, they also increased some of the explicit and implicit costs of using controls, imposed new constraints on the formulation of macroeconomic and structural policies, and raised the issue of whether countries should respond to the reduced effectiveness of capital controls by attempting to tighten capital controls or adapting to a more open capital account.

4.1 The cost of maintaining capital controls

Even as the effectiveness of capital controls eroded over time, they still heavily 'taxed' certain classes of external financial transactions, limited the access of some individuals or institutions to international financial markets, and restricted the degree of competition in domestic financial markets. Moreover, as new channels developed for moving funds abroad, the costs of enforcing the capital controls – investigating suspected violations of the controls, and prosecuting violators of the capital controls code – rose.

Capital controls also create an implicit market value for the licences for approved but restricted capital account transactions. However, these licences are seldom sold at public auctions but are usually allocated to individuals and institutions according to a set of rules administered by the capital controls bureaucracy. These arrangements therefore often provide a strong incentive for individuals to attempt to capture the 'rent' inherent in these licences through bribery, corruption, and political influence.

4.2 The potential benefits of a more open capital account

As the costs of maintaining capital controls increased, attention began to focus on the potential benefits and costs of an open capital account. Crockett (1991) summarises several efficiency and welfare gains associated with the removal of capital controls. First, freedom of capital flows allows the international economy to attain the efficiency gains created by specialisation in the production of financial services.[14] Just as with trade in goods, countries will find it more efficient to import rather than produce some financial services.

Second, capital account convertibility can also promote dynamic efficiency in the financial sector. Increased competition from abroad will force domestic producers to become more efficient and can stimulate innovation and productivity improvement.

Removing capital controls can also improve the global intermediation of resource from savers to investors if international financial markets appropriately price the risks and returns inherent in financial claims. In addition, enterprises will be able more easily to diversify their activities abroad and to adopt new technologies and managerial techniques, especially those involving the use of new financial products to manage risks and finance investments.

In addition, capital account convertibility allows residents to hold an internationally diversified portfolio of assets, which reduces the vulnerability of their income streams and wealth to domestic financial and real shocks. A further benefit associated with the removal of capital controls is that it may facilitate access to international financial markets and reduce borrowing costs.

4.3 Constraints on the formulation of macroeconomic and structural policies

As the effectiveness of capital controls eroded, new constraints were imposed on the formulation of macroeconomic and structural policies. Even with unchanged external financial market conditions, for example, the increasing willingness and ability of domestic residents to evade capital controls implied that unstable domestic monetary and financial policies, which created a large differential between the expected real returns on domestic and external assets, induced capital outflows, and thereby resulted in smaller real sizes of the domestic monetary system and the domestic tax base. As the real size of the domestic financial system declined, the revenues that the authorities could obtain from an inflation tax (at a given rate of inflation) were also reduced.

The reduced effectiveness of capital controls also affected fiscal policy by making it increasingly difficult for the authorities to tax financial incomes, transactions, and wealth. As a result, new taxes and/or cuts in government spending were needed as the effectiveness of capital controls eroded and led to reduced real tax revenues.

As capital controls were relaxed or lost their effectiveness, large-scale capital flows at times occurred, especially when macroeconomic policies diverged across countries. While there have been many analyses of how best to deal with these capital flows, policy recommendations have generally focused on three alternatives: (1) sterilisation of capital flows, (2) tightening capital controls, and (3) implementing measures which allows a country to live with the risks created by a more open capital account.

In the industrial countries, the authorities often attempted to offset the effects of capital flows on the domestic economy market through 'sterilised' foreign exchange market intervention, where any purchase (sale) of foreign exchange was offset by a corresponding sale (purchase) of open market securities (or central bank advances or discounts). The experiences of a number of European countries in late 1992 suggest that, when there is considerable uncertainty about the authorities' exchange rate commitments, capital flows can easily reach a volume that makes it difficult for the authorities both to undertake large-scale sterilised intervention and to maintain monetary control. Even strong currency countries facing large capital inflows may find it difficult to sterilise, since their central banks must engage in either large-scale open market sales of securities or be authorised to issue additional government securities. In practice, central banks may be reluctant to operate in this manner, or may face legal restrictions on issuing additional debt, or may be constrained to accommodate using assets already on their existing portfolios.[15] Such intervention can also expose the strong-currency central bank to large foreign exchange losses if the exchange rate commitment is not sustained.

If capital flows cannot be effectively sterilised, another policy alternative would be to tighten capital controls. The effectiveness of tighter capital controls is likely to depend on whether the capital flows are motivated primarily by short-run speculative considerations or alternatively represent a desire of residents to adjust their external asset over the medium term. A tightening of capital controls could give the authorities some additional control over short-term capital flows and thereby some influence on the real exchange rate. As has been discussed, however, the effectiveness of such additional control would be of uncertain duration; and, if residents are motivated primarily by medium-term considerations, historical experience suggests that they would eventually find channels for evading the new controls. Moreover, capital controls could weaken the long-term willingness of investors to hold domestic claims since they may fear that they will be unable to adjust their net asset position during a future crisis.

The potentially adverse effects of a severe tightening of capital controls have raised the issue of whether there are fiscal, financial and structural policies that would allow a country initially to 'live with' any capital flows, limit the potentially adverse effects of asset price volatility and eventually help achieve and sustain an open capital account.

5 Establishing and sustaining capital account convertibility

The benefits of a more open capital account can be obtained only if a country can sustain capital account convertibility. This section reviews the experiences of selected industrial countries to identify: (1) what difficulties are likely to be encountered when capital controls are initially relaxed and subsequently removed and (2) what policies can be used to facilitate the transition to an open capital account and to sustain capital account convertibility.

5.1 Experiences with capital account liberalisation

Industrial countries have followed quite divergent strategies when attempting to establish capital account convertibility. While some industrial countries (such as the United Kingdom) removed most of their capital controls in a short period, other countries have followed a more gradual approach of first relaxing constraints on trade-related capital flows, then on longer-term foreign direct and portfolio investment flows, and finally on short-term financial flows.

New Zealand and the United Kingdom, which removed their capital controls relatively quickly and sustained current account convertibility, nonetheless provide examples of the types of asset price movements and capital flows that accompanied the opening of the capital account in a number of other industrial countries. New Zealand's capital controls, which had been in place since 1938, encompassed surrender requirements on the receipt of foreign exchange, limitations on holdings of foreign securities, restrictions on overseas borrowing, and limits on raising of funds on the New Zealand capital market by overseas companies. In the United Kingdom, investors were required to obtain prior approval for most categories of foreign currency investments and were denied access to the 'official' foreign exchange market for certain types of foreign investments. In addition, holdings of other foreign currency assets, such as bank deposits, were restricted to those needed for trade purposes, and lending of sterling to nonresidents, including trade credit, was also restricted.

In both countries, the removal of capital controls was only one element in comprehensive stabilisation and structural reform programmes. Although there was some relaxation of capital controls in the United Kingdom in June and July 1979, the final abolition occurred in October of that year. During that period, fiscal policy reforms were introduced in the context of the Medium Term Financial Strategy (MTFS) which encompassed changes in both spending and tax policies. In addition, the practice

Table 12.2. *Capital flows and real exchange rates, New Zealand and the United Kingdom, billion $ US*

	New Zealand capital flows				
	1984	1985	1986	1987	1988
Capital account balances	2.2	1.3	3.3	– 1.6	0.7
Direct investment abroad	– 0.2	– 0.1	– 0.4	– 0.5	– 0.2
Direct investment in New Zealand	0.3	4.2	0.3	0.2	0.4
Portfolio investment	—	—	—	—	—
Net errors and omissions	1.1	0.9	0.4	0.9	– 0.1
Real exchange rate (1985 = 100)	98.2	100.0	101.1	116.8	124.5
	United Kingdom capital flows				
	1978	1979	1980	1981	1982
Capital account balances	– 8.0	1.9	– 8.2	– 20.6	– 6.4
Direct investment abroad	– 6.8	– 12.5	– 11.2	– 12.2	– 7.2
Direct investment in the United Kingdom	3.8	6.5	10.1	5.9	5.4
Portfolio investment	– 2.3	1.5	– 4.5	– 8.7	– 13.3
Net errors and omissions	3.4	1.9	1.9	1.8	– 3.7
Real exchange rate (1985 = 100)	82.5	96.1	115.4	121.9	114.5

Sources: International Monetary Fund, *Balance of Payments Yearbook* and *International Financial Statistics.*

of announcing monetary aggregate targets was continued, with a gradual deceleration in the rate of monetary expansion envisaged. Moreover, when the actual budget deficit and the rate of monetary expansion exceeded the MTFS's first-year targets, the second-year budget proposed higher taxes and lower targets for the rate of monetary expansion than had been aimed at in the previous two years.[16]

New Zealand abolished exchange and capital controls in December 1984 as part of a general financial liberalisation which also encompassed the removal of most interest rate controls (July 1984), withdrawal of credit expansion guidelines (August 1984), the removal of all reserve and other ratio requirements, and the adoption of a floating exchange rate (March 1985). A fiscal reform introduced a medium-term perspective to the formulation of the budget and measures were announced that would remove a wide range of subsidies and tax incentives, progressively increase energy prices, and establish tax and transfer policies designed to provide an improved safety net for low-income groups. More gradual, and less comprehensive, trade liberalisation and labour market reforms were also initiated.

In both countries, the removal of capital controls and the implementation of the other reforms was followed by sharp adjustments in capital flows and an initial appreciation of the real exchange rate (Table 12.2). In the United Kingdom, for example, the Bank of England (1981) noted that pension funds, insurance companies, and unit investment trusts sharply increased the proportion of their cash flows devoted to the purchase of external assets. In addition, the financing of overseas investment, which had previously been done in foreign currency, was increasingly financed by borrowing denominated in sterling. Foreign currency deposits held by UK residents also increased by £5 billion (approximately a 100% increase) between end-September 1979 and end-June 1981. While these outflows by UK residents were partially offset by foreign private capital inflows, net identified capital outflows (including net errors and omissions) totalled $18.8 billion in 1981, compared with $6.3 billion in 1980 and an inflow of $3.8 billion in 1979. Despite this pattern of capital flows, the real effective exchange rate appreciated by 16% in 1979, by 20% in 1980 and, by 6% in 1981.

In New Zealand, there was initially a historically large net capital inflow and a real appreciation of the exchange rate. Net capital inflows (including errors and omissions) reached $2.1 billion in 1985 and $3.7 billion in 1986. The real effective exchange rate also experienced uneven but substantial appreciation (by roughly 27% between 1984 and 1988).

These capital account liberalisations were thus accompanied by large increases in *gross* and *net* capital inflows and outflows that were large relative to the size of the domestic financial system. Moreover, there was a real exchange rate appreciation despite differences in exchange rate arrangements, or even whether there was a *net* capital inflow or outflow.

5.2 Preconditions for establishing capital account convertibility

The capital flows and asset price movements (including the appreciation of the real exchange rate) that have often accompanied the opening of the capital account can make it more likely that a country can sustain capital account convertibility. One of the key macroeconmic preconditions for opening the capital account is a fiscal reform which significantly reduces any fiscal deficit and finances any remaining deficit in a noninflationary manner. Even a large fiscal deficit financed by bond issuance may not be compatible with an open capital account if a rising stock of external and internal debt leads to doubts about a country's ability to service these debts, and thereby its creditworthiness.

Maintaining capital account convertibility also requires carefully formulated financial policies that establish more flexible interest rates, restructure and recapitalise domestic financial institutions, and more clearly define the scope of the protection offered by the official safety net underpinning the domestic financial system, as well as strengthening prudential supervision of financial institutions. At a minimum, this will require the restructuring of any financial system with large holdings of bad debts or nonperforming loans, and eventually a rebuilding of the capital position in domestic financial institution (especially banks) to those comparable to the capital adequacy standards such as those established for international banks by the Bank for International Settlements Committee on Banking Supervision.

Opening the capital account will also require that the authorities examine the scope and coverage of any official safety net underpinning the domestic financial system. The stability of most national financial systems has historically been supported by the provision of short-term emergency liquidity assistance by central banks, some form of private or official deposit insurance, and direct short- or medium-term emergency liquidity assistance for large troubled institutions. While such policies help contain the effects of a financial crisis, they expose the authorities to a 'moral hazard' problem and associated credit risks through lending at the central bank's discount window, lending to troubled institutions, or deposit insurance obligations. The credit risks associated with an official safety net have traditionally been limited by establishing minimum capital adequacy standard, codes of behaviour in financial markets, restrictions on risk-taking, systems of prudential supervision, and institutional arrangements for managing the risks inherent in payments, clearance, and settlement systems.

Removing capital controls and establishing capital account convertibility will lead to the introduction of new financial techniques and instruments, new sources of funds, and new participants into domestic financial markets. While such changes increase competition and yield important efficiency gains, they can potentially introduce new and highly complex elements of risk – some of a systemic nature – that make the pricing of financial instruments more difficult and that can contribute to abrupt changes in credit flows once previously unforeseen risks become evident. The potential official credit risks arising from the institutional failures that can be created by the mispricing of risk or widespread fraud provide a strong case for improving the domestic system of prudential supervision and coordinating supervisory efforts with those undertaken by the home supervisors of foreign institutions operating in the domestic market prior to the opening of the capital account.

Domestic taxes on financial income, wealth and transactions can also strongly influence residents' choices regarding the location of financial activities, the composition of their portfolios, and where financial transactions occur. The experiences of industrial countries with capital account convertibiity have repeatedly demonstrated the need to harmonise domestic taxes on the financial sector with those prevailing in other countries.[17] Such harmonisation should be done prior to the complete removal of capital controls if large-scale, tax-motivated capital flows are to be avoided.

While establishing prudent macroeconomic, financial and fiscal policies can facilitate obtaining the greatest efficiency and risk-diversification benefits from an open capital account, it is evident from the experience of the 1980s that periods of high asset price variability have characterised international financial markets; and economies with capital account convertibility must adapt their domestic economic and financial structures to withstand the effects of such variability. Such asset-price variability can have an especially adverse effects on employment, output and wealth in economies with regulations and institutional arrangements which inhibit wage, price, and interest rate adjustments. Eliminating or reducing such regulations and institutional arrangements could play a significant role in allowing an economy to adjust more smoothly to both real and financial shocks.

Even if countries put in place the policies needed to sustain capital account convertibility, there is still the question of how quickly to move to full convertibility. Fischer and Reisen (1992) have argued that capital account liberalisation can be facilitated if there is a gradual phasing out of capital controls with controls on foreign direct investment and trade-related flows being removed first and those on other flows removed only after extensive progress has been made on the stabilisation and reform programmes. While such a phased reduction has been followed by a number industrial economies, this process creates new avenues for disguised capital flows and can work effectively only if domestic and external financial market conditions do not markedly differ. Moreover, countries such as New Zealand and the United Kingdom have successfully sustained an open capital account after an abrupt removal of capital controls early in their reform process. The speed with which a country can move to full capital account convertibility appears to depend both on how far it has proceeded in implementing the policies that are preconditions for such convertibility and on its willingness to take further policy measures that credibly establish that it will carry on with the implementation of the remaining policy steps. Historical experience moreover suggests that the consistency of macroeconomic, financial and exchange rate policies is more important for sustaining an open capital account than is the sequencing of the removal of capital controls.

NOTES

This chapter has benefited from the comments of Morris Goldstein, Timothy Lane, Orlando Roncesvalles, Frits van Beek, Jan van Houten, and Eran Yashiv, other colleagues at the Fund. Any remaining errors are the responsibility of the authors. The opinions expressed in this chapter are those of the authors and are not necessarily those of the International Monetary Fund.

1 While Meese (1986) concluded that the exchange rates between the United States and some other major industrial countries followed a pattern in the early 1980s consistent with the existence of such bubbles, Flood, Rose and Mathieson (1991) used daily exchange rate data from the 1980s and found little evidence that such bubbles existed.
2 For a simple model of the relationship between the inflation tax and capital controls, see McKinnon and Mathieson (1981).
3 See Aizenman and Guidotti (1993) and Giovannini and de Melo (1991) for discussions of this possibility.
4 See Greene and Isard (1991) for a discussion of this experience.
5 For example, Yeager (1976) provides an overview of the experience of the major industrial countries in the 1950s and 1960s and provides an extensive bibliography. Baumgartner (1977) analyses the experience of a number of European countries (including Germany) with capital controls in the 1970s, and Argy (1987) compares the Australian and Japanese experience with capital controls in the 1960s and 1970s. Dooley and Isard (1980) provide a general framework for analysing the effects of capital controls.
6 For example, Argy (1987) argued that such controls were much more effectively and efficiently administered in Japan than in other industrial and developing countries.
7 As noted by Fukao (1990), one indication of the effectiveness of these controls was that there was an almost one-to-one relationship between the level of Japan's foreign exchange reserves and its cumulative current account balance between 1945 and 1962. Supplement A in Fukao's article provides a detailed listing of the various controls that were used between 1945 and 1990.
8 Official foreign exchange reserves rose from $4.4 billion at the end of 1970 to $7.9 billion at the end of July 1971. Moreover, capital inflows in the 11 days between 16–27 August 1971 amounted to $4 billion.
9 Horiuchi (1984) showed that officially-controlled real interest rates in Japan were relatively high by international standards, which may have played a key role in limiting incentives for residents to shift funds abroad.
10 Fukao (1990) shows that the differentials (in absolute value) between the 3-month gensaki (repo) interest rate and the 3-month Euro-yen interest rate

were at most 6% per annum in the period 1974–87 but reached 20–40% per annum during the period 1971–4.

11 These interest rates included (in order of expected international tradability): (1) the 3-month Dublin interbank market rate, (2) the 90-day exchequer bill rate, (3) the 5-year-to-maturity government security yield, (4) the clearing banks' rate on deposits in the 5,000–25,000 Irish pound range, (5) the clearing banks' prime lending rate, (6) the building societies, share account rate, and (7) the building societies' mortgage rate. Their data covered the period from 1971:1 to 1986:4.

12 The close relationship between the interbank rate and international rates could have reflected the fact the Authorised Dealers (selected banks) were not prohibited from acquiring foreign exchange deposits and incurring foreign currency debts as long as their total spot against forward position did not exceed the long and short limits set by the central bank.

13 Gros (1988) reached a similar conclusion regarding the Belgium dual exchange rate system.

14 These efficiency gains can be reduced if assets prices are distorted by such factors as tax differentials.

15 By early October 1992, for example, the Bundesbank's stocks of domestic securities which could be used to sterilise its foreign exchange operations had fallen from DM 150 billion at the end of August to DM 91 billion.

16 Since this tightening of fiscal policy occurred when the economy was in a recession, Maynard (1988) argued that it was crucial in establishing the credibility of the government's anti-inflation policy.

17 Razin and Sadka (1991) have argued that, unless all countries can agree on a common set of taxes on financial activities and income, then the optimal domestic tax on income from capital would be zero.

REFERENCES

Adams, Charles and Jeremy Greenwood (1985) 'Dual Exchange Rate Systems and Capital Controls: An Investigation', *Journal of International Economics*, **18** (February), 43–63.

Aizenman, Joshua and Pablo E. Guidotti (1993) 'Capital Controls, Collection Costs, and Domestic Public Debt', *Journal of International Money and Finance*, forthcoming.

Argy, Victor (1987) 'International Financial Liberalization – The Australian and Japanese Experiences Compared', *Bank of Japan Monetary and Economic Studies*, **5** (May), 105–67.

Bank of England (1981) 'The Effect of Exchange Control Abolition on Capital Flows', *Bank of England Quarterly Bulletin*, **21** (September), 369–73.

Baumgartner, Ulrich (1977) 'Capital Controls in Three Central European Countries', *Finance and Development*, IMF and World Bank, **14** (December), 46–9.

Browne, Francis X. and Paul D. McNelis (1990) 'Exchange Controls and Interest Rate Determination with Traded and Nontraded Assets: The Irish–United Kingdom Experience', *Journal of International Money and Finance*, **9** (March), 41–59.

Crockett, Andrew (1991) 'Financial Market Implications of Trade and Currency Zones', unpublished.

Dooley, Michael and Peter Isard (1980) 'Capital Controls, Political Risk and Deviations from Interest-Rate Parity', *Journal of Political Economy*, **80** (April), 370–84.

Fischer, Bernhard and Helmut Reisen (1992) 'Towards Capital Account Convertibility', OECD Development Center, *Policy Brief*, **4**.

Flood, Robert P., Andrew K. Rose and Donald J. Mathieson (1991) 'An Empirical Exploration of Exchange Rate Target-Zones', *Carnegie–Rochester Conference Series on Public Policy*, **35** (Autumn), 7–66.

Fukao, Mitsuhiro (1990) 'Liberalization of Japan's Foreign Exchange Controls and Structural Changes in the Balance of Payments', *Bank of Japan Monetary and Economic Studies*, **8** (September), 101–65.

Giddy, Ian H. (1979) 'Exchange Risk Under Exchange Controls and Credit Controls', in R.M. Levich and C.G. Wihlborg (eds), *Exchange-Risks and Exposure: Current Developments in International Financial Management*, Boston: Lexington Books.

Giovannini, Alberto and Martha de Melo (1991) 'Government Revenue from Financial Repression', NBER, *Working Paper*, **3604** (January).

Greene, Joshua E. and Peter Isard (1991) 'Currency Convertibility and the Transformation of Centrally Planned Economies', IMF, *Occasional Paper*, **81** (June).

Gros, Daniel (1988) 'Dual Exchange Rates in the Presence of Incomplete Market Separation; Long-Run Effectiveness and Policy Implications', *IMF Staff Papers*, **35** (September), 437–60.

Horiuchi, Akiyoshi (1984) 'The "Low Interest Rate Policy" and Economic Growth in Postwar Japan', *Developing Economies*, **22** (December), 349–71.

Maynard, Geoffrey (1988) *The Economy Under Mrs. Thatcher*, New York: Basil Blackwell.

McKinnon, Ronald I. and Donald J. Mathieson (1981) 'How to Manage a Repressed Economy', *Princeton Essays in International Finance*, **145** (December).

Meese, Richard (1986) 'Testing for Bubbles in Exchange Markets: A Case of Sparkling Rates?', *Journal of Political Economy*, **94** (April), 345–72.

Razin, Assaf and Efraim Sadka (1991) 'Vanishing Tax on Capital Income in the Open Economy', unpublished paper (July).

Yeager, Leland B. (1976) *International Monetary Relations: Theory, History, and Policy*, New York: Harper & Row, 2nd edn.

Discussion

ERAN YASHIV

The central issues examined by Chapter 12 are the erosion of the effectiveness of capital controls in the 1980s, the implications for stabilisation and structural reform programmes and the benefits of and prerequisites for an open capital account. The chapter first discusses the nature of capital controls. It presents IMF data according to which 123 out of 153 territories and member countries were using some form of capital controls at the end of 1989. It then discusses the rationale for such controls: limiting volatile short-term capital flows; retention of domestic savings and maintenance of the domestic financial tax base. The chapter goes on to list methods for avoiding capital controls and reports several pieces of empirical evidence which show that the effectiveness of these controls has diminished in the 1980s. This sets the stage for a theoretical discussion of the implications of reduced effectiveness: the cost of maintaining controls, the formulation of macroeconomic policy against this background and the potential benefits of a reduction or elimination of controls. Real-world experience with such liberalisation is then reported, focusing on the United Kingdom and New Zealand. Finally the chapter looks at the necessary preconditions for establishing capital account convertibility.

I have found the chapter to be most interesting and quite stimulating. It is certainly a very useful starting point for policy discussions concerning the costs and benefits of capital account liberalisation and the necessary conditions for successful liberalisation. The chapter for the large part avoids (correctly, I believe) the much-discussed issue of the sequencing of balance of payments liberalisation but rather concentrates on its interaction with other aspects of macroeconomic policy.

I do, however, have certain comments that may strengthen the arguments made in the chapter and several others that may prompt the authors to look into related issues. I will pursue these in the order presented in the chapter itself.

Section 2 discusses the rationales for capital controls. With respect to the rationale of maintaining the domestic tax base the following should be noted: as mentioned by the authors it has been established in several theoretical models, most notably by Adams and Greenwood (1985), that in many respects there is an equivalence between capital controls, taxes on capital flows and dual exchange rates. The institution of capital controls may thus be justified from an optimal taxation point of view, whereby the government minimises welfare losses induced by the various distortionary taxes at its disposal, one of which is some sort of a capital-flow tax or control. In a related context one might argue that even if the government does not truly optimise some objective function defined over social welfare, it might still be choosing among several distortionary taxes in accordance with various *political* constraints. This point has important implications for other parts of the chapter: if the government is to loosen controls it might be forced to readjust other tax policies, and there is always the question of the political implications of such a step. (See Alesina and Tabellini, 1989 for a model that formalises political considerations in the determination of controls.)

Section 3 discusses the erosion in the effectiveness of controls. It would be useful to present some data in this context such as the magnitude of capital flows or different estimates of capital flight. As it stands, there is a lot of anecdotal evidence about the techniques to avoid controls.

Section 4 discusses the implications of the reduced effectiveness of controls to the formulation of macroeconomic policy. One issue is that capital flows may cause the monetary base to shrink and thus affect government revenues from seigniorage. Recent experience in Europe, particularly in Italy, Spain and Portugal should provide the necessary data to see how government revenue as affected by the flows generated by the ERM crisis which began in September 1992. The fact that some governments reinstated controls is noteworthy in this context and it would be useful to examine the motivation for this policy and its success. Could it point, for example, to a re-emergence of effective capital controls?

Section 5 documents the experience of New Zealand and the United Kingdom with capital account liberalisation. A common result is real appreciation. However the authors present evidence according to which such appreciation occurred both following increased inflow of capital (New Zealand) and increased outflow (United Kingdom). As the real exchange rate is a key variable in production and consumption decisions it would be natural to examine the real appreciation in more detail. For example, could it concern differential price movements in the traded and nontraded sectors of those economies? Linking appreciation solely to capital account liberalisation seems to be somewhat misleading.

Another important point that is worth examination is the role of expectations and credibility in this context. This is obviously a major topic in the context of EC capital controls, and it would be useful to analyse these differential outcomes in terms of a well-defined model which explicitly incorporates such issues.

There is a discussion in this section of the preconditions for establishing capital account convertibility. These conditions include reducing any fiscal deficit and making domestic interest rates comparable to international ones. It should be emphasised, however, that this type of action has political costs: reducing controls may reduce government revenues and make deficit cutting more difficult, for example. There are also some tradeoffs: lowering interest rates may run counter to a restrictive monetary policy in the context of a stabilisation policy.

There is a short but interesting discussion of the interaction between capital account convertibility and the introduction of new financial techniques. A previous version of the chapter (Mathieson and Rojas-Suarez, 1992) mentioned the use of derivative securities to hedge risks in international borrowing. I believe this point is fairly novel with respect to international portfolio diversification from a macroeconomic (rather than financial) perspective. I would like to encourage the authors to pursue this theme further.

REFERENCES

Adams, Charles and Jeremy Greenwood (1985) 'Dual Exchange Rate Systems and Capital Controls: An Investigation', *Journal of International Economics*, **18** (February), 43–63.

Alesina, Alberto and Guido Tabellini (1989) 'External Debt, Capital Flight and Political Risk', *Journal of International Economics*, **27** (November), 199–220.

Mathieson, D.J. and L. Rojas-Suarez (1992) 'Liberalization of the capital account: Experiences and issues', IMF, *Working Paper*, **WP/92/46** (June); see also Chapter 12 in this volume.

Index

Note: 'n.' after a page reference indicates the number of a note on that page.